The Afterlife of Mary, Queen of Scots

The Afterlife of Mary, Queen of Scots

Edited by
STEVEN J. REID

EDINBURGH
University Press

Edinburgh University Press is one of the leading university presses in the UK. Publishing new research in the arts and humanities, EUP connects people and ideas to inspire creative thinking, open new perspectives and shape the world we live in. For more information, visit www.edinburghuniversitypress.com.

© editorial matter and organisation Steven J. Reid, 2024
© the chapters their several authors, 2024

Edinburgh University Press Ltd
13 Infirmary Street, Edinburgh EH1 1LT

Typeset in 10/13 Giovanni by
Manila Typesetting Company

A CIP record for this book is available from the British Library

ISBN 978 1 3995 2354 7 (paperback)
ISBN 978 1 3995 2353 0 (hardback)
ISBN 978 1 3995 2355 4 (webready PDF)
ISBN 978 1 3995 2356 1 (epub)

The right of Steven J. Reid to be identified as editor of this work has been asserted in accordance with the Copyright, Designs and Patents Act 1988 and the Copyright and Related Rights Regulations 2003 (SI No. 2498).

Contents

List of Tables and Figures   vii
Acknowledgements   xi
The Contributors   xv
Abbreviations and Conventions   xviii

Introduction – The Afterlife of Mary, Queen of Scots:
Themes and Paradigms   1
Steven J. Reid

PART ONE Mary in Contemporary Objects

1. *Damnatio Memoriae*: Mary, Queen of Scots' Iconography and the Ham House Portrait of Sir John Maitland of Thirlestane   33
   David A. H. B. Taylor

2. New Perspectives on the Sheffield Portraits of Mary, Queen of Scots including the Discovery of a New, Related, Contemporary Portrait   53
   Caroline Rae

3. Memorialising (in) Mary, Queen of Scots' Books of Hours   84
   Emily Wingfield

4. The Afterlives of Mary's Letters   106
   Jade Scott and Alison Wiggins

PART TWO Mary in Literature and History

5. Editing and Collecting Mary, Queen of Scots in the Eighteenth Century: James Anderson (1662–1728) and Dr William Hunter (1718–83)   125
   Michelle H. Craig

6	The Battle for Memory: The Reception of Mary, Queen of Scots in the Eighteenth-century British Periodical Press *Rhona Brown*	142
7	'Deeply impressed upon the imagination': The Return of Mary in the Eighteenth and Nineteenth Centuries *Gerard Carruthers*	160
8	'A tracked and hunted creature': Mary, Queen of Scots and the Histories of David Hay Fleming, Andrew Lang, Gordon Donaldson and Antonia Fraser *Catriona M. M. Macdonald*	179
9	Re-imagining Mary, Queen of Scots in Contemporary Scottish Women's Writing *Nia Clark*	197

PART THREE Collecting and Displaying Mary

10	Collecting and Exhibiting Marian Objects in Nineteenth-century Britain *Julie Holder*	221
11	'The most interesting apartment in Scotland': The History and Presentation of Mary, Queen of Scots' Chambers at the Palace of Holyroodhouse *Deborah Clarke*	241
12	Materialising Mary in a Museum: Marian Objects and Authenticity *Anna Groundwater*	267

PART FOUR Mary in Media

13	Minstrels of Maelstroms: Mary's Musical Afterlives *Tim Duguid*	293
14	The Transformations of Mary, Queen of Scots in Early Cinema, 1895–1923 *Ian Goode and Stephen McBurney*	317
15	Long Live the Queen: The Afterlife of Mary, Queen of Scots in Contemporary Visual Culture *Daniel Fountain and Alicia Hughes*	343

Index	371

Tables and Figures

Tables

10.1	Number of Marian objects exhibited at the temporary exhibitions in Peterborough, Glasgow and London	231
10.2	Status of lenders of Marian objects exhibited at the temporary exhibitions in Peterborough, Glasgow and London	231
13.1	Schema for duet between Mary and Leicester, *Maria Stuarda*, Act 2, Scene 2	303
13.2	Instances of the 'Zadok' motif in *Mary Queen of Scots* (2018)	310
13.3	Drum beat patterns in *Mary Queen of Scots*	313
13.4	Translations of Maria's words, *Maria Stuarda*, Act 2	314

Figures

I.1	Gavin Hamilton, *The Abdication of Mary Queen of Scots*, 1765–73	12
I.2	Richard Verstegan, *Theatrum crudelitatum haereticorum nostri temporis*	16
I.3	Frontispiece inserted in Adam Blackwood, *Martyre de la Royne d'Escosse . . .*	17
I.4	Frontispiece to William Udall, *The Historie of the Life and Death of Mary Stuart, Queene of Scotland*	18
I.5	*Das Herz der Königin*, promotional poster	20
I.6	Wall of images of Mary, Room 1, 'The Afterlife of Mary, Queen of Scots' Exhibition, Hunterian Art Gallery	23
I.7	Wall of quotes about Mary, Room 2, 'The Afterlife of Mary, Queen of Scots' Exhibition, Hunterian Art Gallery	23
I.8	'Mary, Queen of Quacks', alongside peg dolls of Mary created by Hope and Euan Reid at a project kids' craft event	25

1.1	*Mary, Queen of Scots*, by unknown artist (currently attributed to or after Rowland Lockey), *c.* 1578	42
1.2	*Mary, Queen of Scots*, attributed to the Wierix brothers, *c.* 1587	46
1.3	*Mary, Queen of Scots*, by Renold Elstrack, *c.* 1618	47
2.1	*Mary, Queen of Scots*, by unknown artist (English school), inscribed 1578	54
2.2	*Mary, Queen of Scots*, Nicholas Hilliard	55
2.3	*Mary, Queen of Scots*, Nicholas Hilliard, 1580s (?)	56
2.4	*Mary, Queen of Scots*, the 'Blairs Memorial Portrait', by an unknown artist (Flemish school), 1604–18	58
2.5	Superimposition of tracings taken of the faces in two portraits (Clouet, BNF and Rijksmuseum)	59
2.6	Superimposition (Hardwick Hall and 'Blairs Memorial Portrait')	60
2.7	Superimposition (Hilliard, Royal Collection and Rijksmuseum)	60
2.8	Superimposition (Hilliard, Royal Collection and 'Blairs Memorial Portrait')	61
2.9	Superimposition (Hilliard, Royal Collection and Hardwick Hall)	61
2.10	Detail, face, *Mary, Queen of Scots*, Hardwick Hall	62
2.11	*Catherine de' Medici*, by an unknown artist (French school), 1550s	64
2.12	Detail, partlet, *Mary, Queen of Scots*, Hardwick Hall	66
2.13	*Portrait of a Woman*, by François Clouet, 1560	67
2.14	John Leslie, *De origine, moribus, et rebus gestis Scotorum, libri decem* . . . (Rome, 1578)	69
2.15	Mary, Queen of Scots, by François Clouet, *c.* 1558–60	70
2.16	*Sir John Maitland, 1st Baron Maitland of Thirlestane*, attributed to Adrian Vanson, inscribed 1589	73
2.17	*Maitland*, Vanson, mosaiced X-radiograph image	74
2.18	*Maitland*, Vanson, infrared image	74
2.19	*Maitland*, Vanson, MA-XRF elemental map of lead	75
2.20	*Maitland*, Vanson, composite tracing of the underlying composition	77
2.21	Superimposition of tracings of the faces in two portraits (female portrait underlying *Maitland*, Vanson and 'Blairs Memorial Portrait')	78
2.22	The Blairs Jewel, by unknown artist, containing a miniature portrait of Mary Queen of Scots, 1580s, early seventeenth-century setting	79
2.23	*Mary Queen of Scots*, by unknown artist, 1580s	80
2.24	*Louise de Lorraine*, by unknown artist (French school), 1580	81
3.1	Mary Queen of Scots, autograph inscription, Sheffield, Guild of St George	90

9.1	Unknown, *Anamorphosis, called Mary, Queen of Scots, 1542–1587. Reigned 1542–1567*, 1580	201
10.1	Queen Mary harp	224
10.2	Sixteenth-century cabinet keys	227
10.3	National Museum of Antiquities of Scotland, c. 1900	229
10.4	Cabinet, seventeenth century	233
11.1	The Palace of Holyroodhouse in the 1560s. James Gordon (1615?–86), *Palatium Regium Edinense, West front of Palace*, c. 1649	243
11.2	Samuel Dukinfield Swarbreck, *Mary, Queen of Scots' Bedchamber*, 1861	249
11.3	From Samuel Dukinfield Swarbreck's *Sketches in Scotland* (1839), Queen Mary's closet and Queen Mary's dressing room	255
11.4	Alexander Fraser, *Mary, Queen of Scots Outer Chamber, Holyroodhouse*, c. 1884	258
11.5	Mary, Queen of Scots' outer chamber, c. 1981	263
11.6	Alec Cobbe, *Design for Mary, Queen of Scots' bedchamber*, 1994	264
11.7	Mary, Queen of Scots' outer chamber, 1995–2019	264
11.8	Mary Queen of Scots' closet, 2019	265
12.1	Penicuik Jewels: necklace	270
12.2	Penicuik Jewels: locket	270
12.3	Craigmillar Crucifix	272
12.4	Cameo heart-shaped locket	282
12.5	Cameo ring	282
12.6	The Renaissance Gallery, Kingdom of the Scots, National Museums Scotland	288
13.1	'Peril motif', Max Richter, *Mary Queen of Scots* (2018)	306
13.2	'Usurper's motif'	307
14.1	Slide 21 of 24, *Mary Queen of Scots* (York & Son, 1885)	321
14.2	Slide 23 of 24, *Mary Queen of Scots* (York & Son, 1885)	322
14.3	A still from Pathé Frères' *Marie Stuart* (1908)	324
14.4	Full-page advertisement for Edison's *Mary Stuart*, printed in *Kinematograph Weekly*	326
14.5	Production still from Edison's *Mary Stuart*, which parallels the mise-en-scène of *Execution of Mary Queen of Scots*	327
14.6	Production still from Edison's *Mary Stuart*, illustrating Mary publicly denouncing Elizabeth	328
14.7	Full-page advertisement for the Romance of History series, printed by *Kinematograph Weekly* in 1922	335
14.8	Film still from *Mary, Queen of Scots* (1922)	336
14.9	Production still from *The Loves of Mary, Queen of Scots* (1923), printed in the *Daily Mirror* in support of the British Film Weeks	338

14.10	Denison Clift on set at Stirling Castle, filming *The Loves of Mary, Queen of Scots* (1923)	340
15.1	Helen Flockhart, *Linger Awhile* (2018)	347
15.2	Helen Flockhart, *Lachrymose Window* (2018)	349
15.3	Helen Flockhart, *I See and Keep Silent* (2018)	351
15.4	Helen Flockhart, *Lover's Eye* (2018)	352
15.5	Helen Flockhart, *Red Bodice* (2018)	353
15.6	Rachel Maclean, *The Queen* (2013)	354
15.7	George Vertue, *Maria Scotorum Regina et Franciae Dotaria*, 1735	354
15.8	Rosé as Mary, Queen of Scots; photography by Robert Postotnik (2021)	362
15.9	François Clouet, *Mary, Queen of Scots*, c. 1558	362
15.10	Rosé as Mary, Queen of Scots with cigarette and candelabra; photography by Robert Postotnik (2021)	364
15.11	Stills from 'Night of the Living Drag' at MGM National Harbor, Maryland on 21 November 2021, with Rosé as Mary, Queen of Scots; YouTube	366

Acknowledgements

This volume originated in '"In My End is my Beginning": The Memorialisation and Cultural Afterlife of Mary Queen of Scots', a research project led by The Hunterian and the University of Glasgow. The project was funded initially (2016–18) by a series of small grants from the University of Glasgow's Centre for Scottish and Celtic Studies, and in its main research phase (2019–21) by a Royal Society of Edinburgh Research Network Award (funder reference 62643). Anne Dulau Beveridge and I are grateful to both funders, and would like to particularly acknowledge Dr Catriona Macdonald, who as Centre Director provided tireless support in the project's early stages. Licence costs for many of the images in this volume have been paid for from the University of Glasgow History Research Support Fund, while a subvention towards its production costs was provided by Glasgow's Centre for Scottish and Celtic Studies. I am very grateful to Dr Andrew Mackillop as current Centre Director for arranging this. I would like to acknowledge the expert help of Ross Crammond, Christelle Le Riguer and Isabel Jones in ordering and invoicing images, the administrative support provided by Alicia Hughes during the project, and the production of the volume index by Beth Cowen.

This volume, like all the project outputs, is the product of teamwork. Anne and I would like to thank all the colleagues in the Hunterian and the University of Glasgow Archives and Special Collections who helped develop the project, whether by providing access to objects, organising their photography and conservation, or helping us refine our thinking and approach to them. We are also hugely grateful to all the academics, curators, librarians, archivists and students who participated in discussions of Mary and her cultural life. Finally, I would like to thank my co-investigator Anne Dulau Beveridge, who has been an exceptional and enthusiastic collaborator, colleague and friend throughout the whole project.

Acknowledgements from specific contributors are as follows:

Chapter 1. The author would like to thank Caroline Rae (former Caroline Villers Research Fellow, Courtauld Institute of Art) for a very productive and enjoyable collaboration beginning when he was curator of pictures and sculpture at the National Trust and during her postdoctoral fellowship, with conversations around the authorship of the Ham portrait of Sir John Maitland and discussions about her technical examination of the portrait and surrounding research, including her discovery of a hidden, underlying image of Mary, Queen of Scots. This in turn led to our two chapters on the queen's visual imagery, which should be read together. The author would also like to thank the Royal Collection Trust for generously supplying images and the University of Glasgow for supporting with image permissions.

Chapter 2. The author would like to thank the trustees of the Caroline Villers Research Fellowship including the project mentor, Professor Aviva Burnstock (Courtauld Institute of Art), for funding the nine-month postdoctoral research fellowship, and Lesley Stevenson, Kate Anderson, Jack Ridge and other National Galleries of Scotland colleagues for supporting and co-hosting the wider fellowship, including providing funding for technical examination and imaging of works in their collection. Great thanks must also be extended to Christine Sitwell and Rebecca Hellen (The National Trust) for their support of the project, including funding dendrochronology, and the loan of the Ham House work for examination and exhibition. The author would like to thank also David A. H. B. Taylor (former curator of pictures and sculpture at the National Trust) for an enjoyable collaboration in relation to our interlinked chapters for this publication, and discussions during the research, in which his expertise in Scottish early modern portraiture was of great benefit and interest to an early career scholar. The author would also like to thank Ian Tyers, Dr Hannah Woodward-Reed and Christine Slottved Kimbriel (Hamilton Kerr Institute) for so generously sharing their unpublished research, the Scottish History Endowment (University of Glasgow) for funding a research trip to Aberdeenshire, Amy Miller (Blairs Museum), Keren Guthrie (Blair Castle) and Dr Susan Kay-Williams, Chief Executive of the Royal School of Needlework, for her contribution. The author would like to acknowledge the History of Art Department at UCL for granting funding for images, the Royal Collection Trust, the National Trust and the Hamilton Kerr Institute for generously supplying images, and the University of Glasgow for supporting with images and permissions.

Chapter 3. Initial research into the books of hours owned by Mary, Queen of Scots was funded by the Neil Ker Memorial Fund, and furthered by internal funding from the University of Birmingham. Work in this chapter is more fully developed within the author's *Scotland's Royal Women and European Literary Culture 1424–1587* (Turnhout, 2023).

Chapter 4. This research was enabled with the support of an AHRC Leadership Fellowship, Project title: *Archives and Writing Lives*, PI Alison Wiggins, RA Jade Scott, University of Glasgow 2017–19 (AH/P009735/1). The authors are grateful to contributors to the RSE Project '"In my End is my Beginning": The Memorialisation and Cultural Afterlife of Mary Queen of Scots', especially Steven Reid and Anne Dulau Beveridge, for the opportunity to participate in events during 2019–20. For their insight and for taking the time to talk with them about these letters, they especially thank Jana Dambrogio, Helen Newsome, Steven Reid, Danial Starza Smith, Emily Wingfield and Ronnie Young.

Chapter 7. The author wishes to acknowledge that research for this essay was in part enabled by the AHRC-funded project 'Editing Robert Burns for the 21st Century: Correspondence and Poetry' (AH/P004946/1) [Principal Investigator: Gerard Carruthers]. He is most grateful to Dr Sarah Dunnigan for very helpful advice on the trajectory of this essay.

Chapter 8. The author wishes to acknowledge the support of the Royal Society of Edinburgh in funding the research that contributed to the writing of this essay.

Chapter 9. The author wishes to acknowledge the support of the Arts and Humanities Research Council in funding my doctoral research, which contributed to the writing of this essay. I would also thank the Scottish National Portrait Gallery for supporting with image permissions, and the University of Glasgow History Research Support fund for funding the licence cost.

Chapter 10. The author would like to thank National Museums Scotland (particularly the library staff) for supporting this research and for generously supplying images. I would also like to thank Historic Environment Scotland and The Royal Collection Trust for supporting this work with image permissions.

Chapter 11. The author would like to thank Emma Stead (Royal Collection Trust), Ailsa Hutton and Julie Holder (National Museums Scotland), and Ian Gow for their help and Royal Collection Trust for generously supplying the images.

Chapter 12. The author would like to thank National Museums Scotland for waiving reproduction fees for the use of images of their objects, and curators of material at NMS relating to Mary, Queen of Scots, particularly David Forsyth, former Principal Curator, Modern and Contemporary History at National Museums Scotland, and the curator of the critically acclaimed exhibition *Mary, Queen of Scots* in 2013. This chapter owes a huge debt to him; his work laid the foundations for it. It also drew heavily on the knowledge and support of previous curators at NMS, Lyndsay McGill and Jackie Moran. Many thanks also to Steven Reid and Anne Dulau, and all participants in the RSE-funded project workshops. All errors that remain are of course the author's.

Chapter 14. The authors would like to thank Tony Fletcher and Bob Geoghegan for kindly sharing their beautifully restored version of *The Loves of Mary, Queen of Scots* (1923). We would also like to thank Kay Foubister of the Scotland Moving Image Archive, for her continuous generosity of time. With thanks also to the Media History Digital Library, Cambridge University Library and The British Newspaper Archive.

Chapter 15. The authors would like to thank Helen Flockhart, Rachel Maclean and Rosé for the time they took to speak to us about their work and artistic practices. Their testimonies supported the development of our chapter, and we hope that the quotations used may draw further scholarly attention to their practices. We would also like to acknowledge their generosity for sharing images of their work, and the University of Glasgow for supporting with image permission. The research for this chapter evolved from the authors' conversations during the RSE Project '"In my End is my Beginning": The Memorialisation and Cultural Afterlife of Mary Queen of Scots'. This included Fountain's blog contribution to the project website in 2021 and Hughes's contribution to the development and delivery of 'The Life and Afterlife of Mary, Queen of Scots' Massive Open Online Course (MOOC), launched in November 2021.

The Contributors

Rhona Brown is Professor of Scottish Textual Cultures at the University of Glasgow. Her research interests include eighteenth-century Scots-language poetry, the history of the Scottish periodical press and textual editing.

Gerard Carruthers, Scottish Literature, School of Critical Studies, is Francis Hutcheson Professor of Scottish Literature at the University of Glasgow and general editor of the multi-volume edition of the *Complete Works of Robert Burns* for Oxford University Press.

Nia Clark is a PhD graduate from the University of Glasgow. Her research interests include contemporary Scottish literature, ekphrastic poetry and the relationship between visual art and writing in Scotland.

Deborah Clarke is an independent art historian and former Senior Curator for Royal Collection Trust at the Palace of Holyroodhouse. Her research interests include the history, contents and residents of the Palace of Holyroodhouse.

Michelle H. Craig is a rare books cataloguer in Archives and Special Collections at the University of Glasgow. Her PhD was on the library of Dr William Hunter and her research focuses on late medieval and early modern book and library history.

Tim Duguid is a Lecturer in Digital Humanities and Information Studies at the University of Glasgow. His current research interests lie in the intersection between digital humanities and historical musicology.

Daniel Fountain is Senior Lecturer in Art History and Visual Culture at the University of Exeter. Their research focuses on contemporary art, craft and queer visual culture.

Ian Goode is a Senior Lecturer in Theatre, Film and Television Studies at the University of Glasgow. His research interests include contemporary Scottish and British film and television, particularly representations of the past, and auto/biographical representation.

Anna Groundwater is Principal Curator, Renaissance and Early Modern History, at National Museums Scotland. Her research interests include the material culture and social history of early modern Scotland, cultural exchanges and the construction of meaning in heritage settings.

Julie Holder is Assistant Curator of Modern and Contemporary History in the Scottish History and Archaeology department at National Museums Scotland. Her recent research focuses on Scottish antiquarianism, museum and collecting histories and Scottish disability history.

Alicia Hughes is a curator and historian of art and collecting at the British Museum, and formerly the Project Assistant on the RSE Project '"In my End is my Beginning": The Memorialisation and Cultural Afterlife of Mary Queen of Scots'. Her research focuses on intersections in histories of art, science, collecting and image-making.

Stephen McBurney is a PhD graduate from the University of Glasgow, currently working on his first monograph *Colour in Early Scottish Cinema: Materiality and Social Context, 1896–1906* (Edinburgh University Press).

Catriona M. M. Macdonald is Reader in Late Modern Scottish History at the University of Glasgow, a former editor of the *Scottish Historical Review* and past President of the Scottish History Society. Her recent research focuses on the evolution of Scottish historiography since 1832.

Caroline Rae is an Associate Lecturer in History of Art at University College London. Her research centres on art produced in the early modern period in northern Europe with a focus on émigré Netherlandish artists working at the English and Scottish Jacobean, and Elizabethan, courts.

Steven J. Reid is Professor of Early Modern Scottish History and Culture at the University of Glasgow. He has published widely on intellectual, religious and political culture in the reigns of Mary, Queen of Scots and James VI and I.

Jade Scott is a Lecturer in English Language and Linguistics at the University of Glasgow. Her research interests include historical Scots and medieval literature, with a particular focus on the epistolary culture of early modern Scottish women, including Mary, Queen of Scots.

David A. H. B. Taylor is an independent art historian and curator, who specialises in sixteenth- and seventeenth-century portraits, including the work of Peter Lely, female patronage at the Restoration court and portraiture in early modern Scotland.

Alison Wiggins is Reader in English Language and Manuscript at the University of Glasgow. She was AHRC Leadership Fellow for *Archives and Writing Lives* and PI for the AHRC *Letters of Bess of Hardwick Project*. She has collaborated on projects with the National Trust, Chatsworth House Archive, The National Archives, The Bodleian Library and National Library of Scotland.

Emily Wingfield is a Senior Lecturer in English Literature at the University of Birmingham. Her research specialism is Older Scots literature, particularly Older Scots romance and the history of the book. She is also especially interested in the history of women's reading and writing.

Abbreviations and Conventions

BL	British Library
BNFL	British National Film League
CIA	Courtauld Institute of Art
CSP Scot.	Joseph Bain et al. (eds), *Calendar of State Papers Relating to Scotland and Mary, Queen of Scots, 1547–1603*, 13 vols (London, 1862–1954)
ESTC	British Library, English Short Title Catalogue
EUL	Edinburgh University Library
Fraser, *Mary Queen of Scots*	Antonia Fraser, *Mary Queen of Scots* (London, 1969)
GU	Glasgow University
Guy, *My Heart is My Own*	John Guy, *My Heart is My Own: The Life of Mary Queen of Scots* (London, 2004)
Labanoff (ed.), *Lettres*	Prince Alexandre Labanoff (ed.), *Lettres, Instructions et Mémoires de Marie Stuart, Reine d'Écosse*, 7 vols (London, 1844)
NLS	National Library of Scotland
NMAS	National Museum of Antiquities of Scotland
NMS	National Museums Scotland
NPG	National Portrait Gallery
NRAS	National Register of Archives of Scotland
NRS	National Records Scotland
ODNB	*Oxford Dictionary of National Biography* (www.oxforddnb.com)
PSAS	*Proceedings of the Society of Antiquaries of Scotland*
SHR	*Scottish Historical Review*
SoAS	Society of Antiquaries of Scotland

Strickland, *Letters*	Agnes Strickland (ed.), *Letters of Mary, Queen of Scots, and Documents Connected with her Personal History*, 2 vols (London, 1842)
TNA	The National Archives, Kew

Mary's correct formal title is 'Mary, Queen of Scots' (as in 'David, King of Scots'), but this is often rendered without the comma ('Mary Queen of Scots'), which can lead to considerable confusion. Where contributors use Mary's full title in their own words we use the formal version (with comma), but have preserved the usage without comma in quotations and titles of texts where other authors have done so.

Links to all online sources were checked and functional at the time of publication.

Introduction
The Afterlife of Mary, Queen of Scots: Themes and Paradigms
Steven J. Reid

> To all of these fans of Mary Queen of Scots, as to me, she lives. And it is we, all of us, who give her life.
>
> Lady Antonia Fraser, 'Foreword to the New Edition', *Mary Queen of Scots*[1]

The quotation that opens this collection comes from Lady Antonia Fraser's foreword to the 2009 edition of her biography, *Mary Queen of Scots*. She explains that, like so many people, she had an intense and abiding passion for Mary, in her case from childhood onward.[2] Like many female authors over the past three centuries in particular, Fraser both identified with and drew strength from Mary's story in the process of writing, the tale being dramatic enough to combat the 'desperation' and loneliness she felt as a mother-of-six and unpublished author working on her first book.[3] In recounting the travels of the book around the world, she also noted the legions of equally passionate fans of Mary who had contacted her after reading it. Many fervently believed that they were related to Mary, owned a personal relic of hers, or had actually been her in a past life. Fraser was in no way mocking of these Marian enthusiasts. As she herself recognises, even though Mary died almost four and a half centuries ago, she is still able to generate feelings in those who become entranced by her story that can be as deeply intense and intimate as any 'real' relationship.

Mary's life was certainly dramatic, but as a ruler of Scotland her impact on its political history is highly debatable. Born in 1542, Mary was personally active as monarch of Scotland for just six years between 1561 and 1567, after

---

[1] Originally published in 2009 edition; cited here from the 2015 edition (London), pp. xxv–xxx (quote at p. xxx).
[2] She describes Mary as her 'first love' and had fantasies of being a fifth handmaid among her companions, the 'four Maries': Fraser, 'Foreword', p. xxv.
[3] Fraser, 'Foreword', p. xxvi.

spending most of her childhood in France. After fleeing Scotland in 1568, she spent the remainder of her life in English captivity, where she was executed in 1587.[4] Biographies of the queen have variously portrayed her as a sympathetic victim of circumstance with modest political ability and a talent for the art of courtly display, through to an excoriating failure when set against her fellow Stewart monarchs, whose sole interest in Scotland was as a stepping stone to the English throne.[5] A range of additional mitigating factors can be brought into play when considering Mary's relative success. A prosopographical study of political factions in her reign by Gordon Donaldson revealed just how complex and shifting alliances were in 1560s Scotland, where dynastic and personal interests mixed with religious affiliations in ways that were unique to every family and did not follow neat confessional divides.[6] This would have made managing Scottish politics difficult for any monarch, let alone a young queen who returned to Scotland in 1561 as an essentially French cultural outsider. Michael Lynch's forensic assessment of the politics of Mary's reign notes the relative lack of extant governmental manuscripts for the period. If they had survived, they might well reveal Mary as a more engaged and active legislator than appears to be the case. He has also suggested that we do not fully appreciate how important the 'soft power' of her court was in her approach to effective rule.[7] The most significant new assessments of Mary are those that take a gendered approach and articulate the inherent constraints on her as a female ruler in a highly patriarchal society.[8] Retha Warnicke's biography of Mary shows just how essential a political currency Mary's honour was to her, and explains how her rape by James Hepburn, fourth earl Bothwell, would have left her with no choice but to marry him to ensure that honour was not lost in the eyes of the public. Yet from all these differing accounts Mary emerges as a figure who neither restored the Catholic faith in Scotland nor legalised the Protestant Reformation, who produced almost no substantive legislation and whose one enduring legacy was

---

[4] See 'Timeline for Mary's Life' at the end of this chapter for further details.
[5] There are innumerable biographies of Mary, but key modern texts include Fraser, *Mary Queen of Scots*; Gordon Donaldson, *Mary Queen of Scots* (London, 1974); Guy, *My Heart is My Own*; Jenny Wormald, *Mary Queen of Scots: A Study in Failure* (London, 1988).
[6] Gordon Donaldson, *All the Queen's Men: Power and Politics in Mary Stewart's Scotland* (London, 1983).
[7] Michael Lynch, 'Introduction', in *Mary Stewart: Queen in Three Kingdoms*, ed. Michael Lynch (London, 1988); also published as *Innes Review* 38 (1987). There has been a range of subsequent research addressing this gap, for an entry point into which see Sarah Carpenter, 'Performing Diplomacies: The 1560s Court Entertainments of Mary Queen of Scots', *SHR* 82 (2003): 194–225.
[8] Retha Warnicke, *Mary Queen of Scots* (Abingdon and London, 2006); Kristen Post Walton, *Catholic Queen, Protestant Patriarchy: Mary, Queen of Scots, and the Politics of Gender and Religion* (Basingstoke and London, 2007); for Mary's female networks, see also Rosalind K. Marshall, *Queen Mary's Women: Female Friends, Family, Servants and Enemies of Mary, Queen of Scots* (Edinburgh, 2006).

the production of a male heir, James VI, who became the first ruler of a united British Isles in 1603.

However, Mary did have runaway success in one regard. She fervently hoped that the indignities she had suffered would be remembered as a direct assault on an anointed and lawful Catholic monarch. Her extensive deployment of Catholic ritual at her execution, including wearing a red bodice (the colour of martyrdom), constituted a final dramatic performance, whose aim was neatly summed up in Mary's own phrase: 'in my end is my beginning'. Her subsequent role in popular culture and imagination has far surpassed her contemporary impact, and her story has enjoyed perpetual retelling in every medium and reached a global audience over the past four and a half centuries. This collection is the culmination of a large, multi-partner, research project on Mary's cultural afterlife, which began in 2016 in collaboration with Anne Dulau Beveridge, art curator at the Hunterian, home to the University of Glasgow's fine art and museum collections.[9] It represents the fruits of research developed at workshops over four years by the main project contributors, plus additional essays specially commissioned to explore key aspects of Mary's afterlife not addressed during the life of the project. What follows is thus a collaborative and holistic assessment of Mary's reputation and depiction in popular culture, from the end of her personal reign in Scotland (1567) to the present. The authors variously address what changing representations of Mary over the past five centuries tell us about evolving attitudes towards gender, monarchy, power and religion in Scotland, and to Scotland's own perception of its history. This introduction provides an overview of the project's key research findings and posits a series of key themes and paradigms for interrogating and understanding Mary's cultural afterlife, which are informed by recent research trends in material culture and the history of objects, gender history, and communal memory and public history. It also reflects on the new methodologies and approaches that the project has helped to create for engaging public opinion in the curation and display of Marian objects, which have potential application to ambiguous and contested historical material more generally. A central feature of Mary's afterlife, as will be seen, is that her story is continually repurposed to reflect the society telling it.

Object afterlives: ambiguity, emotion, and material culture in perpetuating Mary's legacy

The project began as two workshops scoping the University of Glasgow collections for Marian objects, funded by the university's Centre for Scottish and Celtic Studies. This revealed that the university had a world-leading collection

---

[9] Named after William Hunter (1718–83), the famed Scottish physician and anatomist whose gift forms the core of the present-day collection.

of Marian items, particularly of contemporary coinage within the collection of the late Lord Stewartby (1935–2018) currently held by the Hunterian, and in a key painting of Mary, Gavin Hamilton's *Abdication of Mary Queen of Scots* (1776, discussed below: Figure I.1). The project then became a Royal Society of Edinburgh-funded research network between 2019 and 2021. It brought together more than 40 academics, museum curators and heritage specialists from every major Scottish heritage collection, the British Library and the Royal Collection Trust, to compile a complete census of Marian objects within their respective collections. In total just under 2,000 physical objects relating to Mary were uncovered, along with almost four times as many printed texts, ranging from contemporary pamphlets to modern biographies.

The survey resulted in several major discoveries of Marian material culture, discussed in Parts One and Three of this collection. Considerable attention has rightly been paid in previous scholarship to the surviving embroideries produced by Mary's own hands, the majority of which now reside in the Victoria and Albert Museum collection.[10] Mainly created during Mary's captivity, in collaboration with Bess of Hardwick, the wife of her chief jailor the earl of Shrewsbury, Mary's embroidery acted as an important creative outlet during the long boredom of her confinement. The embroideries were also active forms of protest, featuring anagrams and animal and plant motifs which spoke to triumph and rebirth after adversity – for example, Mary's depiction of a red-haired 'catte' pawing at a small brown mouse in a panel now held by the Royal Collection leaves little doubt that the two animals represent her and Elizabeth.[11] However, as Emily Wingfield shows in Chapter Three, the various devotional books that Mary owned and gifted across her lifetime were also active sites of self-commemoration, not fully appreciated until now due to their global dispersal. Mary frequently added verses of dedication to the recipients of these volumes, enjoining them to remember her, which project an image of her as deeply pious and show her skill at poetry. They also served as textual repositories which she used to mark significant events, as seen in the St Petersburg Book of Hours, which she signed and filled with verse at many points across her life.

The objects logged in the census are notable for their exceptionally wide range of analogue material forms, including images (portraits and other depictions, coins, photographic portrayals of young women as Mary); objects (clothing, furniture, purported relics such as locks of hair); and commemorative items (jewellery, dolls, stained glass). Unlike the embroideries and books, most of these items have what might kindly be termed 'ambiguous' links to Mary.

---

[10] See (for example) Michael Bath, *Emblems for a Queen: The Needlework of Mary Queen of Scots* (London, 2008); Clare Hunter, *Embroidering Her Truth: Mary, Queen of Scots and the Language of Power* (London, 2022). Most of the embroideries are now on long-term loan to the National Trust, where they are displayed at Oxburgh Hall in Norfolk.

[11] Royal Collections Trust, 'A Catte' (*c.* 1569–84), RCIN 28224.

For example, multiple crucifixes in British heritage collections (including the Craigmillar Crucifix discussed by Anna Groundwater in Chapter 12) are said to have belonged to Mary, but none have a demonstrable link to her. There are, to take another example, three different variants of an alleged cast of her face made at death, none of which bear a similarity to the others. Their ambiguity is further compounded by the proliferation of multiple and competing physical and digital copies of individual items. As Alison Wiggins and Jade Scott note in Chapter Four, there are numerous transcripts and editions of Mary's original letters, which in the digital age have become even more complex as 'copies of copies', for example microfilms or .jpg and .pdf files of calendared transcripts of original letters. In processing and reprocessing these texts we have often lost sight of the physical artefacts that underpin them. Much of what we take as their 'authentic' text is in fact mediated through imperfect summary translation and decryption of early modern French and cipher.[12] The fact that so many original letter packets have been separated across different repositories, then bound and flattened into themed codices, means we are missing vital context as to how these packets were used by Mary to present herself to different audiences.

A common trait in many objects examined by the project, but especially ones well-known or on display, is their capacity to generate strong 'evocative' responses in those who engage with them, often at the direct expense of acknowledging their highly contested provenance and past itineraries. Julie Holder shows (Chapter Ten) that this issue was already apparent in the treatment of Marian items during the development of the National Museum of Antiquities of Scotland collection in the nineteenth century. Several key items associated with Mary, including the Queen Mary Harp that she allegedly gifted to Beatrix Gardyn of Banchory and a multitude of keys from Loch Leven, were viewed in this period with increasing scepticism or reframed to prioritise a different narrative of their cultural importance, in the case of the harp by showcasing its beauty as a surviving example of late medieval Highland woodwork. However, the tercentenary exhibitions relating to Mary at Peterborough, London and Glasgow in 1887 all made extensive use of personal relics from private lenders and were far more subjective and romantic in their approach, to appeal to the interests of the broader public. This tension between entertaining and educating is also apparent in Deborah Clarke's narrative of Mary's long afterlife at the Palace of Holyroodhouse, the site of Mary's court for most of her personal reign and of the brutal murder of David Rizzio in March 1566 (Chapter Eleven). Visitors, tourists and artists are often highly affected by the physicality of this core site of Marian history, even willingly suspending disbelief over some of its

---

[12] For an important new discovery in this regard, see George Lasry, Norbert Biermann, and Satoshi Tomokiyo, 'Deciphering Mary Stuart's lost letters from 1578–1584', *Cryptologia* 47 (2023): 101–202.

more spurious claims to authenticity, such as the miraculous survival of Rizzio's bloodstain on the timber floor of Mary's apartments for four and a half centuries. The projection of a Marian provenance onto the seventeenth-century Duchess of Hamilton's 'Red Bed' was a myth first perpetuated by the housekeeper, who gave private tours of Mary's chambers, and was only reluctantly abandoned in the early twentieth century. This anecdote neatly captures the blending of historical fact with accreted layers of myth often found in the history of Marian objects, and the difficulties curators face in disentangling the two.

However, as Anna Groundwater notes in her reflections on curating Mary for the twenty-first century at the National Museums of Scotland (Chapter Twelve), a broad range of disciplines have increasingly acknowledged the value of problematic and non-textual historical artefacts over the past four decades. Their own itinerant lives and the problems in reconstructing these have been debated, as has the nature of their entanglement with our own temporal existence as objects created in the past and in use or on display now, and their ability to generate empathetic and non-rational responses in their viewers. Mary's place in the communal memory of Scotland, she argues, is similarly contested, and shaped by emotion and supposition rather than critical evaluation of the queen's life and reign. This is particularly the case with much of the rich jewellery and personal ornaments associated with Mary, such as the Penicuik Jewels and her alleged pomander beads, which give the viewer an immediate sense of intimacy with the queen, even though they cannot physically touch them. As Groundwater suggests, the central role of the public in perpetuating this process of memorialisation must be acknowledged and incorporated into their narratives. When allegedly Marian objects have a spurious or unclear provenance, how they have been remembered or interwoven into Mary's story across time becomes the true signifier of their historical value.

Textual afterlives: Mary in literature

The cultural afterlives of many key sixteenth century historical figures, particularly queens, has been a growing scholarly field over the past two decades.[13] Mary is no stranger to this historiography, particularly in examinations of literary depictions of her life, which in its neat divisions between her time in France, her personal reign and her captivity in England could easily be adapted into a three-act play (and frequently has been). This began with James Emerson Phillips' study of Mary's portrayal in propagandistic texts during her own

[13] Michael Dobson and Nicola J. Watson, *England's Elizabeth: an Afterlife in Fame and Fantasy* (Oxford, 2002); Stephanie Russo, *The Afterlife of Anne Boleyn: Representations of Anne Boleyn in Fiction and on the Screen* (London, 2020); Estelle Paranque (ed.), *Remembering Queens and Kings of Early Modern England and France* (London, 2019); for the afterlife of a single text, see Bruce Gordon, *John Calvin's* Institutes of the Christian Religion: *A Biography* (Princeton, NJ, 2016).

lifetime and shortly afterwards, where it became apparent that a highly divisive, binary narrative developed from the final moments of her personal reign. On one side lay anti-Marian texts written by men like George Buchanan, in which Mary was portrayed as a willing accomplice in Darnley's murder and as an adulteress with Bothwell. On the other side, John Leslie the bishop of Ross and several authors in France responded to Buchanan's ideas, depicting Mary as a devout Catholic, a loving wife to Darnley and above all a fit and able monarch from the longest-serving royal dynasty in Europe who had been forcibly ousted by a group of rebels.[14]

Mary's literary afterlife has been studied in multiple contexts, with John Staines and Jayne Lewis mapping out her place in British texts from her own time until the late nineteenth century.[15] Staines has shown that Mary remained a politically live figure in cultural debates for as long as the Stuart dynasty remained on the British throne, with her story filtered according to the need of various factions – Protestant and Catholic, republican and royalist – to portray her as either the virtuous and blameless mother of a dynasty facing unjustified persecution from its subjects, or as the first in a line of would-be tyrants who needed to be removed from power. While Mary retained some resonance as a political figurehead in the material culture of the Jacobites,[16] Lewis notes that in the eighteenth and nineteenth centuries she became unmoored entirely from historical consideration and turned into a source of inspiration for plays, novels and art.[17] However, in this period literary and historical portrayals alike of Mary were heavily romanticised and actively reflected the gender constructs of Georgian and Victorian society. The tragedy and pathos associated with the Marian legend triggered a series of 'affective' portrayals of a chaste and submissive Mary in the eighteenth century, before giving way to more liberated, independent and occasionally sexually transgressive versions in the nineteenth.[18]

Unsurprisingly, a central element running through these texts was gendered response to Mary. Men like the historians Walter Goodall, William Robertson

---

[14] James Emerson Phillips, *Images of a Queen: Mary Stuart in Sixteenth-Century Literature* (Berkeley, CA; Berlin, 1964).

[15] John D. Staines, *The Tragic Histories of Mary Queen of Scots, 1560–1690: Rhetoric, Passions and Political Literature* (London and New York, 2009); Jayne Elizabeth Lewis, *Mary Queen of Scots: Romance and Nation* (London and New York, 1998).

[16] Murray Pittock, 'Treacherous Objects: Towards a Theory of Jacobite Material Culture', *Journal for Eighteenth Century Studies* 34 (2011) no. 1: 39–63; Murray Pittock, *Material Culture and Sedition, 1688–1760: Treacherous Objects, Secret Places* (London, 2013).

[17] Jayne Elizabeth Lewis, 'Hamilton's "Abdication", Boswell's Jacobitism and the Myth of Mary Queen of Scots', *ELH* 64 (1997): 1069–90.

[18] Joy Currie, 'Mary Queen of Scots as Suffering Woman: Representations by Mary Stuart and William Wordsworth', in *'High and Mighty Queens' of Early Modern England: Realities and Representations*, ed. Carole Levin, Jo Edgridge Carney and Debra Barrett-Graves (London, 2003), pp. 187–202; Paula de Pando, *John Bank's Female Tragic Heroes: Re-Imagining Tudor Queens in Restoration She-Tragedy* (Leiden, 2018).

and David Hume and the novelist Sir Walter Scott wished to judge, excuse and even own Mary – literally in Scott's case, as he installed a wooden engraving of her death mask on his library ceiling and hung what was believed to be a picture of her severed head painted shortly after death in his dining room. As Michelle Craig's examination of Dr William Hunter's collection of Marian books reveals (Chapter Five), Scott was not alone in this preoccupation. Mary was the only person within Hunter's extensive library to be given her own subject heading and he devoted considerable investment over the space of some fourteen years to assembling the latest texts on her during the height of the controversy over the authorship of the Casket Letters (the letters allegedly written by Mary that proved her complicity in the murder of Darnley and her willing adultery with Bothwell) in the late eighteenth century. Women, by contrast, particularly those on the margins of society, were historically more interested in identifying and empathising with her. Key texts in this regard include Sophia Lee's gothic novel *The Recess*, centring on a pair of twin sisters secretly born to Mary from the Duke of Norfolk and hidden in the eponymous ruins of a convent destroyed in the Henrician purges; the emotionally charged accounts of Mary's life produced by Eliza Haywood, Agnes Strickland and by Jane Austen in her juvenile manuscript masterpiece, the *History of England*;[19] and the homoerotically charged portrayal of Mary and her handmaids in *The Tragic Mary*, written by 'Michael Field' (the pen name for the lesbian aunt-and-niece couple Katharine Harris Bradley and Edith Emma Cooper).

Conversely, Alexander Wilkinson has shown that in French literary culture there was a distinct lack of interest in the former queen of France after her return to Scotland, until her death triggered a huge outpouring of pro-Catholic propaganda.[20] This led to the formation of an enduring reputation for Mary on the continent quite separate to its British counterpart, where she was remembered first and foremost as a Catholic martyr and secondly as a renaissance queen of France. The seventeenth and eighteenth centuries saw a proliferation of novels, plays, tragedies and operas across Europe, but particularly in Spain, Italy, Germany and France. These ranged from Jean De Bordes' unpublished *Maria Stuarta Tragoedia* (first performed at the College of Brera in 1589–90) through to Edme Boursault's *Marie Stuard* (1683).[21] This tradition arguably

---

[19] Jayne Lewis, '"Ev'ry lost relation:" Historical Fictions and Sentimental Incidents in Sophia Lee's *The Recess*', *Eighteenth-Century Fiction* 7 (1995): 165–84; Matthew J. Rigilano, 'The Recess does not Exist: Absorption, Literality, and Feminine Subjectivity in Sophia Lee's *The Recess*', *Eighteenth-Century Fiction* 26 (2013): 209–32; Vickie L. Taft, '*The Tragic Mary*: A Case Study in Michael Field's Understanding of Sexual Politics', *Nineteenth-Century Contexts* 23 (2001): 265–95.

[20] Alexander S. Wilkinson, *Mary Queen of Scots and French Public Opinion, 1542–1600* (Basingstoke and New York, 2004).

[21] Stefano Villi, 'From Mary Queen of Scots to the Scottish Capuchins: Scotland as a Symbol of Protestant Persecution in Seventeenth-Century Italian Literature', *The Innes Review* 64 (2013): 100–11.

culminated in Friedrich Schiller's *Maria Stuart* (1800), a verse tragedy focusing on Mary's later imprisonment and execution, which was then transformed by Gaetano Donizetti into the tragic operetta *Maria Stuarda* (1835). Both have enjoyed a unique cultural afterlife of their own, with regular revivals across the world as Gerry Carruthers (Chapter Seven) and Tim Duguid (Chapter Thirteen) note. Alongside this, new literary and dramatic portrayals have continually been generated in the twentieth and twenty-first centuries, including Maxwell Anderson's Broadway play *Mary of Scotland* (1933), the basis for the film of the same title starring Katharine Hepburn that premiered three years later; Robert Bolt's *Vivat! Vivat! Regina*, which premiered in Chichester in 1970 and later travelled to Broadway; and the 2019 dramatic monologue *Mary Said What She Said* by Darryl Pinckney, featuring Isabelle Huppert with music by Ludovico Einaudi in sell-out shows across Europe.

As Parts One and Three of this collection offer fundamentally new ways of considering how to approach and value Marian objects, so too do the five chapters of Part Two constitute a significant new intervention in studies of Mary's literary reception, focussing on Scottish literary and historical responses from the eighteenth century through to the present day. Key themes that emerge are the role gender plays in the positioning of authors, historians and critics writing about Mary; the ambiguity of stance that writers can take when discussing the queen; and the enduring applicability of Mary's story to contemporary political and societal concerns. Michelle Craig (Chapter Five) charts the reception of James Anderson's early attempt to create an 'objective' corpus of Marian documents with his four-volume *Collections Relating to the History of Mary Queen of Scotland* (1727–28), and the lengths to which he went to demonstrate to his readers that his sources had been rigorously synthesised from archives across Europe. Rhona Brown (Chapter Six) explores periodic responses across the eighteenth century to the debates over Mary's culpability in her own downfall and to the new histories that emerged in the wake of Anderson's efforts, such as Walter Goodall's *Examination of the Letters said to have been written by Mary Queen of Scots* (1754). Collectively, they show that a new spirit of Enlightened objective enquiry was being applied to the textual evidence of Mary's life. However, this was by no means a linear process, and religious sympathies, the lingering spectre of Jacobitism and pro- or anti-Union feeling continued to shape the views of authors. The rise of the literature of Sensibility and affective sympathy further complicated this evolution, particularly along gendered lines. Despite the assertions of cool rationality, male authors aggressively attacked or defended Mary in a curiously intense and personal way, perhaps most notably exemplified by Gilbert Stuart, whose *History of Scotland from the Establishment of the Reformation till the Death of Queen Mary* (1782) won praise for its sympathetic portrayal of the queen's plight. Stuart publicly pursued his fellow historian William Robertson to recant his view of Mary, first published in the latter's

History of Scotland, during the Reigns of Queen Mary and King James VI (1759), as guilty of her alleged crimes. This literary joust, played out in front of Edinburgh high society, was notable both for its portrayal of Stuart and his fellow combatant as vigorously masculine knights competing for Mary's honour, and for the widespread support Stuart's active defence of Mary garnered from key society figures including the Earl of Buchan, President of the Society of Antiquaries.

The affective portrayal of Mary also proved central to literary presentations of Mary in the late eighteenth and early nineteenth century, as Gerry Carruthers's examination of 'Romantic' texts by authors including Robert Burns, William Wordsworth and Sir Walter Scott shows (Chapter Seven). Burns and Wordsworth created defiant and tragic versions of Mary, portraying the queen as closely attuned to nature and yet constrained by her captivity in England. Burns' 'Lament for Mary Queen of Scots' was directly influenced by William Tytler, whose *Historical and Critical Enquiry* (1759) into the evidence presented against Mary at the York-Westminster trial was lauded for its objectivity. However, the poet's comments on Mary to both Tytler and Lady Winifred Maxwell Constable show a sympathetic engagement with the queen, tailored to his respective audiences, that appeared almost Catholic and Jacobite in tone. Affective versions of Mary culminated in Scott's *The Abbot* (1820), which recounted her escape from Loch Leven and depicted her as a siren radiating royal power and a bewitching sexuality. Scott, whose deep and conflicted affection for Mary was most visible in the macabre collection of Marian curios he owned, epitomises the view of her under the late Georgian male gaze as an object of both sympathy and desire.

Gender and religion continued to play central roles in Scottish historical and literary presentations of Mary in the modern era, as Catriona Macdonald and Nia Clark confirm (Chapters Eight and Nine). Macdonald's examination of two pairs of Mary's biographers – David Hay Fleming and Andrew Lang, and Antonia Fraser and Gordon Donaldson – reflects a broader narrative of the professionalisation of the historical discipline in Scotland and the slow progress made in gaining purchase for the views of both non-academics and women within that space. Hay Fleming's empirical and exceptionally detailed life of Mary was frequently perceived as more objective than Lang's material culture-led approach to the queen. Yet Hay Fleming was just as driven by subjectivity, in his case by his desire to defend the centrality of the Protestant Reformation in Scotland's national history and to quash all interest in the Catholic Mary. Neither men were university professionals, and nor was Lady Fraser, while Donaldson was very much part of the mid-century historical establishment at the University of Edinburgh. While Fraser's work became (and remains) the standard general biography of Mary's life, it was greeted on its first publication in 1969 with considerable scepticism. This mixed reception was shaped by observations of her dramatic private life, her physical beauty and her outsider status as an 'amateur' historian. In a process showing surprising parallels with Enlightenment developments in historical criticism, the retelling of Mary's story in the twentieth century, while ultimately incorporating novel material approaches and perspectives, remained constrained by establishment dictations of what 'history' should be, and by whom it should be practised.

The broader impact of misogyny and sectarianism in Scottish culture was addressed in the most famous and subversive modern commemoration of Mary's life, Liz Lochhead's *Mary Queen of Scots Got Her Head Chopped Off* (1987). Written to coincide with the quatercentenary of Mary's execution, it shows Lochhead's enduring concern with religion and gender in modern Scotland, and the impact of cultural and social decline following a decade of Thatcherism. Clark shows these themes were a central feature of much of Lochhead's early corpus, and places Lochhead within a broader group of female authors who, since the late 1980s, have used Mary's story as a lens through which to examine pressing social issues. While poems and plays by Marion McCready, Gerda Stevenson and Linda McLean all tap in to the long history of portraying Mary as an affective figure, they also take this view in distinct new directions, whether directly tackling the horror of the miscarriage that Mary endured at Loch Leven in the summer of 1567 or highlighting the role sexual violence and patriarchal control played in dictating her political fortunes. Collectively, these works – and indeed all those surveyed for this volume – show the infinite capability of Mary's story to be retold in ways that accord with changing values in Scottish society, and particularly in relation to shifting conceptions of gender.

Imaged afterlives: Mary in art and on screen

While Mary has been commemorated extensively in text, she is best known in the public consciousness as an iconic image – of an austere queen resplendent in black dress, with auburn hair, a white cap and ruff, and (usually) some form of religious accessory, such as a prayer book, crucifix or rosary. The project has explored the transmission of this image in depth, and in fact the project originated in a discussion between the co-investigators over coffee regarding a key Marian painting owned by The Hunterian, Gavin Hamilton's *The Abdication of Mary Queen of Scots*, commissioned by James Boswell and first displayed at the Royal Academy in London in 1776. Based in Rome for most of his career, Hamilton was famed as a neo-Classical artist, and extensively deployed Classical dress and architecture in his work.[22] While Boswell exulted in 'being the Patron of so fine a picture from Scottish History', Hamilton made it clear that his Mary was not based on any 'real' portrait of the queen, but was a composite and idealised 'beauty in distress' (as he termed her) developed from known

---

[22] See, for example, his *Hector's Farewell to Andromache*, The Hunterian, GLAHA: 44127.

Figure I.1 Gavin Hamilton, *The Abdication of Mary Queen of Scots*, 1765–73
Courtesy of The Hunterian: GLAHA 43874

portraits and historical accounts.[23] While the dress in the painting owes more to Georgian fashions than those of the sixteenth century, a recent cleaning of it following technical conservation has revealed how central is the cap on her head, previously obscured by layers of dirt, in identifying the queen for the viewers.

Hamilton's work marks the precise mid-point of an arc of artistic representations, beginning with ostensibly authentic portraits of Mary going back to the fragile chalk sketches done at the French court by François Clouet in 1558, and culminating in the highly stylised painting sequence completed by Helen Flockhart in 2018 (discussed by Daniel Fountain and Alicia Hughes in Chapter Fifteen).

---

[23] Charles N. Fifer (ed.), *Correspondence of James Boswell, with Certain Members of the Club* (New York, 1976), p. 56; Lewis, 'Hamilton's "Abdication"'.

The known corpus of painted and coin portraits of Mary was catalogued in a series of works across the twentieth century, particularly the *catalogue raisonné* produced by Helen Smailes and Duncan Thomson for their 1987 exhibition 'The Queen's Image', which showcased Mary in a range of static media.[24] Two core themes emerge from these surveys. Firstly, whether we have any true recorded likenesses of Mary is highly debatable, as the details in each of the early portraits vary significantly beyond the general features of hazel eyes, high forehead, soft chin and sharp nose. Secondly, posthumous renderings of Mary, as Lionel Cust noted, are even more suspect because artists have always invested images of Mary with 'that particular attributed likeness which tallied most with their own preconceived idea'.[25] This trend is certainly apparent in Forrest P. Chisman's study of the multiple copies of Mary's *en deuil blanc* or mourning veil portraits, where her face initially hardens in seventeenth-century versions to reflect growing criticism of the Stuarts as a corrupt dynasty, only to soften and round out over the eighteenth century to match changing aesthetics of feminine beauty.[26]

Mary and her supporters worked hard to frame her within an iconography of Catholic martyrdom, both at the time of her death and immediately afterwards. This remained an important strand of Marian cultural expression, visible in the calls for Mary's beatification as late as the 1930s.[27] That iconography is captured in a sequence of paintings known as the Sheffield portrait type, featuring Mary in three-quarter or full-body pose (see Chapter One, Figure 1.1). There has been considerable debate surrounding the origins of these portraits, but nearly all are redolent with the imagery of Catholic martyrdom.[28] They include tableaus of scenes from Mary's execution, Latin panegyrical text commemorating her piety

---

[24] Precursors to this process include Sir George Scharf, 'Observations on the Principal Portraits of Mary I, Queen of England and Mary, Queen of Scots', *Proceedings of the Society of Antiquaries*, 2nd series, 7 (1876): 49–66; Lionel Cust, *Notes on the Authentic Portraits of Mary, Queen of Scots* (1903); and Andrew Lang, 'Portraits and Jewels of Mary Stuart', SHR 3 (1906): 129–56, 274–300. Helen Smailes and Duncan Thomson, *The Queen's Image: A Celebration of Mary Queen of Scots* (London, 1987).

[25] Cust, *Notes on the Authentic Portraits of Mary*, p. 2.

[26] Forrest P. Chisman, 'The Portraits of Mary, Queen of Scots, "En Deuil Blanc": A Study in Copying', *The British Art Journal* 6 (2005): 23–27.

[27] The papers of Scotland's Eastern District Vicariate record a serious attempt to begin a process of beatification for Mary at the tercentenary of her execution in 1887: Scottish Catholic Archive (Columba House), ED4/85-92. My thanks to Andrew R. Nicholl for this information. See also John Quinlan, 'Was Mary Stuart a Martyr?', *The Irish Monthly* 61, no. 725 (1933): 665–70.

[28] See Chapters One and Two for a fuller discussion. Jeremy L. Smith, 'Revisiting the Origins of the Sheffield Series of Portraits of Mary Queen of Scots', *Burlington Magazine* 152 (2010): 212–18; Jeremy L. Smith, 'The Sheffield Portrait Types, Their Catholic Purposes, and Mary Queen of Scots's Tomb', *British Catholic History* 33 (2016): 71–90; Marguerite A. Tassi, 'Martyrdom and Memory: Elizabeth Curle's Portrait of Mary, Queen of Scots', in *The Emblematic Queen: Extra-Literary Representations of Early Modern Queenship*, ed. Debra Barrett-Graves (Basingstoke, 2013), pp. 101–32.

and suffering for the faith, and coded allegorical symbols such as a depiction of Susanna and the elders on Mary's crucifix.[29]

As David Taylor shows in his comprehensive survey of extant contemporary portraits of Mary (Chapter One), the iconography in the Sheffield portraits played a central role in fixing and transmitting a globally recognisable image of the queen, one that compensated for the highly changeable facial presentation of the central 'Mary' in each portrait. While a wide variety of sketched and coin likenesses survive from Mary's early life and her time in France, only one image – a joint portrait with Darnley from around 1565 – can be dated with confidence to her personal reign, and we are wholly dependent on the Sheffield paintings to get a sense of her adult features. The Sheffield type was modified in a variety of painted, engraved and sculpted examples across Europe between the late 1570s and the 1610s. A new examination of the visual evidence of the Sheffield portraits by Caroline Rae (Chapter Two) makes a compelling case that Mary herself led the creation of this portrait type, precisely with her own memorialisation in mind. A comparison of facial tracings taken from the various portraits reveals that the leaner and more angular physical appearance of Mary in the latter grouping fits better with contemporary descriptions of her in the late 1570s. Moreover, the portrayal of decor, furnishings and Mary's own costume in the Sheffield portraits is more in keeping with the fashions of the French Valois court with which Mary was intimately familiar, suggesting that as patron she was influencing their style and content.

Rae links the Sheffield portraits to her astounding discovery of a 'hidden' image of Mary beneath a painting of James VI's secretary John Maitland of Thirlestane by the court artist Adrian Vanson. Found using x-radiography, the 'Maitland Mary', completed at some point between the late 1570s and 1589, is closer in appearance to the Sheffield type and appears to have been the basis for other portraits that appeared in Scotland in the early 1580s (such as the *c.* 1583 double portrait of Mary and James VI, now at Blair Atholl). This further suggests that it was Mary herself, in the late 1570s, who inaugurated the tradition of painted memorials so decisive in shaping her later visual commemoration. However, the deliberate over-painting of Mary in the Maitland example, rightly described by Taylor as a *damnatio memoriae*, possibly reflects a wider campaign of destruction by the party around the young king as they sought to remove any

---

[29] Only the 'Dalmahoy' or 'Morton' portrait, now in the Glasgow Life Collection, is devoid of any overt religious symbolism, though the jewelled pendant that Mary holds in the painting may have once been a crucifix, now painted over: Glasgow Life, 'Mary, Queen of Scots (1542–1587)', accession no. 1685. Susanna was a character in the Book of Daniel (chapter 13) falsely accused of adultery by two elders after she refused to have sexual intercourse with them. Her pursuers are struck down by their community for their false allegations, making the story an apt parallel for Mary's own. Jeremy L Smith, 'Mary Queen of Scots as Susanna in Catholic Propaganda', *Journal of the Warburg and Courtauld Institutes* 73 (2010): 209–20.

trace of her memory from Scotland, which would also explain the near-complete absence of images from her personal reign.

A key discovery in research by the co-investigators on the project was the role played by the thriving early modern European market for engravings and woodcuts in establishing Mary's iconographical fixity across Europe. Cheap to produce and easy to adapt, these images could be sold as standalone single broadsheets, or inserted as illustrations in larger works, and were accessible to a much wider range of purchasers than elite paintings.[30] A central image of Mary could also be modified and embellished with a high degree of specificity to accommodate a particular didactic purpose, whether that was to convince citizens of the British Isles that Mary was a regal mother of the Stuart dynasty, or to show Europe that she was the martyred and rightful queen of France, Britain and Ireland. While a range of engravings of Mary circulated during her time at the French court, the earliest example of a didactic engraving was published in 1578, in John Leslie's *Ten Books on the Origin, Customs, and Deeds of the Scots* (see Chapter Two, Figure 2.14).[31] The Mary in this engraving shares marked facial similarities with those seen in the early Sheffield portraits, and is linked to a smaller portrait of Mary's young son, James VI, via a range of paratext. In the year of publication James had technically declared himself an adult ruler as part of a coup led by the earls of Atholl and Argyll against his last regent, James Douglas, earl of Morton, a fact which furthered diminished Mary's already slim chances of successfully reclaiming her throne.[32] The image is designed to project her royal authority to a Europe-wide public at the direct expense of her son. Displaying Mary with a large royal crown, it proclaims her firm place as '107th in the line of kings' (*ordine regum CVII*) and deliberately emphasises James' status as both a prince and a minor, his physical features looking more akin to those of a 6-year-old than his actual 12 years.

While this image established an important parallel track in the creation of a Marian iconography, the sheer volume of engravings and woodcuts of Mary quickly outpaced the limited production and circulation of painted portraits.[33] These broadly follow three typologies: an engraving of Mary in full- or half-length portrait; an engraving of Mary's head and shoulders; or an engraving of her execution scene. Richard Verstegan's *Theatrum Crudelitatum*, a history of English martyrs produced within six months after Mary's death, features a

---

[30] For further details see the forthcoming article by Anne Dulau Beveridge and Steven J. Reid, 'A Queen Engraved: the Evolution of Mary Queen of Scots' Image in Print, *c.* 1578–1800'.

[31] John Leslie, *De origine, moribus, et rebus gestis Scotorum, libri decem* (Rome, 1578), p. 440.

[32] Steven J. Reid, *The Early Life of James VI: A Long Apprenticeship, 1566–1585* (Edinburgh, 2023), Chapter Four.

[33] A volume of these engravings collected by John Allan contains over 260 examples of this phenomenon, most of which are distinct. 'Portraits of Mary Queen of Scotland with graphic illustrations of her Life and Reign Collected by John Allan Esqr', National Galleries Scotland, PGE 86.

Figure I.2 Richard Verstegan, *Theatrum crudelitatum haereticorum nostri temporis* ('The spectacle of the cruelties of the heretics of our time', Antwerp, 1587)
Courtesy of University of Glasgow Archives & Special Collections: Sp. Coll. BC32-f.27

highly stylised woodcut of her execution at Fotheringhay, which was copied in reverse format into Adam Blackwood's *Histoire et Martyre de la Reyne d'Escosse*.[34]

Mary's head-and-shoulder image could appear plain and unadorned save for a note of her title, as was the case with an example pasted into the frontispiece of a copy of Blackwood's *Martyre de la royne d'escosse* (1587), or the same image could be amplified with cherubs, Mary's royal arms, scenes of her execution and a Latin account of her life (see Chapter One, Figure 1.2).[35]

---

[34] Adam Blackwood, *Histoire et Martyre de la Royne d'Escosse . . . Avec un petit livret de sa mort* (Paris, 1589), opposite p. 12; Richard Verstegan, *Theatrum crudelitatum haereticorum nostri temporis* (Antwerp, 1587), p. 85.

[35] For other examples, see National Galleries Scotland PGE 86.002 (Wierix Brothers, late sixteenth century); PGE 86.038 (J. Leipoldt, 1587).

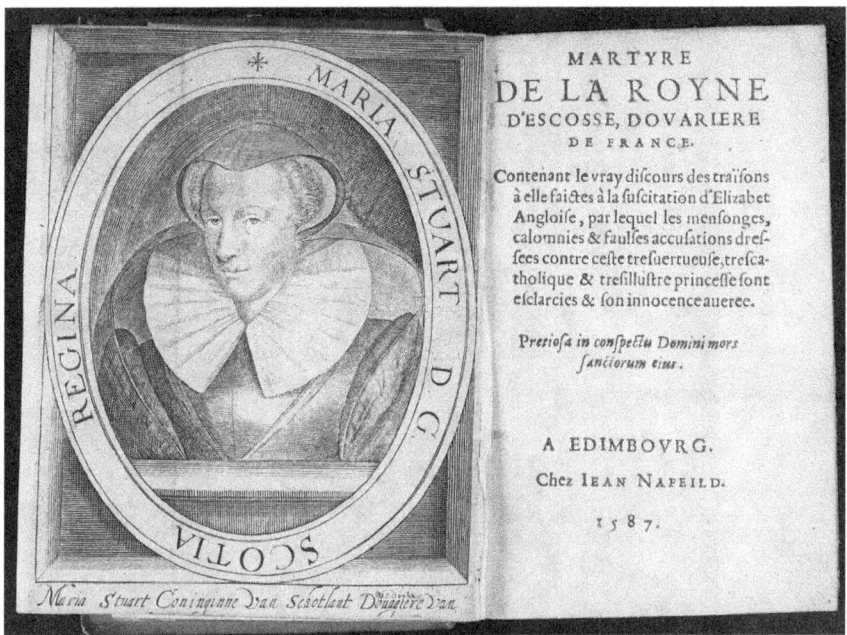

Figure I.3 Frontispiece inserted in Adam Blackwood, *Martyre de la Royne d'Escosse* . . . (Paris, 1587) Courtesy of University of Glasgow Archives & Special Collections: Sp. Coll. Hunterian Cn.3.39

These images became more elaborate over the course of the seventeenth century, and featured Mary variously with the four crowns of France and the British Isles, crucifixes and rosaries, and even implements from her execution (see Chapter Fifteen, Figure 15.7). Mary could even be made to appear distinctly Elizabethan, as was the case in the frontispiece of the first account of Mary's life in English by William Udall.[36]

Udall's account was based on the Latin *Annales* of Elizabeth's reign by William Camden, who had been under some pressure from James VI and I to give a sympathetic account of his mother and thus bolster the image of the Stuart monarchy as descending from an honourable matriarch. The image of Mary in Udall's version (based on an earlier print by Renold or Reginold Elstrack) retains Mary's usual cap and ruff but is given a royal sceptre and a dress and hair very similar to that of her cousin (see Chapter One, Figure 1.3).[37] In all these images, however, the iconographic elements – cap, cross/rosary and to a lesser extent ruff and dress – play the central role in conveying to the viewer that they are looking at a version of Mary, Queen of Scots, even if that version's

---

[36] William Udall, *The Historie of the Life and Death of Mary Stuart, Queene of Scotland* (London, 1636). Copy consulted: University of Glasgow, Sp. Coll. Hunterian Cn.3.36.

[37] For the Elstrack print, see National Galleries Scotland SP I 23.14 (*c.* 1618).

Figure I.4 Frontispiece to William Udall, *The Historie of the Life and Death of Mary Stuart, Queene of Scotland* (London, 1636)
Courtesy of University of Glasgow Archives & Special Collections: Sp. Coll. Hunterian Cn.3.36

facial features look markedly different to those found in images believed to be more historically accurate. This iconography became a fixed element in nearly all images thereafter, to the extent that by the mid-eighteenth century engravings featuring women with virtually no physical resemblance to Mary could be claimed as Mary simply by virtue of it. It was this silent revolution in more affordable black and white prints that established the queen in the popular global consciousness.

In the modern era the iconographic shorthand for Mary has continued to flourish in an array of popular media, ranging from girls' magazines and children's books through to mature graphic novels and Disney cartoons. It is in film and television that Mary's image has featured most.[38] The first ever film to depict Scottish history on screen was an 18-second clip portraying Mary's execution at Fotheringhay, produced by the Edison company in New York in 1895.[39] Featuring the actor Robert Thomae dressed as Mary, the piece was also the first to use a 'jump cut' special effect, where filming was paused and the figure of 'Mary' replaced with a mannequin with detachable head. The resulting reels were then spliced together to produce a realistic-looking beheading. Mary has been the titular subject of multiple full-length feature films since, ranging from Pathé Frères' *Marie Stuart* (1908) through to Josie Rourke's *Mary Queen of Scots* (2018).[40] She has also appeared as either the central figure or main foil to Elizabeth in a range of television adaptations of the lives of the queens, from the BBC's highly acclaimed six-part miniseries *Elizabeth R* (1971, starring Vivian Pickles as Mary) through to *Reign*, a highly watched (and wholly inaccurate) TV series based on her early life in France produced by the CW network which ran for four seasons between 2013 and 2017.[41]

Perhaps the most surprising instance of filmic Marian afterlife is *Das Herz der Königin* (dir: Carl Fröelich, 1940), produced in Berlin by Universum-Film Aktiengesellschaft and starring the German-Swedish actress and cabaret star Zarah Leander in the title role.[42] As well as featuring an unusual revenge plot against Mary involving Bothwell's first wife, Jean Gordon, the film portrays an imagined rustic Scotland and its folk culture, represented by Leander's frequent diversions into minstrel songs and the portrayal of puppet shows and other 'traditional' performances, as under threat from the imperialist aggression of Elizabeth I and her council, making the piece a thinly disguised piece of Nazi propaganda. The quality and accuracy of films of Mary's life has been heavily debated,[43] and gendered readings of the 1936, 1971 and 2018 films have been particularly

---

[38] Elizabeth Ford and Deborah C. Mitchell, *Royal Portraits in Hollywood: Filming the Lives of Queens* (Kentucky, 2009); Ingibjörg Ágústsdóttir, 'Mary Queen of Scots as Feminine and National Icon: Depictions in Film and Fiction', *Études écossaises* 15 (2012): 75–93 (https://doi.org/10.4000/etudesecossaises.603).

[39] William Heise (camera), 'The Execution of Mary Queen of Scots', National Library of Scotland Moving Images Archive (https://movingimage.nls.uk/film/4413).

[40] See Chapter Fourteen for films before 1923. Denison Clift (dir.), *The Loves of Mary Queen of Scots* (1923); John Ford (dir.), *Mary of Scotland* (1936); Carl Froelich (dir.), *Das Herz der Königin* (1940); Charles Jarrott (dir.), *Mary, Queen of Scots* (1971); Thomas Imbach (dir.), *Mary Queen of Scots* (2013); Josie Rourke (dir.), *Mary Queen of Scots* (2018).

[41] Other instances include *Gunpowder, Treason and Plot* (BBC, 2004), starring Clémence Poésy as Mary; *Elizabeth I* (2005), starring Helen Mirren as Elizabeth and Barbara Flynn as Mary; and *The Serpent Queen* (Starz, 2022), starring Samantha Morton as Catherine de' Medici and Antonia Clarke as Mary.

[42] Geoff Brown, 'The Heart of a Queen', *Monthly Film Bulletin* 49, issue 576 (1982): 115.

[43] John Guy, 'Mary, Queen of Scots (1971)', pp. 136–49; Steven J. Reid, '*Mary Queen of Scots*: Don't Worry about Movie Accuracy, Historians Can't Agree on Who She Really Was Either', *The Conversation*, January 2019 (https://theconversation.com/mary-queen-of-scots-dont-worry-about-movie-accuracy-historians-cant-agree-on-who-she-really-was-either-109993).

Figure I.5 *Das Herz der Königin* (dir: Carl Fröelich, 1940), promotional poster
Cinematerial.com

divided. Jennifer M. DeSilva and Emily K. McGuire have welcomed the turn in screen portrayals over the past decade from framing Mary's life within a context of confessional and religious conflict towards one where her main enemy is the entrenched patriarchy she encounters in France and Scotland.[44] Shelley Anne Galpin, by contrast, has suggested that the 2018 film especially presents the story of Mary and Elizabeth as a reductive and binary narrative, in

---

[44] Jennifer M. DeSilva and Emily K. McGuire, 'Revising Mary Queen of Scots: From Protestant Persecution to Patriarchal Struggle', *Journal of Religion & Film* 25 (2021) (DOI: 10.32873/uno.dc.jrf.25.1.003).

which women cannot have success unless they sacrifice their feminine identity. That sacrifice results in a pyrrhic victory at best, represented most clearly by Elizabeth's despair throughout the film at her lack of a husband or family.[45]

Ian Goode and Stephen McBurney provide a very different perspective in this volume on Mary's place in film history (Chapter Fourteen), focussing on the almost entirely overlooked body of black and white films produced between 1895 and 1923. Collectively, these serve as a case study in the attempted use of cinema to perpetuate the cultural hegemony of the British Empire in the late nineteenth and early twentieth centuries, just as America increasingly used film to assert its own cultural superiority. *The Execution of Mary Queen of Scots* (1895) was part of a wider set of cultural artefacts circulating in late Victorian Britain – including waxworks, community performances and lantern sets – that celebrated Mary's execution as a suppression of Scottish identity and Catholicism within a Protestant and imperial British framework. The jealous guarding of a 'true' historical narrative of Mary's life in film was apparent in the censorship by British film distributors of the French Pathé Frères production, which highlighted Mary's French upbringing and Catholic piety, while the Edison-produced *Mary Stuart* (1913) was lauded for portraying Mary as a self-destructive plotter executed for aspiring to overthrow the English imperial throne. Over the decade that followed no less than three Marian films were attempted by British directors and production companies, including Walter West's unfinished *Mary, Queen of Scots* (1921), the British National Film League-endorsed *Mary, Queen of Scots* (1922) and Denison Clift's *The Loves of Mary Queen of Scots* (1923). All three sought, with varying degrees of success, to promote Mary's history as part of a grand imperial past. They were also more austere in style and narrative, and purported to be more historically authentic and of greater educational value, than their American counterparts. The failure of these films to make a significant public impact reflects the broader failure of British attempts to counter America's domination of film, neatly exemplified by the fact that today the best-known early Marian biopic is *Mary of Scotland* (1936), produced in Golden Age Hollywood as a vehicle to relaunch Katharine Hepburn's ailing career, while the preceding forty years of filmic representations have been largely forgotten – until now.

Contemporary afterlives: commercialisation, controversy, and inclusivity

The enduring public interest in Mary was starkly brought home to the project's team over its lifetime. The funded element launched in January 2019, just as the

---

[45] Shelley Anne Galpin, 'Leaning in or Opting out? Women's Choices in *Little Women* and *Mary Queen of Scots*', *Feminist Media Studies* (2021): 1–14 (https://doi.org/10.1080/14680777.2021.19 79070).

new filmed biopic *Mary Queen of Scots* (dir: Josie Rourke) went on general release in the UK. Although not a direct critical response to the #MeToo movement then sweeping the film industry in the wake of extensive sexual assault charges brought against the director Harvey Weinstein, the film was certainly read as one, and enjoyed arguably even more international exposure as a result.[46] The combination of this with the general public's appetite for Mary led to media interest that was unprecedented in the experience of the co-investigators.[47] The project has directly engaged, and been informed by, contemporary public views of Mary as part of its research. This began during the COVID-19 pandemic with the development of a blog site populated with short articles by the research team, and the online public hosting of the project's research workshops (originally intended to be closed, in-person events).[48] The project launched a Massive Open Online Course (MOOC) on Mary's life and afterlife in November 2021, where project research formed the basis of a full third of the course, and which actively sought public reaction to our material through carefully curated discussion exercises.[49] The initial run of the course attracted 3,800 visitors, and the range of responses that learners posted significantly informed our approach to the project's final public offering, a major exhibition showcasing all the Marian items from the university's collection relating to Mary's afterlife, which ran in The Hunterian Art Gallery between October 2022 and February 2023.[50] Opinions on Mary from the course and from social media were displayed on one wall, with other walls showcasing a multiplicity of quotes from texts and images from Mary's time until today.

Reaction to the curated material was sought in exit questionnaires and during tours. This chapter concludes with some thoughts, in part derived from this material, on where Mary's afterlife stands in the early twenty-first century, and suggests directions for further research.

---

[46] Steve Rose, 'How Casting across Racial Lines Exposes Hollywood's Power Imbalance', *The Guardian*, 1 April 2019 (https://www.theguardian.com/film/2019/apr/01/how-casting-across-racial-lines-exposes-hollywoods-power-imbalance); Rosalind Smith, 'Mary, Queen of Scots is Newly Relevant in the Age of #MeToo', *The Conversation*, 27 February 2019 (https://theconversation.com/mary-queen-of-scots-is-newly-relevant-in-the-age-of-metoo-111604).

[47] A short video outlining the project, posted on Twitter and Facebook, garnered over 21,000 views within 24 hours; a short article for *The Conversation* looking at historical inaccuracies in portrayals of Mary accrued 27,815 views and became the second-most-viewed article on the site in the first month after posting; and the co-investigators were sought for interviews for a host of radio and TV outlets around the UK, Australia and New Zealand. Reid, '*Mary Queen of Scots*: Don't Worry About Movie Accuracy'.

[48] Mary Queen of Scots Project, '"In my End is my Beginning": The Memorialisation and Cultural Afterlife of Mary Queen of Scots' (https://mqs.glasgow.ac.uk/).

[49] University of Glasgow, 'The Life and Afterlife of Mary, Queen of Scots' (https://www.futurelearn.com/courses/the-life-and-afterlife-of-mary-queen-of-scots).

[50] For the exhibition, see https://www.gla.ac.uk/hunterian/visit/exhibitions/exhibitionprogramme/maryqueenofscots/.

Figure I.6 Wall of images of Mary, Room 1, 'The Afterlife of Mary, Queen of Scots' Exhibition, Hunterian Art Gallery
Courtesy of The Hunterian

Figure I.7 Wall of quotes about Mary, Room 2, 'The Afterlife of Mary, Queen of Scots' Exhibition, Hunterian Art Gallery
Courtesy of The Hunterian

Apart from Rachel Maclean's use of Mary in her *The Lion and the Unicorn* film that responded to the 2014 Scottish independence referendum (discussed in Chapter Fifteen by Daniel Fountain and Alicia Hughes), Mary has not emerged in our research as a significant figure of interest for the Scottish nationalist movement or in identification with the contemporary royal family. Yet she has proven to be a powerful commercial tool for the heritage industry and products related to it, the value of which remains to be fully quantified for the Scottish economy and should be investigated further. The most recent exhibitions on Mary at the National Museums of Scotland in 2013 and at the British Library in 2021 drew huge interest, with the 2013 exhibition drawing a record crowd of around 79,000 attendees.[51] The display of Mary's last letter at the National Library of Scotland on the anniversary of her execution had to be extended into the late evening due to viewing demand.[52] More broadly, every major heritage organisation in Scotland uses Mary in their historical trails and castle tours, seen most visibly in a dedicated guidebook, *Mary Was Here*, published by Historic Environment Scotland.[53] The project logged a staggering array of Mary-themed merchandise ranging from bespoke bookmarks, purses, tea towels and Christmas decorations to an online virtual marathon series run by Secret London Runs, where runners can collect six Mary- and Elizabeth-themed medals for logging miles.[54] A rubber duck known as 'Mary Queen of Quacks', sold in various museum gift shops, became the project's unofficial mascot and a star item in the exhibition. While amusing, it shows that Mary's iconographic shorthand is now so well known that it can be easily replicated on a novelty item.

Many of these items are light-hearted in nature, but in audience responses tensions remain apparent between inherent conservatism and reverence for an enduring 'saintly' and 'true' image of Mary and new imaginings of Mary's story that reflect contemporary values. As Fountain and Hughes note, the accretion of multiple 'Marys' over centuries of retelling is a stimulating source of creative potential for artists. Depictions of Mary by Maclean and the artist Helen Flockhart (for her 'Linger Awhile' series of paintings) actively 'refract' the various icons and phrases associated with the queen, in Maclean's case mixing it with symbols denoting a militant 'British' identity and Scotland's economic dependence on oil. Flockhart creates modern affective portrayals of Mary that deliberately muddy fable and fact, for example by drawing maps of the places associated with Mary onto her dress, but which encourage a sympathy for the ways in which her detractors have continually tried to erase her voice. Mary has also proven an inspiring figure for the international drag community, with multiple

---

[51] On the NMS exhibition, see Chapter Twelve; for the British Library exhibition, see Susan Doran (ed.), *Elizabeth and Mary: Royal Cousins, Rival Queens* (London, 2021).

[52] 'Last Letter of Mary, Queen of Scots: Display Extended by Three Hours', *BBC News*, 8 February 2017 (https://www.bbc.co.uk/news/uk-scotland-38907013).

[53] Andrew Burnet, Nicki Scott and Sally Gall, *Mary Was Here: Where Mary Queen of Scots Went and What She Did There* (Dollar, Fife, 2013).

[54] For examples, see https://www.etsy.com/uk/search?q=mary+queen+of+scots&ref=search_bar; for the marathon medal series, see https://www.secretlondonruns.com/the-rivals.

Figure I.8 'Mary, Queen of Quacks', alongside peg dolls of Mary created by Hope and Euan Reid at a project kids' craft event
Editor's own

performers on *RuPaul's Drag Race* portraying the Mary–Elizabeth relationship, particularly the Scotland-born artist Rosé. The story of Mary and Elizabeth has been actively repurposed over the past decade to celebrate sexual and gender fluidity, a fact that reflects Mary's own interest in masquing and gender inversion through dress. Moreover, as RuPaul and Pangina Heals' striking re-imaginings of Elizabeth show, drag artists are producing versions of the two queens that incorporate elements of their own cultural heritage into the established iconography, and that create a more racially inclusive retelling of their narrative.

Despite the fact (as this volume attests) that Mary's story has constantly been re-imagined as society changes, these modern Marys have often faced vocal criticism. Images of Maclean and Rosé were included in both the exhibition and our MOOC. While viewers were uniformly comfortable with romantic representations of Mary such as the Hamilton painting and the various engravings of her, there was a highly divided response to the modern images, particularly that of Rosé:

> Disappointed at the choice of images in this section. I knew [i]t was too good to be true to have a whole MOOC free of tiresome wokism! MQoS as drag – what would John Knox have said??[55]

[55] Response to learning step 3.17, 1 December 2021.

> I think this is a disrespectful way of treating Mary Queen of Scots. She was a woman of her age and should be portrayed as such. These ways of depicting the Queen do not in any way enhance my understanding of the woman . . . Stick to real history.[56]
>
> I didn't know about Mary's afterlife in popular culture – I'm glad I didn't as it is utter tripe. These people cannot think up anything original so they will stigmatise, degrade, be rude & call it 'Drama/Comic/Satire'. Pathetic !!![57]

A sub-theme to negative responses was the view that there was a singular 'true' and venerable Mary that existed for some learners, which exposure to new portrayals seemed to threaten:

> This was entertainment, not history, and fortunately none of it has influenced the memories of my visit to Edinburgh where I walked where Mary had trod.[58]
>
> I can understand the need to bring Mary screaming and kicking into the twenty-first century. But for me, I would rather she wasn't brought up to date but remained the dignified mystical martyr who has transcended history.[59]
>
> Maybe these portrayals of Mary Queen of Scots represent contemporary views of Mary but for me they do not represent Mary as I have conceived of her in my mind.[60]

Although these comments are reactionary and conservative, they raise valid points, deserving of further research, on how we approach a contested historical figure with sensitivity. Humour is increasingly used in modern representations of Mary, whether in Rosé's performance showing Mary's beheading, in children's educational programmes like *Horrible Histories* or, most notably (and with much swearing), in Michelle Gomez's portrayal of Mary for the Sky Arts series *Psychobitches*.[61] A result of Mary's story becoming so unmoored from historical fact, while being so well known, is that viewers have become desensitised to the brutality of it. It is right to raise the question 'can we, or should we, ever laugh at a historical figure who was the victim of forced marriage, sexual violence, captivity and a vicious (and botched) execution?'

---

[56] Response to learning step 3.17, 9 December 2021.
[57] Response to learning step 3.17, 22 February 2022.
[58] Response to learning step 3.18, 8 January 2022.
[59] Response to learning step 3.17, 23 January 2022.
[60] Response to learning step 3.17, 5 March 2022.
[61] Simon Gibney (dir.), *Horrible Histories: Mardy Mary Queen of Scots Special* (2015) (https://www.imdb.com/title/tt7045788/); Jeremy Dyson (dir.), *Psychobitches* (2013) (https://www.youtube.com/watch?v=5ADGrq8cQco).

However, positive responses to these portrayals showed an appreciation of both the drag performance itself and how the revised view of Mary linked to a long-term pattern of Marian reinvention:

> I love Maclean's kitsch representation of Mary and how it draws on the George Vertue, *Maria Scotoru[m] Regina et Franciae Dotaria*, 1735, engraving for inspiration. I also loved Rosé's scarlet reveal stunt. She slayed in this performance, great energy and perfectly on point. Yaass Queen![62]
>
> I like seeing how people are continuing to push the boundaries on how Mary Queen of Scots is portrayed . . . I think the temptation for us to say Mary should be portrayed in one particular way or another could be reflecting how she was viewed during the Marian civil wars with the propaganda saying she was like this or like that, rather than seeing her as a complex figure made up of lots of different aspects who was, above all, a human being.[63]

One of the most striking responses to this discussion was a connection made by an older learner between historical revisionism as it pertains to Mary and to the ongoing decolonisation of history, accelerated by recent work on the legacy of slavery in many educational and civic institutions and the Black Lives Matter movement:

> [I]t depends how you define history. History is fluid and forever changing, in my opinion. An action took place and that action is fixed (if we can depend on the sources) but the interpretation of the action is constantly evolving, depending on the social *mores* of the time. I think of my history classes in Primary School where it was accepted that sugar cane was produced by slave labour and that the British Empire was wonderful and brought benefits to our colonies. I remember the map of the world on the wall in my primary class coloured in red, and that was meant to be a good thing. Thanks to the Black Lives Matter movement we are now looking at those days through different eyes. My granddaughter will be taught that period of history in a different way. So yes, I do think this section on MQS should be on this course, for it is making me analyse our present society using an iconic figure from the past, who became an icon after her death and was used by different factions – Protestants and Catholics – to suit their own ends.[64]

Mary's role in perpetuating an imperial identity in British colonies, and the retelling of her story in relation to race, are topics that urgently require attention. A great deal of important research has been done in recent years on the

---

[62] Response to learning step 3.17, 5 February 2022.
[63] Response to learning step 3.17, 23 January 2022.
[64] Response to learning step 3.17, 19 December 2021.

role of Burns Clubs and other societies in perpetuating a Scottish identity and mythology abroad.[65] Where did Mary fit into this? A scoping exercise carried out for the project revealed that Mary is mentioned in a range of Australian and New Zealand periodicals, but this needs to be augmented with a fuller study of her place in teaching curriculums, in community celebrations and in other forms of cultural expression. This would give us a sense of the queen's global and imperial reach that builds on the discussion of this issue by Goode and McBurney.[66] Linked to this, the reception of racially inclusive portrayals of Mary also warrants further study. Josie Rourke's 2018 film was widely praised for its inclusive casting, but faced significant online backlash, with a strong racist overtone, for being historically inaccurate.[67] Gemma Chan (who played Bess of Hardwick) defended the film as an active response to racially insensitive casting in old Hollywood and as part of a new wave of historical fiction portraying the past in an inclusive way:

> 'Why are actors of color, who have fewer opportunities anyway, only allowed to play their own race? And sometimes they're not even allowed to play their own race', she said. 'In the past, the role would be given to a white actor who would tape up their eyes and do the role in yellowface. John Wayne played Genghis Khan. If John Wayne can play Genghis Khan, I can play Bess of Hardwick . . . I feel like [the musical] *Hamilton* opened minds a lot. We have a black man playing George Washington. They describe it as "America then, told by America now". And I think our art should reflect life now . . .'[68]

Chan's sentiments brilliantly capture the sense of Mary's afterlife that has emerged in this project – her history has always been used to tell stories about the past that reflect us now. Perhaps this is the most important aspect of Mary's enduring cultural afterlife, and the reason why retellings of her story show no sign of ending soon. As Lady Fraser astutely observed: 'it is we, all of us, who give her life'.

---

[65] See, for example, Tanja Bueltmann, *Scottish Ethnicity and the Making of New Zealand Society, 1850–1930* (Edinburgh, 2011).

[66] I am very grateful to Professor Tanja Bueltmann for undertaking this initial research and confirming its potential value.

[67] See, for example, https://www.quora.com/Is-the-inclusion-of-black-actors-in-the-movie-Mary-Queen-of-Scots-based-on-reality-or-is-it-historical-revision; https://www.reddit.com/r/asiantwoX/comments/aag8nc/the_colorblind_casting_in_mary_queen_of_scots/.

[68] Jessica Chia, 'Gemma Chan Wants to End Whitewashing – in Hollywood and in History Books', *Allure*, 19 March 2019 (https://www.allure.com/story/gemma-chan-cover-story-2019).

Timeline for Mary's life

1542	Born at Linlithgow Palace, Scotland; Mary's father James V dies a week later
1543	Crowned Queen of Scots
1543–7	Henry VIII tries to seize Mary as a bride for his son, the future Edward VI

The French princess

1548	Sent to France as the future bride to the crown prince of France, François
1559	Mary and François become Queen Consort and King of France Scottish Reformation Rebellion begins
1560	Reformation Parliament outlaws Catholicism in Scotland François II dies, still in his teens

The Queen of Scots

1561	Returns to Scotland aged 18 to exercise direct rule as Queen of Scots
1565	Marries her cousin, Henry Stuart, Lord Darnley
1566	Gives birth to Prince James, the future James VI and I
1567	Lord Darnley is murdered at Kirk o'Field on 10 February Mary is abducted by James Hepburn, 4th Earl of Bothwell, on 24 April Mary and Lord Bothwell marry on 15 May

The captive

1567	Imprisoned at Lochleven Castle on 17 June Abdicates in favour of her one-year-old son James VI on 24 July
1568	Escapes from Lochleven Castle Defeated at Langside, outside Glasgow Flees to England seeking the support of her cousin Elizabeth I
1568–87	Held in captivity in various English castles
1586	Tried for treason against Elizabeth I and found guilty
1587	Executed at Fotheringhay Castle

Part One
Mary in Contemporary Objects

ONE

Damnatio Memoriae: Mary, Queen of Scots' Iconography and the Ham House Portrait of Sir John Maitland of Thirlestane

David A. H. B. Taylor

An essential part of our understanding of Mary, Queen of Scots lies in our perception of her image. During her lifetime and through the centuries since, Mary's portraiture has played an important role in defining her queenship, and in disseminating ideas (both positive and negative) around her gender, nationality and religion. The discovery of a new depiction of the Scottish queen, hidden under a later portrait of a male sitter and revealed through x-radiography during technical analysis (see Chapter Two), offers the opportunity to re-examine her iconography and its significant role in her cultural afterlife.

The recent discovery revealed an unfinished portrait of Mary, Queen of Scots, unseen since 1589 when it was painted over with a portrait of Sir John Maitland, 1st Lord Maitland of Thirlestane (1543–95), James VI's lord chancellor.[1] Maitland's portrait, painted on panel and inscribed with the date it was produced and the sitter's age (44), descended in ownership within his family. His grandson, John Maitland, Duke of Lauderdale, brought the picture to Ham House in Surrey, the Thames-side palace of his second wife Elizabeth Murray, Countess of Dysart, following their marriage in 1672, where it was placed in the Long Gallery and where it has remained since.[2]

Maitland of Thirlestane, the son of Mariotta Cranstoun and Sir Richard Maitland of Lethington, was the younger brother of the better-known William Maitland of Lethington, Mary, Queen of Scots' secretary of state, and was himself the queen's keeper of the privy seal. After Mary's forced abdication in 1567,

---

[1] The portrait is in the collection of the National Trust (NT 1139943).
[2] Ham House was gifted to the National Trust in 1948, by Sir Lyonel Tollemache, 4th Bt (1854–1952) and his son Sir Cecil Tollemache, 5th Bt (1886–1969), descendants of Elizabeth Murray, Countess of Dysart and Duchess of Lauderdale. The National Trust transferred ownership to HM Government, who purchased the collection, including the current portrait, and entrusted it to the care of the Victoria and Albert Museum, until 1990, when it was returned to the care of the National Trust, to which ownership was transferred back in 2002.

Maitland initially joined her opponents, working for the regency of her half-brother the Earl of Moray. He supported the queen during the Marian civil war and during her early years of English captivity, and he was imprisoned after the 'Lang Siege' of Edinburgh Castle.[3] In 1578, after four years of house arrest, Maitland was freed, and three years later he was fully rehabilitated by the young James VI. By 1583 he had been appointed a privy councillor and was one of the authors of the so-called Black Acts, which increased the monarch's jurisdiction over the Kirk and promoted episcopacy.

In 1584 the king appointed Maitland secretary of state and in 1587 he created him lord chancellor. His political dominance at court was attributed to the fact that 'he gained complete ascendancy over the mind of the young King, who was sagacious enough . . . to appraise . . . the talents of the man to whose political guidance he resigned himself wholly'.[4] This influence over the king led to Maitland's increasing unpopularity at court, with a libel against him stating 'Justice is brought in lamenting, that one of Cameleon's clan, one of the disciples of Matchiavell, had so great a place in the commonwealth to the ruin of justice'.[5] His increasing wealth and political power were also being discussed at the English court, where he was described as 'the wisest man in Scotland . . . and worth winning'.[6] Further discontent amongst many of the Scottish nobles arose when Maitland encouraged non-aristocratic members on the privy council, aimed at making the king less reliant on support from a traditional, elite, social power base. Eventually, in 1588, there was a failed plot to murder Maitland, organised by a group of Catholic-dominated nobles. The following year the king thought it best to take his chancellor with him, for safety's sake, when he travelled to Scandinavia to marry the Danish king's sister Anna, refuting the charge that Maitland was 'leading me, by the nose as it were . . . as if I were an unreasonable creature, or a bairn that could do nothing of myself'.[7]

Maitland's portrait at Ham, dated 1589, may have been produced to commemorate surviving the assassination plot, being part of the king's marriage party or his recent elevation at court. Following a failed second assassination attempt in 1591, the potential danger his unpopularity represented to the security and reputation of the crown resulted in his dismissal from court in 1592.

---

[3] David Masson (ed.), *The Register of the Privy Council of Scotland*, vol. 14, *Addenda ad 1545–1625* (Edinburgh, 1898), p. 50.

[4] William Cook Mackenzie, *The Life and Times of John Maitland, Duke of Lauderdale (1616–1682)* (London, 1923), p. 12.

[5] David Calderwood, *The History of the Kirk of Scotland*, ed. T. Thomson and D. Laing, 8 vols (Edinburgh, 1843), vol. 5, p. 121.

[6] Maurice Lee, Jr, *John Maitland of Thirlestane and the Foundation of Stewart Despotism in Scotland* (Princeton, NJ, 1959), p. 68 and n. 89, citing a letter to Sir Francis Walsingham from the English ambassador to Scotland, Sir Edward Wotton.

[7] Lee, Jr, *John Maitland*, p. 3.

Maitland and Adrian Vanson

The portrait shows Maitland wearing a fashionable black doublet with white linen, lace-edged collar and cuffs, and a black hat decorated with an embroidered band, with his left hand holding the upright hilt of his sword. Traditionally attributed to an anonymous painter of the Scottish School, the position of the sitter's head and body and the painterly style of the face and clothes are strongly reminiscent of the Netherlandish émigré painter Adrian Vanson (Adriaen van Son), a suggestion first posited and then verified through technical analysis by the present author and Caroline Rae (see Chapter Two).[8]

Vanson, who came from Breda in the duchy of Brabant, was working in Scotland by 1581.[9] In June that year he was paid by James VI's treasurer for two portraits, of John Knox and of either the king or George Buchanan, which had previously been sent to Geneva to be engraved as illustrations for *Icones*, Theodore's Beza's book of images of key supporters of the Protestant Reformation (1580).[10] In 1584 he was appointed James VI's painter, and the following year he was made a burgess of Edinburgh, with the hope that he would train apprentices and increase the number of portraitists working in the Scottish capital and their quality. Vanson followed the court to London, following the king's accession to the English throne in 1603. Little is known of his time there, although he was paid for decorating a triumphal arch, commissioned by the city's Dutch community, for the king's official entry into London on 15 March 1604.[11] He died at some point between 1604 and 1610, in which year his wife was referred to as his widow when she sued for the artist's unpaid wages.

Maitland sat to other artists but commissioning Vanson meant he was painted by the highest regarded artist working in Edinburgh, and because the artist was the king's official painter it was also an act of monarchical loyalty

---

[8] David A. H. B. Taylor, 'Questions of Attribution: A Portrait of Sir John Maitland of Thirlestane at Ham House', *Apollo, National Trust House & Collections Annual* (London, 2013), pp. 55–9; Caroline Rae, with curatorial input from Kate Anderson and David A. H. B. Taylor, 'New Thoughts on Adrian Vanson: Findings from a Technical Examination of Selected Works, including the Discussion of an Interesting Panel Join', *The Picture Restorer* 61 (Autumn 2022): 35–46.

[9] David A. H. B. Taylor, 'Gesture Recognition: Adam de Colone and the Transmission of Portrait Types from the Low Countries and England to Scotland', in *Painting in Britain 1500–1630: Production, Influences and Patronage*, ed. Tarnya Cooper, Aviva Burnstock, Maurice Howard and Edward Town (Oxford, 2015), p. 290.

[10] For a discussion of the image of James VI used as the frontispiece of Beza's *Icones*, see Michael Bath and Theo van Heijnsbergen, 'Paradin Politicized: Some New Sources for Scottish Paintings', *Emblematica* 22 (2016): 43–68.

[11] See Astrid J. Stilma, '"As Warriouris in Ane Camp": The Image of King James VI as a Protestant Crusader', in *The Apparelling of Truth: Literature and Literary Culture in the Reign of James VI*, ed. Kevin J. McGinley and Nicola Royan (Newcastle, 2010), pp. 241–51, at p. 247. The triumphal arch included images of the king, of Edward VI and of Lucius, the legendary first Christian king of Britain.

from the second most powerful man in the kingdom.[12] And of course Vanson was probably the painter of the unfinished image of Mary – regrettably something that might not be ascertainable, given the unfinished state of her portrait underneath Maitland's.

Mary, Queen of Scots' iconography

For such an important figure in her own lifetime, as queen regnant, queen consort and prisoner, we have to wonder why there are so few contemporary likenesses of Mary.[13] As a female royal figure with the prospect of an eminent marriage in mind when she was young, and as ruler of an ancient kingdom and a key figure in the politico-religious turmoil of the second half of the sixteenth century, you would expect there to have been a large body of portraits of Mary during her life. Furthermore, there appears to be only one surviving large-scale portrait type from the nearly seven-year period she spent in Scotland as an adult, between her return from France in 1561 and her 1568 flight to England.[14]

Mary's iconography is richest from the period of her childhood and youth. The earliest and only image of Mary as a very young child, before she was sent to the French court for safety during the war of the so-called 'Rough Wooing', is on a billon penny first minted in 1547, although this is a relatively generic depiction showing her full face, wearing an open crown.[15] Two coins made six years later in France show images of the queen in profile, probably both designed by John Acheson, the engraver to the Scottish mint.[16] These are more sophisticated than the Scottish coin and attempt a proper portrait of the young queen, depicting her wearing a closed, imperial crown in the first and crownless in the second. Permission for Acheson to cast dies for both coins was given from the

---

[12] For example, Maitland sat to the anonymous miniaturist who painted him in c. 1588 (National Portrait Gallery, London – NPG 2769). The same artist was probably the painter of the double-sided miniature of James Hamilton, Duke of Châtelherault and 2nd Earl of Arran, and his son John Hamilton, later 1st Marquess of Hamilton and 3rd Earl of Arran (National Galleries of Scotland – PG 3412).

[13] See David A. H. B. Taylor, 'Why Are There so few Portraits of Mary, Queen of Scots?', *Apollo*, 15 November 2017 (https://www.apollo-magazine.com/why-are-there-so-few-portraits-of-mary-queen-of-scots/).

[14] The double portrait is at Hardwick Hall, Derbyshire, in the collection of the National Trust (NT 1129218).

[15] Edward Burns, *The Coinage of Scotland*, 3 vols (Edinburgh, 1887), vol. 2, pp. 307–9; vol. 3, fig. 864; Lionel Cust, *Notes on the Authentic Portraits of Mary, Queen of Scots* (London, 1903), pp. 21–22; Helen Smailes and Duncan Thomson, *The Queen's Image* (Edinburgh, 1987), p. 18, no. 1.

[16] Augustus W. Franks, 'Notice of Permission given at Paris to John Acheson to make Dies with the Portrait of Mary Queen of Scots, 21st October 1553, and to Nicolas Emery to make a Die for Jettons, with the Arms, &c., of the Queen of Scots, from a Register preserved at Paris', *Proceedings of the Society of Antiquaries of Scotland*, vol. 9, 1870–72 (Edinburgh, 1872): 506.

Paris mint, and the uncrowned image of Mary (the latter coin was apparently never officially issued) was re-used for a gold three-pound piece or ryal, minted three times in the second half of the 1550s.[17]

In France she was drawn and painted several times by the court artist François Clouet, including the earliest surviving drawing of her, of 1549 when she was around 7 years old (now held by Yale University Art Gallery).[18] Other portraits by or attributed to Clouet include the 1552 drawing ordered by Catherine de' Medici as one of a set, to record the health of the royal children,[19] and two drawings dated to *c*. 1555, in the Bibliothèque Nationale de France, Paris[20] and in the National Ossoliński Institute, Wrocław.[21] Clouet's finest surviving image of the queen is the watercolour from the time of her 1558 marriage to the *dauphin*, the future François II, showing her placing a ring on the fourth finger of her right hand.[22] The face type was copied in 1559 in a double portrait of Mary and François as king and queen of France, crowned and in prayer, from Catherine de' Medici's book of hours.[23] Another, now lost, Clouet image of Mary and François, from before his accession, was in Charles I's collection when he was still Prince of Wales; a miniature described by Balthasar Gerbier as 'the Queene of Scotland with the Dolphin of Fraunce of Gennetts doeinge'.[24] Clouet's last, much-copied portrait of Mary showed her in white mourning, around the time of the deaths of her father-in-law, her mother and her husband.[25] After Mary became queen consort of France she employed Jean Decourt as her painter, retaining him as her *peintre ordinaire* following her return to Scotland, although no extant portraits of her by him are known.[26]

---

[17] See John Kenneth Ronald Murray, 'The Scottish Gold Coinage of 1555–8', *The Numismatic Chronicle* 19: 139 (1979): 155–64.

[18] Yale University Art Gallery – 2009.46.1.

[19] Musée Condé, Château de Chantilly – MN 38. A painting based on the drawing, formerly in the Colworth Collection, was sold at Christie's, 2 July 1892, lot 22.

[20] Bibliothèque Nationale de France, Paris – Reserve NA 22 (17) Boîte Planche 3.

[21] National Ossoliński Institute, Wrocław – 8695.

[22] RCIN 401229. The portrait may have been in the Royal Collection since the reign of Elizabeth I, who famously kissed a miniature of her cousin in front of Sir James Melville, the Scottish ambassador, in 1564.

[23] Bibliothèque Nationale de France – N.a.lat.82 fol. 154v.

[24] W. N. Sainsbury, *Original Unpublished Papers Illustrative of the Life of Sir Peter Paul Rubens As an Artist and a Diplomatist* (London, 1859), p. 355, no. 19; Graham Reynolds, *The Sixteenth and Seventeenth-Century Miniatures in the Collection of Her Majesty the Queen* (London, 1999), p. 60. François Clouet was sometimes called Janet, the diminutive nickname of his father, artist Jean Clouet.

[25] There are many versions of this type, including the picture in the Royal Collection, first recorded there during the reign of Mary's grandson, Charles I (RCIN 403429).

[26] The enigmatic Jean Decourt remained living in France and travelled to Scotland to undertake royal commissions (none of which survive), including to paint miniatures of the queen, her second husband Darnley, and their son Prince James, for a jewelled girdle book, around the time of the prince's christening.

Further portraits survive in Mary's coinage and as printed engravings. A 1558 gold ducat, cast in Edinburgh, shows Mary and François facing each other under a single imperial crown, and commemorates their marriage, describing them as 'King and Queen of Scots, Dauphin and Dauphiness of Vienne', thus introducing the future king of France as the Scots' new co-monarch. The same year, paired engravings of Mary and François by Pieter van der Heyden were published in Antwerp by Hieronymus Cock.[27] Also made in c. 1558 is a glazed ceramic profile medallion of Mary, from the workshop of Bernard Palissy,[28] which in turn relates to a full-length Flemish engraving of her by Frans Huys that was one of a series of European rulers.[29] This engraving incudes an inscription that describes Mary as queen of Scotland only but a version was reproduced in half-length format that was paired with an image of François, both of which were part of another series of monarchs and dated 1559.[30] Other early portraits of Mary, although essentially emblematic, can be found on the various iterations of her official seals. These show her seated and crowned and holding sceptres; on her own as queen of Scotland, with François II as king and queen of France, Scotland, England and Ireland,[31] and finally as queen of Scotland and dowager queen of France.[32]

John Acheson designed a silver testoon of Mary in 1561, showing her in her widowhood, with her profile presumably based on or influenced by the Hieronymus Cock engraving.[33] Three 1565 coins cast in Scotland following Mary's second marriage, to her cousin Henry Stuart, Lord Darnley, show profile portraits of the royal pair, facing each other. Two versions of a silver medal celebrating their marriage were cast, the first showing Mary and Darnley crowned, the queen with loose hair,[34] the second with the same composition but showing the couple uncrowned, the queen with her hair in a caul and wearing a feathered bonnet.[35] The circumscription around both states they are 'Queen and King of Scots', following Mary creating her husband king consort. A silver ryal from the same year includes an inscription translating as 'Henry and Mary, by the Grace of God, King and Queen of Scots', but as his title, given without

---

[27] Royal Collection Trust – the engraving of Mary is RCIN 618174.
[28] Musée National de la Renaissance, Écouen – EP1601.
[29] British Museum, London – 1884, 0412.20.
[30] Royal Collection Trust – the image of Mary is RCIN 618171.
[31] Musée du Louvre, Paris – OA779.
[32] See Walter de Gray Birch, *History of Scottish Seals*, vol. 1 (Stirling, 1905), pp. 68–76.
[33] Burns, *The Coinage of Scotland*, vol. 2, pp. 332–33. An example of the coin is in the British Museum, London – E.2626.
[34] On loan to The Hunterian Museum, University of Glasgow – IN.2017.4.
[35] Hunterian Museum, University of Glasgow – GLAHM:37190.

parliamentary approval, was placed before the queen's, the coin was subsequently removed from circulation.[36]

An extant double painted portrait of Mary and Darnley, depicted at three-quarter-length, was presumably produced in Scotland, c. 1565.[37] It commemorates not only their calamitous marriage but also the production of possibly the only large-scale portrait of Mary painted during her short personal rule of Scotland. There are two other versions of this type of the queen, wearing a standing collar and feathered cap, both of which are in reverse and show Mary at head-and-shoulder length. The first is a small-scale portrait of her in the National Portrait Gallery, London, given a conjectural date range of 1560–92, following dendrochronological examination.[38] A second version is a miniature in the Uffizi Gallery, Florence, dated to c. 1560–65.[39]

Portraits of Mary, Queen of Scots in captivity

The newly discovered Ham portrait of Mary appears to be after the so-called Sheffield portrait type of the queen, and to contextualise its production we should consider the circumstances of her English imprisonment, and the continued production of her image during that time. Following the murder of Darnley and Mary's subsequent third marriage to James Hepburn, 4th earl of Bothwell, the chief suspect in the murder, the queen was defeated by the rebel Confederate Lords at the Battle of Carberry Hill in 1567, imprisoned and forced to abdicate. She escaped from captivity in Loch Leven Castle the next year, and was again defeated, at the Battle of Langside, by an army led by her half-brother Regent Moray, in the name of her son, the infant King James VI. She fled to England to seek support from her cousin Queen Elizabeth but was put into custody. After nearly twenty years in English captivity, she was tried for treason for her involvement in the Babington Plot and executed at Fotheringhay Castle in Northamptonshire on 8 February 1587.[40]

---

[36] British Museum 1849, 0626.1; Edward Hawkins, with Augustus W. Franks and Herbert A. Grueber (eds), *Medallic Illustrations of the History of Great Britain and Ireland to the Death of George II*, 2 vols (London, 1885), vol. 1, p. 114.

[37] National Trust – 1129218.

[38] National Portrait Gallery – NPG 1766.

[39] Uffizi – 1890, no. 4443. A second version of the Uffizi miniature, previously in the Dutch royal collection and now in the Rijksmuseum, appears to be a nineteenth-century copy (Rijksmuseum – SK-A-4392).

[40] For further discussion see Conyers Read (ed.), *The Bardon Papers: Documents Relating to the Imprisonment and Trial of Mary, Queen of Scots* (London, 1909); Emanuel Tomascon (1587) in Victor von Klarwill (ed.), *The Fugger News-Letters, Being a Selection of Unpublished Letters from the Correspondents of the House of Fugger, 1568–1605* (London and New York, 1924), pp. 97–105; and Jayne Elizabeth Lewis, *The Trial of Mary, Queen of Scots: A Brief History with Documents* (London, 1999).

Despite the lack of any sort of programmatic production of the queen's image during her personal reign in Scotland, Mary was active in using portraiture to promote her cause during her captivity. She displayed Stuart family portraits during her initial years in England and the year before she was executed she wrote from Chartley Castle to the French ambassador in Scotland, Charles de Prunele, baron d'Esneval, 'I beg you to send me a whole length portrait of my son, as large as life, drawn from his own person', to which he replied he was having a copy made 'from a good portrait lately painted of him' (probably a portrait by Vanson).[41] During this time Mary also corresponded with foreign allies to procure new miniatures of herself. Quicker to produce and easier to transport and distribute than full-scale portraits, miniatures were a suitable art-form to utilise for garnering widespread politico-religious support. In 1575 Mary wrote to her ambassador in France, James Beaton, former archbishop of Glasgow: 'Among my friends in this country there are some who ask for my portrait. I pray you have four of these made for me, all of which must be set in gold, and send them to me secretly.'[42]

Mary was also permitted to sit to portraitists while she was imprisoned. Jacopo Primavera's profile portrait medal of Mary, probably cast in the Netherlands around 1572, was likely after a miniature produced during the queen's English imprisonment.[43] Mary sat to the celebrated limner Nicholas Hilliard, who painted at least two miniatures of her.[44] Another portrait from her imprisonment was referred to in 1577, when Mary's secretary Claude Nau de la Boisseliere wrote to ambassador Beaton: 'I was thinking to accompany this letter with a portrait of Her Majesty, but the painter has not managed to finish it in time for me to send it with this'.[45]

Mary owned portraits of herself at the end of her life, including a jewelled miniature that she gave to a lady-in-waiting, Elizabeth Curle, on the day of her execution. In her will, Curle described the object as 'a jewel in gold . . . which contains a small portrait of Mary Queen of Scotland my mistress, an object which I esteem greatly, because it was given to me by her Majesty on the very morning that she was martyred'.[46] This is traditionally thought to be the 'Blairs Jewel' miniature of her, incorporated into a reliquary in the early seventeenth

---

[41] Strickland (ed.), *Letters*, vol. 2, p. 172.
[42] Labanoff (ed.), *Lettres*, vol. 4, p. 256.
[43] British Museum – M.6880.
[44] Royal Collection Trust – RCIN 420641; Victoria and Albert Museum, London – P.24–1975.
[45] Labanoff, *Lettres*, vol. 4, p. 390. The translation, and that regarding n. 42, both appear in David A. H. B. Taylor, 'A Derbyshire Portrait Gallery: Bess of Hardwick's Picture Collection', in *Hardwick Hall: A Great Old Castle of Romance*, ed. David Adshead and David A. H. B. Taylor (New Haven, CT and London, 2016), p. 76.
[46] See Marguerite A. Tassi, 'Martyrdom and Memory: Elizabeth Curle's Portrait of Mary, Queen of Scots', in Debra Barrett-Graves (ed.), *The Emblematic Queen: Extra-Literary Representations of Early Modern Queenship* (London, 2013), p. 106.

century, in the collection of the Scottish Catholic Heritage Trust. A second version of the miniature, apparently by the same hand, is in the Rijksmuseum, Amsterdam.[47]

The Sheffield portrait type

A portrait of the queen that was potentially painted from life is the well-known Sheffield portrait, of which several versions exist. The discovery of the unfinished image of Mary under the portrait of Maitland of Thirlestane, with the recognisable details of the sitter's physiognomy and clothes, adds another version of this portrait type to the queen's iconography. The Sheffield composition shows the queen, usually at full length, wearing black, with a white cap and ruff, standing on an Anatolian carpet and in front of a green curtain, resting her right hand on a table covered with a red cloth and holding her rosary beads with her left hand. The full-scale versions include a Latin inscription at the top-left of the design, which translates as 'Mary, by the Grace of God, Most Pious Queen of Scotland, Queen Dowager of France, in the 36th year of her age and reign, and the 10th of her English captivity, In the year of the salvation of men, 1578'.

Several versions survive and despite twentieth-century presumptions that the Sheffield portraits were posthumous Jacobean images, produced to restore the late queen's reputation and utilise her imagery for Stuart genealogical purposes, some at least are instead likely to be contemporary to Mary's lifetime.[48] The version at Hardwick Hall in Derbyshire, owned by Elizabeth Hardwick, Countess of Shrewsbury ('Bess of Hardwick') is potentially the prime version.[49]

Bess's fourth husband, George Talbot, sixth earl of Shrewsbury, was Mary's longest-serving English gaoler, and Bess knew the queen well. The portrait is mentioned as one of the 'pictures of the Quene of Scottes' at Hardwick, where it was displayed in the Withdrawing Chamber there, alongside a double portrait of the Queen with her second husband Lord Darnley (see above) and a double portrait of her parents, James V and Mary of Guise.[50]

Two other versions are painted on panel – another full length at Hatfield House, Hertfordshire and a former full-length image cut down in the later seventeenth century to three-quarter-length, with subsequent alterations to

---

[47] Rijksmuseum – SK-A-4391. For a discussion of the Blairs and Rijksmuseum miniatures' relationship with the Ham portrait of Mary, including significantly similar facial features, see Chapter Two by Caroline Rae.

[48] For further discussion of the date of the Sheffield type, see Jeremy L. Smith, 'Revisiting the Origins of the Sheffield Series of Portraits of Mary, Queen of Scots', *Burlington Magazine* 152 (2010): 212–18.

[49] National Trust – NT 1129104.

[50] Lindsay Boynton (ed.), 'The Hardwick Hall Inventories of 1601', *Furniture History* (London, 1971), p. 27.

Figure 1.1 *Mary, Queen of Scots*, by unknown artist (currently attributed to or after Rowland Lockey), c. 1578; oil on panel, 194.3 × 113.0cm
Hardwick Hall, Derbyshire (National Trust – NT 1129104) © National Trust Images/ John Hammond

the sitter's posture, in the National Portrait Gallery, London (NPG).[51] The Hardwick picture remained in the Cavendish collection until it was transferred to the National Trust in 1959. The Hatfield picture, previously in the famous Lumley collection, is likely the portrait described in their 1590 inventory as 'Mary Quene of Scottes, executed in Englande', before being left to Sir Robert Cecil and moved to Hatfield in 1609.[52] The NPG version (possibly from the

---

[51] NPG 429.
[52] Lionel Cust, 'The Lumley Inventories', *Walpole Society* 6 (Oxford, 1918): 25.

same workshop as the Hardwick picture) was previously in Charles I's collection, where it was displayed in the Tennis Court Chamber at Whitehall Palace and described as 'the picture of Queene Marie of Scotland kinge James Moother at length' and 'Brought from Scotland'.[53] This latter point, placing a Sheffield-type portrait of the queen within Scotland, suggests a possible prototype for whoever painted the queen on the panel now at Ham, over which Maitland's portrait was painted in 1589.

Three other full-length Sheffield portraits survive, painted on canvas rather than panel. The well-known Scottish National Portrait Gallery version came from the collection of the dukes of Lennox, cousins of the Stuarts, at Cobham Hall in Kent.[54] A second Cavendish family picture, from the collection of the dukes of Portland, is at Welbeck Abbey, Nottinghamshire.[55] The third copy is in the Palacio de Liria, Madrid, possibly left to the 14th duke of Alba by Cardinal York, a fellow descendant of James VII and II.[56]

This type is called the 'Sheffield' portrait as the original was thought to have been painted at either Sheffield Castle or Sheffield Manor, both of which were owned by the earl of Shrewsbury between 1569 and 1584. In the twentieth century the Sheffield portraits were thought to be posthumous Jacobean images, based on Hilliard's miniatures (depicting her with a similar face type and clothes), dated to *c.* 1576 (two years before the date inscribed on the Sheffield portraits).[57] A more determinative factor in dating the portraits is the technical analysis undertaken on the Hardwick and NPG versions. This included dendrochronology on their respective wooden panels, showing timbers cut within the queen's lifetime and, in the case of the Hardwick picture, using timbers from an area that includes Derbyshire. This suggests that the Hardwick and NPG pictures could have been painted from life in 1578, with the prime version painted by a now unknown artist.

Who commissioned the Sheffield portrait remains unknown. The picture is overtly Catholic, with two prominent crucifixes, one of which includes a circular jewel with an image of Susanna and the Elders, the biblical story (Daniel 13:22) reminding the viewer of a virtuous woman found innocent of a crime of which she was earlier accused and for which she had been sentenced to death. The Latin circumscription around the jewel translates as 'trouble on all sides',

---

[53] Oliver Millar (ed.), 'Abraham van der Doort's Catalogue of the Collections of Charles I', *Walpole Society* 37 (Glasgow, 1960): 1.

[54] National Galleries of Scotland – PG 1073.

[55] William John Arthur Charles James Cavendish-Bentinck, Duke of Portland, *Catalogue of the Pictures Belonging to His Grace The Duke of Portland, at Welbeck Abbey, and in London* (London, 1894), p. 153, no. 537.

[56] La Fundación Casa de Alba, Madrid – P.64. Ángel M. de Barcia, *Catálogo de la Colección de Pinturas del Exmo. Sr. Duque de Berwick y de Alba* (Madrid, 1911), p. 61, no. 36.

[57] See Chapter Two by Caroline Rae regarding the Sheffield type not being connected with Hilliard's miniatures of the queen.

and along with the partisan inscription describing the queen being 'most pious' and referring specifically to her English captivity, presents a resolutely political, pro-Mary image. As such it is unimaginable that Elizabeth I commissioned the portrait (although she may have sanctioned its production, and the Hilliard miniatures that likewise show Mary with a crucifix), which presumably came from Mary or one of her key supporters instead.

The Hardwick version has been attributed to or was after Rowland Lockey, an artist closely connected with Bess of Hardwick and her second son William Cavendish, later 1st earl of Devonshire. Lockey worked for Bess and her son between 1592 and 1613, providing miniatures, portraits and copies of portraits. He was in fact too young to have painted the Hardwick portrait in 1578, but the Hatfield version may be a copy by him or someone in his workshop. Lockey, however, is connected with the picture in other ways, as part of his Hardwick patronage. In January 1610, 'Mr Lockey's Man' was paid 3s. for travelling, with two porters, to London 'with the Queene of Scotts Picture', and on 21 June 1613 Lockey's men, 'who brought the Scotch queen's picture', were then paid 2s. for taking the portrait back to Hardwick, possibly a reference to the portrait being taken to the capital to use as a model for the queen's tomb effigy at Westminster Abbey, completed in 1613 (see below).

A version of the portrait, in reverse, was reproduced at bust-length in a tondo engraving of the queen, surmounting another portrait, of her young son James VI, as an illustrative plate in John Lesley, Bishop of Ross's history of Scotland, *De Origine, Moribus, et Rebus Gestis Scotorum*, published in Rome, while he was acting as the queen's ambassador there, in 1578 – the year of the production of the Sheffield portrait.[58] While emphasising the young Scottish king's heritage, the image reiterates Mary's monarchical legitimacy. Her portrait is larger, and she is shown crowned, and her inscription calls her 'Maria Regina', while James is described as 'Princeps'. Another example is an undated French engraving made after the Sheffield portrait type, but possibly produced within the queen's lifetime, engraved and published by Jean Rabel.[59]

The image was certainly reproduced as engravings in the years following the queen's death, their easy dissemination allowing the importance of the portrait type within Mary's iconography to grow. It also exemplifies part of the process of how this image became a visual signifier for the queen during her English captivity. An example of an engraved portrait of the queen that reproduces the Sheffield portrait, at half-length and in reverse, made in France potentially in the year of her execution, is the *c.* 1587 engraving of Mary titled 'La Feu Royne

---

[58] Examples include National Galleries of Scotland, SP I 23.1A. A version of the same engraving but with a different image of the young James VI, after a portrait by Arnold Bronckorst, is in the Metropolitan Museum of Art, New York (58.549.248).

[59] Musée National du château de Pau – P2016-2-1-12.

d'Écosse' by Léonard Gaultier, published by Pierre Gourdelle.[60] As well as the title referring to Mary as the late queen, four lines of French verse inscribed below give biographical details, translated as 'I have no equal to my divine beauty/I was queen twice, daughter and mother of a king/With eyes open you can see my death not my ruin/And I was appointed to die for the Faith' – an apposite response to Mary's execution from Catholic France, where she was still queen dowager. The composition of the engraving is similar to a number of royal and aristocratic portraits produced by Gaultier and Gourdelle in 1587, and by Jacques Granthomme and Gourdelle in 1588, according to dated examples from the group, hence the proposition that the engraving could have been produced very soon after Mary's death.[61]

A French bust-length engraving of Mary by Thomas de Leu, possibly made while she was still alive and very loosely based on the Sheffield type, was part of a group of Catholic images created around the end of her life.[62] The image was re-used, in reverse, in a 1587 Catholic propagandist engraving by the Wierix brothers (Jan, Hieronymus and Anton), showing the queen's portrait flanked by angels holding martyr's palms and crowns of immortality, allegorical figures representing Faith and Fortitude, and two scenes from her execution, above a verse by George Chrichton.[63]

One of the execution scenes, showing the executioner raising the axe for the second strike (the queen's neck is shown partly cut) appears to have been copied from the last illustration in Richard Verstegan's *Theatrum Crudelitatum haereticorum nostri temporis* (Antwerp, 1587) showing atrocities committed against Catholics by Protestants, and from the section on those undertaken in Elizabeth's I's England. The potent image of Mary's Catholic martyrdom was further disseminated by the publication two years later of Adam Blackwood's *Histoire de la martyre de la Royne d'Écosse* (Paris, 1589), which was illustrated with a woodcut version of the same engraving. Similarly, the image of the execution was the pattern for the same scene behind the full-length Flemish portrait of Mary, now known as the Blairs Memorial Portrait, commissioned by Elizabeth Curle,[64] in which the figure of the queen is based on either a 1587 print of her, standing next to the executioner's block, attributed to Jan Wierix,[65]

---

[60] BM 1928,0417.30.
[61] Taylor, 'A Derbyshire Portrait Gallery', p. 78. Dated examples of compositionally similar works engraved by Gaultier and published by Gourdelle include Anne, duke of Joyeuse (1587) and Louis II, cardinal of Guise (1588).
[62] An example of the engraving is in the collection of the National Galleries of Scotland – PGE 86.113.
[63] One of the finest extant examples is in the Royal Collection Trust – RCIN 618301.
[64] See Tassi, 'Martyrdom and Memory', pp. 101–32.
[65] National Galleries of Scotland – SP I 23.26.

Figure 1.2 *Mary, Queen of Scots*, attributed to the Wierix brothers, c. 1587; engraving, 35.2 × 27.1cm Royal Collection Trust (RCIN 618301) Royal Collection Trust/© His Majesty King Charles III, 2023

or a later, smaller engraving after the same, by Martin Baes.[66] A second version of the painting exists, copied by another artist.[67]

The face pattern from the Sheffield portrait was used for later depictions of the queen, for example for a Jacobean image used to illustrate the 1618 *Baziliogia, A Booke of Kings . . .*,[68] produced for the purpose of rehabilitating the king's mother in the public imagination.

The image shows Mary at half-length, her face, cap and ruff after the Sheffield portrait, but in different clothes, wearing an imperial crown and holding an

---

[66] Three examples, printed from the same plate, are in the collection of the National Portrait Gallery, London – NPG D42994, NPG D42995 and NPG D42996.
[67] RCIN 404408.
[68] BM 1848, 0911.264.

Figure 1.3 *Mary, Queen of Scots*, by Renold Elstrack, c. 1618; engraving, 18.6 × 10.8cm Royal Collection Trust (RCIN 680687) Royal Collection Trust/© His Majesty King Charles III, 2023

orb and sceptre.[69] It was engraved by Renold Elstrack, with an inscription below the queen's portrait that includes '[t]he most excellent Princesse Mary queen of Scotland/... Mother to our Soueraigne/ lord James of greate Brittaine France & Ireland king'. Six years later Elstrack's image was reproduced to illustrate William Udall's *The Historie of the Life and Death of Mary Stuart Queene of*

---

[69] Freeman O'Donoghue, *Catalogue of Engraved British Portraits Preserved in the Department of Prints and Drawings in the British Museum*, vol. 3 (London, 1912), p. 192, no. 25; Arthur Mayger Hind, *Engraving in England in the Sixteenth and Seventeenth Centuries*, vol. 2 (Cambridge, 1955), p. 132, no. 24.

Scotland (1624), the queen's first English biography.[70] The engraving must have been seen as an appropriate visual depiction for this positive propagandist, literary portrayal of the queen, with descriptions including 'the most worthy and royall Princesse Mary Stuart Queene of Scotland, who in all her life being tossed and turmoiled with infinite misfortunes concluded it with an untimely death' and 'a woman most constant in her religion, adorned with a wonderfull piety toward God'. In 1636 a second edition of Udall's life of the queen was published in 1636, illustrated with a new version of Elstrack's depiction of Mary, engraved in reverse by William Marshall.

Another aspect of the survival of the Sheffield portrait type as a visual signifier, and its re-interpretation, is the argument that the portrait was the source for the queen's marble tomb effigy, made when her coffin was removed from Peterborough Cathedral on the orders of her son James VI and I and reinterred in Westminster Abbey in 1612. The tomb was begun by Cornelius Cure, the king's master mason, and completed after his death by his son and successor as royal mason, William Cure II. Recent research posits the Sheffield type being the model for the effigy, through discussing the movement of a portrait of Mary from Hardwick to London in 1610 and back to Hardwick in 1613, concurrent with the payment of materials for work on creating the tomb and effigy, relating to dates recorded in Cavendish family archives and exchequer records.[71]

The recently rediscovered portrait of Mary at Ham, hidden for centuries under a portrait of John Maitland of Thirlestane, was not the only painted version of the Sheffield portrait type of the queen, produced in her lifetime or soon afterwards – for example, a potentially contemporary miniature in the Bibliothèque Nationale de France (the face type suggests a possible connection to the Uffizi miniature, discussed above) shows the queen, facing to her left, wearing the same clothes as the Sheffield type.[72] The appearance of several extant large-scale panel portraits of Mary suggest a coordinated production of pictures after the Sheffield portrait type, presumably copied from printed versions. Images that share specific details of dress or painting technique include the pair of portraits in which she holds a fan in her right hand,[73] and the pair of pictures, both dated 1585, with the lion rampant of the royal banner of Scotland displayed in a lozenge in the top-left corner of the panel.[74] Another, well-known, panel portrait

---

[70] Udall's biography was a translation of part of William Camden's history of the reign of Elizabeth I, in Latin, *Annales Rerum Anglicarum et Hibernicarum Regnante Elizabetha, ad Annum Salutis, M.D. LXXXIX* (1615). George Buchanan's 1568 *Detectio Mariae Reginae* was published in Latin, and his 1571 *De Maria Scotorum Regina* was published in Scots and Latin versions.

[71] See Jeremy L. Smith, 'The Sheffield Portrait Types, their Catholic Purposes, and Mary, Queen of Scots' Tomb', *British Catholic History* 33 (2016): 71–90.

[72] Bibliothèque Nationale de France, Paris – NAL MS 82, fol. 190 r.

[73] Trinity College, University of Cambridge – TC Oils P113; Falkland Place, National Trust for Scotland – NTS 52.715.

[74] Government Art Collection – 17; Montacute House, National Trust – NT 597950.

from the early seventeenth century based on the Sheffield type, is the so-called Morton portrait in the Kelvingrove Art Gallery and Museum, Glasgow.[75]

The most intriguing of the large-scale paintings is a fanciful double portrait of Mary and her son James, dated 1583 – four years before the queen's execution – showing the pair at half length, with the date, surmounted by a thistle and imperial crown, between them. In reality the two last saw each other in 1567, some sixteen years before the painting was produced, when James was less than a year old. The purpose of the double portrait may have been to commemorate a potential co-rule of Scotland that the queen had proposed for herself and James, the subject being debated on and off from 1579 until 1585, when he wrote to both Mary and Elizabeth denying any intent to rule his kingdom in association with his mother.[76]

Around the time the unlikely co-monarchy was suggested, a double portrait of Mary and James was being discussed on the continent. Mary's ambassador John Lesley, bishop of Ross, during an audience with Rudolf II in Prague in 1578, considered the emperor's wish for a portrayal of the queen and king, 'that a true and natural portrait of each be shown, that he may see each of the princes as it were face to face'.[77] The details of the commissioning of the Blair double portrait are not known, but it imagines an important (if unrealised) politico-religious association and represents one element of the machinations made between Scotland and England, and their three living monarchs, during Mary's long imprisonment.[78] One aspect of the composition clearly links the picture with the Ham portrait, in that the queen's left hand in the Blair picture is the same design, in reverse, as the right hand in the Ham picture. The fact the hand is reversed suggests the involvement of a printed reproduction used for the second image. The queen's left hand holds a pearl on the bottom of a pendant necklace in the Blair picture and presumably would have done the same in the portrait of Mary in the Ham picture, had that been completed – instead it was incorporated into Maitland's portrait, resulting in a rather redundant posture for the subsequent sitter. The same printed source may have been the prototype for the woodcut of Mary, after the Sheffield portrait showing the queen holding the base of a pendant crucifix, included in Thomas Trevelyon's 1608

---

[75] Kelvingrove Art Gallery and Museum, Glasgow – 1685.
[76] See *CSP Scot.*, vol. 7, nos 573 and 577; Patricia Basing, 'Robert Beale and the Queen of Scots', *The British Library Journal* 20:1 (1994), p. 72. On the 'Association', see Steven J. Reid, *The Early Life of James VI: A Long Apprenticeship, 1566–1585* (Edinburgh, 2023), esp. Chapters Six and Nine.
[77] *CSP Scot.*, vol. 5, no. 389.
[78] The second double portrait at Blair Castle, of Mary's parents, is presumably by the same artist; it shows similarities in the painting of the sitter's faces and clothes, and includes painted inscriptions and an imperial crown that appear to be by the same person who worked on both elements in the portrait of Mary and James VI.

Miscellany, illustrating a chronology of 'the noble race the Stewards: succeeding lyneallye to the crowne of Scotland, to this day: with their lively protraitures'.[79]

The year after the Blair portrait was painted John Lesley published a second Marian propagandist volume, *A Treatise Towching the Right, Title, and Interest of the Most Excellent Princesse Marie, Queene of Scotland, and of the Most Noble King James, Her Grace's Sonne, to the Succession of the Croune of England* (Rouen, 1584). The bottom of the title page states 'All Britaine . . . will grow to one at last', and the book includes a genealogy showing Mary's right to the English throne through her descent from Henry VII and Elizabeth of York. An image of Mary within the *Treatise* is a cruder version of the engraving after the Sheffield type, published in Lesley's 1578 history of Scotland (see above). However, here the queen is paired with an image of James VI, with both sitters depicted in tondos of equal size. Both mother and son are shown crowned, with the circumscription around Mary reading 'Maria Scotorum Regina' and that around James 'Jacobus VI Scotorum Rex'. Thus they appear as monarchical equals, although they are presented above a cautionary verse, reading 'Through princelie grace and pietie/Great is the mothers fame/The king her sonne dothe yeeld much hope/To imitate the same'.[80]

In the earlier seventeenth century the Sheffield portrait image became less potent in its political and religious overtones. Around 1627, Charles I commissioned Daniel Mytens to make a full-length copy of the version that he owned (Royal Collection Trust).[81] The portrait reproduced the Sheffield type in reverse, after which there are a large number of reduced-length copies. It was displayed in the Bear Gallery at Whitehall, along with two other posthumous Stuart portraits that the king commissioned from Mytens, of James IV and Margaret Tudor.

Iconoclasm and the Ham portrait of Mary, Queen of Scots

When we examine the unfinished image of Mary at Ham, over which Maitland's portrait was painted, we have to consider the reasons for the cessation of its production and the erasure of that image. The charismatic potency of an image of Mary, with the potential to inspire both established and new followers, was symbolically dangerous in late 1580s Scotland, for both supporters and opponents of a restoration of Marian politics and religion in the kingdom. Reproductions of Elizabeth I were also the targets for iconoclasm, both in England and on the continent, that saw representational images of her, symbolic of the royal

---

[79] Folger Shakespeare Library, Washington DC – MS V.b.232. The quotation is fol. 121r and the woodcut of Mary is fol. 125r.
[80] University of Edinburgh, Center for Research Collections – De.10.121/1.
[81] Royal Collection Trust – RCIN 401182.

body, being stabbed, stoned, burned and hanged by her opponents.[82] Ironically Elizabeth herself sanctioned the destruction of many of her portraits, albeit for aesthetic reasons. In 1563 an unrealised, draft decree attempted to control the number of portraits being produced, to eliminate those showing 'errors and deformities' in the queen's likeness, and in 1596 the Privy Council ordered the destruction of unflattering pictures, to manage the royal image, leading to 'an official holocaust of portraits of her judged unseemly and improper'.[83]

Similar iconoclasm to Mary's, re-using a panel or canvas to cover a potentially problematic subject, can also be seen in a portrait of her son, based on a portrait of the young king by Arnold Bronckorst.[84] Infrared photography of the panel revealed a much earlier portrait underneath James's, showing a man at prayer, and subsequent cleaning uncovered elements of the older composition, including the earlier sitter's hands holding a small chalice, above which is the sacramental bread or host. A religious picture showing the symbols of the eucharist ritual would have been a highly provocative image in post-Reformation Scotland and the picture would likely have been destroyed had it not been for the value of the oak panel and integral frame, both of which were perfectly acceptable for re-use for a portrait of the Protestant king during his minority.

While Mary was alive there was always the possibility of her escaping her captivity, or being released, following the potential sudden death, including by murder, of Elizabeth. The prospect of a liberated Mary taking power in England or returning to take power in Scotland imbued her painted portrayal with a power beyond the purely representational reproduction of her image. Following the queen's execution in 1587 that potency ceased to exist, yet owning and displaying a painted portrait of her remained a potentially dangerous act in itself. The destruction of the image exemplifies a post-Reformation visual *damnatio memoriae*, where the sitter's memory was condemned and a reign that many thought best forgotten was unambiguously decommemorated. The act of destroying her image made her invisible – as if not seeing her removed the threat of displeasing the English queen and court, and removed any shame for not avenging that same queen for the judicial murder of the Scots' anointed monarch. The Sheffield portrait type is however the best-known and most influential example of Mary's likeness, and it has come to represent the whole of her complex iconography. While previously misunderstood in its date and purpose, it is a credible image of the Scottish monarch that was highly religious and political in its intent and reception.

---

[82] See Roy Strong, *Gloriana: The Portraits of Queen Elizabeth I* (London, 1987), p. 41.
[83] David Piper, *The English Face* (London, 1992), p. 46.
[84] See Bendor Grosvenor's *Art History News* blog entry: https://www.arthistorynews.com/articles/992_New_discovery__a_portrait_of_the_young_James_I_amp_VI.

Conclusion

The representation of the Scottish queen's likeness through coinage, painted portraits, miniatures and other media, and through their reproduction and wide dissemination in printed form, helped to serve both pro- and anti-Marian propagandist programmes of sanctification or vilification. A key significance of a group of images from her lifetime is that there was a body of contemporary work from which later imagemakers, historians, playwrights, composers, novelists, filmmakers and others could draw on for similar ends, be they supporting a partisan agenda or just offering a more nuanced and less sentimental understanding of who Mary was. Mary's portraiture offers clues, real and imagined, to both the physiognomy and the psychology of a hugely important historic figure.

The Sheffield portrait type discussed here has become a sort of visual shorthand for Mary during her English imprisonment, appearing in black, wearing symbols of her religion and innocence, and with an inscription that explains her regal position, her captivity and her piety. We are presented with a clear idea of the queen's real body, although the sympathy for the queen's misfortune, through images such as this, mutated into the cultish desire to create an enduring tragic persona in the centuries that followed her execution.

One of the ways in which Mary's iconography is so significant to her reputation is how it was utilised for her to become a symbolic personification or an icon – as a representative and allegorical object either worthy of reverence, or deserving of demonisation for her notoriety. Mary's iconography plays a hugely important part in the fabrication of a cultural afterlife for Scotland's most famous monarch. It gives the queen a recognisable visual identity, with which we can conceptualise the attributes of both her contemporary and posthumous fame, and it helps to secure Mary's enduring presence long after her famous death.

TWO

New Perspectives on the Sheffield Portraits of Mary, Queen of Scots including the Discovery of a New, Related, Contemporary Portrait

Caroline Rae

This chapter is the second of two in this volume to discuss Mary, Queen of Scots (frequently referred to here as 'the sitter') and visual imagery. The research and conclusions of this chapter will provide a foundation for Taylor's arguments in Chapter One, which focus in more detail on the memorialisation of this sitter. The first part of this chapter aims to reassess the evidence, and to bring new perspectives to bear, in relation to a group of full-size painted portraits of Mary inscribed 1578 (this group includes Figures 1.1 and 2.1).

This group are commonly known as the 'Sheffield' type due to the provenance of the assumed primary version at Hardwick Hall. This portrait type was hugely influential in the creation of the Catholic visual afterlife of this sitter. A key conclusion of this study is that the primary version of this group can probably be dated to the inscribed date, and that the available evidence suggests Mary's direct involvement in this work's creation. Thus, this significant strand of visual Catholic memorialisation can be considered to have originated with the sitter during her own lifetime.

The second part of the chapter focuses on the discovery and analysis of an unfinished painted portrait of Mary which lies beneath a further contemporary male portrait (attributed to Adrian Vanson, *Sir John Maitland, 1st Baron Maitland of Thirlestane*, National Trust at Ham House; henceforth referred to as *Maitland*; see Figures 2.16 and 2.17). The underlying portrait will be argued to have been produced in Scotland in the 1580s prior to the sitter's execution. It will be demonstrated that this portrait can clearly be linked to the Sheffield group (alongside other exemplars), providing further evidence for the existence of these hugely important Catholic images at this early date. The wider significance of the discovery of the underlying portrait and its obliteration will be also considered briefly here; this aspect is developed further by Taylor in Chapter One.

Figure 2.1 *Mary, Queen of Scots*, by unknown artist (English school), inscribed 1578, National Portrait Gallery, oil on panel, 79.1 × 90.2cm (NPG 249)
Lifestyle Pictures/Alamy Stock Photo

The Hilliard and 'Sheffield' portraits

This section will bring new perspectives to bear on the dating and origins of the Sheffield group of portraits and their relationship to two miniature portraits created by the English court limner and goldsmith Nicholas Hilliard (1547–1619) from the collections of the Royal Collection and the Victoria and Albert Museum (Victoria and Albert Museum).

These two groups, their potential date of creation and their inter-relationship has sparked much scholarship and debate over the years. A notable example is work by Roy Strong, who suggested that the Sheffield type were Jacobean portraits created as part of James VI and I's rehabilitation of his mother's image after his accession to the English throne in 1603, utilising the Hilliard miniatures as

Figure 2.2 *Mary, Queen of Scots*, Nicholas Hilliard, Royal Collection, watercolour on vellum laid on card, h 4.5 cm × w 3.7 cm (RCIN 420641)
Royal Collection Trust/© His Majesty King Charles III, 2023

a basis for the face and costume.[1] A key factor in shaping Strong's argument was that he omitted to note the presence of the supposed prime version at Hardwick Hall [Figure 1.1] in the 1601 inventory of Bess of Hardwick. Strong's influential argument has recently been disputed by Smith who, focussing his discussion on the Catholic iconography present in the works in relation to the socio-historical context, opined that the Sheffield portraits contain demonstrable patron-led choices, and that they are likely related to a sitting in 1578. On the basis of documentary evidence (in the accounts of Bess of Hardwick) Smith argued the

[1] Roy Strong, *Tudor and Jacobean Portraits* (London, 1969), vol. 1, 220–21.

Figure 2.3 *Mary, Queen of Scots*, Nicholas Hilliard, 1580s (?), Victoria and Albert Museum, watercolour on vellum, h 4cm × w 5.1 cm (P.24-1975)
© Victoria and Albert Museum, London

Hilliard miniatures were later and possibly derivative of the Hardwick Sheffield portrait.[2] His arguments for the involvement of the patron in the composition of the Sheffield portraits and for the influence of the Sheffield type on Mary's tomb in Westminster Abbey are compelling. However, a potential weakness in his argument that the Hilliard miniatures were created after 1590 is his reliance on the presumption that Bess of Hardwick was the initial patron.[3]

Provenance, evidence from technical studies, summary of previous scholarship

There is no extant archival evidence that can be used to verify whether the Hilliard miniatures or Sheffield variations were painted from life. As noted, the Hardwick Hall Sheffield portrait is included in the 1601 inventory of Bess of

---

[2] Jeremy L. Smith, 'Revisiting the Origins of the Sheffield Series of Portraits of Mary Queen of Scots', *The Burlington Magazine* 152: 1285 (2010): 217–18; Jeremy L. Smith, 'The Sheffield Portrait Types, their Catholic Purposes, and Mary Queen of Scots' Tomb', *British Catholic History* 33 (2016): 71–90.

[3] Smith, 'Revisiting the Origins', pp. 214–15.

Hardwick (Bess of Hardwick was the wife of the earl of Shrewsbury, who was the gaoler of Mary, Queen of Scots between 1569 and 1584). Dendrochronology carried out on the supports of the Sheffield and NPG works has recently provided evidence that both may have been created during the sitter's lifetime, although the possibility of trees being felled and planks stored prior to usage cannot be ruled out.[4]

The two miniature portraits by Hilliard are similar in costume and composition. Although the V & A version is slightly extended and embellished, both depict a head-and-shoulders view. Technical study revealed the presence of the costly blue pigment ultramarine in the background of the Royal Collection version. This has been utilised to argue for the latter work as the prime version, although it has also been argued that the treatment of the face in the V & A version is more vivacious and suggestive of a sitting from life.[5]

That the sitter was able to sit for her portrait at least once whilst in the charge of Shrewsbury is evidenced by a letter sent to Cardinal Beaton on 31 August 1577 by her personal secretary, Claude Nau de la Boisseliere, which presumably refers to the creation of a miniature portrait or portraits:

Je pensois faire accompagner la presente d'un portrait de Sa Majestie, maid le peintre ne luy a sceu donner sa perfection avant le partement de cetter despeche.

(I thought to accompany this letter with a portrait of Her Majesty, but the painter has not managed to finish it in time for me to send it with this).[6]

Neither the Sheffield portraits (inscribed 1578) nor the Hilliard miniatures can be linked to this letter (Hilliard was in France between September 1576 and 1578). Previous scholars have argued that the queen may have sat for Hilliard in an undocumented sitting, perhaps in 1576, before the limner travelled abroad. Logically, this also opens the door to the suggestion that other undocumented sittings may potentially have occurred during the sitter's captivity. The fact that Hilliard more frequently utilised an oval format, as opposed to circular, following his return from France is another factor that should be considered in relation to dating, although the potential for the format to have been a patron-led choice by this dowager queen of France should also be considered.[7]

---

[4] Ian Tyers, 'The Tree-Ring Analysis of Panel Paintings from the National Portrait Gallery: Group 5.2', unpublished report (September 2011), registered packet NPG 1807, Heinz Archive, National Portrait Gallery, pp. 11–15.
[5] Elizabeth Goldring, *Nicholas Hilliard: Life of an Artist* (New Haven, CT, 2019), p. 153.
[6] Labanoff (ed.), *Lettres*, vol. 4, p. 390.
[7] On Hilliard's use of both formats, see Catherine MacLeod, Rab MacGibbon, Nicholas Hilliard and Isaac Oliver, *Elizabethan Treasures: Miniatures by Hilliard and Oliver* (London, 2019), p. 51. For a comparative example, see Clouet's miniature portrait of Catherine de' Medici, *c.* 1555 (Victoria and Albert Museum, London [P. 26 - 1954]).

Comparison between the Hilliard and Sheffield portrait types

With the aim of casting new perspectives on the debate, and in order to interrogate the argument that the Sheffield likenesses were potentially later images based on the Hilliard miniatures, an object-focussed approach was taken. A key component of the methodology was the comparison of face tracings. Tracings taken from both groups were compared to each other and also to extant 'authentic' likenesses of the sitter. The latter group included portraits produced during the sitter's time at the French court and the 'Blairs' group comprising a highly significant full-length posthumous portrait (commonly referred to as the 'Blairs Memorial Portrait') and two potentially related miniatures, discussed later in this chapter.[8] The Blairs Memorial Portrait can be argued to be an important,

Figure 2.4 *Mary, Queen of Scots*, the 'Blairs Memorial Portrait', by an unknown artist (Flemish school), 1604–18, Blairs Museum, oil on canvas, 227 × 139cm
Reproduced by permission of the Scottish Catholic Heritage Collections Trust

[8] The Blairs Memorial portrait and associated miniatures are typically considered derivative of the Sheffield type in the literature. However, there are subtle differences in the face patterns utilised between the two, and accordingly they are considered as separate groups in this chapter. It seems plausible that the Sheffield likeness may have been updated to reflect the sitter's increased age/weight in the later portrait.

authentic likeness, as it was commissioned in the early seventeenth century, likely in Antwerp, by Elizabeth Curle, the sitter's lady-in-waiting and close companion during her imprisonment in England.[9]

Contemporary descriptions of Mary were also considered as part of the study in relation to the 'authentic' likeness depicted in the two groups of painted portraits. A further approach was the comparison of the images (including elements of costume and background) to contemporary French portraiture, in the hope of uncovering further aspects that could arguably be evidence of patron-led choices.

Results from comparison of face tracings

The comparison revealed that (perhaps unsurprisingly) portraits of Mary depicted her as having similar facial features and proportions throughout her life. For example, if a tracing of the Rijksmuseum miniature, which depicts the sitter later in life, is superimposed on a drawing of Mary as a young girl, it can be seen that although these are not a perfect match, and the sitter is depicted at a slightly different angle, the proportions of the face and the features broadly correlate.

Figure 2.5 Superimposition of tracings taken of the faces in two portraits (François Clouet, *Mary, Queen of Scots*, 1559, drawing, Bibliothèque Nationale de France, Paris, and *Mary, Queen of Scots*, 1580s, Rijksmuseum)
C. Rae

---

[9] The painting can be argued to have created between 1604 and 1618. For a recent discussion of this work, see Marguerite A. Tassi, 'Martyrdom and Memory: Elizabeth Curle's Portrait of Mary, Queen of Scots', in Debra Barrett-Graves (ed.), The Emblematic Queen: Extra-literary Representations of Early Modern Queenship (New York, 2013), pp. 101–32.

Figure 2.6 Superimposition of tracings taken of the faces in two portraits (unknown artist (English school), *Mary, Queen of Scots*, Hardwick Hall, and 'Blairs Memorial Portrait')
C. Rae

Most of the portraits have similar general proportions to the Sheffield portraits.

However, the Hilliard portraits, also associated with this later period in the sitter's life, are a slight outlier, in that the face is consistently shorter, if the

Figure 2.7 Superimposition of tracings taken of the faces in two portraits (Hilliard, *Mary, Queen of Scots*, Royal Collection, and *Mary, Queen of Scots*, Rijksmuseum)
C. Rae

Figure 2.8 Superimposition of tracings taken of the faces in two portraits (Hilliard, *Mary, Queen of Scots*, Royal Collection, and 'Blairs Memorial Portrait')
C. Rae

Figure 2.9 Superimposition of tracings taken of the faces in two portraits (Hilliard, *Mary, Queen of Scots*, Royal Collection, and *Mary, Queen of Scots*, Hardwick Hall)
C. Rae

bottom of the upper chin is taken to represent her natural jaw line, although the facial features are consistent and match well with the other portraits.

It is not possible to infer from this finding that Hilliard did or did not paint the sitter from life. What can be argued is that, like many artists at the time,

Figure 2.10   Detail, face, *Mary, Queen of Scots*, Hardwick Hall
National Trust

he interpreted her face through his own artistic lens or characteristic mode of interpretation. Hilliard's consistently flattering approach to his sitters can be observed similarly in comparison of portraits of James VI and I by Hilliard and by John de Critz the Elder, the king's official painters in miniature and in large.[10]

The plumper face and double chin of the sitter in the Hilliard miniatures matches well to a description of the sitter given at her execution in 1587: 'Her face full and flat, double chinned, and hasel eyed'. However, the sitter in the Sheffield type has a gaunt visage that is incongruous with this description, and also with the depiction of the sitter in Hilliard's portraits.

A review of the correspondence of Bess of Hardwick during the period of Mary's imprisonment was undertaken by the author with the hope of finding an additional, first-hand description. Bess, writing to Sir Francis Walsingham on 28 December 1578, states that the queen has grown 'lean and sickly' and

---

[10] For example, see John de Critz the Elder, *James VI and I*, 1608, Galeria Palatina, Palazzo Pitti, Florence (2389) and Nicholas Hilliard, *James VI and I*, c. 1609, Collection of the Buchanan Society on long-term loan to the National Galleries of Scotland (PGL 153).

she blames her captive's weak state on the lack of exercise necessitated by her captivity:

> euer yn affecte synce my comynge she ys growed lene and seckely and say the wante of exarcyse ys brynge har yn to that weke statte
> (effectively, since my coming she has grown lean and sickly and says the want of exercise has brought her to that weak state).[11]

It is striking that this description matches so much better the likeness in the portrait than it does that depicted in the Hilliard works, where the sitter has a notable double chin. Building on this point is the fact that evidence from comparing face tracings reveals the Sheffield artist depicted the proportions of the sitter's face more in keeping with the 'authentic' portraits than did Hilliard. This would seem unlikely to have occurred if the artist only had the Hilliard miniatures to utilise as the basis for their likeness.

Costume and composition

Further insight into the veracity of the Sheffield-type portraits was garnered from consideration of composition and costume. A first point of consideration was examination of the works in relation to contemporary French court portraiture. Such an approach may seem somewhat alien as the Sheffield-type portraits are so clearly naive and English in execution. However, the significance of the potential identification of any arguable influence of French portraiture in the full-size portraits, not present in the Hilliard works, should be noted in seeking evidence of the direct involvement of this particular sitter in the former works.

The composition of the Sheffield type, consisting of an Anatolian carpet, a table covered in a red velvet cloth, and green taffeta curtains, is, as Strong notes, highly unusual for a full-size portrait produced in the 1570s in England.[12] This atypical composition was one of the notable factors that led him to opine that these full-length works were created in the early Jacobean era. Several authors have disputed Strong's argument by citing a further sixteenth-century work with a similar composition. This portrait, of Arbella Stuart (1575–1615), is inscribed 1589 and is also in the Hardwick collection. As noted by these authors, it seems plausible that the composition of the latter work was directly influenced by the full-length portrait of Mary in the same collection, as a means for Bess to

---

[11] Hatfield House, Cecil Papers, 10/77, fols 137–38 (http://www.bessofhardwick.org/letter.jsp?letter=123).
[12] Strong, *Tudor and Jacobean Portraits*, vol. 1, p. 221.

visually emphasise the dynastic connection linking the two families (Stuart was Mary's niece by marriage, and Bess's granddaughter).[13]

However, the question of the source for the composition of the Sheffield series has not been explored further in the extant literature. If the portrait is considered in the context of the portraiture at the Valois court in which Mary

Figure 2.11 *Catherine de' Medici*, by an unknown artist (French school), 1550s, Palazzo Pitti, oil on canvas, 194 × 100cm
Gabinetto Photigraphico delle Galerie degli Uffizi, Florence

[13] David A. H. B. Taylor, 'A Derbyshire Portrait Gallery: Bess of Hardwick's Picture Collection', in *Hardwick Hall: a Great Old Castle of Romance*, ed. David Adshead and David A. H. B. Taylor (New Haven, CT, 2016), p. 80, Smith, 'Revisiting the Origins', pp. 215–16.

grew up, it becomes apparent that this type of full-length portrait with attendant props was a standard format in that period at that court. For example, a portrait of Mary's mother-in-law Catherine de' Medici depicts the subject in a posture similar to the Sheffield-type portraits, with a red velvet tablecloth and curtains hanging in the background.

The use of curtains and carpets as background props can also be seen in full-length portraits of Henri II and Charles IX.[14] That the composition of the Sheffield-type portraits was a patron-led direction by Mary herself seems a plausible explanation for this artistic innovation (in British art of the period), especially given the apparent lack of sophistication of the painter (although it must be considered a possibility that the Hardwick portrait could be a copy of a lost original). This finding builds on the earlier conclusion from comparison of likenesses that 'authentic' aspects that are not present in the Hilliard miniatures are present in this work. Turning Strong's theory on its head, one could even speculate that Mary herself may have been responsible for importing this type of composition to England, with early Jacobean copies of the Sheffield image, created during and after James VI's accession to the English throne (such as the Scottish National Portrait Gallery or Hatfield versions), influencing fashionable early seventeenth-century artists at such as William Larkin (c. 1585–1619), who made such portrait compositions his hallmark.[15]

As has been noted by Smith in relation to costume, a difference between the two groups is the presence of ruff ties: these are included in the Sheffield portraits but not in the Hilliard miniatures. Ruffs commonly tied at the front in the period.[16] Visible ties are rare in French and English portraiture of this time, although they can be seen in portraits of significant figures at the sixteenth-century Scottish court including James Stuart, first earl of Moray, Mary's half-brother.[17] It is possible, therefore, that wearing the ties visible may reflect a Scottish fashion, or alternatively that Hilliard, a sophisticated painter *au fait* with modes of representation at European courts, omitted these as he did not believe they were an appropriate inclusion. The ties in the Sheffield portrait are trimmed with pearls. Such a luxurious detail can be argued to be an authentic addition to the traditionally austere black and white French mourning garb

---

[14] See, for example, Clouet, *Charles IX*, 1569, Kunsthistorisches Museum, Vienna, oil on canvas, 222 × 115 cm and François Quesnel, *Henri III*, Ambras Castle, oil on canvas, 199 × 117cm.

[15] On Larkin, see Caroline Rae, 'William Larkin', in *Allgemeines Künstlerlexikon. Die Bildenden Künstler aller Zeiten und Völker*, ed. A. Beyer, B. Savoy and W. Tegethoff (Berlin, 2015), p. 207.

[16] Anna Reynolds, *In Fine Style: The Art of Tudor and Stuart Fashion* (London, 2013), p. 59.

[17] See the 1561 wedding portrait by Hans Eworth (private collection), and also portraits of Mary's father, James V, and Archibald Douglas, 4th earl of Angus: unknown artist (French school), *Archibald Douglas*, c. 1530, Palace of Holyroodhouse, Royal Collection (RCIN 402700); Corneille de Lyon, *James V*, c. 1536, National Trust at Polesden Lacey (NT 1246456).

worn by this elite sitter. Brantôme (1540–1614), discussing the sumptuous clothing worn by aristocratic widows, writes:

> Nos vefves d'ennuy n'osent porter de pierreries sinon aux doigts et à quelques miroirs et à quelques heures et à de belles ceintures, mais non sur la teste ny le corps: ou bien force perles au col et au bras . . .
>
> (Our bored widows dare not wear precious stones except on their fingers and a few mirrors and at certain hours and on beautiful belts, but not on the head or the body: or else force pearls on the collar and on the arm . . .)[18]

Further departures in depiction can be noted between the two portrait groups. Hilliard, a sophisticated court artist, understood that the wired veil should be represented with two perfect arcs extending above Mary's shoulders (as can be seen in paintings and engravings of French aristocratic sitters of the period), whereas the Sheffield artist has depicted the collar of this garment with a less impressive and more asymmetrical outline. Hilliard created the illusion of Mary's diaphanous, lozenged partlet in a confident and skilled fashion by utilising simple grey strokes over a white underlayer without extraneous detail, whereas the Hardwick artist observed that this garment was a two-part construction and painted in both elements of the embroidered lattice and diaphanous fabric beneath it in laborious detail.

In contemporary French court portraiture, and earlier Florentine elite portraits, partlets are often depicted as being constructed similarly, with a lattice placed over a light fabric that was pulled through the overlying structure to create puffed lozenge shapes.

Figure 2.12 Detail, partlet, *Mary, Queen of Scots*, Hardwick Hall
National Trust

---

[18] Pierre de Bourdeille, Seigneur de Brantôme, *Oeuvres Complètes*, vol. 9 (Paris, 1876), p. 638.

Figure 2.13 *Portrait of a Woman*, by François Clouet, 1560, Barnes Foundation, oil on panel, 29.2 × 22.9 cm (BF809)
The Barnes Foundation, Philadelphia, PA

Dr Susan Kay-Williams, Chief Executive of the Royal School of Needlework, advised that, in her view, the partlets in both the Hardwick Hall and NPG Sheffield versions could indeed be faithful depictions of real garments, with the lattice created using a diamond pattern and chain stitch embroidery, worked by a needle.[19] Although the difficulties in identifying lacework from painted depictions should be acknowledged,[20] it is notable that this artist should choose to take such a different approach to depicting this element from that of Hilliard, and yet manage to create something authentic in appearance, if he had only had the Hilliard miniatures as a basis for his work.

A final comparison was undertaken of the gold crucifixes worn by Mary in both groups of portraits. Inventories of the queen's jewellery were examined in relation to this part of the study. Although it was not possible to identify

---

[19] Private correspondence by email, 24 January 2020.
[20] Reynolds notes the difficulties of identifying lace from painted depictions alone (Reynolds, *In Fine Style*, p. 61).

these items, the inventory of the sitter's possessions taken in 1586 at Chartley suggests that Mary may have habitually favoured one gold crucifix ('[l]a croix d'or que Sa Majesté avoit accoustomé de porter').[21] At her execution in 1587, the queen was described by a witness as wearing 'about her necke a crucifix of gold'.[22] On the basis that Elizabeth Curle, a fellow Catholic and companion in Mary's captivity who was present at her execution, was intimately familiar with this item, it can be argued that the depiction in the Blairs Memorial Portrait is likely a faithful rendition of a crucifix owned by the sitter. The great care typically taken to represent regal jewellery accurately in this era is a further compelling aspect in this regard. The layers of paint on the crucifix worn by the queen in the Hardwick Hall portrait appear to have suffered losses, and related overpainting is visible. However, the jewel can be seen to have once been similar in form to the crucifix depicted in the NPG version.[23] The crucifixes in these Sheffield-type portraits are closer in appearance to the crucifix worn by the sitter in the Blairs Memorial Portrait than those worn in the Hilliards, although they are not identical (the Blairs crucifix appears flat whereas the Sheffields are more rounded). The Sheffield and Blairs Memorial crucifixes have similar pointed, tapered ends with gold edging, whereas the Hilliards differ in a few ways. The miniature crucifixes are depicted as having parallel 'INRI' bands which somewhat resemble crosses of Lorraine, and the ends of the crossbars are square.[24] The extended V & A version has the addition of a hanging pendant pearl. Of course, Mary owned several crucifixes during her life, and it may be possible that the Sheffield artist was simply depicting a generic type commonly worn by Catholics. However, it is notable that the Sheffield artist has again departed from Hilliard in their depiction of this significant detail, and that their interpretation can be linked more compellingly to the depiction of the same item on an authentic portrait of this sitter.

Relation of the Hilliard and Sheffield types to contemporary painted and engraved works and circulation of these likenesses in the 1570s and 1580s

Due to the lack of relevant documentary sources, arguments for the creation of both of these groups of portraits during the sitter's lifetime have often been

---

[21] Inventaire de la Garde-Robe de Marie Stuart, Chartley, 13 June 1586, included in Labanoff (ed.), *Lettres*, vol. 7, p. 242.
[22] Anonymous account contained in a MS in the Bodleian Library (labelled E.Museuo.178), printed in Thomas Hearne, Charles Edward Doble, David Watson Rannie and Herbert Edward Salter (eds), *Remarks and Collections of Thomas Hearne* (Oxford, 1898) vol. 4, p. 76.
[23] The similarity between the crucifixes worn by the sitter in the Sheffield type and Blairs Memorial portraits was also noted by Scharf, as quoted in Lionel Cust, *Notes on the Authentic Portraits of Mary Queen of Scots* (London, 1903), p. 105.
[24] The house of Guise was a branch of the house of Lorraine. Such crosses are featured on the verso of French coinage featuring Mary and the *dauphin* struck in 1558.

based on evidence for the dissemination of the original designs in various secondary painted or printed forms during or soon after the sitter's lifetime. Needless to say, print media was a technology that was highly influential in disseminating images and propaganda in the sixteenth century. However, a reassessment of the evidence suggests that these previous comparisons with the Sheffield and Hilliard groups can be argued to be inconclusive in terms of deliberating between the groups and their circulation at the time.

An engraved portrait of the sitter in roundel form included in Bishop Lesley's *De origine, moribus, ac rebus gestis Scotia libri decem*, Rome 1578 has been used to argue for the existence and circulation of the Hilliard likeness in the year of publication, which year is also inscribed on the Sheffield group of full-size portraits.[25]

Figure 2.14 John Leslie, *De origine, moribus, et rebus gestis Scotorum, libri decem* . . . (concerning the origin, behaviour and deeds of the Scots, in ten books, Rome, 1578), p. 440
Courtesy of University of Glasgow Archives & Special Collections: Sp. Coll. Bi3-h.2

---

[25] Goldring, *Nicholas Hilliard*, p. 153.

However, comparison with a wider range of likenesses undertaken during the study suggests that the basis for the facial likeness in this image was more probably instead a French model associated with the court artist Clouet's workshop, such as the miniature portrait of the sitter now in the Uffizi collection.[26]

This portrait is mounted amongst a series of Valois family miniature portraits that probably once belonged to Catherine de' Medici.[27] The 1578 engraved

Figure 2.15 Mary, Queen of Scots, by François Clouet, c. 1558–60 (detail of *Henri II of Valois and Caterina de' Medici, Surrounded by Members of Their Family*, by François Clouet) Uffizi, tempera on parchment, 5 × 3.6cm
Gabinetto Photigraphico delle Galerie degli Uffizi, Florence

[26] Smailes and Thomson also suggest the potential influence of an earlier French model on the likeness depicted in this engraving, and also note that the elongated proportions of the face in the engraving (and French portraits) correspond more closely to the Sheffield likenesses than they do to the Hilliard miniatures. However, following on from Strong, these authors argue that the Sheffield works are most likely posthumous likenesses: Helen Smailes and Duncan Thomson, *The Queen's Image* (Edinburgh, 1987), pp. 40, 53. The Uffizi miniature (or a similar portrait) seems a more likely source for the likeness in the engraving than the *En Deuil Blanc* series, as suggested by Smailes and Thomson, as it includes Mary's characteristic large ear.

[27] Anon. curatorial/provenance information, Uffizi online catalogue (https://catalogo.uffizi.it/it/29/ricerca/detailiccd/1504549).

portrait shares with the Uffizi miniature larger eyes and a youthful visage, alongside a distinctively shaped, prominent, right ear (also present in other portraits of Mary produced during her time in France) which is omitted from all of the variations of the Hilliard and Sheffield portraits.[28] The smaller open collar worn by the sitter in the engraved portrait corresponds more closely to that in the earlier Uffizi portrait and seen in French fashion around 1565, and differs from the larger ruff worn in the Sheffield and Hilliard portraits.[29]

Affirming Mary's continued use of the Uffizi miniature type after she left France is the fact that this was also used as the model for a double portrait of the sitter and her second husband, Henry, Lord Darnley (at Hardwick Hall) which may have been painted in Scotland during her brief reign.[30] A further version of the Uffizi portrait type exists, perhaps once part of a portrait set, which can be argued on the basis of technical analysis to have been produced in England in the sixteenth century, either during or shortly after the sitter's life (perhaps between 1560 and 1592).[31] It seems plausible, due to the existence of this work and the influence of the Uffizi portrait type on the Lesley engraving, that this likeness may also have been in wider circulation in the 1570s. Indeed, it may have been this type to which the queen was referring when, in 1575, she wrote to James Beaton, the former archbishop of Glasgow and her French ambassador:

> Il y a de mes amis en ce pays qui demandent de une peinctures. Je vous prye m'en faire quatre, don't il fauldra qu'il en soyent quatre enchassex en or, et me les enboyez secrètement.
>
> (Among my friends in this country some ask for my portrait. I pray you have four made for me, all of which must be set in gold, and send them to me secretly.)[32]

The circulation of the Hilliard or Sheffield likenesses at the French court in the 1580s has been more convincingly argued. Taylor has suggested the influence of the Sheffield portraits on an engraved likeness by Leonard Gaultier,

---

[28] Cust also considers the large ear to be a characteristic feature of Mary's in portraits created at the French court (for example: Cust, *Notes on the Authentic Portraits*, pp. 28, 32).

[29] Francis M. Kelly and R. Schwabe, *Historic Costume: A Chronicle of Fashion in Western Europe 1490–1790* (London, 1929), p. 76.

[30] Woodward-Reed suggested that the double portrait was most possibly a copy or composite commissioned by Bess of Hardwick for her collection, to further elucidate her Stuart dynastic ties: Hannah Elizabeth Woodward-Reed, 'The Context and Material Techniques of Royal Portrait Production within Jacobean Scotland: The Courts of James V and James VI' (PhD thesis, University of Glasgow, 2018) vol. 1, p. 123. Taylor (Chapter One) has argued that this item may have been commissioned by the sitter during her Scottish reign.

[31] For further discussion of this work, see Tarnya Cooper, *Elizabeth I and Her People* (London, 2014), p. 208.

[32] Labanoff (ed.), *Lettres*, vol. 4, p. 256.

published by Pierre Gourdelle, dating from after the sitter's execution in 1587.[33] Cust, and later Goldring, suggested that a miniature portrait inserted into a book of hours once owned by Catherine de' Medici is a copy after the Hilliard portraits (although the viage has been replaced with a portrait of the Queen more similar to those created when she was a younger age than those created by Hilliard, such as those produced by the Clouet workshop).[34] The latter comparison (of the miniature contained in the book of hours to the Hilliard portrait) is visually compelling. A notable factor is that the 1587 miniature depicts the sitter in reverse of the Hilliard portraits, which could potentially suggest the influence of an engraving in its creation (such as that by Gaultier, which faces in the same direction, and which also depicts the sitter with a younger appearance than the Hilliard). However, a limitation in developing this comparison further is the lack of specific details, such as repetitions of face patterns or costume, that could be used to argue more definitively for the influence of the Hilliard or Sheffield types on these works. More loosely related to the latter types but even further removed, in terms of authentic detail of costume or likeness, is an engraved portrait produced in the year of the sitter's execution by the Wierix brothers in Antwerp (Figure 1.2, discussed by Taylor in Chapter One).

A new portrait of Mary, Queen of Scots and its relationship to the Blairs and Sheffield types

In 2016 the author was awarded nine months' funding by the Trustees of the Caroline Villers Research Fellowship to carry out a research project, hosted by the Department of Conservation and Technology, Courtauld Institute of Art (CIA) in collaboration with National Galleries of Scotland and the National Trust. The aim of the fellowship was to reassess the *oeuvres* of two significant *émigré* Netherlandish artists who lived and worked in Scotland in the late sixteenth and early seventeenth centuries – Adrian Vanson (*fl.* 1581–1602) and Adam de Colone (*c.* 1593–1628) – by utilising technical examination in combination with a re-evaluation of the art historical and documentary evidence.[35]

Sir John Maitland (inscribed 1589) was examined at CIA in 2016.

---

[33] Taylor, 'A Derbyshire Portrait Gallery', p. 78. He notes that a version of this print is in the collection of Fitzwilliam College, Cambridge.

[34] Bibliothèque Nationale de France, Paris, NAL MS 82, fol. 90r. This portrait and its relation to the Hilliard miniatures is discussed by Cust (Cust, *Notes on the Authentic Portraits*, pp. 77–78) and Goldring (Goldring, *Nicholas Hilliard*, p. 153). Goldring suggests that the French copy may have been created at the time of the sitter's execution in 1587.

[35] For further discussion of key findings of the fellowship in relation to Vanson, see Caroline Rae, with curatorial input from Kate Anderson and David A. H. B. Taylor, 'New Thoughts on Adrian Vanson: Findings from a Technical Examination of Selected Works, including the Discussion of an Interesting Panel Join', *The Picture Restorer* 61 (Autumn 2022): 35–46.

Figure 2.16 *Sir John Maitland, 1st Baron Maitland of Thirlestane*, attributed to Adrian Vanson, inscribed 1589, National Trust at Ham House, oil on panel, 74.7 × 58.5cm (NT 1139943)
National Trust/C. Rae

This portrait depicts a significant Scottish figure (Maitland was Chancellor of Scotland at the date inscribed on the portrait) that, at the time that it came into the department, had been recently attributed (by Taylor, on stylistic grounds) to James VI's court painter Adrian Vanson.[36] A striking discovery was the presence of an unfinished portrait of a woman beneath the overlying male portrait in X-radiography and infrared reflectography. Further detail of the costume, most notably the veil worn by the sitter, became visible during a later examination carried out at the Hamilton Kerr Institute using MA-XRF (scanning macro X-ray fluorescence).

Who was this mysterious woman, when was she painted and why was she painted over? It will be argued strongly, here, that the woman depicted is Mary, Queen of Scots and the discovery of this work is significant in the present context, as it provides further evidence for the circulation and genesis of the

[36] David A. H. B. Taylor, 'Questions of Attribution: A Portrait of Sir John Maitland of Thirlestane at Ham House', *Apollo (National Trust Historic Houses and Collections Annual)* (2013): 55–59.

Figure 2.17 *Maitland*, Vanson, mosaiced X-radiograph image
National Trust/Courtauld Institute of Art

Figure 2.18 *Maitland*, Vanson, infrared image
National Trust/Courtauld Institute of Art

Figure 2.19 *Maitland*, Vanson, MA-XRF elemental map of lead
National Trust/Hamilton Kerr Institute

Sheffield group of portraits, key to the development of the Catholic memorialisation of this sitter, in the 1580s or earlier. The covering over of this work can also be argued to be of note, in that potentially it bears witness to the obliteration of images of this controversial female monarch shortly after her execution.

Dating of the portraits

Evidence relating to the dating and potential geographic origin of both the underlying and overlying portraits was gleaned from examination of the work's panel support. Dendrochronologist Ian Tyers noted that the unusual asymmetric joints used to join together the boards of the panel support may be something that can be associated with Scottish practice in the period.[37] Although examination of a wider number of works is needed to further contextualise

---

[37] Ian Tyers, 'Tree-ring Analysis of a Panel Painting: A Portrait of Sir John Maitland, 1st Baron Maitland of Thirlestane, aged 44, 1589, from Ham House (Dendrochronological Consultancy Report 1286)', unpublished 2021 report, National Trust Conservation files, NT 1139943, Conservation Department, The National Trust, London, p. 5.

this finding, a Scottish location of production would fit not only with the identity and significance of the overlying sitter but also with the provenance of the portrait within the sitter's family (discussed by Taylor). Tyers concluded that first usage dates for *Maitland*'s panel support likely fell between *c.* 1569 and *c.* 1586.[38] This dating would support a hypothesis that the underlying portrait was painted and then covered over by the male portrait in 1589 (inscribed date). Further evidence regarding the dating of the underlying work was garnered from technical examination. Several *pentimenti* visible at the male sitter's shoulders likely relate to difficulties encountered during the conversion of the portrait. There are several extant contemporary or slightly later painted and engraved copies that repeat the composition of the overlying portrait exactly. It can be inferred from the presence of the *pentimenti* that the Ham House portrait is likely the prime or original version, created at around the inscribed date, which acted as a model for further versions, as previously suggested by Taylor. This is a key finding in that it can be used to strongly argue for the inscribed date on the male portrait as a *terminus ante quem* for the underlying work.

Evidence for the identification of the female sitter

An initial identification of the woman in the underlying portrait as Mary, Queen of Scots, was made due to the striking resemblance of the face to the well-known characteristic features of this monarch. Such features, which can be traced throughout her life in depictions on coinage and in engravings and painted portraits, and in reliable contemporary descriptions, include a long, pale face that grew fatter with age, thin lips with a slightly projecting upper lip, heavy eyelids, a long, straight nose that dipped slightly at the tip (in some images) and a high, domed forehead.[39]

A significant description was given by Mary's grandmother Antoinette de Bourbon, when the future queen was a child at the French court:

> elle est clere, brune et pence qu'estant en eage d'en bonpoint qu'elle sera belle fille, car le taint est beau et cler; et la chair blanche, le bas du vysage bien jolly, les yeux sont petis et ung petit enfoncé, le visage ung petit long, la grace etasurance fort bonne quent tout est dit elle est pour ce contenter.
>
> (She has fair skin, is brunette and we think that when she comes of age she will be a beautiful girl, because her complexion is beautiful and clear; and the white skin, the lower part of the face is very beautiful, the eyes small and a little deep, her face a little long, [she has] grace and very good self-confidence when all is said she is satisfactory.)[40]

---

[38] Tyers, 'Tree-ring Analysis', p. 4.
[39] Cust, *Notes on the Authentic Portraits*, pp. 16–17, 32.
[40] Antoinette de Bourbon to François, duke of Guise, August 1548 (BNF, Department of Manuscripts, fr. 20468, fol. 165).

A further notable description was given by an anonymous witness at the Queen's execution in 1587:

> The Queen of Scots was of Stature high, bigg made, and somewhat round-shouldered. Her face full and flat, double chinned, and hasel eyed.[41]

In comparison to this overall group of likenesses and descriptions, the depiction of the sitter in the underlying portrait resembles most that of the aged queen, due to its heavier jawline. After examination of the technical images, it was concluded that no inscriptions, regalia or other iconographical attributes (such as crucifixes or jewellery) had been present in the underlying portrait, which could have been used to support the suggested identification of the sitter. Therefore, a priority became adopting other means to verify more conclusively her identity. A composite tracing using the technical images was made in order to obtain a clearer view of the sitter and her costume.

Study of picture files in sitter boxes in the library of the Scottish National Portrait Gallery and the Heinz Archive at the National Portrait Gallery, London,

Figure 2.20 *Maitland*, Vanson, composite tracing of the underlying composition
C. Rae

---

[41] Hearne et al. (eds), *Remarks and Collections*, p. 76.

revealed that the portrait is not a direct copy of any known extant work, although it is probable that many contemporary portraits of this controversial queen that may once have existed have now been lost.

The composite tracing was compared with tracings taken from the group of painted and engraved portraits of Mary that can be argued to be 'authentic' likenesses.[42] With the caveat that such a comparative process can never be an exact science, as tracings are created by hand and so there is a very small margin for slippage, a notable finding of this detailed comparative process was that, of the comparison group, the features of the underlying female sitter are an almost exact match in some areas for the outline and features of the face of the Blairs Memorial Portrait.

Details in the tracings taken from the two portraits, such as the irises, peaks of the lips, jawline and eyebrows, align almost perfectly, although there are some slight differences such as at the outlines of the neck, hairline and eyelids. Due to the close likeness in the patterns used to create both portraits, the identification of the woman depicted in the underlying portrait as Mary, Queen of Scots can strongly be argued to be correct. On the basis of this comparison,

Figure 2.21 Superimposition of tracings of the faces in two portraits (female portrait underlying *Maitland*, Vanson and 'Blairs Memorial Portrait')
C. Rae

[42] Coinage and medallions (although excellent sources of authentic likenesses) were not included in either comparative study of tracings as they typically depict sitters in profile and so are not suitable for a comparison based on overlaying outlines of portraits depicted in three-quarter view.

it seems plausible that both portraits were very probably based on a similar source, likely to be a miniature portrait or face pattern (or alternatively a further full-scale likeness), which were commonly used in the generation of portraits in northern Europe at the time.

The underlying portrait, most likely produced in sixteenth-century Scotland during the time of Mary's imprisonment in England, and the Blairs Memorial Portrait, created in the Spanish Netherlands in the early seventeenth century, were clearly both based on a further portrait source, whether painted portrait, pattern or engraving. Curle famously was gifted a miniature portrait of the sitter on the day of the queen's execution, at which the former was present, and this miniature (location now unknown) is assumed to be the source of the likeness for the full-length work. Previous scholars have noted the similarity between the likeness depicted in the Blairs Memorial Portrait and two miniatures: one,

Figure 2.22 The Blairs Jewel, by unknown artist, containing a miniature portrait of Mary Queen of Scots, 1580s, early seventeenth-century setting, Blairs Museum, 3cm diameter
Sandy Young/Alamy Stock Photo

Figure 2.23   *Mary Queen of Scots*, by unknown artist, 1580s, Rijksmuseum, parchment (animal material), d 3.7cm × h 4cm × w 3.8cm × d 0.5cm (SK-A-4931)
incamerastock/Alamy Stock Photo

like the full-length work, in the collection of Blairs Museum; and another in the Rijksmuseum collection.[43]

By examining the sitter's costume and pose in the portrait underlying *Maitland* (see Figure 2.20) in relation to portraits potentially produced during Mary's imprisonment in England, it was possible to draw further inferences regarding dating and relationships of the underlying portrait to extant portrait types. The wired cap and fashionably curved bodice of the gown worn by the sitter accord with several portraits of the queen that may have been produced at this time, including the Sheffield group.

The underlying portrait can also be linked to a further type by examination of costume. Mary has been depicted wearing a standing collar as opposed to a ruff, as in the Blairs Memorial Portrait and the Sheffield and Hilliard types. Such a collar is only worn by Mary in two other extant portraits, thought potentially to have been painted during her imprisonment in England – the Rijksmuseum and Blair miniatures – thus further establishing a potential link between the underlying portrait and these two works. Such collars were not popular in England

---

[43] Neither miniature has a provenance that can be used to confirm that they were produced during Mary's lifetime: the Rijksmuseum miniature has a Stuart family connection that goes back to 1759 (it is mentioned as a legacy in the will of Anne of Hanover: anon. curatorial/provenance information, Rijksmuseum). The Blairs Museum miniature has a provenance going back to 1809 only, but it is housed in a reliquary that can be argued to have been produced between 1610 and 1622: Smailes and Thomson, *The Queen's Image*, pp. 37–38.

until the 1590s (although a few earlier examples can be found in portraiture from 1580 onwards). As has been often mentioned by earlier scholars, the correspondence of the sitter, a former queen of France, reveals that she attempted to keep up with the latest French fashions during her time in confinement. Similar collars are depicted in French court portraiture of the later 1570s and more prominently in the 1580s (for example, Figure 2.24) (although they were also worn earlier by Mary's former mother-in-law, Catherine de' Medici, elements of whose style can be related to the modes of Florence, from where she originated).[44] This observation provides further evidence that the portrait underlying *Maitland* is likely based in part on an authentic source (or a copy of one) from later in the queen's confinement.

The potential pose of the sitter's proper right hand and its gesture, potentially shared by the queen and also the overlying portrait of Maitland in outline, is of note in that it is very similar in placement and shape to the hands of several

Figure 2.24 *Louise de Lorraine*, by unknown artist (French school), 1580, Louvre, oil on panel, 32 × 26cm (M1852)
The Picture Art Collection/Alamy Stock Photo

[44] This style of collar is considered characteristic of French fashion *c.* 1580 in the historic fashion literature (see Kelly and Schwabe, *Historic Costume*, p. 72, fig. 48).

extant portraits of Mary. Most relevant to this discussion is the similarity to two works with a Scottish provenance: a half-length double composite portrait of Mary and James VI (duke of Atholl, Blair Castle, inscribed 1583) and a three-quarter-length portrait, the 'Morton' portrait (Glasgow Life Museums) that appears to be a slightly later work, based on the former double portrait or a similar source. These pictures are closely related in their derivative interpretation of the Sheffield-type full-length portraits, both in likeness and in costume. In the Blair Castle work the sitter makes such a gesture with her proper left hand, and in the 'Morton' portrait her proper right (as in the portrait underlying *Maitland*). This compositional similarity between the underlying composition and these works is a compelling factor in support of the argument that this hand may have formed an initial part of the composition of the hidden portrait. However, this can only remain speculation at this stage, as it could not be confirmed either way in the technical examination – the painting technique present is more similar to that utilised for the face of the male sitter, but it is possible the hand was left at outline stage when the unfinished female portrait was abandoned. If indeed the proper right hand was included in the underlying portrait, then it seems plausible that the queen may have been depicted holding a pendant, as in the 'Morton' and Blair Castle portraits – such a pendant may have been more palatable for a Scottish Protestant audience than the crucifix worn by the sitter in the Sheffield full-length portraits.[45] If this is the case, then the position and placement of the proper hand would make more sense compositionally, as it fits gracefully with the female sitter's arm, whereas in relation to the portrait of Maitland, it is a notably awkward addition in terms of composition, scale and placement. It seems plausible that the artist, most likely working in Scotland, may have been influenced by depictions such as the Blair Castle double portrait, or that they utilised this gesture (as plausibly did the Blair Castle artist) to visually place the sitter in a chain of accession with portraits of earlier Scottish monarchs.

Covering over of the image

It was of interest to consider further, as part of the study, evidence relating to the covering over of the image. As noted, potentially this palimpsest also bears witness, through its physical history, to the contemporary destruction of images of one of the most controversial of female rulers in sixteenth-century Europe. Taylor rightly discusses in Chapter One the concept of *Damnatio Memoriae*, and questions why there are so few remaining portraits of this sitter. Such iconoclasm must be considered in the context of societal tensions about female rulers at the time. From John Knox's *The First Blast of the Trumpet Against the Monstruous Regiment of*

---

[45] Cust, *Notes on the Authentic Portraits*, p. 86.

Women (1558) to the ongoing popularity in European renaissance visual culture of the theme of the Fatal Power of Women (including ambiguous depictions of female heroines such as Judith), and the destruction and defacement of images of Mary's cousin (Elizabeth I, discussed in Chapter One), it can be demonstrated that there was cultural unease about powerful women in the period.[46] We must also consider this case in relation to the wholesale destruction and covering over of religious images and those of prominent Catholics during and immediately after the Protestant Reformation. Tensions about visual imagery, during and after the Reformation in Scotland, for example, had led to the drowning of religious statues by Knox.[47] Recent studies at the National Portrait Gallery, London have uncovered, using X-radiography, Catholic images underlying later Protestant works.[48] However, is also possible that a more pragmatic reason may exist – due to the common re-use of expensive materials in the period, such a work may simply have been painted over if there was a lack of demand, as Mary lost her role as figurehead of the Catholic cause in Scotland alongside her life.

Conclusion

In conclusion, it can be strongly argued that the work underlying *Maitland*, discovered by the author in a recent technical study, is an unfinished portrait of Mary, Queen of Scots. The painting was most likely produced between the late 1570s and 1589 in Scotland. It seems plausible that the execution of the sitter in 1587 may have played a role in the unfinished portrait being painted over. The artist who created the underlying work had access to the Scottish variant of the Sheffield type (such as the Blair Castle double portrait, dated 1583) as well as other exemplars that were in circulation at the time. This finding can be used to build on the argument that the Sheffield-type portrait was likely created, and in international circulation, during the sitter's lifetime. Overall, this study, including evidence from the first part of the discussion, can be argued to provide compelling evidence that the significant strand of visual Catholic memorialisation represented by the 'Sheffield type' originated with Mary, Queen of Scots during her own lifetime.

---

[46] For example, for a discussion of tensions relating to the display of Donatello's sculpture of Judith and Holofernes, see Yael Even, 'The Loggia Dei Lanzi: A Showcase of Female Subjugation', *Woman's Art Journal* (1991): 10–14.

[47] For discussion, see Pamela C. Graves, 'From an Archaeology of Iconoclasm to an Anthropology of the Body: Images, Punishment, and Personhood in England, 1500–1660', *Current Anthropology* 49 (2008): 35–60. https://doi.org/10.1086/523674.

[48] 'Hidden: Unseeen Paintings Beneath Tudor Portraits', former display at the National Portrait Gallery, London, in relation to findings from the Making Art in Tudor Britain research project. https://www.npg.org.uk/collections/research/programmes/making-art-in-tudor-britain/case-studies/hidden-unseen-paintings-beneath-tudor-portraits.

THREE

Memorialising (in) Mary, Queen of Scots' Books of Hours

Emily Wingfield

In offering a new critical evaluation of autograph poetry written into the margins and blank spaces of known and previously unknown devotional books belonging to Mary, Queen of Scots, the following chapter reveals the extent to which the Scottish queen engaged in continuous and often fraught reflection on themes of identity, ill fortune, imprisonment and piety. In using her verse to consider her past, present and future identities, Mary, Queen of Scots signally engaged in a continuous, reflective and often notably metatextual process of self-memorialisation within the covers of volumes that now themselves are frequently treated as Marian relics.

The Memorial Portrait of Mary Queen of Scots, now housed at Blairs Museum, Aberdeen, is one of the most famous portraits of the Scottish queen.[1] It was produced somewhere between *c.* 1604 and 1618 by an unknown artist in the city of Antwerp and commissioned by Elizabeth Curle, one of the ladies-in-waiting who accompanied Mary to the scaffold at Fotheringhay Castle on 8 February 1587. A full-length depiction of Mary dominates the painting's foreground: she is dressed in black with a contrasting white ruff, head-dress and veil to complement the chiaroscuro effect of the entire piece; a crucifix hangs from her neck and a rosary from her waist; and she holds another crucifix in her right hand, and a white-bound prayer book in her left (with her fingers marking particular passages). Elizabeth Curle is depicted to the left of Mary in a background vignette, along with another of Mary's attendants, Jane Kennedy; an inset scene to the right depicts Mary kneeling on the block with the executioner and his axe poised to strike another blow to her already-bleeding neck. The royal arms of Scotland are presented in the top left-hand corner, and the visual imagery is glossed throughout by three Latin inscriptions documenting Mary's imprisonment in England, the bloody execution process (it took three strikes of the axe

---

[1] The painting (see Figure 2.4) can be viewed on the museum's website: www.blairsmuseum.com/Collection/paintings.html, accessed 6 September 2023.

to sever Mary's head from her neck) and devotion to the Catholic faith. In sum, *The Memorial Portrait* is designed to present Mary, Queen of Scots as a martyr; indeed, as Marguerite Tassi observes, the 'large crucifix held by Mary above the scene of the execution invites the comparison between Christ's sacrifice and her martyrdom'.[2]

Strikingly, *The Memorial Portrait of Mary Queen of Scots* is just one of almost fifteen images depicting Mary with a book.[3] The other examples, ranging in date from the sixteenth through to the twentieth century, include an eye-witness ink-and-pencil sketch of the execution by Robert Beale, where Mary and her two ladies-in-waiting stand alongside a *prie-dieu* with open prayer book and crucifix, and a watercolour from some time after 1613 showing Mary kneeling at the scaffold alongside a red-bound prayer book. Two woodcut illustrations from the martyrologist Adam Blackwood's *Histoire et Martyre de la Royne d'Escosse* (Paris, 1589) also show, first, Mary reading aloud to her ladies when she is interrupted by the delivery of her death warrant and, second, Mary at prayer prior to her execution, with three books and writing tools on the table standing next to her. Blackwood further states that Mary carried a book of hours to the scaffold, and spent the evening before her execution 'in prayer and orations, in the reading of the passion of our lord, and in similar consolations of the soul and holy meditation'.[4]

Most of the images depicting Mary with a devotional volume are part and parcel of the same repeated attempts to present her as a martyr to the Catholic faith, but an eye-witness account of the execution prepared for William Cecil, Lord Burghley (1520–98) by Sir Robert Wingfield of Upton in Northamptonshire (*c.* 1558–1609) confirms that Mary did indeed take a book with her to the scaffold. He describes how the queen 'sat upon a stool, having about her neck an Agnus Dei, in one of her hands a crucifix, at her girdle a pair of beads with a golden cross at the end of them with a Latin book of vain prayers in her other hand'; he reports too how she repeated 'diverse other prayers in Latin', including two verses (2, 6) from Psalm 30.[5] We know too that she owned a diverse collection of books; indeed, Mary is the first Scottish monarch for whom we have evidence for the existence of a royal library (or even libraries) at Edinburgh Castle and Holyroodhouse.[6]

---

[2] Marguerite A. Tassi, 'Martyrdom and Memory: Elizabeth Curle's portrait of Mary, Queen of Scots', in *The Emblematic Queen: Extra-Literary Representations of Early Modern Queenship*, ed. Debra Barrett-Graves (New York, 2013), pp. 101–32, at p. 123.

[3] Helen Smailes and Duncan Thomson, *The Queen's Image* (Edinburgh, 1987).

[4] Quoted in Alexander S. Wilkinson, *Mary Queen of Scots and French Public Opinion, 1542–1600* (Basingstoke, 2004), p. 135.

[5] *The Execution of Mary Queen of Scots: An Eyewitness Account by Sir Robert Wingfield of Upton* (with a foreword by Antonia Fraser) (Mount Stuart, 2007), p. 26.

[6] See John Higgitt (ed.), *Scottish Libraries* [with an introductory essay by John Durkan] (London, 2006), S11, S16 and S17. Also: John Durkan, 'The Library of Mary, Queen of Scots', in *Mary*

After the execution, Mary's clothes and ornaments were burned so that no relics could be acquired by her Catholic supporters, but the prayer book she held may have escaped this fate if, as Guy suggests, it had already been promised to one of the queen's ladies-in-waiting.[7] Alternatively, even if Mary's own book was burned, others carried by or given previously to her female attendants may not have been. Some fourteen surviving books of hours with varying degrees of known or plausible connection to Mary survive in libraries across the world,[8] and many of the libraries in which they are held claim that the volumes were present with Mary at the scaffold. In most cases, there is little or no evidence of Marian provenance to match this desire to associate a specific volume with the moment of Mary, Queen of Scots' execution, but such posthumous memorialising of Mary is intriguingly anticipated by the queen herself in the signatures and poetic inscriptions she added to her books of hours.

In turning now to analysis of these inscriptions, I build upon and develop observations by Sarah Dunnigan and Rosalind Smith. They have suggested that Mary's inscriptions 'can only be fully comprehended in their original iconographic content'; '[w]hile they are added at a different time from the other content of the Book of Hours, they frame and interpret the earlier texts and images as much as that text determines their meaning'.[9] Taking key manuscripts in turn, I will demonstrate how Mary's autograph inscriptions, largely composed during her imprisonment, relate both thematically and materially to the biblical material they accompany, and in doing so I reveal how Mary self-consciously transformed her books into memorial artefacts, witnesses to her Catholic faith and markers of her shifting identity.

Stewart: Queen in Three Kingdoms, ed. Michael Lynch (Oxford, 1988), pp. 71–104; J. Sharman, *The Library of Mary, Queen of Scots* (London, 1889); *Inventaires de la royne descosse douairiere en France. Catalogue of the Jewels, Dresses, Furniture, Books and Paintings of Mary Queen of Scots*, ed. J. Robertson, Bannatyne Club (Edinburgh, 1863); and chapter 10 of Emily Wingfield, *Books Beyond the Border: Scotland's Royal Women and European Literary Culture 1424–1587* (Turnhout: in press).

[7] Guy, *My Heart is My Own*, p. 7. In 1566 Mary added to an inventory of her personal belongings a note in her own hand in which she requested that after her death her Latin and Greek books be left to the University of St Andrews, and the rest (i.e. the vernacular texts) to Mary Beaton (c. 1543–97), one of the four 'Queen's Marys'. See NRS, MS E35/3(13); *Inventaires de la royne descosse*, p. 124 ('[i]e laysse mes liuures qui y sont ceulx en Grec ou Latin a luniuersite de Sintandre pour y commancer vne bible Les aultres ie les laysse a Beton').

[8] Durkan, 'The Library of Mary, Queen of Scots', Appendix II, pp. 103–04.

[9] Sarah Dunnigan, 'Scottish Women Writers c. 1560–c. 1650', in *A History of Scottish Women's Writing*, ed. Douglas Gifford and Dorothy McMillan (Edinburgh, 1997), pp. 15–43 (p. 25); Rosalind Smith, '"Le pouvoir de faire dire": Marginalia in Mary Queen of Scots' Book of Hours', in *Material Cultures of Early Modern Women's Writing*, ed. Patricia Pender and Rosalind Smith (Basingstoke and New York, 2014), pp. 55–75, at p. 63.

The Christie's manuscript

On 29 July 2020, a prayer book containing an inscription by Mary, Queen of Scots sold at Christie's for £311, 250.[10] The manuscript was produced for Mary's great-aunt, Louise de Bourbon (1495–1575), abbess of Fontevraud (Fontevrault), and it contains a cycle of forty miniatures attributed to the so-called Master of François de Rohan (fl. 1525–46). The latter was patronised by the French king François I (1494–1547), as well as his sister Margaret of Navarre (1492–1549), and he produced upwards of eighteen surviving manuscripts and four printed books.[11] It seems likely that the manuscript was produced towards the beginning of Louise's tenure as abbess, and it complements the wider programme of self-fashioning and architectural renovation in which she engaged.

A quatrain in Mary's hand occurs towards the end of the manuscript (fol. 206r). It reads:[12]

Puis que voules quissi me ramentoiue
en vos prieres et deuotes oraisons
ie vous requiers premier quil vous souiene
quele part aues en mes affections

Since you wish to remember me here
in your prayers and devout orations,
I ask you first that you remember
what part you have in my affections

Mary's inscription has a memorial function. It is designed to encourage Louise and Mary to remember one another in the act of reading (or prayer), and it is likely that the book was part of an exchange of gifts between the two women during Mary's time in France – rather like another surviving book of hours (Reims, Bibliothèque Carnegie, MS Reserve CR I 100 M) which Mary seems to have gifted to a different aunt, Renée de Lorraine (abbess of Saint-Pierre de Reims from 1553 until her death in 1602).[13] Similar memorial inscriptions –

---

[10] See www.christies.com/features/Christies-to-offer-the-prayer-book-of-Mary-Queen-of-Scots-10775-7.aspx, accessed 6 September 2023.

[11] Myra D. Orth, 'The Master of François de Rohan: A Familiar French Renaissance Miniaturist with a New Name', in *Illuminating the Book: Makers and Interpreters. Essays in Honour of Janet Backhouse*, ed. Michelle P. Brown and Scot McKendrick (London, 1998), 69–91; Gabrielle Esperdy, 'The Royal Abbey of Fontevrault: Religious Women and the Shaping of Gendered Space', *Journal of International Women's Studies*, 6 (2005) no. 2: 59–80, at pp. 73–78.

[12] My transcription and working translation.

[13] H. Jadart, 'Le Livre d'heures de Marie Stuart à la Bibliothèque de Reims', *La Bibliofilia*, 4 (1902–03): 145–57, at p. 155. Also Joanne Baker, 'Female Monasticism and Family Strategy: The Guises and Saint Pierre de Reims', *The Sixteenth Century Journal*, 28 (1997) no. 4: 1091–1108. Christie's suggest that Mary took the manuscript with her to Scotland and from there to England, since it was owned in the seventeenth century by the Hale family of Gloucestershire. Sir Matthew

including another by Mary discussed below – appear commonly in surviving sixteenth-century books of hours. They served to transform books into acts of remembrance and as a means of maintaining ties between separated family and friends. They could also be as much public as private gestures since the inscriptions always had the potential to be seen by a wider audience than the direct addressee.[14]

Mary concludes the verse in the volume sold by Christie's with a partially anagrammatic motto based on her name, 'Va Tu Meriteras' ('Go, you shall be worthy'), as well as a monogram based on the initial 'M' of her name and 'ϕ' (the initial phonetic letter of the name of her husband François II). The same motto appears at the end of Mary's sonnet 'L'ire de Dieu', which was included by John Leslie in the 1574 printed edition of his *Libri Duo: Quroum vno, Piae Afflicti Animi Consolationes, diunaque remedia: Altero, Animi Tranqvilli Mvnimentum et conservatio, continentur*, two pious Latin treatises that he wrote for Mary between 1572 and 1573.[15]

'L'ire de Dieu' is an adaptation of verses 18 to 21 of Psalm 51. This psalm is one of the so-called Penitential Psalms and during the Reformation it was strongly appropriated to doctrinal debates concerning the relative worth of good works and divine grace. It was also associated particularly with female writers;[16] it was translated by Anne Lock and Mary Sidney, for instance, and recited by Lady Jane Grey (c. 1537–54) at her execution.[17] In contrast to these women's Protestant uses of the psalm, Jane Donawerth has suggested that Mary offers a 'traditional Catholic version' by emphasising the importance of 'works

---

Hale (1609–76) inherited from John Selden (1584–1654) a collection of manuscripts relating to Mary, Queen of Scots which had belonged to Henry, 6th Earl of Kent (1541–1615), one of the organisers and witnesses of Mary's execution. It is worth noting here that the mother of Renée de Lorraine and Mary of Guise (Mary's grandmother), Antoinette de Bourbon, served in Mary's French household; also that another of Mary's ladies-in-waiting, Mary Seton, retired from Mary's service to the Abbey of Saint-Pierre-les-Dames, where Renée was abbess. See Rosalind K. Marshall, 'In Search of the Ladies-in-Waiting and Maids of Honour of Mary, Queen of Scots: A Prosopographical Analysis of the Female Household', in *Politics of Female Households: Ladies-in-Waiting Across Early Modern Europe*, ed. Nadine Akkerman and Birgit Houben (Leiden, 2014), pp. 209–29, at pp. 217, 227. Fraser notes that Seton sent Mary a book from France: Fraser, *Mary Queen of Scots*, p. 521.

[14] Eamon Duffy, *Marking the Hours: English People and their Prayers 1240–1570* (New Haven, CT, and London, 2006), pp. 49–52.

[15] Mary Stuart, *Œuvres littéraires*, ed. Sylvène Édouard, Irène Fasel and François Rigolet (Paris, 2021), p. 294; Pamela Robinson, 'John Leslie's "Libri Duo": Manuscripts Belonging to Mary Queen of Scots?', in *Order and Connexion: Studies in Bibliography and Book History*. Selected Papers from the Munby Seminar, Cambridge, July 1994, ed. R. C. Alston (Cambridge, 1997), pp. 63–75; Jane Donawerth, 'Stuart's "L'Ire de Dieu"', *The Explicator*, 59 (2010) no. 4: 171–73. Unless otherwise noted, all quotations of Mary's poetry are taken from the edition by Édouard et al.

[16] See Margaret P. Hannay, '"Wisdome the Wordes": Psalm Translation and Elizabethan Women's Spirituality', *Religion & Literature*, 23 (1991) no. 3: 65–82.

[17] Male writers (such as Wyatt) did also translate the psalm, and it was recited by Protestant male martyrs too.

as a requirement of salvation', and she proposes that the final anagram contributes to this by echoing words from the Mass: 'non sum dignus . . . sed tantum dic verbo, et sanabitur animal mea' ('I know that I am not worthy . . . but only say the word and I shall be healed'); 'ite, missa est' ('go, the mass is done'). Donawerth states: 'Mary's anagram, rather than addressed to the poem, is God's answer to her through the mass: although you are not worthy, your faith, your works, and the efficacy of the mass make you worthy in God's sight'.

The use of the same anagram in the Christie's manuscript might also bear a relationship to the sacrament of penance. Although it occurs on what would originally have been a blank page, the quatrain appends the final words of the *Ave gratia plena* – a liturgical text for the feast of St Anne – which emphasise the Virgin's sinless state; it is also surrounded by a prayer known as *O excellentissima* (in which Mary is asked to petition Christ for forgiveness of the speaker's sins).[18] Although this prayer was added at a later date, it seems that Mary's inscription was first designed to – and later did – encourage prayer for her own spiritual salvation. In turn, the anagram's apparent echo of words from the Mass might further contribute to the quatrain's memorial function, given that the Mass is itself a memorial sacrament. Certainly, as we shall see, Mary forged similar links between memorialisation, biblical text and the sacraments in her other books of hours.

The 'De Croy Hours'

A variation of the Christie's quatrain appears on fol. 17r of a manuscript now better known as the 'De Croy Hours' after its later sixteenth-century owner, Diana de Croy (*née* Dommartin) (1552–1625) (Sheffield, Guild of St George, MS R.3546).[19]

Before Diana, the manuscript seems to have been owned by her husband's mother, Anne de Lorraine (1522–68),[20] who was herself a cousin of Mary's mother, Mary of Guise. Apparently at Anne's behest, Mary, Queen of Scots

---

[18] The words of the full prayer can be accessed here: www.preces-latinae.org/thesaurus/BVM/OExcellentissima.html, accessed 6 September 2023.

[19] There is a large volume of manuscript signatures and inscriptions in French, Spanish and Italian scattered throughout, most written by the friends and relatives of Diana and her husband, Charles-Philippe. See further Emily Wingfield, 'Re-Reading a Quatrain by Mary Queen of Scots', *Renaissance Studies*, 35 (2021) no. 5: 788–810.

[20] Interestingly, Anne owned a collection of books, including a manuscript of *c.* 100 (largely love) poems presented to her by her first husband, René of Châlon (1519–44), a genealogy of the house of Nassau and a large number of printed books that she acquired in Paris around 1560. See Anne S. Korteweg, 'Anna van Lotharingen, vrouw van René van Chalon (1522–1568), een liefhebster van mooie boken', *Jaarboek De Oranjeboom*, 61 (2008): 54–75. I thank Professor Alasdair MacDonald for help with this Dutch article. Also: Hanno Wijsman, *Luxury Bound: Illustrated Manuscript Production and Noble and Princely Book Ownership in the Burgundian Netherlands (1400–1550)* (Turnhout, 2010), pp. 317–42.

Figure 3.1 Mary Queen of Scots, autograph inscription, Sheffield, Guild of St George, MS R.3546, fols 16v–17r
© Museums Sheffield

placed in the manuscript (sometime between July 1559 and December 1560) a memorial inscription like that in the Christie's manuscript.[21] I provide below a transcription of the original French text and an edited version in modern French. (In the transcription square brackets indicate text lost due to damage to the manuscript and asterisks estimate the most likely number of letters missing.) I publish too a proposed new translation in which I attempt to capture something of the sophisticated wordplay of Mary's original French.

> Si ce Lieu est pour ecrire ordon [**]
> cequil vous plest auoir en souena [***]
> Je vous requiers que lieu me soit d [****]
> Et que nul temps nen oste lordonnan [**]
> Royne de france
>   [monogram] Marie

---

[21] The fact that Mary signs herself as 'Royne de france' allows us to date the poem. She was only queen for a short time before François' untimely death in December 1560. After that date she instead described herself as 'Marie Royne d'Escosse, douairière de France'.

Si ce Lieu est pour écrire ordonné
Ce qu'il vous plaît avoir en souvenance,
Je vous requiers que lieu me soit donné
Et que nul temps n'en ôte l'ordonnance.
Reine de France
    Marie.

If this place is arranged for writing
That which it pleases you to hold in memory,
I ask you that the place be given to me,
And that no time take from its arrangement.
Queen of France.
    Mary.

Previous readings of the quatrain by Lisa Hopkins and Peter Herman have focused on the repetition of *ordonné* and *l'ordonnance*, relating such word-play to themes of governance and control: additionally, the quatrain is carefully arranged in formal terms (regular pentameters, *abab* rhyme scheme) and Mary is never herself the subject of any command. Hopkins attends too to the quatrain's striking relationship to Mary's maternal French family – the author addresses her mother's cousin, writes in French and signs herself as 'Queen of France' – and she notes the repeated emphasis on place and space.[22] I have elsewhere developed such work on Mary's word-choice to propose that with the repetition of *ordonné* and *l'ordonnance* she might additionally have been playing on the notion of *dispositio* or rhetorical organisation of arguments, since these words could refer also to the ordering and arrangement of textual material. With her concluding focus on the effects of time, arguably Mary also plays throughout the quatrain on *memoria* or 'memory', the discipline of recalling the arguments of a discourse.[23] Indeed, in classical treatises on rhetoric, *dispositio* and *memoria* were intimately connected to one another; for instance, in the Ciceronian *Rhetorica ad Herennium* (which Mary owned),[24] *dispositio* is defined as 'the ordering and distribution of the matter', and *memoria* as 'the firm

---

[22] Lisa Hopkins, 'Writing to Control: The Verse of Mary, Queen of Scots', in *Reading Monarch's Writing: The Poetry of Henry VIII, Mary Stuart, Elizabeth I, and James VI/I*, ed. Peter C. Herman (Tempe, AZ, 2002), pp. 35–50 (esp. pp. 36–39); Peter C. Herman, *Royal Poetrie: Monarchic Verse and the Political Imaginary of Early Modern England* (Ithaca, NY and London, 2010), pp. 54–55.
[23] Mary Carruthers, *The Book of Memory: A Study of Memory in Medieval Culture*, 2nd edn (Cambridge, 2014), p. 8.
[24] Higgitt, *Scottish Libraries*, p. 198. Mary also owned 'The Offices of Cicero' (p. 114) and several other works on poetics, including Ronsard's *Abrégé de l'art poétique françoyse* (Paris, 1565) (p. 123) and Joachim du Bellay's *La déffence et illustration de la langue françoyse* (Paris, 1549) (p. 123).

retention in the mind of the matter, words, and arrangement'.[25] Mary similarly brings the two faculties together. In the first two lines she writes of how space has been set aside in the book of hours for writing memorial inscriptions and in the third and fourth lines she requests that the words she now writes in that place will acquire a permanence, both on the page and in the mind or memory. In essence, Mary figures her quatrain as an epitaph, and uses wordplay to suggest that her carefully ordered words are themselves both that epitaph and the means whereby the epitaph and she herself will be remembered.

The 'arrangement' referred to in the final line further encompasses not just the arrangement of Mary's verse *per se*, but also the meaningful arrangement of the entire manuscript opening (fols 16v–17r) on which it appears, for the inscription appears below an earlier sixteenth-century image of Christ's side wound (accompanied by the words 'Hec est mensura plaga domini', 'This is the measurement of the wound of the Lord'), and opposite a miniature of a priest celebrating the eucharist. This miniature also contains an image of Christ displaying his *stigmata* alongside the Cross and instruments of the Passion. Such scenes were rich in contemporary meaning. Firstly, the representation of Christ's wounded body alongside the instruments of the Passion recalls the tradition of the Mass of St Gregory in which Christ as the Man of Sorrows appeared to the saint as he celebrated the eucharist. Fols 16v and 17r also form a part of the late medieval and early modern practice of devotion to the Holy Wounds of Christ and *arma Christi*. The set of instruments of the Passion (fol. 16v) are matched by the spear piercing the lozenge on fol. 17r, whilst the centre of that lozenge both depicts Christ's sacred heart and functions as a representation of the wound placed in Christ's side by the spear. Kathryn M. Rudy has shown how such visual representations of the *arma Christi* 'were visual stand-ins for the tangible remains of Christ' and she discusses an apparent desire on the part of readers to fill in the blank spaces of sacred books with images of Christ's body. She also analyses the popularity of so-called 'metric rubrics' – such as that surrounding the lozenge in the Sheffield manuscript ('this is the measurement of the word of the Lord') – which formed part of a broader desire 'to envision the Passion with increased particularity and attention to detail, and a sense of objective reality that was measurable'. Unlike some of the other measurements of Christ (e.g. his height) the wound in Christ's side could easily fit into a manuscript, and Rudy argues that in the process the book was itself 'reconsidered as a wounded corpus'.[26] This transformation would of course have been all the more apparent in the case of a manuscript made of parchment (skin) rather than paper.

---

[25] Cicero, *Rhetorica ad Herennium*, trans. Harry Caplan, Loeb Classical Library 403 (Cambridge, MA, 1954), p. 7.

[26] Kathryn M. Rudy, *Rubrics, Images and Indulgences in Late Medieval Netherlandish Manuscripts* (Leiden, 2017), pp. 55–100 (esp. pp. 55, 59–60, 73, 77). Also: David S. Areford, 'The Passion

This idea of a slippage between Christ's wounded body and the manuscript page is further reinforced when we remember that the eucharist, the wounds of Christ (especially that to his heart) and Christ's body functioned all three additionally as symbols of the divine Word, represented of course by the book of hours itself, on fol. 16v by the image of the Bible and by the added image of the Annunciation on fols 18v–19r.[27] Moreover, hearts and books also functioned throughout the medieval and into the early modern period as two of the most significant and related metaphors for memory, such that books were understood to have a mnemonic function.[28] As Mary Carruthers has written, 'books themselves are memorial cues and aids, and memory is most like a book, a written page or wax tablet upon which something is written'. She cites a passage from the aforementioned *Rhetorica ad Herennium*:[29]

> those who have learned mnemonics can set in backgrounds what they have heard, and from these backgrounds deliver it by memory. For the backgrounds are very much like wax tablets or papyrus, the images like the letters, the arrangement and disposition of the images like the script, and the delivery is like the reading.[30]

The placement of Mary's quatrain on fol. 17r very much keys into these ideas. The queen focuses through wordplay on notions of 'arrangement and disposition' and she prays that her 'arrangement' will stand the test of time. We might note, furthermore, the potential sacramental connotations of the French verb *ordonner* and noun *ordonnance*; both verb and noun appeared in contemporary French texts in the context of references to the eucharist more generally and last rites in particular.[31] In emphasising the visual nature of her words and drawing repeated attention to the 'place' in which they appear, Mary appears to be asking her reader to recall not just her words, but also the images with which they appear, and both of these images are connected to ideas of memory; the

---

Measured: A Late-Medieval Diagram of the Body of Christ', in *The Broken Body: Passion Devotion in Late-Medieval Culture*, ed. Alasdair Macdonald et al. (Groningen, 1998), pp. 210–38.

[27] For discussion of Christ's body as a book in the later Middle Ages see D. H. Green, *Women Readers in the Middle Ages* (Cambridge, 2007), pp. 45–46, citing S. Huot, 'Polytextual Reading: the Meditative Reading of Real and Metaphorical Books', in *Orality and Literary in the Middle Ages*, ed. M. Chinca and C. Young (Turnhout, 2005), pp. 203–22 and V. Gillespie, 'Strange Images of Death: The Passion in Later Medieval English Devotional and Mystical Writing', in James Hogg and Erwin Stürzl (eds), *Zeit, Tod und Ewigkeit in der Renaissance Literatur* (Salzburg, 1987), pp. 111–59.

[28] Carruthers, *The Book of Memory*, chapter 1; E. Jager, *The Book of the Heart* (Chicago, 2000). The link between the heart, the book and notions of memory originates in the Bible, e.g. Proverbs 3:3, Ezekiel 40:4 and 2 Corinthians 3:3. See also Helen Smith, '*Grossly Material Things*': *Women and Book Production in Early Modern England* (Oxford, 2012), p. 195.

[29] Carruthers, *The Book of Memory*, pp. 18, 32–33.

[30] Cicero, *Rhetorica ad Herennium*, p. 209.

[31] See 'Sacrement, subt masc', www.atilf.fr/dmf/definition/sacrement, accessed 6 September 2023, definition 2.

eucharist was by its very nature a memorial act whilst the Latin words surrounding the wounded heart of Christ quite possibly functioned as a rubric, cueing some kind of prayer to Christ's wounds. Thus, in positioning her inscription on fol. 17r Mary produces a seemingly simple memorial verse that in fact conceives of the arrangement of text and image as itself mnemonic, and in so doing she constructs for herself a memorial and cultural afterlife using the simple, but meaningful and durable, media of pen, ink and parchment.

The Manchester and St Petersburg books of hours

Manchester, John Rylands, MS Latin 21 is a tiny book of hours, small enough to fit in the palm of the hand.[32] Mary added inscriptions to two previously blank folios. Although undated, the nature of these annotations suggests that they were made either during Mary's English imprisonment or during the course of her final months in Scotland. The first occurs on fol. 114r, after a prayer for the faithful departed (fol. 113v) and cue for the prayer 'De profundis', based on Psalm 129. This prayer begins *de profundis clamavi ad te Domine/Domine exaudi vocem meam fiant aures tuae intendentes ad vocem deprecationis meae* ('out of the depths I have cried to thee, O Lord: Lord, hear my voice. Let thy ears be attentive to the voice of my supplication'). Mary's annotation – *Mon Dieu/confondez mes ennemys* ('my God, confound my enemies') – is well placed in this context; her personal prayer for divine aid during her own time of trouble echoes the psalmist's subsequent call to God in the remainder of the psalm and hope that *redimet Israhel ex omnibus iniquitatibus eius* ('he shall redeem Israel from all his iniquities'). It also parallels reference to enemies in poetry inscribed in the St Petersburg book of hours (examined below).

Mary's second annotation on fol. 125r follows suit: *Dieu viuant/mon seul Iuge/ olyez mes plainctes & mes gemissementz* ('living Lord/my only Judge/hear my complaints and my lamentations'). It is positioned immediately after a prayer to the Virgin at the end of the Office of the Virgin in Advent (*ora pro nobis*, 'pray for us') and it precedes an image of King David in prayer (fol. 126v) at the start of the penitential psalms (Psalm 6): *Domine ne in furore tuo arguas me neque in ira tua corripias me* ('O Lord, rebuke me not in thy indignation, nor chastise me in thy wrath'). In the first half of this psalm, David laments his misfortune – he refers, for instance, to how *consumptus sum ab universis hostibus meis* ('I have grown old amongst all my enemies') and how his body suffers – *conturbata sunt ossa mea*

---

[32] M. R. James, *A Descriptive Catalogue of the Latin Manuscripts in The John Rylands Library at Manchester*, vol. 1 (Manchester, 1921), pp. 61–64; https://luna.manchester.ac.uk/luna/servlet/s/3yxhc6, accessed 7 September 2023 (University of Manchester login required); Schoenberg Database of Manuscripts, https://sdbm.library.upenn.edu/entries/126489, accessed 7 September 2023.

('my bones are troubled').³³ He records too how he has 'laboured' in his 'groanings' (*laboravi in gemitu meo*) and he repeatedly prays for forgiveness. In the final verses he gives thanks that the Lord has heard his complaints and predicts that his enemies will now themselves be troubled. If the striking verbal parallel between David's phrase *in gemitu* and Mary's French *gémissementz* encourages elision of their suffering, we might think it equally possible for Mary to have taken comfort from David's release.

Interestingly, Mary's prayer echoes a version of Psalm 13, verse 4 by the French poet, Clément Marot (1496–1544): *Regarde moy, mon Dieu puissant/Responds à mon cueur gémissant* ('Look upon me, my powerful Lord/ And respond to my complaining heart'). Marot in fact produced a number of French paraphrases of the psalms, including Psalm 6.³⁴ Although his translations were subsequently associated strongly with the cause of the Protestant Reformation in France, they were initially popular at and sponsored by members of the French court.³⁵ Unidentified works by 'Clement Marot' also appear in the inventories of Mary's library.³⁶ It is therefore possible that the queen had Marot's translations in mind as she herself responded in French to the original Latin found in her books of hours. Given the shared use of the word *gémissement* and Mary's imprisonment, it is particularly interesting to note that Marot used this word in relation to prisoners in his version of Psalm 79, verse 11. He thus renders 'Let the sighing of the prisoners come in before thee' (*ingrediatur coram te gemitus vinctorum*) as 'Des prisonniers le gemissement vienne/Jusques au ciel'.

Mary's verse is similarly aligned with the (penitential) psalms and related office for the dead in St Petersburg, National Library of Russia, MS Lat. Q. v. I. 112, a richly decorated Latin and French parchment book of hours from the second quarter of the fifteenth century that was owned and written in by Mary over a period of more than twenty years.³⁷ As Rosalind Smith's detailed essay

---

³³ Mary's own body suffered as a consequence of her imprisonment. See Guy, *My Heart is My Own*, pp. 445–47, 458.
³⁴ Clément Marot, *Cinquante pseaumes de David*, ed. Gérard Defaux (Paris, 2022).
³⁵ Barbara B. Deifendorf, 'The Huguenot Psalter and the Faith of French Protestants in the Sixteenth Century', in *Culture and Identity in Early Modern Europe (1400–1800): Essays in Honour of Natalie Zemon Davis*, ed. Barbara B. Deifendorf and Carla Hesse (Ann Arbor, MI, 1993), pp. 41–63, at p. 43.
³⁶ Higgitt, ed., *Scottish Libraries*, S11.116.
³⁷ A. de Laborde, *Les Principaux Manuscrits à Peintures conservés dans l'Ancienne Bibliothèque Impériale Publique de Saint-Pétersbourg*, 2 vols (Paris, 1936–38), no. 64, pp. 63–66; T. P. Voronova, 'Chasovnik Marii Stuart [Mary Stuart's Book of Hours]', in *Istoria v rukopisyah i rukopisi v istorii*, ed. G. P. Enin (St Petersburg, 2006), pp. 95–100. I am grateful to the National Library of Russia for sending me a copy of this article and to Maria Artamonova for producing an English translation of it. We currently know little of the manuscript's whereabouts after its ownership by Mary and before its acquisition in France by the Russian diplomat, Peter P. Dubrovskii (1754–1816), who sold his collection of manuscripts in 1805 to the Emperor Alexander I, thereby forming the foundations for the manuscripts department at what was then the Imperial Public Library. It is not known how or when Dubrovskii acquired this particular manuscript, but he is thought to

on this manuscript has shown, it was also accessed (and signed) during Mary's imprisonment – and after her death – by her friends and family members, and, interestingly, also by her enemies (e.g. Sir Francis Walsingham, *c.* 1532–90).[38]

Mary herself signed the book on six occasions, twice with a date:

fol. 1r: 'A moi Marie R'
fols 12v–13r: 'Ce livre est a moi Marie royne 1553'[39]
fol. 81: 'Marie R', twice
fol. 110r: 'Marie R 1579'
fol. 145r: 'Marie R'

In 1553, she was 11 years old and living at the French court; in 1579 she was 39 years old and imprisoned at Sheffield Castle. The volume thus accompanied Mary through several significant stages of life in France, Scotland and England. It is notable that the queen stresses her royal status in the signatures, but that status changed signally as Mary and her book moved from the French court, where she was child queen of Scots and queen consort of France, to Scotland, where she was widowed queen of France and queen regnant of Scotland, and then to England, by which point she had been forced to abdicate.

In addition to signatures, Mary added fourteen verses to the manuscript at different stages,[40] and seven of these verses occur, as in the Manchester

---

have purchased a number of his volumes as a result of the depredations of monastic libraries that occurred during the French Revolution. If he acquired MS Lat. Q. v. I. 112 in the same way, it must have previously found its way to France, perhaps via Jesuit connections. See T. P. Voronova, 'Western MSS in the Saltykov-Shchedrin Library', *Book Collector*, 5 (1956): 12–18; T. P. Voronova, 'P. P. Dubrovskiĭ 1754–1816 and the Saint-Germain Manuscripts', *Book Collector*, 27 (1978): 469–78; Patricia Z. Thompson, 'Biography of a Library: The Western European Manuscript Collection of Peter P. Dubrovskii in Leningrad', *The Journal of Library History (1974–1987)*, 19 (1984) no. 4: 477–503.

[38] Smith, '"Le pouvoir de faire dire"'. See also: Rosalind Smith, 'Narrow Confines: Marginalia, Devotional Books and the Prison in Early Modern Women's Writing', *Women's Writing*, 26 (2019) no. 1: 35–52 (pp. 47–49). Those signing the book include Elizabeth Talbot [Bess of Hardwick], countess of Shrewsbury (1527?–1608), in whose household Mary was imprisoned between 1569 and 1584; Thomas Radcliffe, third earl of Sussex (1527/8–83); Charles Howard, first earl of Nottingham (1536–1624); Walter Devereux, first earl of Essex (1539–76); Sir Francis Walsingham (*c.* 1532–90); Matthew Stewart, fourth earl of Lennox [and father of Darnley] (1516–71) (not certain); Arabella Stewart, wife of William Seymour (1575–1615); Ambrose Dudley, earl of Warwick (*c.* 1530–90); Edward Clinton, first earl of Lincoln (1512–85); and Sir Nicholas Bacon (1510–79).

[39] Some scholars print this date as 1554, but my own examination of the manuscript suggests that it is more correctly 1553.

[40] The verses (and translations of them) have been printed, with various degrees of accuracy, in the following: Labanoff (ed.), *Lettres*, vol. 7, pp. 346–51; *Queen Mary's Book*, ed. P. Stewart-Mackenzie Arbuthnot (London, 1907), pp. 113–15, 167–69; Bell, *Bittersweet within my Heart: The Collected Poems of Mary, Queen of Scots*, ed. Robin Bell (London, 1992), pp. 87–93; David Angus, 'Mary's Marginalia', *Review of Scottish Culture*, 3 (1987): 9–12. See also: Rosalind Smith, ed., 'Quatrains

manuscript, on what was previously a blank folio (81v), opposite an image of King David in prayer. The latter miniature again prefaces the sequence of penitential psalms (fols 82–95). The verses, written at different times and with different pens, are as follows:

1. qui jamais davantage eust contraire le sort	Whoever had fortune more against [them]?
si la vie mest moins utile que la mort	life is thus less use to me than death.
Et plus tost que cha[n]ger de mes maus lad-uenture	And rather than alter the occurrence of my ills,
Chacune change pour moi dhumeur et de nature	Everyone alters their character and bearing towards me.
2. Co[m]me autres fois la renom[m]ee	Unlike before, [my] good name[41]
ne vole plus par lunivers	no longer flies through the universe.
isy borne son cours divers	[Lo,] here and now, the thing most loved by her
la chose delle plus aimee	is here limited in its varied way!
3. Les heures ie guide & le iour	I follow the hours and the day
par lordre exacte de ma carriere	according to the precise order of my life course,
quittant mon triste seiour	leaving my sad abode
pour icy croistre ma lumiere.	to here increase my light.
4. celle qui dhonneur sait combler	She who knows how to lavish honour on each [person]
chacun du bruit de sa louange	by the noise [i.e proclamation] of her praise [of them],
ne peux [sic][42] moins qua soi ressembler	cannot be less like herself,
en effet nestant que un bel ange.	being indeed only a good angel.
5. il faut plus que la renomee . . .	It takes more than good name
pour publier dire . . . [incomplete]	to publish say [–][43] . . . [incomplete]
6. [or] mais nous avons	But [now] we have
un bel ange	a beautiful angel
[pou]r suiet de notre louange	as the subject of our praise

in Mary Stuart's Book of Hours', https://c21ch.newcastle.edu.au/emwrn/index.php?p=hours, accessed 7 September 2023, and Stuart, Œuvres littéraires, pp. 319–46. I here present my own transcriptions and working translations. My thanks to Jane Bliss, Elizabeth L'Estrange, Olivia Robinson and Graham Roberts Edwards for discussion of and assistance with these notably elliptical quatrains.

[41] Or a personification, Fame.
[42] As I note below, Mary's use of the first person here may not be a mistake; it is likely instead that she is identifying herself with the 'she' who lavishes honour on others.
[43] Traces of illegible letters here.

7. ma voix & mes accord . . .	My speech and my [opinions?]
si ne vous touch . . .	if [they?] do not touch/concern you . . .
com[m]ent pourr . . .	how can . . .
& dire que le [incomplete]	and say that the . . . [incomplete]

As across the verses in the manuscript as a whole, we can trace several repeated words, phrases and themes across these seven, indicating that Mary meditated on similar topics over time and wrestled with how best to express herself. In the first verse, she laments her misfortune and the way in which she is treated unfairly by others, stating that death would be of more value to her than life (perhaps because of the rewards she might find in heaven), whilst in verse 2 she notes that good name (or renown) (most probably her own) is confined to the pages of the books of hours in which she writes.[44] Mary here establishes a paradox by suggesting that the devotion on which her good name is based is precisely the only sphere in which that good name can now exist; in using the verb *borner* (to block/limit), she additionally establishes a carceral theme and aligns the bound pages of the manuscript with her own imprisoned state. This idea is further developed in the third verse where Mary observes how she follows the routine of the hours in which she writes, and she seems to suggest that this regular devotional activity will allow her to regain something of her previous fame ('light').[45] The second and third verses are therefore notably metatextual – the literal binding of the book of hours mirrors Mary's own physical imprisonment – and in them the queen makes use of some of the same wordplay as in her earlier poem 'Si ce Lieu est'. In addition to using again the word *ordre*, Mary plays on the similarity of the French words *heure* (referring both to the division of time, and the book of hours itself) and *heur* (meaning [particularly good] fortune),[46] thereby again aligning her fortune with the bound manuscript. It is notable too that these three verses each reflect on the notion of change, particularly constrained movement or diverted journeys.[47]

---

[44] The appearance of the signature 'Marie R' beneath this quatrain strengthens this likely alignment.

[45] Murray's comments on the seventeenth-century prison poems of Sir Walter Slingsby might apply equally well to Mary's quatrain here: 'his vows and prayers constitute a kind of provisional self-sentencing, an effort to render the deeply irregular experience of imprisonment logical and intelligible': Molly Murray, 'Measured Sentences: Forming Literature in the Early Modern Prison', *Huntington Library Quarterly*, 72 (2009), 147–67 (p. 161). The word 'light' might bear several layers of meaning, referring also to the lack of natural light (to which Mary had limited access); she might additionally have had in mind the parable of the lamp under a bushel (Matthew 5:14–15; Mark 4:21–25; Luke 8:16–18); one of her mottoes, *sa Vertue m'attire*, seems to allude to the sun's light since she used it in one of her embroidered emblems depicting a marigold turning towards the sun's rays.

[46] Stuart, *Bittersweet within my Heart*, p. 87.

[47] DeVos offers interesting comments on Mary's use in the Oxford sonnet 'O Signeur Dieu, rescevez ma priere' of the noun *carrière*, also used here: 'In addition to a way, path, or route, "carrière" also denotes the circuit around which horses raced. The road the poet must travel is thus not simply

In the fifth and seventh incomplete verses, Mary reflects further on renown, and this time establishes a link between it and the spoken rather than written word. In the fifth, she wavers between the verb *dire* (to speak) and the more long-lasting *publier* (to make public/known) before seeming to settle on the more ephemeral act. In the seventh verse, Mary makes reference to her own speech and opinions, which form the subject too of verse 4. Here she describes the power an unnamed woman has to bestow praise on others and she likens this woman to a beautiful angel. The use of the first-person form of the verb (*peux*) is grammatically incorrect, but not necessarily a mistake – instead it might point towards Mary's self-identification with the woman, and therefore with the angel. The angel and the notion of praise (*louange*) appear again in verse 6 (both once more in rhyming position), where Mary states that the beautiful angel (considered in further detail below) is the object of her prayer.

As well as verses, fol. 81 contains two further instances of Mary's signature 'Marie R', as well as the dates 'xviii octobre' and 'xxx may', and the words 'aduertir fl:' and 'escrire au segretaire pour doug[l]as', all in her hand. The repeated signatures see Mary perhaps endeavouring to assert her monarchical status, whilst the dates and notes reveal something of her less poetic but still politically important everyday domestic life. Labanoff suggested that the abbreviation 'fl:' might be expanded to 'Fleming' and linked this name, but without further comment, to John, fifth lord Fleming (*d.* 1572).[48] He was in fact one of Mary's most loyal supporters, and the brother of Marie Fleming (1542–*c.*1600), one of her closest serving women. Mary wrote two letters to him on 30 May 1568 from Carlisle, just after her escape from Lochleven. These letters instructed him first to seek aid from Elizabeth I and then, if this was not forthcoming, from her uncle the Cardinal of Lorraine.[49] The dual appearance on fol. 81r of the date 'xxx may' and phrase 'aduertir fl:' might well refer to these sets of instructions.

Several candidates present themselves for the Douglas mentioned in the second note, including Margaret Douglas (1515–78) (mother of Mary's second husband, Darnley) who visited Mary in 1574; James Douglas, fourth earl of Morton (*c.* 1516–81); or either of George Douglas or 'Little Willie' Douglas – brother and page, respectively, to Sir William Douglas, laird of Lochleven (*c.* 1540–1606) – who helped Mary to escape from that castle in 1568.[50] The latter is a particularly strong possibility. He joined Mary during her imprisonment

---

an existential journey, but one that is also physically demanding': Jessica DeVos, 'Renewing the Auld Alliance: Marie Stuart's Poetics and the Catholic League's Politics', *Renaissance Studies*, 35 (2021), 600–20 (p. 614).

[48] Labanoff (ed.), *Lettres*, vol. 7, p. 348.

[49] Labanoff (ed.), *Lettres*, vol. 2, pp. 85–93; John Simmons, 'Fleming, John, fifth Lord Fleming (*d.* 1572)', *Oxford Dictionary of National Biography*, new version (2006) <https://doi.org/10.1093/ref:odnb/9701>.

[50] Fraser, *Mary Queen of Scots*, pp. 401, 416–17, 426–29; Guy, *My Heart is my Own*, pp. 366–68.

in England, but was one of the servants she was forced to let go in September 1571. Mary wrote a moving letter to these servants, thanking them for their loyalty and directing them towards France for aid, and she addresses 'Little Willie' directly on two occasions: 'et à vous maistre Jehan Gordon et Guillaume Douglas, je prie Dieu qu'il vous veuille inspirer le coeur' ('and as to you, Master John Gordon and William Douglas, I pray God to inspire your hearts!'); '[j]e vous prie, consollés vous en Dieu; et vous, Guillaume Douglas, soyés asseuré que la vie qu'avés hazardée pour la mienne, ne sera jamais destituée tant que j'auray un ami vivant' ('I implore you to find consolation in God; and you, William Douglas, be assured that the life you hazarded for mine will never be neglected while I have a living friend').[51] A pension to Douglas is also mentioned in her final testament.[52] That scraps of notes related to Mary's domestic affairs occur mixed with drafts of her poems stands witness to the close relationship of the queen's life and writing documented throughout this chapter.

Mary's next quatrain occurs on the bottom margin of fol. 129v:

un Coeur que loutrage martire
par un mepris ou dun refus
A le pouvoir de faire dire
ie ne suis plus ce que ie fus
    Marie

A Heart which is tormented by insults
through contempt or disdain
Has the power to say
I am no longer what I was
    Marie

Mary here points towards the mistreatment she has suffered and articulates the extent to which her identity has changed. Indeed, the final line interestingly parallels once again a sentiment voiced by Clément Marot, this time in one of his epigrams: *plus ne suis ce que j'ay esté* ('I am no longer what I once was').[53] The quatrain nevertheless remains open to two readings. On one hand, it might function as a pessimistic summary of the extent to which Mary's private and public self has changed for the worse – and in support of this it is perhaps telling (albeit surprising) that Mary appends just her Christian name to the verse, rather than the usual 'Marie R' – and yet, by asserting that she has '*the power* to say/I am no longer what I was' (my emphasis), the former queen

---

[51] Labanoff (ed.), *Lettres*, vol. 7, pp. 378–82 (pp. 380, 381).
[52] Labanoff (ed.), *Lettres*, vol. 6, p. 488.
[53] See https://clementmarot.com/epigrams.htm#De_soi-m%C3%AAme, accessed 7 September 2023.

simultaneously asserts a strong sense of self-authorship and retains a degree of control over her identity and its articulation.

The quatrain's balance of pessimism and optimism is further highlighted when we consider its position in the manuscript alongside material from Job 14:13–16 belonging to the office of the dead: *quis mihi hoc tribuat ut in inferno protegas me ut abscondas me donec pertranseat furor tuus et constituas mihi tempus in quo recorderis mei* ('who will grant me this, that thou mayst protect me in hell, and hide me till thy wrath pass, and appoint me a time when thou wilt remember me?'). The office of the dead was designed to help relieve the suffering in purgatory of those who had died, but its position within books of hours also ensured that it functioned as an allegory for the reader's own life on earth (and subsequent life in purgatory). In this particular portion of the biblical narrative, Job articulates his despair but retains a confidence in God's redemption: *vocabis et ego respondebo tibi operi manuum tuarum porriges dexteram* ('thou shalt call me, and I will answer thee: to the work of thy hands thou shalt reach out thy right hand'). The positioning of Mary's verse alongside these verses might suggest that even if she identified with Job's sufferings during her imprisonment she nevertheless attempted to share something of his hope for salvation.

Another quatrain occurs on the very next folio (130r), this time appending a Latin prayer from the third nocturne of the office of the dead which begins: *libera me domine de morte eterna* ('free me O Lord from eternal death'). Mary's quatrain reads:

> si nos pensers sont esleves
> ne lestimes pas chose etrange
> ils meritent estre aprouver
> ayant pour obiet un bel ange

> If our thoughts are raised upwards
> do not think them strange;
> they deserve to be acknowledged
> having as their object a beautiful angel

Mary's description of the object of her devotion as 'a beautiful angel' recalls the fourth and sixth verses on fol. 81v, and she returns again to the topic of angels in the next verse, on fol. 137v:

> Pour recompense et pour sala[i]re
> de mon amour et de ma foie
> rendes men ange titulaire
> autant comme ie vous en doye

As a reward and wage
for my love and faith,
O, titular angel, give me in return as
much therefore as I may owe you.

In drawing on a monetary lexeme, and using a model of prayer known as *da quia dedi* ('give because I gave'), Mary here figures the relationship between herself and the angel as a quasi-feudal pattern of service and reward. She motivates the very roles of early modern lordship and patronage she referred to in verse 4 of fol. 81, but this time places herself in the position normally held by her own subjects.[54] The quatrain occurs in the bottom margin of fol. 137v, below text from Psalm 41:3 (*sitivit anima mea Deum fortem viventem quando veniam et parebo ante faciem tuam*; 'my soul hath thirsted after the strong living God; when shall I come and appear before the face of God?') and a cue for the Lord's Prayer, *Pater Noster. Et ne nos inducas sed libera nos*, which interestingly echoes the Latin prayer accompanying the first angel verse on fol. 81. Accompanied as they are by the circular framework of two similar Latin prayers, Mary's vernacular prayers to the Virgin Mary thus both echo the psalmist's prayer and express her hopes for a similar spiritual and physical freedom.

Mary's three references to angels in the St Petersburg manuscript are matched by another in her 100-line 'Meditation'. Here Mary prayed '[p]ermets, Seigneur, que tousjours mon bon Ange/Soit pres de moy, et t'offre ma louange' (83–4, '[g]rant, Lord, that my good Angel always/Be close to me, and offer you my praise'). The shared reference to angels – and use of the same rhyme (*Ange* and *louange*) – thus creates an intertextual link between Mary's manuscript and print poetry to match the more intratextual echoes across the verses of the St Petersburg Book of Hours and the Latin text they accompany. It remains uncertain, however, precisely who Mary had in mind when referring to the angel, described variously as *bel*, *bon* or *titulaire*. The latter phrase is often translated as guardian angel, but the French for this would ordinarily be *ange gardien*. It is therefore perhaps more likely that Mary had in mind her namesake the Virgin Mary who, in her role as Queen of Heaven, was also figured as Queen of Angels. This would fit with Mary's use of the adjective *titulaire*, and with the fact that she claimed 8 December (the feast of the Immaculate Conception of the Virgin Mary) as her date of birth (when instead, perhaps, she was born on 7 December).[55]

---

[54] For the prayer model see: Virginia Reinburg, *French Books of Hours: Making an Archive of Prayer, c. 1400–1600* (Cambridge, 2012), p. 153.

[55] Jenny Wormald, *Mary Queen of Scots: A Study in Failure* (London, 1988), p. 11. For an alternative reading which links the angel to Elizabeth I see Stuart, Œuvres Littéraires, pp. 327–28. Guy (*My Heart is My Own*, p. 439) notes that Mary had a servant to whom she referred as the 'Angel Mary' but I have not yet been able to find a source for this.

On fol. 138r Mary writes:

> En feinte mes amis changent leur bienveillance
> tout le bien quils me font est desirer ma morte
> & comme si mourant iestois en deffaillance
> dessus mes uestements ils ont iette le sort

> My friends feign their good will [towards me];
> all the good they do is to wish me dead,
> and, as if I were dying in despair,
> they cast lots for my clothes.

In its complaint against the fickleness and falsehood of those thought to be friends, this quatrain recalls the first verse on fol. 81v where '[a]ll change their mood and bearing' (the verb *changer* is common to both). It also notably echoes Psalm 21:19 (*diviserunt vestimenta mea sibi et super vestimentum meum miserunt sortem*, 'they parted my garments amongst them; and upon my vesture they cast lots') and its fulfilment following Christ's crucifixion when the soldiers cast lots for his clothes (Matthew 27:35 and John 19:24), as well as Job's complaint in the Latin text to which her verse is appended (Job 17): *spiritus meus adtenuabitur dies mei breviabuntur et solum mihi superest sepulchrum. non peccavi et in amaritudinibus moratur oculus meus* ('my spirit shall be wasted, my days shall be shortened and only the grave remaineth for me; I have not sinned, and my eye abideth in darkness'). As previously, however, Mary's pessimism and suspicion of those around her is tempered in the manuscript's next verse, which follows a French prayer to the Virgin Mary (fol. 158v):

> il napartient porter ces armes
> qu a ceus qui d un coeur indomte
> comme nous nont peur des allarmes
> du temps puissant mais sans bonte

> None has the right to bear these arms
> except those who with an indomitable heart
> like us do not fear alarms
> in these powerful but unkind times.

Here, Mary seems to express some confidence in her ability and that of her true supporters to face up to the difficult times in which they find themselves.

The manuscript's final two verses maintain this mixed outlook. In the first, positioned at the end of the Fifteen Joys of the Virgin (159r),[56] Mary adopts a Boethian outlook by asserting that she values the transience of time over

---

[56] Documenting the Virgin's life from the Annunciation to her Assumption into heaven, this prayer presents chronologically the joys Mary experienced as mother of Christ.

fortune – 'bien plus utile est l'heure/que non pas la fortune/puisquelle change autant quelle est oportune' ('time is more useful than fortune/because it changes as much as it is favourable') – and she again aligns, or rather opposes, time (*l'heure*) with (or against) the other kind of *heur* ('fortune'). In the manuscript's final verse (folio 172v) Mary uses that very synonym for good fortune, but here she reflects soberly on the ineluctable fact of earthly mortality:

> la Viellesse est un mal qui ne se peut guerir
> & la ieunesse un bien que pas un ne menage
> qui fait qu'aussitot ne lhomme est pres de mourir
> et qui lon croit heurheux travaille davantage

> Old age is an evil that cannot cure itself
> and youth a good that none can maintain
> as soon as man is born he is close to death
> and he who we think of as happy works all the more.

In the St Petersburg verses, then, we see Mary waver between positions of relative optimism and pessimism as she prays to God and/or the Virgin Mary (her angel), and throughout she echoes the voice of the psalms and prayers alongside which she copies her poems. The poems notably share a form – they are all quatrains (rhyming variously *abab*, *abba* or *abab*) – and repeated vocabulary. They also reflect on a set of common, linked themes: fortune, time, change, identity, devotion, reputation, friendship and falsehood, imprisonment and the relationship between life and death. Moreover, even though the poems were written at different times – and in an unknown order – they nevertheless form a coherent collection. Smith has previously written that 'these poems present a fragmented poetic sequence, one that not only supplements the biblical text that it appends but also forms a new text within it'.[57] My own additional sense is that Mary's quatrains are deliberately, but perhaps sub-consciously, fragmented witnesses to the often-wavering attempts of an imprisoned queen to repeatedly reconstruct and rearticulate her private, public and devotional identities. And perhaps rather than, or in addition to, supplementing and appending the biblical text of her book of hours, what we encounter here is an act of ventriloquism, or co-authorship; like many other prisoners from the period, and indeed many other women who translated or echoed the psalms, including Elizabeth I, Mary here adopts the words of the penitent King David to author and to authorise her own experience.[58]

---

[57] Smith, 'Le pouvoir de faire dire', p. 72.
[58] A detailed consideration of the relationship between Mary's poetry and the psalms is a matter for further study.

Conclusions

Although we cannot tell whether any of the surviving books of hours owned by or associated with Mary, Queen of Scots were present with her at the scaffold, they clearly played an important, and consistent, part throughout her life. Mary's books were very much social volumes, standing testimony both to her relationship with female members of her maternal French family and to those individuals who formed part of – or entered – her increasingly constrained household. They were also notably itinerant objects, acting as witness to her changing domestic and political circumstances. In the verse inscriptions filling the blank pages and margins of her books of hours, Mary consistently meditated on her identity and articulated a notably Boethian but nevertheless reluctant philosophy of patience. She also betrays increasingly personal anxieties concerning the faith with which she was – and is still – so closely aligned, and in doing so forged close, and indeed tantalising, associations between herself and the biblical king, David.

It has often been suggested by historians and biographers that, towards the end of her imprisonment, Mary increasingly sought to establish for herself the reputation she had gained in some circles as a Catholic martyr. In a letter of September 1586 sent to the duke of Guise, for instance, Mary asserted 'je mourray en la foy catholique romane' ('I will die in the Roman Catholic faith') and prayed that God give her 'la grâce de me faire mourir pour sa querèle' ('the grace to die for his cause').[59] Elsewhere, in an unfinished and so-called 'Essay on Adversity' that survives in an autograph copy in National Archives MS SP 53.11 (fol. 64r ff.),[60] Mary explained that her readers would 'learn from the example of persons who have suffered similar miseries before them, and who have found that the remedy is always to turn to God' ('les affligés ... y voiront les exemples de ceulx qui ont souffert pareilles miseres ... trouveront que leur remede a tousjours esté de *se retourner à Dieu*'). She planned to align herself in her own suffering with numerous male and female figures from the Bible, classical literature and earlier periods of history, including John the Baptist, Jeremiah, Hecuba and Dido.

The Sheffield and Christie's manuscripts newly examined in this chapter show how, long before her imprisonment, Mary was already using her books and writings to set about a process of self-memorialisation that mirrors the modern treatment of her books as relics. However, what emerges most strongly from fresh analysis of the later verse added to those books she kept with her during her imprisonment is a portrait of a queen wavering between confidence and caution in her future private and public identity.

---

[59] Labanoff (ed.), *Lettres*, vol. 6, pp. 439, 440. See also her letter to the Pope in the same volume, pp. 447–56.
[60] Stuart, *Œuvres Littéraires*, pp. 297–312. See also: *CSP Scot.*, vol. 5, no. 636; *Calendar of Documents relating to Scotland*, vol. 2: 1589–1603, Appendix 1543–1592, p. 929.

FOUR

The Afterlives of Mary's Letters
Jade Scott and Alison Wiggins

At 10am on 8 February 2017 the 'last letter' of Mary, Queen of Scots went on rare public display at the National Library of Scotland. For preservation reasons the letter was scheduled to be on view for only six hours, until 4pm, although the viewing window was extended to nine hours, until 7pm, due to the long queues forming on the street outside the library in Edinburgh.[1] The demand to see the letter was beyond expectation. The scale of interest might be explained by its intrinsic appeal and dramatic content. The letter was written to Henri III, King of France on 8 February 1587 by Mary, who described herself as his 'soeur & ancienne allyee', to say she had received notice that her nineteen years of imprisonment were to end and she would be executed 'comme une criminelle' six hours later, at eight the following morning.[2] In the letter, she stated herself to be innocent of any crime and described her poor treatment that evening, which included having her personal papers taken away and being denied access to her own chaplain. She asked Henri to pay to her servants their wages, to pray for her soul, to create a memorial mass for her and to give alms. She also mentioned that she had included two precious stones to bring him good health. It is a letter written in a rhetorical style that expresses Mary's own views and instructions with clarity and directness, addressed directly from one royal to another and written at a pivotal and intense moment of historical importance. Added to the intrinsic interest of the letter itself, we might further explain the queuing crowds in Edinburgh as engaged in a commemorative act. The display of the 'last letter' was timed to be 430 years to the day after Mary's execution

---

[1] 'Last letter of Mary, Queen of Scots on display for six hours', 1 February 2017, BBC News, www.bbc.co.uk/news/uk-scotland-38826244; 'Last letter of Mary, Queen of Scots: Display extended by three hours', 8 February 2017, BBC News, www.bbc.co.uk/news/uk-scotland-38907013; 'Display of Mary, Queen of Scots' last letter extended by 3 hours', 8 February 2017, *The Scotsman*, www.scotsman.com/whats-on/arts-and-entertainment/display-mary-queen-scots-last-letter-extended-3-hours-1456471, all three accessed 7 September 2023.

[2] That is, 'sister and old ally' and 'like a criminal'. The letter is NLS, Adv. MS 54.1.1. Images, a transcription, an English translation and background notes are available via the NLS Digital Gallery: https://digital.nls.uk/mqs/, accessed 7 September 2023.

and advertised as marking the anniversary of her death: a space to remember or mourn a Scottish queen executed away from Scotland and whose tomb is in London.[3] The letter offered the promise of getting close to an object with which Mary had had actual physical contact, as the style of handwriting and large clear signature show that the queen had picked up a quill and penned the letter herself. Autograph signed documents stand out amongst all of the objects associated with Marian memorialisation because they are items that we can be demonstrably sure Mary had held in her own hands. Letters in particular, as a text type, give readers the satisfaction of the sense of a direct line to the past and the person. In Erasmian terms, letters 'make the absent person present' as bridges that build rapport and simulate conversations with the rhetorical capacity to connect us to those from whom we are separated.[4] This special quality, of epistolary presence, contributes to the intense and ongoing responses to Mary's letters in their afterlives.

In this chapter we give more examples of responses to the 'last letter' in its afterlife, as an illustrative case study placed in the context of the wider corpus of Mary's correspondence. The discussion proposes that Mary's death in 1587 was not an end point for her letters but a starting point, a point of release, revoicing and creative potential. It highlights how, in their afterlives, her letters were transformed by being infused with the distinctive cultural assumption and practices of subsequent eras. It proposes a conceptual framework for understanding the afterlife of her letters that draws on theories of materiality and is composed of three strands, outlined in the next sections.[5] 'Distributed afterlives' reviews the place of Mary's letters as objects dispersed through libraries, archives and collections, and asks how they reached these locations and are collected, curated, conserved, stored, accessed and displayed there. 'Textual afterlives' considers how Mary's letters have been copied, as modern transcripts, forgeries and replicas, and analyses their treatment in the monumental Victorian editions and calendars more recently made available as digital resources. 'Performative afterlives' highlights how creative writers and filmmakers have responded to the

---

[3] Mary asked in her 'last letter' to be buried in France, although her own hopes or expectations were not, of course, necessarily the same as those of later publics, whose views are part of her afterlife. Her remains were moved from Peterborough Cathedral to her tomb at Westminster Abbey by her son James VI and I in 1612.

[4] A concise summary of the well-documented impact of Erasmus on letter-writing is provided by Alan Stewart, *Shakespeare's Letters* (Oxford, 2008), pp. 12–14. Further relevant studies include Judith Rice Henderson, 'Humanist Letter Writing: Private Conversation or Public Forum?', in *Self-presentation and Social Identification: The Rhetoric and Pragmatics of Letter Writing in Early Modern Times*, ed. Toon Van Houdt, Gilbert Tournoy and Constant Matheeussen, Supplementa Humanistica Louvaniensa 18 (Leuven, 2002), pp. 17–38.

[5] For overviews of approaches and theories in material cultural studies this chapter has benefited from *The Routledge Handbook of Material Culture in Early Modern Europe*, ed. C. Richardson, T. Hamling and D. Gaimster (Abingdon, 2016); and Alexander A. Bauer, 'Itinerant Objects', *Annual Review of Anthropology*, 48 (2019): 335–52.

shadow archive of lost and destroyed letters as a space for feminist responses. This chapter, therefore, conceptualises the letters both as texts and as objects, their materiality encompassing their shifting locations, their stages of textual transmission, and their immersion in evolving animate social and cultural contexts. It defines a permissive and expanding corpus, one that accommodates new letters produced and reproduced *post mortem*. It acknowledges that the value of Mary's letters fluctuates and is situation-specific, their meanings constructed as much as given, generated through collection, curation, remediation, editing and supplementation, among other processes. Mary's letters provide the basis for all of the modern biographical accounts – accounts that strongly disagree with each other about which 'version' of Mary is most acceptable and in which the letters have become sites of struggle over interpretations. This chapter puts those questions of biography to one side and instead considers how ideas about Mary are refracted through responses to her letters. The letters are more Scrabble than Wordl – not puzzles to crack with a single answer, but mobile and multi-vocal points of contact that continually generate freshly made glimpses of Mary through ongoing processes of reading and engagement.

Distributed afterlives: letters destroyed, collected, curated, stored and modelled

At least a thousand letters survive today, to and from Mary, that were produced in her lifetime and can be authenticated as such. While this number is an estimate, it is certainly only a portion of the quantity of letters she actually sent and received. John Guy estimates she must herself have written 'two or three thousand' during her life, which does not include those sent to her.[6] We know some of the reasons for the gap between the letters Mary actually sent and received and those extant today. Elizabeth I's spymaster Sir Francis Walsingham knew Mary's letters were evidence and that objects associated with her could become memorials or relics, so he saw to it that her archive was seized and purged after her death.[7] Control over the archive is control over history and, in Mary's case, there is no doubt that history's victors had a substantive material role in determining which of her letters survived and which did not. The intentional destruction of portions of her papers was the first act in the afterlife of her letters and they remained vulnerable to a range of haphazard incidences of loss. The original Casket Letters disappeared some time after 1581, perhaps intentionally

---

[6] *My Heart is My Own: The Life of Mary Queen of Scots* (London, 2004), p. 500.
[7] Walsingham had Mary's papers seized and carried off in 'three large coffers' to be scoured for evidence against her. Any objects that could have become relics and that had 'special significance' for her supporters, who saw her as a victim of the Protestant state, were removed. Guy, *My Heart is My Own*, pp. 9 and 484–85; Stephen Alford, *The Watchers: A Secret History of the Reign of Elizabeth I* (London, 2012).

destroyed, given their controversial content.[8] Subsequently, important parcels of Mary's autograph letters disappeared after diarist John Evelyn (1620–1706) lent them to friends – casually exchanged as part of 'gentlemanly agreements' but never returned and either carelessly lost or wilfully destroyed. Evelyn expressed regret at having lent an important bundle of autograph letters to historian Gilbert Burnet (later Bishop of Salisbury) for his *History of the Reformation of the Church of England*, Burnet blaming the loss of these and other letters on his printer Richard Chiswell. Evelyn made the same mistake again when he lent a bundle of correspondence, apparently between Mary and William Maitland of Lethington, to the latter's descendant John Maitland, duke of Lauderdale, after a conversation at dinner. The rest of his bundle of letters Evelyn gave to 'a worthy and curious friend of mine' to look after, suspected to be Pepys.[9] As a result of these and other disappearances, the corpus of letters that comes down to us today is incomplete due to a never-fully recoverable pattern of intentional destruction combined with accidental loss and decay. The archive is a far from exact reflection of all the letters originally sent and received, but is filtered, adulterated and tilted.

The surviving letters are now distributed among collections across several countries and reached those locations through a range of archival processes. Some never moved from their earliest collection contexts, while others have passed through the hands of owners, sellers and auction houses, into national libraries, academic institutions, private collections or other repositories. Mary's European network spread her correspondence wide and her letters have been identified in archives from Simanca to Sweden. Of the letters Mary sent to her friends and family in France, many remained in family papers or were transferred to the Bibliothèque Nationale. After the looting of the Bibliothèque du Roi by revolutionaries, many more were sold to collectors beyond France and a large number collected by Prince Alexander Labanoff made their way to the Imperial Library, Saint Petersburg.[10] Of the letters Mary sent to Scottish and English nobles, many remain today in family papers lodged in manor houses, stately homes and castles, at times suffering the risks of fire, water and rodents. Of those sent during her English captivity, a proportion were intercepted by the Elizabethan intelligence service, with copies or originals being kept by men such as Robert Beale and Thomas Phellipes whose personal papers were later

---

[8] Guy, *My Heart is my Own*, p. 398, notes that they were in Scotland in 1581 and went missing after that for an unknown reason, likely 'deliberately destroyed' to preserve James VI's family reputation.

[9] Lauderdale had shown an interest in his ancestor; after the duke's death, at his library sale, Evelyn was unable to find or recover the letters, according to his letter to Archdeacon Nicholson, cited by Strickland, *Letters*, vol. 3, pp. xxi.

[10] Strickland, *Letters*, vol. 1, p. xiv, also mentions letters taken to Warsaw.

absorbed into the State Papers.¹¹ The interests of later buyers subsequently shaped the corpus, such as the Victorian autograph collectors who, interested in personalities more than politics, curated albums of choice specimens by celebrated historical figures and royals.¹² Mary's letters continue to be highly prized by collectors: as recently as 2022 a letter from Mary with a six-line postscript in her own hand made £32,500 at auction, more than double the estimate.¹³ Scribal letters featuring her autograph signature also command high prices at auction, such as the one purchased in April 2017 by the Folger Shakespeare Library, Washington DC.¹⁴ The Folger Library's generous access policy includes Creative Commons licensing for use of photographs from its digital collection, which means that this particular letter has come back into open public view.¹⁵ Other letters, if sold into closed private collections, may be, effectively, lost to history, visible to the public and researchers only for a brief moment when passing through the saleroom.

The afterlives of letters in repositories have included both the linking and the separation of letter-packet elements. To give an example, in 1566 Mary wrote to Elizabeth I in French and in her own hand, and this letter was enclosed with another from her, to Elizabeth's chief minister William Cecil, penned by her

---

[11] These letters shifted from private to public ownership, although the process was not systematic: Alan Stewart, 'Familiar Letters and State Papers: The Afterlives of Early Modern Correspondence', in *Cultures of Correspondence in Early Modern Britain*, ed. James Daybell and Andrew Gordon (Philadelphia, PA, 2016) pp. 237–52. An account of the copying of Mary's intercepted letters is provided by Cathy Shrank, 'Manuscript, Authenticity and "evident proofs" Against the Scottish Queen', *English Manuscript Studies 1100–1700*, Vol. 15: *Tudor Manuscripts 1485–1603*, ed. A. S. G. Edwards (London, 2009), pp. 198–218.

[12] Alan Stewart describes how autograph letters are 'catnip to collectors' and gives examples of collecting practices: 'Early Modern Lives in Facsimile', *Textual Practice*, 23 (2009) no. 2: 289–305.

[13] Mary Queen of Scots from Carlisle Castle, 26 June 1568, to the French ambassador in England, requesting safe passage for George Douglas to France. The letter is in French and penned by a scribe with the postscript in Mary's own hand. The high price at the live online sale was widely reported in the media: 'Mary Queen of Scots letter sells for £32,500 at auction', Anna Bryan, 2 February 2022, *The Scotsman*, www.scotsman.com/whats-on/arts-and-entertainment/rare-letter-written-by-mary-queen-of-scots-sells-for-ps32500-at-auction-3552938. The item was Lot 308 at the sale of the library of William St Clair, 2 February 2022, 10:00 BST, Lyon & Turnbull, Edinburgh: www.lyonandturnbull.com/auction/lot/308-stuart-mary-1542-1587-queen-of-scotland/?lot=252228&sd=1, both accessed 7 September 2023.

[14] Mary Queen of Scots from Edinburgh to William Keith, the Earl Marischal of Scotland, 19 September 1566. The letter is in Scots, penned by a scribe with the signature in Mary's own hand. The item was Lot 259, at 'The Scottish Sale'; it sold for £27,500, 27 April 2017, 11:00 BST, Bonhams, Edinburgh, www.bonhams.com/auctions/24082/lot/259/?category=lis&length=10&page=26, accessed 7 September 2023.

[15] High-quality photographs of this letter can be viewed and linked to for free via LUNA: Folger Digital Image Collection. Use of the images is encouraged under agreement of the Creative Commons License www.folger.edu/copyright-policy. The call number is Folger X.c.206 and the link on LUNA is: https://luna.folger.edu/luna/servlet/detail/FOLGERCM1~6~6~1242325~267717?qvq=q%3Amary%20queen%20of%20scots&mi=33&trs=356, accessed 7 September 2023.

secretary and in Scots.[16] These two letters acted in concert with one another and we can observe how Mary decorously constructed two distinct epistolary personae: textualising herself as more formal and distant for Cecil whereas she was more at ease writing to her royal equal Elizabeth I, as would be expected according to the etiquettes of early modern epistolary culture. To read this packet of two letters as a unit is a reminder that Mary was trained in rhetoric, to fashion her own voice and identity for reasons of decorum and persuasive impact in her letters. These letters sit side-by-side in The National Archives, at Kew, within a bound codex. While they are not stated in the catalogue to have been from the same letter-packet, their relationship is readily apparent to alert users consulting the material in the reading room with the benefits of the haptic process of leafing through the pages. By contrast we find, in other cases, that letters that were originally sent in the same packet have come to be held at two or more different repositories, even though they were originally delivered together. Such is the case with the packet of three letters sent together in 1569 and now distributed between The National Archives and the British Library: one from the earl of Shrewsbury to Cecil, a second from Mary to Cecil and a third from Mary to Elizabeth.[17] Royal and political diplomacy often required that one person did not write directly to another, but would write to that person's secretary or chief administrator, and do so via a trusted bearer. In Mary's case, here, her letters arrived with a covering note from her jailor, Shrewsbury, as a framing context for the reception of her letters to Cecil and Elizabeth.

These examples give us cases of letters bundled together for delivery and then sometimes being unbundled and physically separated in their archival afterlives (but sometimes not). There are numerous possible combinations and permutations of such bundling and unbundling of letters with other letters or documents. These combinations include the scenario in which a letter is linked to another document only in its afterlife. For example, a sheet of paper with a sonnet penned in Mary's own hand is held in the collection of unbound poems that is now Oxford, Bodleian Library, MS Add. C. 92 (fols 22r–v, 24r). This sonnet, written in the first person, opens with Mary asking 'What am I?' and 'what purpose does my life serve?' ('Que sui je, helas, & de quoy sert ma vie?') before going on to express through a series of rhetorical conceits her physical and psychological pain and suffering resulting from exhaustion and ill health.[18]

---

[16] TNA SP 52/12 f. 14 and f. 15, images available from SPOnline, www.gale.com/intl/primary-sources/state-papers-online, accessed 7 September 2023.

[17] TNA SP 53/3 f. 70 (the earl of Shrewsbury to Cecil), BL Cotton Caligula C/I f. 413 (Mary to Cecil) and BL Cotton Caligula C/I f. 409 (Mary to Elizabeth).

[18] We are grateful to Emily Wingfield for sharing a pre-print version of her forthcoming monograph, *Books Beyond the Border: Scotland's Royal Women and European Literary Culture 1424–1587*, and this discussion especially benefits from Chapter 10 on Mary's poetry and associations with European literary culture. We follow Wingfield's translation of the first line of the poem here.

The sonnet, with its tightly bound verse form, is an intellectual exercise that could have come from almost any stage in Mary's life but, based on similarities with other poems she composed, is likely to be from the period of her English captivity. More specifically, its material context (from its former ordering in the State Papers) places it precisely in the third year of her captivity, in 1571, around the time of the Ridolfi plot.[19] Despite the solid evidence pointing to 1571 as the year of composition, it has become traditional to read the sonnet as a record of Mary's feelings the night before her execution in 1587. The association with her last night has become commonplace in the sonnet's afterlife, perhaps derived from a hunch by a previous owner. Whereas the 'last letter' gives us a queen who had long prepared for her final moments, spiritually and pragmatically, by contrast the sonnet – if erroneously imagined as part of the scene – would encourage us to picture Mary on her last night as spiritually and psychologically unprepared, miserably writing poetry about her own distress. To reframe the 'last letter' with the sonnet drastically skews what it might tell us about Mary in her final hours and amplifies hostile voices against her. The incorrect pairing of the sonnet with the iconic 'last letter' is one of the insidious myths about Mary that has been remarkably persistent – the pairing even appeared in The British Library's recent major 2021–22 exhibition, *Elizabeth and Mary: Royal Cousins, Rival Queens*, despite the readily available evidence that the association of the sonnet with her last night is spurious.[20] Such recycling of the myth may seem surprising, and it serves as a reminder that the periodisation of Mary's afterlife is not linear. Ideas about her tend to come in and out of focus and to circle back into view when under cultural pressure, harnessed to align with particular narrative imperatives. Every response to Mary carries cultural information. Each must be situated in its context as evidence of cultural afterlife and reception. Databases and exhibition catalogues dissolve barriers between disparate documents and siloed collections by creating links between them. Such linking can helpfully re-associate letters and documents according to their earlier packets or caskets, to show how they were sent or were collected and curated in later eras, such as through Victorian knowledge frameworks. But, most crucially, the links and adjacencies between documents (i.e. not only the documents themselves but also the material connections and associations between them) must

---

The critical edition of Mary's literary outputs is: Marie Stuart, *Œuvres Littéraires: l'Écriture Française d'un Destin*, ed. Sylvène Édouard, Irène Fasel and François Rigolot (Paris, 2001).

[19] Wingfield provides a literary analysis of the poem and cites the fact that 'prior to its acquisition by its final private owner Captain Montague' it was 'kept as part of the collection of State Papers for the year 1571': *Books Beyond Borders*, Chapter 10. The sonnet is not mentioned in the last letter.

[20] The exhibition did not mention the evidence that the sonnet should be dated to 1571; *Elizabeth and Mary: Royal Cousins, Rival Queens*, ed. Susan Doran (London, 2021), p. 229.

be dated and culturally contextualised if they are to enrich interpretation of the letters from a foundation of factual accuracy.

Letters were sent with other items than documents. Passing mentions indicate they were sent with an extraordinary range of items now long since gone. Ephemeral everyday necessities accompanied the to-and-fro of epistolary exchanges, from blankets, food and medicine to favourite treats such as marmalade and rose-petal conserve. More durable objects may have survived but, detached from their letters, are unidentifiable. Rings were sent as tokens of identification to assure the recipient of the veracity of the bearer's verbal message or the authenticity of the content of a letter. Valuable gifts, such as the heart-shaped diamond for Elizabeth I sent during Mary's reign in Scotland, or the precious stones sent with her 'last letter', played a part in diplomatic negotiations, their metaphorical meanings carefully explained in the accompanying letter-texts or verbal messages. Luxuries were sent from France that included books and the latest fashions, such as the 'head-dresses from Possy' and the watch that Mary admired 'so much for its pretty devices'. Domesticated animals were among the special deliveries Mary asked for and received from her supporters, and these included caged birds and pet dogs: in 1575 she asked the Archbishop of Glasgow and her uncle the Cardinal of Guise for 'a couple of pretty little dogs' to be sent in baskets to keep them warm. Such references give us glimpses of life during Mary's captivity in England and help us unpack the etiquettes and politics of gift-giving for managing interpersonal relations. The diplomatic potentials of these items came to the fore during Mary's captivity, when they had a role in maintaining her powerful network of European connections.[21] They place the letters within a rich context of material exchanges that is no longer available to us in their current storage locations.

---

[21] We know about the rings because they are referred to in the letters; for example, '[b]elieve, in particular, a person who will give you, in my name, a ruby ring, for I assure you, upon my conscience, that this person will tell you the truth agreeably to my desire' (Mary to Mauvissière, September 1584, Strickland (ed.), *Letters*, vol. 2, p. 186). Other examples can be found in Strickland, I, pp. 78, 114, 200; and TNA SP 53/11, fol. 44. Some of the precious objects associated with Mary and now held by National Museums Scotland are discussed at www.nms.ac.uk/explore-our-collections/stories/scottish-history-and-archaeology/mary-queen-of-scots/mary-queen-of-scots/objects-associated-with-mary-queen-of-scots/, accessed 7 September 2023. The references to the head-dresses and watch can be found in Strickland (ed.), *Letters*, vol. 1, pp. 215–16. The reference to sending 'pretty little dogs' is from Mary's letter to the Archbishop of Glasgow, 22 September 1575, Strickland (ed.), *Letters*, vol. 1, p. 205, at p. 209: '[i]f M the Cardinal of Guise, my uncle, is gone to Lyons, I am sure he will send me a couple of pretty little dogs; and you must buy me two more; for, besides writing and work, I take pleasure only in all the little animals that I can get. You must send them in baskets, that they may be kept very warm.' She sent a subsequent reminder on 13 November 1575 to 'send my little dogs' and had evidently received them by 12 February 1576 when she said 'I am very fond of my little dogs; but I am afraid they will grow large' and would also like some 'barbets [now called poodles] and sporting dogs' (Strickland (ed.), *Letters*, vol. 1, pp. 212 and 216).

Storage of letters is culturally specific and part of their ongoing afterlives, not least their physically folded forms. For conservation reasons, letters in archives, libraries and repositories are stored flat in individual slip-case folders or bound into codices with their folds smoothed out to minimise damage. It is as opened sheets or pages that we encounter letters in archives, reading rooms or display cases. However, a recent initiative inspired by their original sending contexts has offered an alternative view. The research value of folded paper models of letters has been spectacularly demonstrated by the MIT and UCL Letterlocking team, whose precision-engineered replicate-letters show formal features previously overlooked. In a remarkable recent discovery, the Letterlocking team reconstructed Mary's 'last letter' to show it was originally spiral-locked; that is, formed into an intricate and highly secure packet for sending using a distinctive paper-folding mechanism (the 'spiral lock') known only to certain elite letter-writers.[22] It is a finding that, we would argue, encourages us to picture Mary, in her last hours, unruffled, steady-handed, supported by her team of women and deliberately focused on effective and secure communication of instructions to the French king.[23] This impression of her demeanour contrasts with eye-witness accounts from that night, which were doubtless hostile and partisan. The high level of manual dexterity required – the steady-handedness needed – to execute a spiral lock has been recovered by the Letterlocking team through hands-on practical workshops that allow participants to learn actively about the process themselves. In addition, the team's video reconstructions available on YouTube have reached unanticipated audiences for Mary's letters and for engaging with assessment of the historical evidence. At the time of writing, Mary's spiral-locked 'last letter' is the most-watched Letterlocking video, having clocked up 305,000 views since its release on 30 March 2018.[24] Thus, the meanings of the materiality of Mary's letters has been reshaped as the letters are dextrously reconstructed outside of slip-cases and display cases. The letters that come down to us today are authentically Mary's letters but resituated, stripped of enclosures, flattened and bound. They have morphed over the centuries, been remediated and remodelled to form a new archive of video reconstructions.

---

[22] It is a rare and complex lock also used by Elizabeth I and Catherine de' Medici, and is the subject of research by the Letterlocking team: http://letterlocking.org/; YouTube, www.youtube.com/@Letterlocking, both accessed 7 September 2023. Other early modern letter locks identified by the team include the Butterfly, Dagger-Trap, Triangle and Anti-Spy locks. The choice of lock can give us information about the identity of the sender, the level of security required or can signify a hidden message.

[23] J. Dambrogio, D. Starza Smith, J. Pellecchia, A. Wiggins, A. Clarke and A. Bryson, 'The Spiral-locked Letters of Elizabeth I and Mary, Queen of Scots', *Electronic British Library Journal*, 11 (2021).

[24] The intricate lock used for the 'last letter' has been reconstructed by Jana Dambrogio, demonstrated in her remarkable video: www.youtube.com/watch?v=dzPE1MCgXxo, accessed 7 September 2023.

Textual afterlives: letters forged, copied, edited and remediated

Handwritten copies of Mary's letters were not penned only during her lifetime. Where a single later copy exists, there is always, inevitably, a question over whether there was ever an original. For example, does the letter penned in the hand of Edinburgh antiquarian and poet John Pinkerton (1758–1826) transmit the text of an authentic letter from Mary's lifetime, or is it a fictionalised text authored by Pinkerton, or a copy of a fake letter that Pinkerton believed to be genuine?[25] The letter purports to be to Bess of Hardwick during the rare period when she was loan keeper, in June 1569, and discusses the plots and 'double dealling' that surrounded Mary during her captivity. The letter is specious on both linguistic and historical grounds. While it is difficult to be sure of Pinkerton's motivations, suspicion seems justifiable given his reputation as a literary forger.[26] The most notorious forger of Mary's letters was Alexander Howland Smith (1859–1913), known as 'Antique Smith', an Edinburgh lawyer's clerk whose fake documents date from the late 1880s until his trial and imprisonment for forgery in 1893. Smith's forgeries number into the hundreds and include documents deceptively claimed to be by celebrated literary figures such as Sir Walter Scott, Charles Dickens and (the especially saleable) Robert Burns, as well as Scottish monarchs. They are now valued themselves as 'authentic fakes' with their own cultural moment. Their sensational story makes them highly collectable and, in 2012, Bonhams sold for £6,875 a 'collection of forgeries' attributed to Antique Smith, a highlight of the collection being forged Marian writings.[27] Smith's hoax letters are scattered through collections, such as the box that is catalogued by the National Library of Scotland as 'containing loose Smith forgeries' and includes a 1564 letter from Mary to Patrick Lindsay about the Chaseabout Raid with Mary's 'fake signature' penned by Smith.[28] These cases have been carefully identified and catalogued by auctioneers and archivists to avoid misunderstanding or misattribution. While these examples have been correctly and accurately recorded as Smithian forgeries, they undoubtedly complicate the corpus of Mary's letters, which has become

---

[25] The letter copied by Pinkerton is from Mary to the countess of Shrewsbury (known as Bess of Hardwick), [June 1569], now NLS, MS 1710, fols 23–24. An image and transcription is available from the online edition of Bess of Hardwick's Letters where it is letter ID 220: www.bessofhardwick.org/letter.jsp?letter=220 and is discussed in the editorial commentary www.bessofhardwick.org/background.jsp?id=150, both accessed 7 September 2023.

[26] Studies of Pinkerton's life include his activities as a forger: Patrick O'Flaherty, *Scotland's Pariah: The Life and Work of John Pinkerton, 1758–1826* (Toronto, 2015); Sarah Couper, 'Pinkerton, John [pseuds. Robert Heron, H. Bennet] (1758–1826), Historian and Poet', *ODNB* (https://doi:10.1093/ref:odnb/22301).

[27] Bonhams, London, 23 May 2023, 14:00 BST: 'The Stuart B. Schimmel Forgery Collection; and other properties'; www.bonhams.com/auctions/20136/lot/85/, accessed 7 September 2023.

[28] NLS MS 2210. Also held by the NLS is the bound vol. MS 2209 from the Society of Antiquaries with clippings about Smith's trial. I am grateful to Ronnie Young for these references.

infiltrated with Victorian specimens. The intense debate over the forged versions of Mary's 'own hand' during her lifetime only adds to the uncertainties. Further research would be necessary to quantify the extent of the problem.

Antique Smith sold his forgeries to buyers eager for materials associated with historical and literary celebrities and keen to possess objects connected with Mary's life. These deceptive copies must be distinguished from legitimate copies, i.e. copies that are reproductions of what we know or believe to be genuine historical materials and that are open about their status as replicates (even if they tap into some of the same interests among purchasers). Legitimate copies made as tributes or artworks include Dundee's magnificent Edward Burne-Jones window produced by William Morris & Co. in 1889 that features Mary holding her charter for the city, which emulates her signature and red wax seal reproduced in the medium of stained glass.[29] Facsimile replicates of Mary's 'last letter' can today be purchased for £10 from the National Library of Scotland gift shop: an educational souvenir and a surrogate that can be studied slowly and up close (a haptic experience not possible with the original or the digital version).[30] Other legitimate analogue copies, that we might permissively include in a corpus of letters in their afterlife, are those that constituted a stage in the production process of editions. The first half of the nineteenth century saw editors, having identified a market for published editions in print, searching for letters in archives, taking notes and making transcripts. The handwritten notebooks by Mary's biographer Agnes Strickland (1796–1874) illustrate her method of visiting archives to find unedited letters, which she transcribed by hand or, very often, had others transcribe for her.[31] Her papers include her cursive hand in blue ink on blue paper (handwriting that is not always easy to decipher) interspersed with papers and notes by others who made copies for her, such as Miss Jane Porter who is credited with making transcripts of letters in the Imperial Library at St Petersburg.[32]

Strickland published three volumes of Mary's edited and annotated letters during the 1840s. Her editorial policy for letters in Scots or English was to

---

[29] The panel was commissioned for the council rooms of Dundee's Town House and is now on display in The McManus art gallery and museum, Dundee (museum number: 1974-748-8): www.mcmanus.co.uk/content/collections/database/stained-glass-window-depicting-mary-queen-scots, accessed 7 September 2023. Mary is depicted holding out the charter, featuring her signature and seal, that confirms the grant of land she had gifted in 1564 to the city for a new burial ground.

[30] The facsimile of the last letter can be purchased here: https://shop.nls.uk/last-letter-of-mary-queen-of-scots-804-p.asp, accessed 7 September 2023.

[31] GU Library Archives and Special Collections, MS Gen. 1076 and 1077. A list of records in UK archives associated with Agnes Strickland can be accessed from TNA and include correspondence, papers and notes in repositories in Edinburgh, Glasgow, Oxford, Suffolk and other locations: https://discovery.nationalarchives.gov.uk/details/c/F31235, accessed 7 September 2023.

[32] Strickland, *Letters*, vol. 3, p. xvi.

preserve most of the original spelling and, for letters in other languages or in cipher, to translate them into modern English.[33] Her aim, she said, was to provide modernised translations for an English-speaking audience that would make accessible to readers a more historically accurate view of Mary. She added heavy Victorian punctuation to show grammatical structure and to flag emotional content using exclamation marks (marks that never appear in the originals). These changes transformed the letter-texts into a hybrid variety of language; that is, Mary's own language and that of her scribes is fused with Strickland's, revoiced as it were by Strickland, which gives us Mary's letters through a nineteenth-century cultural viewpoint and set of conventions. Strickland's texts are correlated with her Introduction, which whets the appetite of readers by promising exciting content. She pitches her edition as a direct response to Sir Walter Scott's 1820 novel *The Abbot*, which took as its topic Mary's 1567 imprisonment and escape from Loch Leven. Strickland asserted her view that, if Scott had been 'so fortunate' as to have seen some of the letters that had since come to light, his 'fine historical romance' would have been greatly improved.[34] She warns other scholars and authors to heed her work as it will provide them with essential new information based on 'closer adherence to the facts', at the same time as framing her edition as of interest to readers of literature and romance.[35]

Strickland's framing commentaries defend Mary's 'epistolary talents' that, in Strickland's view, had been under-rated. Arguing that Mary's letters are superior in style to those of Elizabeth I, she emphasised her opinion of the eloquence and candour of Mary's letters being 'the genuine transcripts of the royal writer's mind' that, she says, reveal a range of passing emotions from her 'feminine earnestness' and 'unaffected simplicity' to flashes of 'sarcastic bitterness'.[36] It is a not unbiased view that describes a mode of reading letters as direct windows into a writer's thoughts – a mode of reading that is now outdated and from which critics have moved away as being naive and sentimental, but that was characteristic of Strickland's era and that she evidently expected to be enjoyed by her readers. While intended as a defence, Strickland may inadvertently have fed into today's tendency to regard Mary as less intelligent and less well educated than Elizabeth.[37] There remains a pressing need for serious reassessment

---

[33] Jeremy J. Smith, *Transforming Early English: The Reinvention of Early English and Older Scots* (Cambridge, 2022).

[34] Strickland (ed.), *Letters*, vol. 1, pp. xxi–xxi.

[35] Other editions of Mary's letters include: T. F. Henderson, *The Casket Letters and Mary Queen of Scots* (Edinburgh, 1889); one letter from Mary is included by Mary Anne Everett Wood in *Letters of Royal and Illustrious Ladies of Great Britain*, vol. 3 (London, 1846), p. 281.

[36] Strickland (ed.), *Letters*, vol. 1, p. xvii, p. xxxiii, p. xl.

[37] The point is made by Emily Wingfield within her discussion of Mary's library and book ownership, where she argues that consideration of the queen's education 'should certainly prompt a reassessment of the common perception that Mary was less intelligent and well-educated than her counterpart Elizabeth': *Books Beyond Borders*, Chapter 10.

of Mary's letters (along the lines that Emily Wingfield has admirably achieved for her poetry), to take account of her humanist education and status as a woman of letters. Strickland was a successful historian of her age who made a living from writing as a career, while always keeping an eye on the marketing of her books and being attuned to the interests of her reading public. Her editorial commentaries and apparatus give us insights into contemporary viewpoints that romanticise Mary. Her career and authoritative subject position benefited from her own gender, which is implicit in her decision to edit Mary's letters, given the contemporary cultural consensus that female historians were best placed to understand historical women.[38] Strickland is now firmly established as a key figure in Mary's feminist historiography and her editions are still very much with us.

Less well known to history is Strickland's assistant in Russia, Miss Porter, who had managed to procure there a copy of Labanoff's 1839 first edition of Mary's letters. Evidently, Labanoff's French-language edition was very difficult to find in Britain and Porter's 'generous exertions', along with the perceived need for an English-language edition, were cited by Strickland as justification for her volumes. Her edition is partly a translation of Labanoff, but there are important differences between their editorial apparatus, policy and choice of letters. Strickland does not include what we today regard as the 'last letter' but instead prints the one Mary wrote the same night to her almoner, calling it her final letter.[39] Labanoff offers less mediation than Strickland, but relies most heavily on the French sources (the archival references of which are now out of date). Both seem to have been unaware of the correspondence held in private Scottish collections (not surprising since these letters were not then available centrally through the National Register of Archives for Scotland, there being no central register at that time). The letters in Scottish collections that are now

---

[38] As discussed by Anne Laurence, 'Women Historians and Documentary Research: Lucy Aikin, Agnes Strickland, Mary Anne Everett Green, and Lucy Toulmin Smith', in *Women, Scholarship and Criticism: Gender and Knowledge, c.1790–1900*, ed. Joan Bellamy, Anne Laurence and Gill Perry (Manchester and New York, 2000), especially p. 126: 'Publishers seem to have felt that, by virtue of their femininity, women could write authoritatively about female historical characters, giving special insights into the private and domestic sides of the lives of public characters, especially of women of the past' and thus 'many women found recognition as historical writers' in the early nineteenth century. Further discussed by Natalie Zemon Davis, 'Gender and Genre: Women as Historical Writers 1400–1820', in *Beyond Their Sex: Learned Women of the European Past*, ed. Patricia H. Labalme (New York, 1980); Rohan Maitzen, '"This feminine preserve": Historical Biographies by Victorian Women', *Victorian Studies*, 38 (1995) no. 3; Una Pope-Hennessy, *Agnes Strickland: Biographer of the Queen of England* (London, 1940); D. R. Woolf, 'A Feminine Past? Gender, Genre and Historical Knowledge in England, 1500–1800', *American Historical Review*, 102 (1997) no. 3.

[39] Strickland (ed.), *Letters*, vol. 2, p. 243, Queen of Scots to her Almoner; Labanoff (ed.), *Lettres*, vol. 6, p. 483, 'Marie Stuart à Préau, son aumonier'; p. 494, 'Marie Stuart à Henri III, Roi de France'; p. 494, 'Dernier Mémoire Adressé par Marie Stuart à Henri III' (17th-century copy from Bibliothèque Royale de Paris).

known shift the focus from France to Scotland during the personal reign in particular, and have repercussions for students who might now access Mary's letters via Labanoff or Strickland and come away with the impression that there are fewer letters written in Scots and fewer sources in Scottish archives than in reality there are. The letters in Scottish collections have been reviewed by the current authors for an Open Access digital handlist intended to go some way towards rebalancing of the corpus.[40] The editions of Labanoff and Strickland, along with the monumental nineteenth-century Calendars of State Papers by Mary Anne Everette Green and Robert Lemon, with their transcriptions and summaries, are now more readily available than ever through resources such as Gale-Cengage's State Papers Online, the Internet Archive and via print-on-demand.[41] While greater access to these resources has undoubted benefits, they risk taking us back more firmly and regularly to the earlier versions and their accompanying frameworks of knowledge. *Caveat lector*: these editions and calendars are not Mary's letters, they are Victorian transformations of Mary's letters with their own cultural contexts as part of their afterlife.

Performative afterlives: the letters reimagined

Mary was all too aware that the moment the ink dried on a letter was not its end but its beginning. She knew that her letters were subject to intense debate and scrutiny during her own lifetime and she regularly expressed her fears that her letters would be intercepted, read by her enemies, copied, forged, tampered with, lost or used as evidence against her – which they often were. Yet she was also aware of posterity and she expressed, in some letters, the hope that her words would pass down to later generations her own version of events – so we are eerily aware, when reading her later letters, that she hoped they would be read in the future. Certainly, her long, essay-like letters to Elizabeth I at the end of her life fall into this category. Mary's awareness of afterlife meant that even in the moment of their authorship her letters were being fashioned for self-memorialisation. Her wish was partly thwarted by the purging of her papers at the end of her life, plus later incidents of loss, although these losses have

---

[40] The catalogue of Mary Queen of Scots letters in Scottish repositories is forthcoming with Early Modern Letters Online: http://emlo.bodleian.ox.ac.uk.

[41] Gale-Cengage State Papers Online, www.gale.com/intl/primary-sources/state-papers-online. Internet Archive scan of Strickland scan available from the Internet Archive, https://archive.org/details/vol1lettersofmar00mary/page/210/mode/2up, both accessed 7 September 2023. Important archival research has gone into unpicking the facts from the extraordinarily complex Babington and Casket letters (Alford, *The Watchers*; Guy, *My Heart is My Own* and Shrank, 'Manuscript, Authenticity'); there is still no modern edition despite this work and the work of John Guy to establish the Casket letters. *Calendar of State Papers, Domestic Series, of the Reigns of Edwards VI, Mary and Elizabeth, 1547–1603*, 12 vols, ed. Robert Lennon and Mary Anne Everett Green (London, 1856–72).

themselves become a point of inspiration for later authors. The violent removal of her papers has been repeatedly returned to by creative writers and the missing letters and archival gaps have become spaces within which to reimagine Mary's predicament and circumstances. Friedrich Schiller's 1800 *Maria Stuart* dramatises the final days of Mary's life and pivots around depictions of the delivery, theft and reception of her letters.[42] Philippa Gregory's 2008 novel *The Other Queen* narrates the early years of Mary's English captivity through historically researched fictional letters that are depicted circulating through the household and fill perceived gaps in the historical record.[43] In these ways, destroyed, lost and never-sent letters have generated their own afterlife of creative responses. The numerous archival gaps and ambiguities offer starting points for thinking again about Mary's meaning and relevance today.

Worthy of special mention is the depiction of letters sent between Mary and Elizabeth I that has become an extension of the now well-established dramatic tradition of a fictionalised meeting between them. The most recent major film, Josie Rourke's 2018 *Mary Queen of Scots*, makes full use of the dramatic potential of letter-writing by being structured around five letters imagined as written between the two queens.[44] These letters are fictional, created for Rourke's film and scripted in present-day English, but historically researched and sited to provide factual exposition of some of the political context. They set the aesthetic tone for the film's promotional material that features stylised quill-pen writing. They are also the focal point for some memorable tableau shots: in a motif referencing Liz Lochhead, Mary dictates a letter to Rizzio surrounded by her women in waiting and, then, later in the film, she composes a letter herself, pen-in-hand, framed by a classic Scottish Highland landscape.[45] Rourke's film depicts Mary as a strong ruler of an independent Scotland. It also inverts the well-worn dramatic cliché of Elizabeth and Mary as rivals constantly scheming against each other.[46] The letters contribute to these feminist perspectives by offering an epistolary space for extended conversation between the two rulers, who are imagined sharing a unique bond of mutual respect forged through

---

[42] For example, Robert Icke's modern version (2016) that dramatises the final days of Mary's life.

[43] Gregory describes her novel as offering 'a fiction which accounts for known facts'. The book features a colour photograph of an original letter on the inside front over, indicating a key theme of the narrative. The novel narrates the early captivity of Mary, from autumn 1569 until June 1572, switching between three narrators: Mary, and her captors the earl and countess of Shrewsbury. The novel features transcriptions of fictional letters and tracks the letters coming into and out of the household.

[44] In addition to these five, there is also a final address from Elizabeth to Mary that is spoken in her mind rather than directly or as a letter.

[45] Liz Lochhead's *Mary Queen of Scots Got her Head Chopped Off* (first performed 1987) features scenes of Riccio taking dictation on a typewriter.

[46] The point is discussed by Thomas S. Freeman, 'Elizabeth I and Mary, Queen of Scots: Afterlives in Film' in *Elizabeth and Mary* (2021), pp. 276–81 (at p. 281).

understanding of each other's gendered position and struggles. In order to depict their leadership of their independent nations, the film uses metaphors of harmony and stability. Such metaphors are reminiscent of the real-life historical letters exchanged between the queens during Mary's reign in Scotland, which play on the diplomatic language of sisterhood, courtship and mutual accord.[47] While not among the best known of Mary's historical letters, they will perhaps gain additional interest as a result of Rourke's film; as Anna Groundwater discusses in Chapter Twelve, creative responses shape public perceptions most widely. Perhaps those who watch Rourke's film will be especially alert to the language of political leadership, its potential to be constructive and inclusive, or otherwise.

Conclusion: an expanding, evolving corpus

The corpus of Mary's letters is neither final nor static but continually expanding and evolving. We might conceptualise three corpora of Mary's letters: (i) the letters actually sent and received that are extant today in archives, libraries and repositories; (ii) the corpus of *post mortem* reproductions and remediations of these historical letters that include editions, transcriptions, facsimiles and artworks; and (iii) the lost letters that we can speculate on and that have prompted a spectrum of creative responses from forgeries to film fictionalisations. These are not fixed categories. Sometimes their boundaries are blurred (if we are unsure whether a letter is lost or not, or we cannot be certain about the status or authenticity of a copy). New letters continue to come to light, either permanently or for a brief moment in the saleroom. We might expect the quantity of new discoveries to diminish over time, yet, just this year, fifty-five new ciphered letters were uncovered and decoded using digital methods, formerly miscatalogued in the Bibliothèque Nationale.[48] In addition to caches of letters lost or found are the myriad treatments and responses that characterise their afterlives. Known letters have been re-presented in new forms or reframed. Forgeries have been confected. Fictional letters have been created for novels, plays and films to fill suspected gaps in the archive and offering opportunities for feminist interventions. Mary's corpus of letters, like Mary herself, is in a constant 'state of becoming'.[49] The letters are never finished, they are remade continually. Their meanings reside not only in their texts, but in their readers and viewers. The scrawled and ciphered obscurity and intractability of many of the historical

---

[47] Discussed by Guy, *My Heart is My Own*, p. 159; Wingfield, *Books Beyond Borders*, Chapter 10.

[48] George Lasry, Norbert Biermann and Satoshi Tomokiyo, 'Deciphering Mary Stuart's Lost Letters from 1578–1584', *Cryptologia*, 47 (2023) no. 2: 101–202.

[49] Eric Ketelaar, 'Cultivating Archives: Meanings and Identities', *Archives and Museum Informatics* 12 (2012) no. 1: 19–33.

letters, their evasive language, as well as the gaps in the records, make them even more open to shifting interpretations. New versions and performances are to be welcomed if they offer ways of envisaging socially beneficial models of good leadership. As Mary's letters – originals, copies and editions, or imagined and fictionalised creations – have reached ever more audiences online, they have gone way beyond their intended reception contexts and now have a global visibility. While the production moment of the original letters recedes further into the past, at the same time novel methods, technologies and imaginative frameworks bring them into the present moment more vividly than ever before. The letters merit serious and scrupulous study in their own right. They hold special importance for contextualising competing opinions of Mary and for unpacking some of the hardened stereotypes that have accrued to her (as tragic and miserable). They give us access to a more poised and intelligent queen than is often presented. The letters are already being read by machines and will continue to be, opening up methods of analysis not previously possible and signalling the direction of the future lives of Mary's letters.

Part Two

Mary in Literature and History

FIVE

Editing and Collecting Mary, Queen of Scots in the Eighteenth Century: James Anderson (1662–1728) and Dr William Hunter (1718–83)

Michelle H. Craig

The publication of two bestselling histories of the British Isles, William Robertson's *History of Scotland* (London, 1759) and David Hume's *History of England* (London, 1754–62), solidified Mary and her story in the eighteenth-century imagination. Robertson's portrayal of Mary was particularly poignant, depicting her as a flawed, but ultimately sympathetic character.[1] As in earlier periods, though, her life still provoked debate and the divisive nature of her story was neatly captured in an anonymous review of Robertson's *History* from February 1759, possibly written by Hume:

> ... by one numerous party [Mary was] held to be illustrious for her virtues; and by another infamous for her crimes. As the violence of both parties has been transmitted down from the times in which she lived to posterity in its full strength, we have not hitherto had any history of her reign, that did not bear strong and marked characters of the spirit of faction.[2]

Intrigue around Mary, and the Casket Letters in particular, was closely linked by the time of Robertson's publication to the discussion of the narration of history itself and the very conscious attempt to create more 'authentic' sources. This chapter will consider the approach to Mary in eighteenth-century society in two different ways. Firstly, it will examine how antiquarians and historians aimed to tackle the problem of Mary and 'historical truth' with empirical methodological approaches. In presenting archival sources related to Mary, as well as scarcely

---

[1] Robertson and Hume will not be discussed here. For more see Jeffrey R. Smitten, *The Life of William Robertson: Minister, Historian and Principal* (Edinburgh, 2017), p. 120.
[2] *The Critical Review or Annals of Literature*, vol. 7 (London, 1759), p. 91. On whether Hume was the author see David R. Raynor, 'Hume and Robertson's *History of Scotland*', *Journal for Eighteenth-Century Studies* 10 (1987) no. 1: 59–63.

available printed books published on her in the sixteenth century, antiquarians such as James Anderson (1662–1728) were able to challenge received partisan narratives on Mary and carve their own approach to Marian scholarship. Particularly because of the divisive nature of Mary's story, this chapter will highlight Anderson's primary aim in encouraging his reader to critically evaluate the sources he presented and to come to their own conclusions. Secondly, it will consider how book collectors supplemented and added to this picture and will use the Scottish physician and collector, Dr William Hunter (1718–83) as a case study. Hunter's donation of his museum and library to his *alma mater*, the University of Glasgow, has ensured that it has remained largely intact. This allows us to view Hunter's Marian books within his wider collection. This chapter does not consider how widely, or in what manner, books related to Mary were read in the eighteenth century. Instead, by focusing on the market for books on Mary and on Hunter's own collecting motivation, we can see how books on her were amassed by someone who acted as a key node in the scholarly networks of London and who was interested in compiling, contrasting and comparing evidence to challenge received thought. Both case studies start to offer a picture of the pathways by which Mary was both written about and discussed within eighteenth-century intellectual circles, and the impact of early empirical approaches to history writing and reading that intended to question the received partisan narratives of Mary and her story.

Editing Mary: James Anderson's *Collections Relating to the History of Mary Queen of Scotland*

Historical understanding of Mary in the eighteenth century was in part shaped by the histories of her story on offer in local bookshops and libraries. With much of the sixteenth-century archival evidence relating to Mary stored in various locations across the British Isles, or in scarce printed volumes, we can assume that readers largely relied on historical accounts drawn by earlier historians, many of whom had their own political or religious angle. James Anderson aimed to counter this in his four-volume *Collections Relating to the History of Mary Queen of Scotland* (Edinburgh, 1727–28). By compiling and publishing a large number of primary sources on Mary found in collections across the country, he made sources related to Mary more accessible to a larger group of people. Although the *Collections* did not directly tell the narrative of Mary in a chronological manner, as had most earlier accounts of her life, the prefaces and introductions to specific papers and printed editions gave much of the contextual information that a reader required to become familiar with her history. Without this overarching narrative, his approach underlines his view of the independence of his reader and thus, by application, their own involvement in the Marian debate if, as he intended, they chose to critically evaluate the sources he provided.

Anderson was born in Edinburgh in 1662. His father Patrick Anderson (*c.* 1626–1690), a Presbyterian minister, was a Covenanter based in Walston, Lanarkshire and had been imprisoned in the 1670s on Bass Rock in the Firth of Forth for non-conformity. James Anderson trained as a lawyer, but quickly found that his chief interest was Scottish history. Arising out of the background to the Act of Settlement in 1701 that secured long-term Protestant succession, Anderson's polemical *Historical Essay Shewing that the Crown and Kingdom of Scotland is Imperial and Independent* (Edinburgh, 1705) challenged English superiority over Scotland. Despite his Protestant and Whig perspective in this publication, it also demonstrated his use of the historical method, with close, critical study of original sources.[3] Antiquarianism and history writing became his primary professional pursuit and in 1708–09 he unsuccessfully petitioned Queen Anne for instatement as historiographer royal for Scotland. He was working on his *magnum opus*, *Diplomata Scotiae*, a compendium of Scottish medieval seals and charters, when he died in 1728.[4]

Anderson does not state in his *Collections* when he turned his attention to Mary, but as with the background to his *Historical Essay*, it may well have arisen out of a desire to respond to the widespread debate around the queen in eighteenth-century literary society. A fellow antiquarian, George Chalmers (1742–1825), writing almost seventy years after Anderson's death in his *Life of Thomas Ruddiman* (London, 1794), claimed that the Whig circles around Anderson were so outraged by Samuel Jebb's positive representation of Mary in *Vita et Rebus Gestis Mariae Scotorum Reginae* (London, 1725) that they had encouraged him to write a counterpublication in response. Chalmers notes that Anderson's 'prejudice made him willingly obey the call upon his industry', with Chalmers also recording that Anderson was possibly influenced 'by the bigotry . . . which he inherited from his father'.[5] Because of Chalmers' Jacobite sympathies, negative portrayals of Anderson in his *Life of Thomas Ruddiman* should be treated with some care, something discussed in more detail below. Yet Chalmers' belligerent tone here serves only to illustrate the entrenched partisan debates around Mary throughout the whole eighteenth century. Moreover, as shall be seen, although Anderson most certainly was both a staunch Whig

---

[3] Alexander Du Toit, 'James Anderson (1662–1728), Historiographer and Antiquary', *ODNB* (https://doi.org/10.1093/ref:odnb/473).

[4] Ibid. This was later completed and published by Thomas Ruddiman (1674–1757), an Edinburgh-based scholar and printer, discussed elsewhere in this chapter: James Anderson, *Selectus Diplomatum et Numismatum Scotiae Thesaurus* (Edinburgh, 1739).

[5] George Chalmers, *Life of Thomas Ruddiman* (London, 1794), pp. 155–56. It should be noted that Jebb's publication also contained printed sources related to Mary.

and Presbyterian, he still made a very concentrated attempt at an impartial approach within his *Collections*.[6]

As documented elsewhere in this volume, the nature of Mary's life and actions provoked debate even within her own lifetime: the humanist George Buchanan (1506–82) was one of her most vehement critics, whilst the exiled Catholic John Leslie, the Bishop of Ross (1527–96), and the lawyer and writer Adam Blackwood (1539–1613) staunchly defended her name and reputation, both while she was alive and after her execution.[7] There was such a fervour around these debates that even Mary's son, James VI and I, was involved. William Udall published his *The Historie of the Life and Death of Mary Stuart, Queene of Scotland* in London in 1624, itself a translation of sections on Mary found in William Camden's *Annales Rerum Anglicarum et Hibernicarum Regnante Elizabetha* (London, 1615).[8] Camden (1551–1623) was a renowned antiquarian, who relied on primary sources to shape his narration of history. For example, when compiling both his *Annales* and his *Britannia* (London, 1586), an account of pre-Roman Britain, Camden undertook extensive 'fieldwork', accessing and evaluating as much literary and archaeological primary evidence as possible.[9] In a move that directly shows how royal censorship affected attempts at historical writing, a warrant was issued with Camden's *Annales* that stated the king himself had examined the text, while the bibliographer John Scott went as far as to note that 'it has been alleged' that James 'corrected many portions pertaining to his mother's history'.[10] By the eighteenth century, Mary was still inviting discussion, something Jenny Wormald attributes to the republication of works by George Buchanan and John Knox, as well as the publication of the *Collections* by Anderson.[11] The introduction to Anderson's *Collections* neatly demonstrates the draw of Mary in the early eighteenth century. He directly alludes to her appeal,

---

[6] Du Toit, 'James Anderson'.

[7] For example, George Buchanan, *De Maria Scotorum Regina* . . . (London, 1571); John Leslie, *A Defence of the Honour of the Right High, Mightye and Noble Princess Marie, Queene of Scotland* (London, 1569); and Adam Blackwood, *Martyre de la Royne d'Écosse* ('Edimbourg' [Paris], 1587).

[8] John Scott, *A Bibliography of Works Relating to Mary Queen of Scots, 1544–1700* (Edinburgh, 1896), p. 74.

[9] Wyman H. Herendeen, 'William Camden (1551–1623), Historian and Herald', *ODNB* (https://doi.org/10.1093/ref:odnb/4431).

[10] Scott, *A Bibliography of Works Relating to Mary Queen of Scots*, p. 74. Herendeen also draws attention to James' desire that Camden refute the critical view of Mary put forward in Jacques Auguste de Thou's *Historia Sui Temporis*. James also asked Camden to write about Scotland during Mary's reign. Herendeen highlights that this was printed as part of Camden's 'Animadversiones in Jac. Aug. Thuani Historiam, in qua res Scoticae memorantur', in de Thou, *V. Cl. Gulielmi Camdeni, et Illustrium Virorum ad G. Camdenum Epistolae* (London, 1691), pp. 356–59. See Herendeen, 'William Camden'. It is possible that further study of this Latin tract and direct comparison with de Thou might prove fruitful and this perhaps raises interesting broader questions over James' involvement in the creation of history, memory and legacy during his reign.

[11] Jenny Wormald, *Mary Queen of Scots: A Study in Failure* (Edinburgh, 2017 edn), pp. 4–6. For a fuller analysis on these debates and their change through time see ibid., pp. 3–11.

both locally and abroad, suggesting that she 'allured the generality of People', to such an extent that an unnamed 'eminent French Author says that her Story is among such Things as are taught to Children from the Cradle to make them fall in love with Books and Reading'.[12]

The very start of Anderson's general preface to volume 1 of the *Collections* also addressed the primary motivation underlying the publication, namely his opposition to polemics and his issue with the traditional published portrayals of Mary, arguing that she 'has been represented to the World in very different Colours' and that 'some Writers have not only widely disagreed in the most material Circumstances, but have even flatly contradicted and opposed each other with great Warmth and Bitterness'.[13] In place of this partisanship, which had led to 'Matters, which are so differently related in her Story', Anderson emphasised the demand for a rather different picture of Mary among his intended readership. He argued they wanted to see aspects of her life 'either supported or disapproved by Records and other authentick Vouchers', manuscript evidence that would highlight, confirm or challenge the aspects of her story described by others in their treatises.[14]

Anderson's historical approach throughout his career involved trawling through and transcribing texts in archives and scarce books, which then could be printed, compared and contrasted. He also clearly emphasises what he believes is the earnest desire of his readers, the 'Lovers of History', to see truth devoid of partisan opinion and to form a more balanced view of Mary, backed up with evidence. It is a 'true' historical Mary that he wished to convey with his volumes, by capturing these records and offering up the evidence to his readers to form their own opinions on Mary and her actions:

> My intention in publishing these Collections, was not to enter into the Argument of that Queen's Conduct in what she is most blamed and accused of by some, and justified and defended by others, but merely for the sake of Truth, the Life and chief Ornament of History; impartially to publish such authentick Records and Papers of State as have come to my Knowledge, and to reprint a very few scarce and curious Books Pro and Con (that is, On both Sides) in relation to a Piece of History, which has been so very much controverted by Authors of great Names, leaving all Men to judge and think of the Matter as they please.[15]

---

[12] James Anderson, *Collections Relating to the History of Mary Queen of Scotland*, 4 vols (Edinburgh, 1727–28), vol. 1, p. ii.
[13] Ibid., vol. 1, p. i.
[14] Ibid., vol. 1, pp. i–ii.
[15] Ibid., vol. 1, p. iii.

Perhaps somewhat to counter this, Anderson clearly discloses in his preface how he viewed his role as editor of the *Collections*, and his role as historian and antiquarian: to collate and present the evidence for both sides of the debate in as impartial a manner as possible, attempting to leave aside his own allegiances and opinions. In doing this, Anderson was not necessarily taking an unusual approach: declarations of impartiality were common at the beginning of history books of this period, so it is possible that he was, in part, reacting to an established form.[16] Anderson discusses his methodology again in the final lines of the general preface to volume 1, where he offers up a succinct synopsis of the role of the historian in the narration of history, noting above all that they should be impartial judges of evidence:

> Whereas all faithful Historians and Publishers of Historical Transactions, ought in Matters of Fact to lay aside all partial Regard to Religion, Country, Interest, Prepossessions, Parties, or other Views; and pay their entire Devotion to the Altar of Truth, considering they become publick Evidences for her, and are accountable at their high Peril, if to their Knowledge they conceal or betray, that which is the very Essence of History: FOR NOTWITHSTANDING ALL ART AND OPPOSITION WHATSOEVER, TRUTH WILL AT LENGTH PREVAIL.[17]

Anderson's publishers, whether at his direction or not, drew attention to this idea with a very noticeable change in the typography of the final lines of the general preface, moving from italics to roman, and capitalising them. They also draw particular attention to the idea of 'truth' which is set in a larger font.

This reader, whom Anderson addresses as his 'candid and unbyassed Reader', is referred to in several parts of his text, with the focus being their role as impartial adjudicator in the Mary debates.[18] Anderson particularly wanted his readers to engage with the failings of previous histories of Mary. In the preface to volume 4, he gives his reader the responsibility to undertake their own evaluation of an earlier published history. When introducing the papers given to Queen Elizabeth's Commissioners in 1568 at the Conferences of York, Westminster and Hampton Court that looked at the Casket Letters and Mary's involvement in Darnley's murder, Anderson notes that Camden does not appear to have used all the evidence available to him in his *Annales*. In particular, Anderson gives a short account of the omission of various sources, including letters to Queen Elizabeth from York and the skirting over of both the Westminster and

---

[16] James A. Harris, *Hume: An Intellectual Biography* (Cambridge, 2015), p. 321.
[17] Anderson, *Collections*, vol. 1, p. lv.
[18] Ibid., vol. 1, p. iv.

Hampton Court sources.[19] He suggests that Camden's aim was 'to favour Q. Mary [more] than those who were her Opposers' and invites his reader to 'give himself the trouble to compare Camden with the Papers I have here printed'.[20] What precisely Anderson means by this will not be examined here but it is possible that these omissions by Camden may say something about the influence James had exerted over Camden in his portrayal of Mary, mentioned above, and is perhaps an avenue worthy of further investigation. In finding issues with previous printed accounts, though, Anderson was also using another technique common to historical writing in the eighteenth century.[21]

Indeed, transparency about the sources and collections included in the volumes is a key part to Anderson's historical method. His preface to volume 1 states in detail how he compiled the sources listed in his volumes. The title page gives an indication of the scope and aim of the *Collections*, noting that the volumes contain 'A great Number of Original Papers never before Printed. Also a few Scarce Pieces Reprinted, taken from the best copies.'[22] He also made sure to list where a source was located and, if applicable, its reference number, something that draws attention to the importance of private and national collections to his endeavour. He claimed to do this so that sources might be checked, while at the same time reminding the reader of his role as impartial conveyor of evidence: 'those who may either doubt or be displeased with any of them, may be satisfy'd whether fairly printed or not, which is all that an Editor is accountable for'.[23]

In volume 4, for example, Anderson transcribes papers from the Cotton Library, citing the volume 'Libr. Cal. C. 1', something which makes clear reference to the pressmark of the volume's placement in Sir Robert Cotton's (1571-1631) original library, where each of the book presses were topped with an imperial bust after which they were named.[24] In his description, Anderson also notes the folio number from which the printed transcription is taken, for example 'Fol. 126' or 'Fol. 57', again allowing for easy comparison if access to the original was available.[25] In these instances he also tries to give a flavour of

---

[19] Ibid., vol. 4, part 1, pp. ii–iii. William Camden, *Annales rerum Anglicarum et Hibernicarum Regnante Elizabetha* (London, 1615).
[20] Anderson, *Collections*, vol. 4, part 1, pp. ii–iii.
[21] Harris, *Hume*, p. 326.
[22] Anderson, *Collections*, vol. 1, p. 1.
[23] Ibid., vol. 1, p. xlix.
[24] 'Libr. Cal.' for example, indicates that this volume was stored in the press topped by a bust of Caligula.
[25] Anderson, *Collections*, vol. 4, part 1, p. iv. This manuscript is now catalogued as Cotton Ms Caligula C 1, British Library, with f. 125 now used for the first reference, and f. 56 for the second. The Cotton Library, originally amassed by Sir Robert Bruce Cotton, was to become one of the foundation collections of the British Museum in 1753 but was likely housed at Ashburnham House in Westminster when accessed by Anderson.

the manuscript and its production for those unable to see it, noting, where he could, who had written it and whether it had been edited. Of a paper recounting the relations between Mary and Elizabeth in 1568, after Mary's escape from Lochleven Castle, Anderson notes that it was '[c]orrected, and in most Places interlined by Secretary Cecil's Hand', showing that he was able to recognise the handwriting of William Cecil (1520-98), close advisor to Elizabeth.[26] In printing copies of these scarce editions or state papers closeted in archives, the *Collections* brought primary evidence of Mary to a wider readership.

In another instance, he discusses at length his printing of an unpublished manuscript text by John Leslie, *A Discourse, Conteyninge a Perfect Accompt Given to the Most Vertuous an Excellent Princesse, Marie Queene of Scots, and her Nobility*.[27] He notes that the text had been used by Camden in the compilation of the latter's account in the *Annales*, but 'has not appear'd in Print, tho there are several Copies of it in Manuscript'. He goes on to discuss the materiality of the manuscript itself, housed in the Faculty of Advocates in Edinburgh, suggesting that not only was the handwriting contemporary, but that it had been written by one of Leslie's secretaries.[28] He touches on the reliability of the manuscript itself, mentioning the donor of the manuscript, the bishop, Dr William Nicholson (1655-1727), and noting that he had also had contact with Nicholson, though again, Anderson does not mention specifics.[29] When discussing the preface and dedication in his copy, he shows the extent of his research into the text by stating that he had accessed another copy of the same manuscript. Comparing their contents, he had noticed differences and used both to compile his printed edition 'to render it [the text] more compleat'.[30]

This scarcity of evidence is picked up elsewhere in the *Collections*, again emphasising the extent of his research. In volume 2 Anderson includes a copy of Buchanan's *Ane Detectioun of the Doingis of Marie Quene of Scottis*, noting in the table of contents that it was 'reprinted from a very rare and scarce Edition'.[31] The collectibility of the book is repeated in his preface to the edition where

---

[26] Anderson, *Collections*, vol. 4, p. 1.

[27] Since 1925 this manuscript has been housed in the NLS, to which it was part of a donation by the Faculty of Advocates on the NLS's foundation: NLS, Adv.MS.35.4.1. This appears to be a very different text to Leslie's better-known *Defence of the Honour*, though its contents have not been examined here.

[28] This manuscript was published in vol. 3 of the *Collections*, the only volume of the *Collections* printed by Thomas Ruddiman, who was also the assistant librarian at the Advocates Library. The volume contains a Faculty of Advocates accession note in Ruddiman's hand, possibly highlighting a collaboration between Ruddiman and Anderson around this text. See NLS, Adv.MS.35.4.1.

[29] Anderson, *Collections*, vol. 3, p. iv.

[30] Ibid. Anderson takes careful attention to note the shift from the manuscript in the Advocates Library to the one in the Cotton Library. See ibid., vol. 3, p. 242. The Cotton manuscript used by Anderson is now in the British Library, with the pressmark Cotton MS Caligula C IV, ff. 152r-237r.

[31] Anderson, *Collections*, vol. 2, p. 3.

he argues that 'it [is] so rare, that the Curious have fought after it'. Part of Anderson's decision to print it in the *Collections* was, in fact, to preserve it.[32] A major piece of the intrigue around this edition seems to be language. Anderson claims, incorrectly, that the edition had been translated into Scots by Buchanan himself, with other editions of the text rendered into English, and it seems to be this feature that attracted collectors.[33]

In his description of *Ane Detectioun*, Anderson refers to the St Andrews imprint, dating to around 1572. He also mentions another edition that was issued without imprint details, but which modern scholars have attributed to the London-based printer John Day and speculate was printed in 1571. Not only is his research into publishing histories apparent here, but also his research across collections and awareness of the general availability of books in the market and within collections. Although he notes that the early English copies in Black Letter 'are indeed very scarce', they are 'not so rarely to be met with as the other [the Scots version]', noting that he had only found one copy of the Scots edition, in the library of the earl of Oxford.[34] Not all of Anderson's statement is correct; he states for example that the St Andrews edition was the earliest, something which is incorrect, although because the first edition, the London edition printed by John Day was printed without a date, Anderson's error here is perhaps not surprising.[35] Errors like this highlight that much of Anderson's framing was somewhat speculative and although pertaining to present truth, could easily, unintentionally perhaps, invite error. Yet his research into this text and its history, thorough by the standards of the period, shows the extent of his knowledge and commitment to his publication.

Anderson's approach highlights the importance of his reader in the process of historical evaluation. More generally, the *Collections* show the scarcity of available evidence for his readers, and his description of the different sources

---

[32] Ibid., vol. 2, p. i.
[33] Ibid. It is possible that the translation was made by the English diplomat Thomas Wilson (1524–81) and was part of English propaganda against Mary. See Tricia McElroy, 'Performance, Print and Politics in George Buchanan's *Ane Detectioun of the duinges of Marie Quene of Scottes*', in *George Buchanan: Political Thought in Early Modern Britain and Europe*, ed. Caroline Erskine and Roger Mason (Farnham and Burlington, VT, 2012), pp. 49–70, particularly pp. 51–60.
[34] Anderson, *Collections*, vol. 2, p. ii. This edition is indeed relatively rare, with only five copies listed on the ESTC (ESTC no. S118393). Scott speculated that Anderson used a copy now housed in the Advocates Library (now NLS, H.32.d.12): see Scott, *Bibliography*, p. 27. The only other copy now in the UK is at the British Library (BL, C.55.a.26). Although the earls of Oxford, Robert and Edward Harley, bound their books in a very noticeable way, the copies in both the Advocates Library and the British Library have been rebound at a later date, so it is impossible to identify for certain which copy Anderson used.
[35] Scott, *Bibliography*, pp. 25–27. Scott also reflects briefly on the change of English and Scots language that Anderson discusses here, something that Anderson reflected had encouraged collectors to make manuscript copies of the St Andrews edition, despite owning copies of the English text. See ibid., p. 27 and Anderson, *Collections*, vol. 2, p. ii.

and their locations implicitly draws attention to the extensive travel needed to access such sources. It also raises the question of the societal connections needed to access the national and private collections he lists. By publishing manuscript papers held in archives and collections he made this evidence more readily accessible, though the content and physical properties – such as its quarto format, and the fact it was issued in a multi-volume set – show that he was still largely writing for an elite and well-educated audience.

Ultimately it is outside the scope of this chapter to consider how successful Anderson was in his aims. However, his account of Mary was heavily criticised several decades after his death by George Chalmers in the latter's *Life of Thomas Ruddiman* (London, 1794).[36] In his account of Ruddiman's association with Anderson, Chalmers attempts an extensive character assassination of Anderson, describing him 'as a man of no vigorous intellect, and a scholar of no extensive erudition'.[37] He suggests that the *Collections* were neither commercially nor publicly successful, stating that '[h]is *Collections* were soon sold at the established price of waste paper'.[38] Despite Anderson's references to impartiality, Chalmers argued the contrary:

> It soon appeared that, in this publication, he had no fairness of principle, nor accuracy of performance, though he talked of candour and impartiality. Under the show of attachment to truth, he acted with enmity to Mary: yet . . . in opposition to his own purpose, his voluminous publication is, at the present hour, supporting the interests of truth, and vindicating the honour of the Queen.[39]

Stating that he had also examined the state papers that Anderson used, Chalmers raised questions over Anderson's editorial reliability, noting that the documents that Anderson includes had 'lost their efficacy from suspicions of his candour'.[40] Chalmers does not explore what he means by this statement. Yet it is clear that Chalmers' Jacobite leanings meant he felt a deep disdain both for Anderson's Whig political background and his esteem of George Buchanan, a Marian critic.[41] Regardless, Chalmers' contradictory conclusion that Anderson's *Collections* had fundamentally failed, yet could still give a positive portrayal of

---

[36] Du Toit, 'James Anderson'.
[37] Chalmers, *Life of Thomas Ruddiman*, p. 155.
[38] Ibid., pp. 156–57.
[39] Ibid., p. 156.
[40] Ibid., p. 157.
[41] See Alexander Du Toit, 'George Chalmers (*bap.* 1742, *d.* 1825), Antiquary and Political Writer', *ODNB* (https://doi.org/10.1093/ref:odnb/5028). Chalmers particularly objected to the formation of a group intending to issue a counterpublication to Ruddiman's edited edition of George Buchanan's *Opera Omnia* (2 vols, Edinburgh, 1715). The group aimed to vindicate 'that incomparably learned and pious author from the calumnies of Mr Thomas Ruddiman'. In the end no such publication was ever printed. See Chalmers, *Life of Thomas Ruddiman*, pp. 74–75.

Mary, surely only stands to reinforce the very nature of Anderson's entire aim: to let the sources speak for themselves and to allow his reader to form their own opinion of Mary and her actions. What this shows us is the use of Mary as part of historical methodology. The aims of impartiality and truth by historians such as Anderson, although not always met, were instrumental in their approach to tackling the topic of the queen.

Collecting Mary in the eighteenth century: Dr William Hunter

The antiquarian motivation to gather and disseminate information, demonstrated by the likes of Anderson, was part of a much wider antiquarian approach to books that also involved close study of them and their material histories, and the placing of these books, and their ideas, within both the history of print and the history of ideas. We have limited information on private book-collectors in early modern Scotland, but a remarkable exception is that of the library of the Scottish physician and collector, Dr William Hunter (1718–83). A collector of museum objects, such as medical and natural history specimens, and of coins, Hunter's library of around 10,000 books is particularly useful for studying eighteenth-century intellectual culture because it survives almost completely intact.[42] Many of Hunter's working papers, some of his correspondence and his manuscript book catalogues also survive, meaning that the books can be placed in their wider context.[43]

Like Anderson, Hunter was interested in returning to original sources and comparing books in his library, using these comparisons to construct different historical narratives: his books were tools, not merely collected for curiosity's sake, highlighting how antiquarianism, knowledge of history and collecting went hand-in-hand in the pursuit of knowledge.[44] The library was a place for Hunter to research and digest ideas but also for the exchange of ideas and community access. Book collections like Hunter's, which contained a large number of early imprints, were invaluable for scholars and antiquarians in a period before routine and ready access to fully national collections: although there were university libraries, the Advocates Library and the British Museum from

---

[42] Hunter's museum collections are now housed in The Hunterian Museum and Art Gallery, with his library and working papers stored in Glasgow University Archives and Special Collections.

[43] We know for example that Hunter had at least one Marian object, a cameo ring, in his personal effects. With thanks to Anne Dulau Beveridge for drawing my attention to this item. See 'Lot 76: Mary Queen of Scots, an exceedingly fine cameo, in agate, set in gold as a ring', 'Sale Catalogue of William Hunter's Personal Effects, 1783' in M. Campbell and N. Flis (eds), *William Hunter and the Anatomy of the Modern Museum* (New Haven, CT, 2018), p. 412.

[44] Michelle Craig, 'The Library of Dr William Hunter: Collection, Usage and Management of a Personal and Professional Library in the Eighteenth Century' (unpublished PhD thesis, University of Glasgow, 2021).

1753, the private library continued to act as a space for the borrowing and use of books within and across social networks. The importance of collections in the dissemination of knowledge is apparent from close study of much of Anderson's *Collections*, and nicely exemplified in his use of the Cotton Library noted above.[45]

Although we have little direct evidence of contemporary interaction with Hunter's books related to Mary, we can use surviving evidence to chart his involvement in the debate more broadly. Firstly, Hunter's library catalogue betrays a noticeable interest in Mary. There are two book catalogues dating to Hunter's life, one of his medical books, one of his non-medical books.[46] They are arranged by format of the book and author name; in theory, for example, all folio-sized books of Aristotle are listed together in the catalogue. As an author catalogue it has limited use for those interested in searching by subject or theme. Unusually, Mary is given her own section in the catalogue. Although not all of these are now attested in the Hunterian Library, with some noted mistakenly, there are thirteen separate works listed under 'Maria Stuarta'.[47] Mary is not the author of any of the works listed under her name; instead, they all relate to her, as they might in a subject catalogue. Indeed, the catalogue even acknowledges that these works are not by Mary by stating 'by Udall' or 'par Leslie' in the entry descriptions. The list is also not a complete synopsis of books on Mary in Hunter's collection but is more an account of book titles that relate to Mary, showing that she was deemed an important category in her own right.

We can identify when Hunter purchased some of these Marian books, primarily by examining auction records to identify earlier provenance.[48] When we specifically consider books related to Mary that Hunter bought, we can also begin to see a few patterns. There were a small cluster of materials bought in the mid-1760s. For example, he purchased two books related to Mary at the sale in 1766 of the books of the eighteenth-century book collector John Baber (d. 1765).[49] One was *Los Doze Libros de la Eneide de Vergil* (Antwerp, 1557),

---

[45] In his account of Mary, William Robertson also talks of various public and private collections that he used in compiling his *History*: see William Robertson, *A History of Scotland* (London, 1759), pp. iv–viii.

[46] It is distinctly hard to identify when these catalogues were started but evidence may suggest a heightened interest in consolidating and describing the collections in the late 1770s. See Craig, 'The Library of Dr William Hunter', pp. 43–45, 230–32.

[47] 'Maria Stuarta', Museum Record 2 (MR2), p. 149. There are also two entries under 'Maria Stuarta' on p. 144. For some reason these were not consolidated in the trustee catalogue, made on Hunter's death. See 'Maria Stuarta', Museum Record 3 (MR3), p. 259.

[48] Much of the transcription from these catalogues was carried out by previous Keeper of Glasgow University Special Collections, Jack Baldwin, in the 1980s at the British Library.

[49] At this sale he bought, for example, Robert Turner's *Maria Stuarta Innocens* (Ingolstadt, 1588), GU ASC, Sp. Coll. Hunterian Cn.3.35.

potentially containing an ownership inscription of Mary herself.[50] Through an agent he also bought several books from a sale in Mechelen in late 1764. Aside from this, the year 1778 stands out as particularly noteworthy. In March of that year he purchased Leslie's *A Treatise Touching on the Right . . . of the . . . Princess Marie, Queene of Scotland . . .* ([Rheims], 1584) and the same author's *A Defence of the Honour of the Right Highe, Mightye and Noble Princesse Marie Quene of Scotlande* (London [i.e. Rheims], 1569).[51] Then, in May, he bought another copy of Leslie's *Defence* from 1569 in another sale, a duplicate of the edition he had bought a couple of months earlier.[52]

His contemporary books on Marian scholarship more broadly also suggest that the 1770s were an important peak for his interest in the debate. Despite being first published in 1759, Hunter's copy of Robertson's *History of Scotland* was purchased in 1771 and his copy of Anderson's *Collections* was bought at the British Museum duplicates sale of 1769. Casting doubt on Chalmers' suggestion noted above, that the *Collections* had been sold for the price of waste paper quickly after publication, Hunter bought his set for the not inconsiderable sum of seventeen shillings, something which may point towards high demand for the volume in the rare books market.[53] Hunter's copy of Hume's *History of England* was also the 1770 edition, perhaps all indicative of some kind of particular personal interest in Mary in the 1760s and 1770s.[54] It also suggests a sustained desire to collect items on Mary over quite a long period, at least fourteen years.

---

[50] Now GUASC, Sp. Coll. Hunterian Bb.4.16. The authenticity of this inscription is still debated. John Durkan concluded that the signature is a forgery, before speculating that it might in fact be in the hand of a juvenile Mary: see John Durkan, 'The Library of Mary Queen of Scots', *The Innes Review* 38 (2010): 80–81. Recent study suggests that it may well be the type of book a young Mary might have read and owned: see Catriona MacLaughlin, 'Los Doze Libros de la Eneida', unpublished blog post, on Art, Culture and Patronage in Renaissance Scotland, 1406–1625: A Showcase of Material Relating to Renaissance and Reformation Scotland Housed in the Historic Collections of the University of Glasgow (2018) https://glasgowuniscotrenaissance.wordpress.com/2018/03/06/los-doze-libros-de-la-eneida-1557, accessed 8 September 2023.

[51] GUASC, Sp. Coll. Hunterian Cn.3.40 and Sp. Coll. Hunterian Cn.3.37 respectively.

[52] Identified from annotated records of both the Hoblyn sale, BL, S.C.S. 11(4), and the Channing and Wilson sale, BL, S.C.S. 11(5). There is now only one copy in his collection.

[53] BL, S.C.S. 12(5). Many of Hunter's volumes were bought for only a few shillings at auction, though sets of volumes were invariably bought for higher prices. It is likely that Anderson's editions more generally reached high prices. An advertisement at the beginning of a translation of Ruddiman's introduction to the *Diplomata Scotiae* notes that the original edition of the work, discussed in note 4 above, was 'a book of high price, exceeding scarce, and only to be found in the cabinets of the curious': see Thomas Ruddiman, *An Introduction to Mr James Anderson's Diplomata Scotiae* (Edinburgh, 1773), p. 3.

[54] It is, of course, altogether possible that Hunter had earlier copies of both Robertson's and Hume's histories, replacing them with later, updated editions. His copies of both Robertson and Anderson contain no marginalia. The story behind Hunter's volumes of Hume's *History* on the other hand are unknown: they were part of a small number of books destroyed by mould when the Hunterian Library was stored in caves during the Second World War.

This is intensified when we look elsewhere. Firmly part of the Scottish intellectual and social circles of London, Hunter was a friend of David Hume and shared mutual friends with William Robertson. Debates around Mary were intensified in the mid-eighteenth century by new evaluations of the Casket Letters, triggered by William Goodall's *An Examination of the Letters Said to be Written by Mary Queen of Scotland to James Earl of Bothwell; Shewing by Intrinsick and Extrinsick Evidence that they are Forgeries* (Edinburgh, 1754). Both William Robertson in his *History of Scotland* (London, 1759) and David Hume in his *History of England* (London, 1754–62) took issue with Goodall's account, arguing that the Casket Letters were genuine, whilst William Tytler's *Historical and Critical Enquiry into the Evidence Against Mary Queen of Scots* (Edinburgh, 1760) believed the opposite.[55] The intrigue and debate caused by the Casket Letters in the middle of the eighteenth century very much triggered a secondary debate around the personal character and morality of Mary herself. Robertson and Hunter may have met when the former was in London in 1758, especially as Robertson is known to have met others in Hunter's close social sphere, such as the writer and critic Tobias Smollett (1721–71), on the same trip.[56] The love of Mary and her story became more intense when Robertson pre-circulated his manuscript and concluded talks with his future publisher, Andrew Millar (1705–68), allowing him to state 'you will wonder even in this great place [London], how I have got Mary Queen of Scots to be a subject of conversation'.[57] Gavin Hamilton's painting 'The Abdication of Mary Queen of Scots', now owned by The Hunterian but originally commissioned in 1765 by writer and lawyer James Boswell (1740–95), was emblematic of the move to see Mary as a sympathetic figure, likely directly inspired by Robertson's own portrayal of the queen.[58]

Although Hunter's interaction with these debates is largely unknown, we can assume that he was part of the hubbub growing around Robertson at this point. Although the library was collected as a private one, it very much had a social function and, as part of these scholarly and literary elites, others were invited to use Hunter's books. Although it is notably incomplete and thus offers an unreliable study of books read and borrowed by others, a short borrower register

---

[55] Wormald, *Mary Queen of Scots*, p. 6. David Hume's *History* was published in six volumes, with the volume covering the period of Mary and Elizabeth (vol. 4) published in 1759.
[56] Hunter will also have known Robertson's cousin William Pitcairn (1712–91) who, like Hunter, was a Scottish physician based in London. Pitcairn is known to have entertained Robertson on his trip: see Smitten, *The Life of William Robertson*, p. 113.
[57] Ibid., p. 115.
[58] With thanks to Anne Dulau Beveridge. The painting now has the modern reference number GLAHA: 43874.

exists that lists books borrowed from the library.⁵⁹ Interestingly, even within this short list, there is one book on this register related to Mary. A 'Dr Franklin, Queen St.' borrowed the 'Defence of Mary Queen of Scots'.⁶⁰ Although Hunter knew Dr Benjamin Franklin (1706–90), the American was known to live on Craven Street in this period, so this is perhaps unlikely to refer to him. The addition of the address in the entry is also interesting from another perspective: not added to many of the entries, it may indicate that this individual was not part of Hunter's immediate social sphere. A note at the start of the register is dated to September 1771, suggesting the volume was borrowed in the 1770s, again perhaps indicative of avid discussion amongst Hunter and his circle over Mary at this point.

Hunter was thus a useful contact for borrowing rare and older books. Yet often it is useful to consider both what is in a collection, and what is missing from it. One might argue that Hunter in fact did not actually own many books on Mary. There are several sixteenth-century editions of Leslie's works, and a copy of Adam Blackwood (1539–1613), alongside the important 1715 edition of George Buchanan edited by Thomas Ruddiman, said to have had an impact on early eighteenth-century reassessments of Mary.⁶¹ Although there is no edition of Camden's *Annales*, there is Udall's translation *The Historie of the Life and Death of Mary Stuart, Queene of Scotland*, originally published in 1624 but found in Hunter's collection in the later 1636 edition.⁶² There are also the eighteenth-century accounts we would expect: Anderson, Hume and Robertson. Missing, however, are many of the more partisan accounts of the later periods that triggered or intensified much of the debate through the period: there are no editions of William Tytler, Samuel Jebb or William Goodall, for example. It is unclear what the precise reasons for this might be. It is possible that these editions were simply harder to source, something that may perhaps be unlikely since Hunter would have been able to buy both William Tytler and William Goodall's publications new. It is also possible that Hunter was simply less interested in these debates, and more interested in returning to original, contemporary sources or viewing more impartial attempts at history and source criticism, typical of the methodology of many of the eighteenth-century authors already noted. Such an approach would also fit with the empirical approach that Hunter and the circle of scientists, physicians and antiquarians around him adopted both in their daily professional work and also in their

---

⁵⁹ The register only notes thirty-five volumes borrowed from Hunter's collection over a ten-year period from 1771 to 1781 so is very likely only a picture of borrowing and use of his books. For more on borrowing and use of the library see Craig, 'The Library of Dr William Hunter', pp. 137–46.
⁶⁰ GUASC, Sp. Coll. MS Hunter 315.
⁶¹ See Wormald, *Mary Queen of Scots*, pp. 5–6.
⁶² GUASC, Sp. Coll. Hunterian Cn.3.36.

more general approach to books and manuscripts of all ages in their collections. As with Anderson, what underpinned the methodological approaches within Hunter's circle was detailed and sustained critical evaluation and the questioning of received histories. This was achieved through the close reading and comparison of printed books and manuscripts, awareness of the place of books and authors within the history of ideas and their wider contemporary contexts, and the study of the physical properties of the books themselves.[63] Interested in establishing chronologies in his own research, Hunter would have been very interested in Anderson's attempt to comprehend the printing history of Buchanan's *Ane Detectioun*, for example. Moreover, Hunter's library served an important social function, existing as a platform for the creation and exchange of ideas, so he would have seen the value of these Marian volumes in his collections for future debate, research and publications on the topic.

Conclusion

The anonymous reviewer of William Tytler's *Historical and Critical Enquiry* (Edinburgh, 1760) concluded that, despite Tytler's bold attempt to rescue Mary's legacy, the truth regarding her involvement in the death of Lord Darnley would always be illusive, and instead allowed for nothing more than literary sparring and the display of an author's rhetorical skill and technique: '[s]uch indeed are the allegations on both sides, that the truth must ever remain problematical; and this a question which may afford scope for the display of talents, but never proofs or presumptions that can amount to conviction'.[64]

This chapter has explored how the question of Mary and her life became closely tied to the nature of history writing itself in the eighteenth century, at least amongst elite readers, writers and collectors. Although true impartiality was impossible, and accounts that attempted to be as impartial as possible always found their critics, efforts were actively made by some to move away from strict polemic. Both the writers of Marian history and those, like Hunter, who were tangentially involved in the debates by providing access to books and manuscripts but ultimately left no evidence as to what they thought, were providing different platforms for debate around Mary in the eighteenth century. That such platforms were successful is highlighted by the fact that Mary appears to have been actively discussed in the circles around Hume, Robertson and Hunter in the 1760s and 1770s and in the coffee houses and salons of London and Edinburgh. Showing a pattern across the eighteenth century, then, both Hunter and Anderson were interested in laying out chronologies and provenance and in assessing the reliability of texts. Their scholarly motivation

---

[63] For more on this see Craig, 'The Library of Dr William Hunter'.
[64] *The Critical Review or Annals of Literature*, vol. 9 (London, 1760), p. 432.

is also linked, providing platforms by which individuals might access and evaluate sources on their own accord. It is difficult to judge the impact of such endeavours on how Mary was seen and considered in the eighteenth century, let alone whether such an approach had any impact outside these scholarly, literary and intellectual circles. New big-data projects such as the Books and Borrowing, 1750–1830 project based at the University of Stirling will allow for more analysis of what Marian books were borrowed and, potentially, read by users from different social strata in Scotland, allowing us to start to understand the impact of these approaches and eighteenth-century thinking on Mary much more broadly.[65]

---

[65] Katherine Halsey (PI) et al., 'Books and Borrowing, 1750–1830: An Analysis of Scottish Borrowers' Registers', University of Stirling, https://borrowing.stir.ac.uk, accessed 8 September 2023.

SIX

The Battle for Memory: The Reception of Mary, Queen of Scots in the Eighteenth-century British Periodical Press

Rhona Brown

In the eighteenth century, Mary, Queen of Scots was what she remains today: a contested, controversial figure with a contested and controversial legacy. As eighteenth-century commentators grapple with a complex icon and a difficult moment in Scottish history, assumptions are made about the queen's morality, sovereignty, guilt and innocence. However, the century also sees a conscious break from the stark polarity exhibited by some of Mary's contemporaries in seeing her as either diabolically bad or saintly good, and a move towards examining the evidence of her guilt or innocence in its original form, scrutiny of the divarication of her historical context and an attempt – at least in some quarters – at producing a balanced picture of her life and reign. In this context, we see Scottish Enlightenment thinkers advertising their own supposedly evolved and rational state, but also sincere advancement towards an objective approach to Mary's strengths and weaknesses as woman and as monarch, as well as to her guilt or innocence in the crimes for which she died. Significantly, eighteenth-century commentators focus almost exclusively on whether or not Mary could have had a hand in the violent death of her second husband, Henry Stuart, Lord Darnley (1545–67), and on the still-vexed question of whether the 'Casket Letters' and accompanying poems were the queen's own work or forged in a fabrication of evidence against her. Although schisms still exist in eighteenth-century debates about Mary, the context of Enlightenment writings on, for example, Francis Hutcheson's (1694–1746) conception of an innate human 'moral sense' and the understanding of sympathy and empathy through the writings of Adam Smith (1723–90), alongside the rise in popularity of the literature of Sensibility, embodied in Scotland by Henry Mackenzie's (1745–1831) tear-stained novella *The Man of Feeling* (1771), means that a new kind of feeling enters long-standing debates on Mary's life and fate.

The reception of Mary in British periodicals of the first half of the century consisted mainly of reviews and often barbed responses to the latest histories with Mary as their subject. As the century wore on, new research was undertaken on the 'Casket Sonnets' by Scottish historian Walter Goodall (1706?–66), sources were examined in attempts at authentication, and Mary's poetry and correspondence were sought and published in magazines. Towards the end of the eighteenth century, Mary became an increasingly common subject for fiction, with new novels, plays and poems on her life and loves discussed in magazines. As the nineteenth century dawned, and the 'magazine for women' was more securely established, she became a subject for women's moral reflection and instruction. This chapter analyses these periodical debates, positing that while some of Mary's eighteenth-century commentators could be partisan and bigoted, others made a genuine attempt to treat her story not just with 'enlightened' lucidity, but with humanity and sympathy.

An anonymous review of Samuel Jebb's *The History of the Life and Reign of Mary Queen of Scots* (1725) in London's *New Memoirs of Literature* sets the scene for eighteenth-century debates on the queen. According to the reviewer, '[t]he several Writers . . . who have undertaken to give us the history of Mary Queen of Scots, have been either so extravagant in her praises, as to allow no human errors to have fallen to her share; or have heaped upon her such a load of infamy, as to make her appear a very monster in wickedness'.[1] The reviewer's summation of the body of work on Mary's life as one of extreme, oppositional conflict continues into his characterisation of the sixteenth century, which is all but dismissed as a period of irrational religious revolution:

> The Reformation . . . had then divided the world into parties; and as that Princess was zealous in the cause of the Romish religion, 'twas look'd upon as the distinguishing mark of a good Protestant, to tarnish her character, and blacken her reputation. On the other hand, the Roman-Catholics, respecting her as a Martyr for the Church of Rome, have swelled their Panegyricks, whilst they have represented her as a perfect pattern of purity and virtue, without any blemish.[2]

Although this reviewer indirectly suggests otherwise, polarised responses to Mary remain a fixture of eighteenth-century commentary, and it is undeniable that some are motivated or at least informed by the religious attachments he implies were specifically sixteenth-century challenges. However, if only on the surface, eighteenth-century Marian schisms are represented by authors as being driven by scholarly and moral, rather than partisan religious, concerns. His context allows this commentator to look back on unruly, sectarian sixteenth-century

---

[1] *New Memoirs of Literature* (London), vol. 2 (July 1725), p. 46.
[2] *New Memoirs of Literature*, vol. 2 (July 1725), p. 46.

Scotland with the balanced, rational and (in his implied view) civilised mind of the eighteenth-century thinker. In keeping with Enlightenment ideals of progress and emerging ideas of history as an ever-evolving trajectory, as outlined in Adam Ferguson's (1723–1816) *Essay on the History of Civil Society* (1767) and the stadial theory espoused in *Lectures on Jurisprudence* (1763) by Smith, this commentator looks back on Mary's religious and political contexts with a somewhat patronising eye. As will become clear, this is a common eighteenth-century approach to Mary and to the historical moment in which she found herself. Indeed, as I will discuss, certain commentators wish that Mary had been born two hundred years later, in their own apparently more sympathetic and less savage time, where she would, it is implied, have been treated with dignity, respect and justice.

From the *Memoirs of Literature* review comes another strand in eighteenth-century thinking about Mary's culpability or otherwise in the death of Darnley. Predictably, the Casket Letters take a central role in these debates, with many critics making an oversimplified calculation: if Mary was the author of these documents, she is guilty; if they were forged, she is innocent. Indeed, in a review of William Maitland's (c. 1693–1757) *History and Antiquities of Scotland* (1757), the reviewer states that, following Goodall's conclusion that the Casket Letters were forged, 'the whole charge against Mary's reputation falls to the ground: for, it does not appear in history, that she had the least knowledge or concern in the death of her husband'.[3] Thus continues a drawn-out debate – not quite solved in the eighteenth century or beyond – over the vilification of Mary, which has the analysis of documentary evidence at its heart. At this juncture, commentators profess to be swayed only by corroborating evidence. In reality, of course, other motivating factors come into play in the evolving reception of Mary.

Nowhere is this more apparent than in the case of one particularly vocal, tireless and perhaps unexpected supporter of Mary. Tobias Smollett (1721–71), Scottish novelist, historian, journalist, periodicals editor, physician and prominent unionist, is extraordinarily consistent in his rational defence of Mary in the face of what he sees as blinding partiality. Indeed, Smollett's sustained plea for sympathy for the queen may in fact be a component of his unionist strategy: while focusing on a moment at which Scotland and England were pulling in different directions may seem counterintuitive in Smollett's programme of support for the British union, Scotland was facing comparable challenges at mid-century under the premiership of Britain's first Scottish prime minister, the unpopular John Stuart, third earl of Bute (1713–92). The violently vocal, often Scotophobic opposition to Bute's ministry by figures such as John Wilkes (1725–97) prompted the launch of a pro-government periodical entitled *The Briton* (1762–63), edited by Smollett. In indignant response, Wilkes created his

---

[3] *The Critical Review, or, Annals of Literature* (London), vol. 3 (April 1757), p. 290.

The North Briton (1762–63), a paper loudly critical of Bute, whose libellous proclamations saw Wilkes imprisoned.[4] Smollett's plea for sympathy for the historical Mary is akin to his appeal for compassion for Bute and his government in *The Briton*, and to his petition for an understanding of the Scots and Scotland in his novel *The Expedition of Humphry Clinker* (1771): pouring cold water on vitriolic attacks, Smollett asks for calm reflection on the facts, and rational curiosity and sympathy for the human beings involved. In this, his journalistic work is also significant. The review of Maitland's *History and Antiquities of Scotland* quoted above is likely to have been written by Smollett. Here, he enters the debate on the devastating role of the Casket Letters in Mary's death and reputation:

> We likewise perceive that [Maitland] has chosen to follow those authors who have endeavoured to blacken the character of Mary queen of Scots. His severity upon the memory of that amiable and unfortunate princess is the more remarkable, as he seems to have perused the performance of Goodall, who, in our opinion, has proved the forgery of the letters in the casket, in such a manner, that a man must be strangely warped by prejudice, who can refute his assent to the truth of the demonstration.[5]

For Smollett, that Maitland could remain 'prejudiced' against Mary in the face of exculpatory evidence is proof of irrational bias. Central to Smollett's argument is a crucial text in Mary's eighteenth-century reception: Walter Goodall's *Examination of the Letters said to have been written by Mary Queen of Scots* (1754). Goodall's is a foundational text for contemporary pro-Marian commentators in that it purports, through forensic literary and linguistic analysis, to provide evidence that the Casket Letters were forged and, therefore, that Mary had been wrongly condemned on their testimony. Many contemporaries accepted Goodall's conclusions, with one reviewer describing the *Examination* as providing 'evidence . . . in her vindication',[6] and another regarding Goodall's as one of 'the most masterly pens of the age'.[7] On the other hand, some accused Goodall of allowing his evidence to lead him to a pro-Marian portrait. For a contributor to the *Monthly Review*, 'it is obvious, that he is not disinterested enough to be depended on as to facts, and therefore his performance merits not a serious refutation'.[8] Goodall's *Examination* garnered more plaudits than criticisms, albeit mainly in Smollett's own *Critical Review*, and it provides an evidential underpinning for the arguments of eighteenth-century Marian apologists.

---

[4] See Rhona Brown, 'Wilkes and Scottish Liberty: The Reception of John Wilkes in the *Weekly Magazine, or Edinburgh Amusement*' in *Before Blackwood's: Scottish Journalism in the Age of Enlightenment*, ed. Alex Benchimol, Rhona Brown and David Shuttleton (London, 2015).
[5] *The Critical Review, or, Annals of Literature* (London), vol. 3 (April 1757), p. 290.
[6] *The Critical Review*, vol. 6 (December 1758), p. 483.
[7] *The Critical Review*, vol. 9 (June 1760), p. 421.
[8] *Monthly Review, or, Literary Journal* (London), vol. 13 (October 1755), p. 300.

Smollett's review of Maitland's *History* moves from its surprise at the author's rejection of Goodall's conclusions to a depiction of Mary's contemporaries as hopelessly corrupt:

> Her enemies and calumniators were a set of gloomy, rancorous, hypocritical religionists, blind to every attraction of elegance, dead to the sentiment of honour and generosity . . . In a word, the Scots were so degenerate at this period, that there does not seem to have been a wise or an honest man in the whole kingdom.[9]

Smollett here demonstrates the belief that Mary's circumstances were impossible, but simultaneously brings those black-and-white religious polarities he decries into the eighteenth century by portraying the Protestant reformers simplistically as 'blind' and 'dead' to the beauty, honour and 'elegance' offered by Mary. Indeed, in a review of Smollett's *Complete History of England* (1757–65), the *Critical Review* for June 1757 states that '[t]he catastrophe of the beauteous Mary queen of Scots, is an affecting proof of the author's talent for the *pathetic* . . . which the humane reader will not peruse without emotion'.[10] Building on Goodall's linguistic analysis, Smollett's approach is one of sympathy for Mary's tragic plight. For this reviewer, Smollett's Mary becomes an object of pathos and the perfect theme for an author of the literature of Sensibility, which emphasises emotional responses to 'pathetic' people and situations and the application of the 'moral sense'. Smollett's contemporary, Mackenzie, would create a paragon of Sensibility in Harley, the protagonist of *The Man of Feeling* whose 'concern is with the arousing of emotion in the reader',[11] for emotional responsiveness 'was considered to indicate the truly perceptive mind'.[12] For Smollett, the evidence exonerates Mary, but so too does the 'humane' and sympathetic response to her life that the literature of Sensibility encourages.

William Robertson's (1721–93) *History of Scotland, during the Reigns of Queen Mary and King James VI* (1759), another core text in the eighteenth-century reception of the queen, is reviewed in the *Critical Review* for February 1759. Here, Robertson is praised for his ability to rise above Mary's historical context, in which she was:

> by one numerous party held to be illustrious for her virtues; and by another, infamous for her crimes . . . Queen Mary is presented to us, neither as a divine nor an infernal, but a human object; a woman with female failings; a character mixed with virtues and vices, such as merits, on many accounts, or condemnation, whilst there is much room left for our pity in deploring her misfortunes.[13]

---

[9] *The Critical Review*, vol. 3 (April 1757), pp. 290–91.
[10] *The Critical Review*, vol. 3 (June 1757), p. 490.
[11] Kenneth Simpson, *The Protean Scot: The Crisis of Identity in Eighteenth-Century Scottish Literature* (Aberdeen, 1988), p. 145.
[12] Kenneth C. Slagle, 'Introduction' to Henry Mackenzie, *The Man of Feeling* (London, 1958), p. vii.
[13] *The Critical Review*, vol. 7 (February 1759), p. 91.

Robertson's text was not, however, without its critics. It was, in fact, central to the eighteenth-century 'Marian Controversy', 'the battle between Mary's detractors and partisans over the authenticity of the famed "Casket Letters"'.[14] Robertson stood with David Hume (1711–76), who argued in his *History of England under the House of Tudor* (1754–61) that Mary was worthy of compassion but guilty of all alleged misdeeds, on the supposedly anti-Marian side of the 'battle', while William Tytler (1711–92) argued in his *Inquiry, Historical and Critical, into the Evidence against Mary Queen of Scots, and an Examination of the Histories of Dr Robertson and David Hume with Respect to that Evidence* (1759) on the opposing side. According to Laurence L. Bongie, Tytler's *Inquiry* 'was immediately viewed as a complete vindication of Mary Stuart and one which triumphantly drove the malicious Hume and Robertson from the field'.[15] At the heart of the controversy was evidence: while Hume denounced Tytler as 'a very mangey Cur' who deserved 'a sound beating or even a Rope' for challenging his authority on Mary so publicly, his vitriol probably arose from the fact that, as Bongie has argued, 'Tytler had caught Hume out on several easily verifiable points of fact, the account of which he saw himself obliged to modify for succeeding editions of his *History*'.[16]

At this point, documents purported to have been authored by Mary – or at least transcriptions of documents that did not surface in their originals – make their way into periodicals. One is a particularly scandalous letter, presented as having been written by Mary to Elizabeth I but either intercepted or unsent, that first appeared in the *London Magazine* for February 1759 and was thereafter reprinted in numerous periodicals across the next twenty years, including the *Annual Register*, the *Newcastle General Magazine*, the *British Magazine* and the *Town and Country Magazine*. The letter was also published in several late eighteenth- and early nineteenth-century sources, including John Whitaker's *Mary Queen of Scots Vindicated* (1788) and Hugh Campbell's *Love Letters of Mary Queen of Scots, to James Earl of Bothwell* (1824), and although the manuscript has not survived, it is regarded by some twenty-first-century Marian scholars, including Retha M. Warnicke, as genuine.[17] Presented as Mary's apparently dutiful but nonetheless hurtful reporting of gossip she has heard spoken against Elizabeth by Elizabeth Cavendish (*c.* 1527–1608), later Elizabeth Talbot, countess of Shrewsbury (also known as Bess of Hardwick), the letter is full of scurrilous details about Queen Elizabeth's active but dysfunctional sex life,

---

[14] Laurence L. Bongie, 'The Eighteenth-Century Marian Controversy and an Unpublished Letter by David Hume', *Studies in Scottish Literature*, 1 (1964) no. 4: 236–52, at p. 236.
[15] Bongie, 'The Eighteenth-Century Marian Controversy', p. 241.
[16] Bongie, 'The Eighteenth-Century Marian Controversy', pp. 242–43.
[17] See Retha M. Warnicke, *Mary Queen of Scots* (London, 2006), pp. 217–18.

her overweening vanity and violence towards subordinates. The *British Magazine* for April 1760 gives details of its apparent provenance:

> For the entertainment of the reader we have endeavoured to translate a very curious letter, written in old French by Mary Queen of Scots, during her imprisonment at Chatsworth, to queen Elizabeth, dated July 10, 1586. This is one of the letters which . . . were intercepted and prevented from coming to the knowledge of Elizabeth, by lord Burghley, who nevertheless preserved them carefully . . . they were afterwards buried two feet under ground, in his son the earl of Salisbury's house at Hatfield in Hertfordshire, where they were found a few years ago in a stone chest, rolled up in woollen; and shewn by the publisher of Burghley's papers to the late master of the rolls . . . This account, however, is disowned by a late reverend editor of state papers.[18]

Some facts presented here stand up to scrutiny: from early 1569, Mary was in the custody of George Talbot, sixth earl of Shrewsbury (*c*. 1522–90) and his wife, Bess of Hardwick, and is known to have been confined at Chatsworth House, Derbyshire, one of the Talbots' homes. William Cecil, first baron Burghley (1520/21–98), Elizabeth's chief advisor who was key to the condemnation of Mary, was succeeded by his son, Robert Cecil, first earl of Salisbury (1563–1612), as Elizabeth's Lord Privy Seal. Following his role in securing the Union of the Crowns in 1603, King James VI and I gifted the younger Cecil the estate of Hatfield House, Hertfordshire, which Cecil spent many years remodelling. The *British Magazine* editor's implication is that the Cecils were motivated to retain and conceal evidence connected to Mary, given their pivotal role in her downfall.

The letter, as it is printed in the *London Magazine*, is explained as having been 'lately made publick'[19] in *A Collection of state papers relating to affairs in the reign of Queen Elizabeth, from the year 1571 to 1596* (1759), as transcribed and edited by William Murdin (1703–60). It is lengthy, packed with gossip and accusations, and strikes a curious balance in tone between indirectly berating Elizabeth and exposing her tyrannical behaviour, while at the same time pleading for her mercy and protection. It begins with the detail that 'a person, to whom you had promised marriage in presence of a lady of your bed chamber, had lain with you an infinite number of times, with all that freedom and intimacy of a husband with his wife; but that you certainly were not like other women',[20] and continues with reports of Elizabeth's 'unqueenly' behaviour, including her 'wantonly dallying . . . with new lovers', particularly her favourite, Sir Christopher Hatton

---

[18] *The British Magazine, or, Monthly Repository for Gentlemen and Ladies* (London), vol. 1 (April 1760), p. 189.
[19] *London Magazine, or, Gentleman's Monthly Intelligencer* (London), vol. 28 (February 1759), p. 78.
[20] *London Magazine* (February 1759), p. 78.

(1540–91), to whom 'you also revealed the secrets of state, thus betraying your own counsels'.[21] 'Mary' goes on to charge Elizabeth with extreme vanity, alleging that it was said that 'you were so vain, that you had as high an opinion of your beauty, as if you were some celestial goddess . . . people could not look you full in the face, because the brightness of your countenance was like that of the sun'.[22] Elizabeth is accused of petulant violence, such as giving Chamberlain of the Exchequer Sir William Killigrew (d. 1622) 'a blow to the ear',[23] and against John Scudamore (1542–1623), 'whose finger you broke, and gave out at court, that it was done by the falling of a candlestick; and that another of your servants you cut across the hand with a great knife'.[24] After revealing these details in the ostensible role of dutiful messenger, Mary ends by beseeching Elizabeth: 'it never once entered into my thoughts to injure you by revealing it; and . . . I shall never speak of it, as I look upon it to be very false'.[25] Mary pleads for 'an hour to speak with you' and finishes her letter thus: 'For God's sake secure to yourself her who is both willing and able to do you service'.[26]

Apart from the *British Magazine*'s notes on the letter's provenance, Mary's letter is presented without commentary, leaving *London Magazine* readers to make up their own minds about the letter's authenticity and the veracity of its contents. They are also left to decide on the editors' motivations for publishing it. On one hand, it shows Mary's spitefulness; on the other, it demonstrates Elizabeth's vain cruelty. In any case, the lack of a surviving manuscript and centuries of Mary-centred rumour raise questions about the letter's validity. Given that Mary's letters to Elizabeth are generally formal, deferential and supplicatory, the tone and content of the 'Scandal Letter', as it is sometimes known, is provocative and confrontational, even if the author presents herself as the mere mouthpiece for gossip she does not believe, and even if the letter never made it to Elizabeth's hands. While rumours of Elizabeth's abusive behaviour towards her courtiers survived into the twentieth century,[27] the almost novelistic account of the scurrilities of Elizabeth's court in the 'Scandal Letter' resembles the salacious depictions of 'low life' in contemporary texts such as Daniel Defoe's *Moll Flanders* (1722), bringing the concerns of moralist picaresque fiction into accounts of the historical elite.

Perhaps as a result of the wide distribution of the 'Scandal Letter', commentators grew louder in their criticism of Elizabeth in relation to Mary from the 1750s onwards. In a review of Robertson's *History of Scotland* in the *Monthly*

---

[21] *London Magazine* (February 1759), p. 78.
[22] *London Magazine* (February 1759), p. 78.
[23] *London Magazine* (February 1759), p. 78.
[24] *London Magazine* (February 1759), p. 79.
[25] *London Magazine* (February 1759), p. 79.
[26] *London Magazine* (February 1759), p. 79.
[27] See Elizabeth Jenkins, *Elizabeth the Great* (London, 1958).

Review for February 1759, the reviewer states that, '[h]owever vicious Mary was, we cannot forbear condemning Elizabeth; who, out of policy as a Queen, and perhaps more out of jealousy as a woman, treated her sister with such unnatural rigour'.[28] As is common in debates about the relationship between Mary and Elizabeth, their 'rivalry' is driven by female jealousy as much as queenly 'policy'. Just as the *Critical Review* commentator describes Mary as suffering from 'female failings', here Elizabeth is motivated by a jealousy that is gendered female.

A review of David Hume's *History of England* in the *Monthly Review* for May 1759 returns to the 'Scandal Letter', as attributed to Mary, in its criticism of Elizabeth's actions. Although the reviewer questions how far 'all these imputations against Elizabeth can be credited' and 'may, perhaps appear doubtful', Elizabeth's relationships with noblemen 'render her chastity very suspicious'. In support of the accusations in the 'Scandal Letter', the reviewer describes Hume's view of Elizabeth's self-conceit as 'extravagant', and states that she was known to 'beat her maids of honour: and the blow she gave to Essex, before the privy council, is another remarkable instance'.[29] Although Hume is later vilified alongside Robertson for his 'partial' account, he is, via this review, unapologetic in his portrayal of Elizabeth's faults, and indirectly substantiates the accusations made in the 'Scandal Letter'. Elizabeth's hypocrisy as the 'Virgin Queen' is highlighted, and implicit comparisons are made between Elizabeth's promiscuity and the oft-cited 'female failings' of Mary in her relationships. And again, the reviewer's emphasis is on contemporary expectations of female virtue and purity.

At the close of the 1750s, another Marian fixation appears in the pages of the periodical press: the obsessive preoccupation with representations of Mary's execution, death and attendant minute, macabre details. The *Gentleman's Magazine* for September 1759 prints the entire passage on Mary's death from the 1759 publication of the *Life of Mary Queen of Scots*, and in doing so emphasises details upon which other publications will also dwell: the tears of her courtiers and maidservants, Mary's quiet and humble patience in death, her steadfast faithfulness to her Roman Catholicism despite attempts to lead her to conversion, and the fact that, when she was beheaded, she was revealed to have been wearing a wig over cropped, greyed hair. This portrayal of Mary's death features the reported speech of Mary, including her plea to be commended to her son James – 'tell him I have done nothing injurious to his kingdom, to his honour, or to his rights; and God forgive all those who have thirsted, without cause, for my blood'[30] – and her wish for 'mercy only thro' the death of *Christ*, at the foot of whose image she now willingly shed her blood; and lifting up and kissing the crucifix, she thus addressed it, "As thy arms O *Jesus*, were extended

---

[28] *Monthly Review*, vol. 20 (February 1759), p. 177.
[29] *Monthly Review*, vol. 20 (May 1759), p. 410.
[30] *The Gentleman's Magazine: and Historical Chronicle* (London), vol. 29 (September 1759), p. 480.

on the cross; so with the outstretched arms of thy mercy, receive me, and forgive my sins."'[31] The review ends as follows:

> Thus died *Mary*, and thus lived *Elizabeth*. Over that part of *Mary*'s character which virtue cannot approve, humanity will ever draw the veil of compassion, and incline every tender and generous mind to impute her faults rather to her situation than disposition ... But the conduct of *Elizabeth* is such as cannot fail to excite a degree of abhorrence and indignation, which we know not how to think any misfortunes would soften into pity. Her dissimulation was not extorted by present distress and inextricable difficulty, but practised to gratify the wanton wishes of ambition and resentment; and her cruelty was not prompted by intolerable injuries or sudden and impetuous passion, but was the deliberate and voluntary tribute of cunning, to interest.[32]

In place of partisan views of her frailties, this commentator unites all 'feeling minds' – reflecting his own eighteenth-century affective sympathy – in Mary's support and in opposition to the 'cunning' Elizabeth. Smollett's black-and-white view of Mary pitted against the Protestant nobles is here replaced by Mary against the cruel Elizabeth, who is understood as having destroyed Mary to protect her own power. In both accounts, Mary is a victim of malice, jealousy and circumstance, and an object of pathos over whom the sensitive reader of 'tender mind' will drop a tear, as they would the wretched characters of a novel of Sensibility.

In 1760, Scottish lawyer and historian William Tytler's (1711–92) *Historical and Critical Enquiry into the Evidence produced by the Earls of Murray and Morton, against Mary Queen of Scots* was published in response to his predecessors, Robertson and Hume, and reviewed in the *Monthly Review* for July 1760. Here, the reviewer is relieved that civilisation has progressed since Mary's time, with a comment that says as much about his own context as it does about the sixteenth century:

> We remember the time when a man who would not believe Mary a monster, without evidence, ran the risk of being stigmatized as a Jacobite. Thank heaven, these narrow prejudices begin to subside; and as the principles of the *Review* are so well established, we shall deliver our sentiments of the article before us, without disguise.[33]

This is a rare mention of an issue bubbling under the surface of eighteenth-century accounts of Mary, and the remnants, two hundred years later, of the Reformation's division of 'the world into parties', as it was put in the 1725

---

[31] *The Gentleman's Magazine*, vol. 29 (September 1759), p. 480.
[32] *The Gentleman's Magazine*, vol. 29 (September 1759), p. 481.
[33] *Monthly Review*, vol. 23 (July 1760), p. 30.

review of Jebb's *History*. This reviewer admits that, during and following the Jacobite uprisings of the first half of the eighteenth century, pro-Marian utterances could betray their author as anti-Hanoverian with potentially dangerous consequences. Although James Francis Edward Stuart (1688–1766) and his son, Charles Edward Stuart (1720–88) – the 'Old Pretender' and 'Young Pretender' respectively – were public icons of the Jacobite cause, Mary was a significant subject of Jacobite memorialisation. One unofficial chronicler of Mary's role in Jacobite debates is Sir James Steuart, third baronet of Goodtrees (1712–80), whose manuscript notes on Hume's *History of England* reassess some of the philosopher's statements on Mary's morality, branding them as naked attempts to dilute the queen's power as a Stuart monarch and to privilege the Hanoverian narrative, while denouncing the author's 'tendency to lay heavy judgments against the weaker sex' in the misogynistic mode 'of John Knox and George Buchanan, whose tracts presented Mary as licentious, lusty, and deserving of her downfall'.[34]

While Steuart's notes remained unpublished until the twenty-first century, the *Monthly Review* commentator states that, a mere fourteen years after Culloden, the 'stigma' attached to Stuart supporters is on the wane, implying that, thanks to the period's self-professed rationality, it is now safe to defend Mary without being branded a Jacobite. Whatever the contemporary reality of this statement, Mary became a symbol through which reviewers could reveal their enlightened sympathy. Indeed, the tide of opinion by 1760 was that the Casket Letters were forgeries and that she had been framed. In the *Gentleman's Magazine* for October 1760, in a review of Tytler's *Enquiry* by prominent author, critic and lexicographer Samuel Johnson (1709–84), this is a matter of confidence: '[t]hat the letters were forged is now made so probable, that perhaps they will never more be cited as testimonies'.[35] Johnson goes on to address the issue of Mary's association with the Jacobite cause:

> It has now been fashionable for near half a century to defame and vilify the house of *Stuart*, and to exalt and magnify the reign of *Elizabeth*. The *Stuarts* have found few apologists, for the dead cannot pay for praise; and who will, without reward, oppose the tide of popularity? Yet there remains still among us, not wholly extinguished, a zeal for truth, a desire for establishing right, in opposition to fashion.[36]

---

[34] Cailean Gallagher, 'Lies, Liberty, and the Fall of the Stuarts: James Steuart's Commentary on Hume's *History of England*', *History of European Ideas* 46 (2020) no. 4: 438–57; see also Murray Pittock, *Material Culture and Sedition, 1688–1760: Treacherous Objects, Secret Places* (London, 2013).

[35] *The Gentleman's Magazine*, vol. 30 (October 1760), p. 456.

[36] *The Gentleman's Magazine*, vol. 30 (October 1760), p. 453.

For Johnson, anti-Marian authors are slavish adherents to the 'popular', while Tytler has 'proved beyond contradiction, that the *French* letters, supposed to have been written by *Mary*, are translated from the *Scotch* copy, and, if originals, which it was so much the interest of such numbers to preserve, are wanting, it is much more likely that they never existed, than they have been lost'.[37] For Johnson, Tytler's *Enquiry* is an objective reading of the facts.

Smollett's review of the second edition of Tytler's *Enquiry* in the *Critical Review* for June 1767 states that the study constitutes 'a full refutation of the false and cruel charges brought by those who had an immediate interest in her destruction, against her person and memory'.[38] Thanks to Tytler's 'vindication', Mary's innocence is established for Johnson and Smollett through an acceptance that the 'Casket Sonnets' had been forged, as Goodall had proved in 1754, to provide the damning evidence that the queen's detractors required. Both James Steuart and Walter Goodall had Jacobite associations: Steuart spent time in Rome with Charles Edward Stuart and, after being present in Scotland in 1745, was forced to remain in Europe until 1771. Goodall was employed by Jacobite Latin scholar Thomas Ruddiman (1674–1757) to his role in Edinburgh's Advocates Library in 1742. By contrast, Smollett has been associated with unionism in his praise for, as Denys Van Renen has put it, 'the well-regulated physical environment in Britain', 'the flourishing state of the country' and its 'interconnectedness',[39] while simultaneously exhibiting pride in Scotland, as seen in *Humphry Clinker*. In this post-Culloden context, Mary has supporters on both sides of the constitutional debate.

In the later decades of the century, a new biographer enters the stage to reignite the 'Marian Controversy'. By then, Gilbert Stuart (1743–86) was established as a historian and journalist, having been published in the *London Magazine* and *Monthly Review* before co-founding the *Edinburgh Magazine and Review* (1773–76). After the failure of the *Edinburgh Magazine*, he focused on historical writing, in which he set himself in opposition to William Robertson. Stuart's *View of Society in Europe* (1778) is a rejoinder to Robertson's *History of Charles V* (1772), in which Stuart takes issue with Robertson's emphasis on 'the gradual improvement of society' at the expense of 'the gradual corruption of feudal institutions',[40] while his *Observations Concerning the Public Law and the Constitutional History of Scotland* (1779) is, according to William Zachs, a 'more direct challenge to Robertson'.[41] Nowhere is Stuart's disagreement with Robertson more marked than in Stuart's *History of Scotland from the*

---

[37] *The Gentleman's Magazine*, vol. 30 (October 1760), pp. 454–55.
[38] *The Critical Review*, vol. 23 (June 1767), p. 401.
[39] Denys Van Renen, 'Biogeography, Climate and National Identity in Smollett's *Humphry Clinker*', *Philological Quarterly* 90 (2011) no. 4: 395–424, at p. 397.
[40] William Zachs, 'Stuart, Gilbert (1743–1786)', *ODNB* (https://doi.org/10.1093/ref:odnb/26704).
[41] Zachs, 'Stuart, Gilbert'.

Establishment of the Reformation till the Death of Queen Mary (1782), in which he moves away from the established eighteenth-century mode of examining the evidence of Mary's life and alleged misdemeanours, and towards 'a more sentimental, immediate, and intentional approach' that portrays Mary 'as a victim of both English oppression and self-interested Scottish alliances'.[42] Such was Stuart's animosity towards Robertson that he published a literary challenge to his predecessor in the press, intended to force Robertson to capitulate his belief in Mary's guilt. The *European Magazine* for April 1782 explains that Stuart's open letter to Robertson was 'handed about in the polite circles at Edinburgh' and was:

> understood to be a very generous, but very resolute call upon Dr. Robertson, to defend what he has written to the prejudice of the honour of Mary Queen of Scots . . . The ground for the encounter is marked out; the subject is a beautiful Queen; and the Judges are appointed. If Dr. Robertson enters the lists, and is successful, he will acquire a new reputation. If he refuses to enter the lists, or enters them and is defeated, he will lose many laurels. This dispute will probably be an æra in the history of Scottish literature.[43]

In the letter, Stuart states that the 'historian who can persist in his mistakes, departs from his duty, and violates the character he has assumed'. To leave these 'mistakes' uncorrected is 'altogether inexcusable', particularly in the case of Mary, 'who has suffered in her honour by misrepresentations, and who with strong and real claims to integrity, has been held out to reproach and infamy'.[44] Although his own account of Mary's life is laden with emotion, in which he weeps 'over the misfortunes, the frailties, and the crimes of this beautiful princess, I will yet pay my devotions to truth, and submit to the law of the victor'.[45] When Stuart's challenge went without response from Robertson, he published a letter to 'the Right Honourable the Earl of Buchan, President of the Society of Antiquaries at Edinburgh', in which he interprets Robertson's silence:

> He followed exactly the track which he ought to have avoided with anxiety; and he has exposed his historic faith and credibility, to every suspicion that is most improper. He provoked a conflict which he was unable to sustain. He turned away with aversion from the lists. He forgot that there is a point of honour which ought to be as dear to an author as to a gentleman. He gave himself airs of superiority, and trembled before the sound of the trumpet.[46]

---

[42] Zachs, 'Stuart, Gilbert'.
[43] *The European Magazine, and London Review* (London), vol. 1 (April 1782), p. 243.
[44] *The European Magazine*, vol. 1 (April 1782), p. 243.
[45] *The European Magazine*, vol. 1 (April 1782), p. 244.
[46] *The Town and Country Magazine, or, Universal Repository of Knowledge, Instruction, and Entertainment* (London), issue 15 (October 1783), p. 509.

Stuart defends his own actions against accusations of 'envy' and 'rivalship' before finishing with a pledge to aid in 'the advancement of those public and national purposes, which employ so honourably your anxieties and toil'.[47]

Buchan responded to Stuart in a letter of 18 April 1783, published in the same issue of the *Town and Country Magazine*. Here the earl, a contemporary arbiter of taste and committed antiquarian, embraces Stuart's approach: 'You, Sir . . . have happily rescued a beautiful and injured queen from the Rhadamanthean tribunal of her partial judges; and you have appealed to the public for a reversal of the cruel sentence had been pronounced against her'.[48] Buchan explains Robertson's unwillingness to meet Stuart in his literary challenge by 'the fear of offending the high presbyterian party, the desire of pleasing the English by an extenuation of the ungenerous conduct of Elizabeth, and the affectation of . . . impartiality and liberality'.[49] Stuart could, therefore, claim a victory for his emotional response to Mary's life; indeed, as Zachs states, it 'won him considerable acclaim, particularly south of the border, and the *History* was soon reprinted and translated'.[50]

Perhaps as a result of responses to Stuart's popular *History*, growing sympathy for Mary as a tragic figure leads to her increasing appearance in imaginative literature that was printed and reviewed in the late eighteenth-century periodical press. The *Town and Country Magazine* for May 1775 publishes a 'Dialogue between the late Queen of Denmark, and Mary, Queen of Scots in the Regions of the Dead'. Mary's counterpart in the 'Dialogue' is Caroline Matilda of Great Britain (1751–75), Queen of Denmark and Norway from 1766 to 1772 by her marriage to King Christian VII of Denmark (1749–1808); she had died in the month of the dialogue's publication. Like Mary's, Caroline Matilda's life and reign were characterised by perceptions of scandal and adultery, and she was divorced from the king following her affair with 'a freethinking physician from Altona'[51] who took the role of doctor to the royal household, Johan Friedrich Struensee (1737–72). Like Mary, she was imprisoned for the final years of her life. In this imaginary conversation, each queen competes with the other as to who had the most miserable life and gruesome death. Mary begins with a welcome to Caroline Matilda into the afterlife, and an acknowledgement of their 'resemblance'.[52] Caroline Matilda insists that Mary's death was 'more to be envied' than her own natural death – 'you had the tears and attention of all the

---

[47] *The Town and Country Magazine*, issue 15 (October 1783), p. 509.
[48] *The Town and Country Magazine*, issue 15 (October 1783), p. 512.
[49] *The Town and Country Magazine*, issue 15 (October 1783), p. 512.
[50] Zachs, 'Stuart, Gilbert'.
[51] D. D. Aldridge, 'Caroline Matilda, Princess (1751–1775)', *ODNB* (https://doi.org/10.1093/ref:odnb/4721).
[52] *The Town and Country Magazine*, issue 7 (May 1775), p. 267.

world, you triumphed even in your fall'[53] – and her tale becomes a moral for princesses of all ranks to 'take warning by my fate, and not become a sacrifice, like me and others, to crooked policy and blind ambition'.[54] Although they differ on whose death was better (or worse), Mary and Caroline Matilda fall victim here to the same fate: the dangerous lure of the 'handsome man'.[55]

The *Gentleman's Magazine* for May 1785 prints an 'Inscription for the (supposed) Tomb of Mary, Queen of Scots, Removed from the Cathedral of Peterborough to the Dean's Garden'. The poem imagines Mary's address to a visiting mourner, as follows:

> Forbear, sweet maid, thy fruitless sorrow heal,
> No more lament what I no more can feel!
> From my freed bosom every passion fled,
> When on the block I bow'd my regal head;
> For then ELIZABETH's stern hatred died,
> DARNLEY's neglect, and BOTHWELL's stubborn pride.[56]

Just as Caroline Matilda's dialogue with Mary held a moral for 'princesses', this inscription warns against 'passion', from which Mary is freed only by death. The queen is here an innocent victim, while the guilty party includes not only Elizabeth, but Mary's second and third husbands, Darnley and James Hepburn, fourth earl of Bothwell (*c*. 1534–78). Indeed, in the *Literary Magazine and British Review* for January 1789, her marriage to Bothwell was, in the author's view, 'a fatal step in Mary; and to this we may in great measure ascribe all those misfortunes which embittered the remaining part of her life'.[57] In these accounts, Mary is portrayed as having been tossed around, not only by malignant fate, but by the ruthless ambitions of those close to her. Far from being guilty, she is the spotless victim whose tragedy sends a warning to those women who would be led by their 'passions'.

On 21 March 1789, a historical tragedy entitled *Mary Queen of Scots* by English Member of Parliament John St John (*d*. 1793) premiered at London's Drury Lane Theatre with the celebrated Welsh actress and tragedienne Sarah Siddons (1755–1831) in the title role. Despite the high profiles of the playwright and leading lady, Smollett echoes contemporary critics in his dismissal of the play in the *Critical Review* for June 1789:

---

[53] *The Town and Country Magazine*, issue 7 (May 1775), p. 268.
[54] *The Town and Country Magazine*, issue 7 (May 1775), p. 268.
[55] *The Town and Country Magazine*, issue 7 (May 1775), p. 267.
[56] *The Gentleman's Magazine*, vol. 55, issue 5 (May 1785), p. 385.
[57] *The Literary Magazine and British Review* (London), vol. 2 (January 1789), p. 10.

The dramatic unities of time and space are violated to a great degree in this Tragedy; and what is worse, there is nothing striking in the incidents, characters, and dialogue, to compensate for these faults. What effect it might have on the stage we know not: in the closet it certainly interests very little.[58]

If Mary's life was difficult to portray on the stage, it appears to have been a more fruitful subject for poetry in the late eighteenth century. 'Mary Queen of Scots, A Monody' by R. B. S. is printed in the *Gentleman's Magazine* for May 1791. This poem, purported to have been written 'near the Ruins of Sheffield Manor', one of the locations in which Mary was held captive, looks back on 'distrustful days, and days of blood'.[59] Echoing the view of Mary as an innocent victim, R. B. S. blames Mary's enemies and self-interested associates for her downfall:

> ELIZA! Britain's glory, and her shame!
> Alternate light and darkness wrap thy name;
> That name, once dreadful over earth and sea,
> While BURLEIGH watch'd, and RALEIGH fought for THEE.
> Thy breast imperious, dark, and big with spleen,
> Could brook no merits in a Rival Queen;
> The fame of MARY mov'd thy envious pride,
> Nor wast thou satiate until MARY died.[60]

For R. B. S., female, queenly 'rivalry' was the cause of Mary's death, for Elizabeth could bear no challenge to her authority. As with the dialogue between Mary and Caroline Matilda in the afterlife, the story of Mary's life becomes a moral to eighteenth-century women:

> Ye fair! who give the liquid pearls to flow,
> O'er baseless incident and fabled woe;
> Reserve your treasures, till of MARY told,
> The refluent crimson strikes your veins with cold;
> Think of her fate, so hapless and so true,
> So may no heartless ruffian injure you.
> Mourn every breast to sympathy allied,
> And ev'ry bright ye weep that MARY died.[61]

---

[58] *The Critical Review*, vol. 67 (June 1789), pp. 554–55.
[59] *The Gentleman's Magazine*, vol. 61, issue 5 (May 1791), p. 471.
[60] *The Gentleman's Magazine*, vol. 61, issue 5 (May 1791), p. 471.
[61] *The Gentleman's Magazine*, vol. 61, issue 5 (May 1791), p. 472.

R. B. S.'s 'Monody' simultaneously casts Mary as an object of pathos for the readers of the literature of Sensibility who are to 'sympathy allied', while castigating female readers for wasting their tears on the fictional characters and invented woes of sentimental novels. Mary thus becomes a 'real' object of sentiment, and a moral lesson to women who would associate with 'ruffians'. No longer is she the profligate harlot driven by her carnal desires: she is now the spotless maid, used roughly by those she trusted. R. B. S. implores female readers to discard their sentimental fiction and instead meditate on the truth and lessons of Mary's life. The 'Monody' is a contemporary of Robert Burns's (1759-96) 'Lament of Mary Queen of Scots on the Approach of Spring', which insists that 'th' balm that draps on wounds of woe/Frae woman's pitying e'e' (ll. 39-40) is unknown to Elizabeth, who is both 'My sister and my fae' (l. 33). In both poems, true sympathy lies with female readers, but they are also the recipients of Mary's moral.

In the late eighteenth century, magazines targeted specifically at a female readership became increasingly commonplace. One such magazine is the *Lady's Monthly Museum*, in which Mary makes frequent appearances. In the issue for November 1799, the queen's womanly (read: physical) charms are emphasised as a model for female readers to imitate:

> The brightness of her complexion dazzled the beholder. Her eyes were of a dark grey, and expressed admirably the varying situation of her mind: they were now languid and lovely, now brisk and enlivening. The gracefulness of her motion was enchanting. She dressed with a propriety that gave a lustre to all her charms . . . When on the scaffold, she displayed a recollection, an ease, and a magnanimity, which could not have been expected from her sex, or her character, and which did the greatest honour to both.[62]

Mary's meekness in suffering and patience in extreme adversity, her beauty and elegant dress make the queen a model of femininity for the eighteenth century. No more are women encouraged to weep on the truth of her tragedy, but to emulate her captivating charms. In the same issue of the *Lady's Monthly Museum*, an article entitled 'Woman. An Apologue' boils the Marian 'lesson' down to its most basic message: 'We admire the masculine mind of Elizabeth, but we love Mary Queen of Scots'.[63] In this equation for the eighteenth-century female reader, Elizabeth's 'masculine' intellectualism is 'admired', but the feminine Mary is 'loved'. Even if, thanks to the many publications and public discussions of her fate, there is a good understanding of Mary's historical circumstances, she

---

[62] *The Lady's Monthly Magazine, or Polite Repository of Amusement and Instruction* (London), vol. 3 (November 1799), pp. 385-86.
[63] *The Lady's Monthly Magazine*, vol. 3 (November 1799), p. 387.

is yet an ideal of compliant womanhood which is defeated by, but simultaneously superior to, Elizabeth's 'masculinity'.

Throughout the eighteenth century, commentators on Mary's life and legacy deal in evidence, in analysis and in the rejection of unexamined prejudice. In a confluence of circumstances, authors become increasingly interested in Mary as an object of pathos and sensibility in the context of Enlightenment affective sympathy. In this, they pit Mary against cruel and unfeeling enemies, whether the Protestant nobles, Knox, Darnley, Bothwell or Elizabeth; and her supporters present themselves as Mary's chivalric protectors. In this supportive and yet patronising context, Mary is depicted as a woman before her time, who would be more at home in the apparently kinder climes of eighteenth-century Scotland. In the *Scots Magazine* for September 1789, the reviewer remarks with pride, that:

> [t]he memory of Mary Queen of Scotland being revived with new lusture, and the dignity of her character restored to justice; it is no small compliment to the liberality of the present age to say, that men of unprejudiced principles, who investigate history with an impartial eye, will now undertake to tear the veil of obloquy which has concealed, or at least cast a dark shade over the fairest personages.[64]

Even if St John's historical tragedy of *Mary Queen of Scots* missed the mark on the stage, its 'Prologue', published in the *Town and Country Magazine* for 1789, catches the mood of the age:

> Oh, had she lived in more enlighten'd times,
> When graces were not sins, nor talents crimes,
> Admiring nations had confess'd her worth,
> And Scotland shone the Athens of the North![65]

Of course, Mary would again fall into disrepute, and often the literary critics who analysed the 'Casket Sonnets' in the ensuing centuries would unequivocally accept her authorship, despite Goodall's minutely argued refutations. Eighteenth-century commentators nevertheless present themselves as injecting humanity and sympathy into Mary's reception, and as rejecting extreme partisan reactions for rationality. The treatment of Mary in the eighteenth-century periodical press shows its commentators adding nuance and detail to the Marian debate, examining the evidence from objective and subjective perspectives, and attempting to reveal the forces at work in her demise.

---

[64] *The Scots Magazine* (Edinburgh), vol. 51 (September 1789), p. 424.
[65] *The Town and Country Magazine* (London), issue 21 (April 1789), p. 185.

SEVEN

'Deeply impressed upon the imagination': The Return of Mary in the Eighteenth and Nineteenth Centuries

Gerard Carruthers

In her afterlife, Mary, Queen of Scots has continuously fascinated the Scottish, British and, indeed, European imaginations. The literary imagining of Mary becomes particularly diverse and extensive through the period of the long eighteenth century and its transition into Romanticism, with Robert Burns, Friedrich Schiller, Jane Austen, William Wordsworth and Sir Walter Scott among many others expending strong energy and feeling in their depiction of Mary Stuart, as if in an intensely affective relationship with the Scottish queen. We might say that the eighteenth century created its own distinctive aesthetic context apt to powerfully imagining and expressing Mary. The age of sentiment and sensibility, by means of theories of tragedy and the sublime, saw a preoccupation with the losing cause as enjoyable – or as morally productive – as anything on the winning side of history. To some extent too, this mentality was obliquely a political qualification of the Whig narrative of natural British advancement in both religious and constitutional terms. The Romantic period saw many of its artists take a rather hesitant, even jaundiced, view of progress, with a preferential option for the marginalised, a proclivity that had been set in train during the sociological and historical enquiries of the Enlightenment. With some validity, then, the Enlightenment may be viewed as an intellectual movement that theorised the rise of 'civilisation', but in the process identified too the marginalised and the 'exotic' (including the concept of the 'noble savage').[1]

One repeated note prior to the later eighteenth century was a recognition of Mary's personal charms, with little sympathy for either her beauty or much else in her circumstances. We might turn to Lady Mary Wortley Montagu (1689–1762), part of the Whiggish Stuart (Bute) dynasty, for an instance here.

---

[1] Among a numerous critical literature on this general point, see, for instance, Kenneth Simpson, *The Protean Scot: The Crisis of Identity in Eighteenth Century Scottish Literature* (Aberdeen, 1988), pp. 41–69.

Montagu wrote her 'Epilogue to Mary Queen of Scots' at some point in the period between 1722 and 1725, intended for a play never finished by Philip Duke of Wharton (1698–1731), a rather dissolute, libertarian figure and a fervid Jacobite. Montagu and Wharton made an odd pair, both as literary and political collaborators (they were lovers, too). Montagu's narrator apostrophises at the opening of the epilogue:

> What could Luxurious Woman wish for more,
> To fix her Joys, or to extend her Power?
> Their every Wish was in this Mary seen,
> Gay, Witty, Youthful, Beauteous, and a Queen!
> Vain, useless Blessings with ill Conduct joyn'd!
> Light as the Air, and fleeting as the Wind.
> What ever Poets write, or Lovers vow,
> Beauty, what poor Omnipotence hast thou![2]

This conjunction between physical beauty, moral laxity and the implication of insubstantiality (political and historical) contrasts with 'Queen Bess [who] had Wisdom, Councel, Power, and Laws/ ... Learn hence, ye Fair, more solid charms to prize'.[3] This hard-headed narrative of Elizabeth (and Protestant Britain) as morally triumphant and Mary as an irredeemable loser with her 'vain, useless blessings' (with its anti-Catholic implication) was, however, to change markedly several decades later.

We see the transformation of attitude to the Scottish queen in 1770 when William Julius Mickle (?1735–88), a son of the manse from Dumfriesshire, publishes 'Mary Queen of Scots, An Elegy'. By this time Mickle had been a minor figure on the cultural scene of both London and Oxford, and, in part, this probably accounts for predilections towards Mary that are far removed from typically Scottish Presbyterian attitudes. In particular, he was an admirer of the pro-Stuart, Tory, Catholic writer, Alexander Pope, and this may be one of the underlying reasons for his receptiveness towards Mary. Evidencing some familiarity with the literary and historical sources, Mickle prefaces his text with an epigraph from George Buchanan, former tutor and ally of Mary, who became one of her most vehement and powerful detractors:

> Quod tibi vitæ sors detraxit,
> Fama adjiciet posthuma laudi;
> Nostris longum tu dolor et honor.[4]

---

[2] Robert Halsband and Isobel Grundy (eds), *Lady Mary Wortley Montagu: Essays and Poems and Simplicity, A Comedy* (Oxford, 1976), p. 240.
[3] *Lady Mary Wortley Montagu: Essays and Poems*, p. 241.
[4] *The Poetical Works of William Julius Mickle Including Several Original Pieces, With a New Life of the Author: By the Rev. John Sim* (London, 1806), p. 73.

> To what the lot of life has drawn for you
> Fame will add posthumous praise;
> Our long suffering and honour.

Mickle's poem brings us to an encounter with Mary's spirit:

> Supreme in grief, her eye confus'd with woe,
> Appears the Lady of th'aërial train,
> Tall as the Sylvan Goddess of the bow,
> And fair as she who wept Adonis slain.
>
> Such was the pomp when Gilead's virgin-band,
> Wandering by Judah's flowery mountains wept,
> And with fair Iphis, by the hallow'd strand
> Of Siloe's brook, a mournful sabbath kept.
> By the resplendent cross with thistles twin'd,
> Tis Mary's guardian genius lost in woe:
> 'Ah, say, What deepest wrongs have thus combin'd
> To heave with restless sighs thy breast of snow!'[5]

Here, we see a deliberate effort to enshrine Mary imaginatively in a highly allusive, literary rhetoric of 'posthumous praise'. Classical mythic and poetic allusions construct Mary as an ethereal, virgin figure with powers akin to a Classical sibylline muse; 'Siloe's brook' in particular is interestingly associated with poetic inspiration by John Milton.[6] Mary is an exalted subject but also imbued with pathos, symbolising an elegiac eloquence that can evoke sympathy: 'Let grief indulge her grand sublimity,/And melancholy wake her melting power'.[7]

Mickle's text depicts the entirety of Mary's life in the relatively compact compass of two lines, deliberately counterpointing the queen's fertility, with celebration of the fact that her son James will occupy the throne, to the barrenness of the Virgin Queen. In explicit and highly charged emotional rhetoric, the poem emphasises Elizabeth's heartlessness and jealousy, qualities suitably rewarded in ignominious death:

> But Tudor as a fruitless gourd, shall die!
> 'I see her death-scene:— On the lowly floor
> Dreary she sits, cold grief has glaz'd her eye,
> And anguish gnaws her, till she breathes no more.'[8]

---

[5] *The Poetical Works of William Julius Mickle*, p. 74.
[6] See Leo Miller, '"Siloa's Brook" in *Paradise Lost*: Another View', *Milton Quarterly* 6 (1972) No. 3: 5–7.
[7] *The Poetical Works of William Julius Mickle*, p. 74.
[8] *The Poetical Works of William Julius Mickle*, p. 80.

This represents an interesting alignment of political allegiances: here Tudor versus Stuart is the central opposition (even though Mary had Tudor lineage), rather than Stuart versus Hanoverian (with William, begetter of the Hanoverian line, associated through marriage with the Stuart line). A striking feature of Mickle's elegy is its jubilant historiographical vindication of Mary, which the narrator attributes to an apparently recent shift in allegiances:

> Falshood unmask'd, withdraws her ugly train,
> And Mary's virtues all illustrious shine—
> Yes, thou hast friends, the godlike and humane
> Of latest ages, injur'd Queen, are thine.

It is clear that Mickle was aware of the mid-century Marian debates among Scottish Enlightenment historians (to which we will return briefly below). He provides a note to his text, which, in his own words, is 'indignant':

> [The] Author of this little Poem to the memory of an unhappy Princess, is unwilling to enter into the controversy respecting her guilt or her innocence. Suffice it only to observe, that the following facts may be proved to demonstration: – The Letters, which have always been esteemed the principal proofs of Queen Mary's guilt, are forged. Buchanan, on whose authority Francis, and other historians, have condemned her, has falsified several circumstances of her history, and has cited against her public records which never existed, as has been lately proved to demonstration. And to add no more, the treatment she received from her illustrious cousin was dictated by a policy truly Machiavellian – a policy which trampled on the obligations of honour, of humanity and morality. From whence it may be inferred, That, to express the indignation at the cruel treatment of Mary, which history must ever inspire, and to drop a tear over her sufferings, is not unworthy of a writer who would appear in the cause of virtue.[9]

In its conclusion, Mickle's poem seems to acknowledge itself as an act of transfiguration as the light of day returns, with its implied restorative and clarifying powers:

> The milky splendors of the dawning ray
> Now thro' the grove a trembling radiance shed;
> With sprightly note the wood-lark hail'd the day,
> And with the moonshine all the vision fled.[10]

In 1776, a little over half a decade after the publication of 'Mary Queen of Scots, An Elegy', James Boswell (1740–95) commissioned a painting entitled 'The Abdication of Mary, Queen of Scots' from Gavin Hamilton (1723–98; see Figure I.1); both writer and artist are associated with more obvious Stuart

---

[9] *The Poetical Works of William Julius Mickle*, p. 80.
[10] *The Poetical Works of William Julius Mickle*, p. 80.

sympathies than is Mickle.[11] Boswell was interested in the historiographical debate over Mary at the end of the 1750s and Jayne Elizabeth Lewis also relates the Boswell–Hamilton Mary project to the recent final failure of Jacobitism itself at Culloden in 1745, identifying a Jacobite opposition to Whig methodology:

> Jacobite sympathizers' tendency, especially through song and putatively mystical image, less to present an authoritative story about the past than to fantasize about it in a way that is, at bottom, wholly subject to the emotional response of those who read about it. So understood, Jacobite history is not what we would properly call historical, at least in the 'Whiggish' sense of being either progressive, or narrative, or evidentiary. In the interest of consolidating the affective power of a central charismatic figure and thus of creating desire for the return of that figure or at least one of its avatars, Jacobite evocations of the past removed the power to determine significance from an author and conceded it to a reader or even beholder.[12]

Hamilton's painting, where an attractive, well-lit Mary is seen in the process of abdication surrounded by shadowy, more physically assertive males, sits well with this diagnosis. It is in the age of sentiment, the early Romantic period, that the causes of Jacobitism and Mary begin to be primed for use in elegiac narratives of Scottish patriotism (one of the long cultural roots of modern Scottish nationalism). Here, ideas of loss (the defeated) return in ways that slowly begin to countermand Whig British history. It is not simply Boswell's Scottish *locus*, however, that provides partiality towards Mary, as a favourable view of her came also from his close friend Samuel Johnson (1709–84). Boswell records one instance from many in Johnson's deprecation of the Scottish people:

> who could let your Queen remain twenty years in captivity, and then be put to death, without even a pretence [sic] of justice, without your ever attempting to rescue her; and such a Queen too; as every man of any gallantry of spirit would have sacrificed his life for.[13]

As he purveys a rather simplistic view here of the politics of Mary's captivity, Johnson demonstrates the susceptibility of the English High Tory, Anglican sensibility to her historic charms. Aside from his own ideological bent, significantly

---

[11] For more generally on the context of Jacobitism, see Jayne Lewis, 'Hamilton's "Abdication", Boswell's Jacobitism and the Myth of Mary Queen of Scots', *English Literary History* 64 (1997) no. 4: 1069–90.

[12] Jayne Lewis, 'The Reputations of Mary Queen of Scots', *Études Écossaises* 11 (2005): 41–55, available at https://journals.openedition.org/etudesecossaises/146, accessed 12 September 2023. See here also the work of Murray Pittock, especially 'Treacherous Objects: Towards a Theory of Jacobite Material Culture', *Journal for Eighteenth-Century Studies* 34 (2011) no. 1: 39–63.

[13] *Boswell's Life of Johnson including Boswell's Journal of a Tour to the Hebrides*, ed. George Birckbeck Hill (New York, 1786), p. 45.

the great lexicographer reviewed William Tytler's *Inquiry* in the *Gentleman's Magazine* for October 1760.[14] In his review, Johnson complains '[i]t has now been fashionable for near half a century to defame and vilify the house of Stuart, and to exalt and magnify the reign of Elizabeth'. He also applauds Tytler for having disproved the authenticity of the Casket Letters, and through the latter's treatment saw Elizabeth as all too conveniently credible as to Mary's guilt and immoral nature.

Mickle's 'Mary Queen of Scots, An Elegy' must have been known to Robert Burns (1759–96) as the latter echoes it throughout his 'Lament of Mary Queen of Scots on the Approach of Spring' (1790). The substantive element of Burns' favourable exposure to Mary, however, occurred via William Tytler of Woodhouselee (1711–92), that pivotal individual, whose pro-Marian efforts in this regard were continuously and widely influential in the second part of the eighteenth century. Tytler was a lawyer, historian and song-collector, and a cornerstone also of Burns's interest in Jacobitism. In January 1793 Burns wrote to the song-publisher, George Thomson (1757–1851). The latter had broken the news to the poet of an intention to collect his edition, *Select Collection of Original Scottish Airs*, and Burns' reply enthusiastically mentions, as a useful authority, '[a]ll the late Mr Tytler's anecdotes [which] I have by me, taken down in the course of my acquaintance with him from his own mouth'.[15] Tytler had strong Jacobite sympathies, which no doubt led to his attempted rehabilitation of Mary, the Stuart queen. In his letter to Thomson, Burns moves from a relishing of Tytler's narratives about song in general to suggesting to his correspondent 'I do not doubt but you might make a very valuable Collection of Jacobite Songs, but would it give no offence?'[16] Contrary to the frivolous 'sentimental Jacobite' label sometimes levelled at the poet, Burns was conscious of (and indeed, cautious about) the possibility of causing cultural 'offence' by means of his Stuart-loyalism, which was reiterated, it might be added, through many years.

For Tytler, Mary was a figure to be reclaimed in a reset historical compass. His *Inquiry Historical and Critical into the Evidence against Mary Queen of Scots* (1759) was a piece of scholarly revisionism at the high point of the Scottish Enlightenment. A 'nationalist' of sorts, or at least a Scottish patriot, in explicitly opposing previous work by David Hume (1711–76) and William Robertson (1721–93) that cast Mary in a culpable light, Tytler presented a narrative that depicted a long historical process of English predation and a campaign of dirty tricks against Scotland, to undermine the Stuart dynasty from the time of

---

[14] See http://www.yalejohnson.com/frontend/sda_viewer?n=112315, accessed 12 September 2023.
[15] *The Letters of Robert Burns*, Vol. II, *1790–1796*, ed. J. De Lancey Ferguson and G. Ross Roy (Oxford, 1985), p. 181.
[16] *Letters of Robert Burns*, Vol. II, p. 181.

James V to that of his daughter Mary.[17] Such history in its overall thrust was strikingly different from the Whiggish, unionist version of Mary's history as set out by Hume and Robertson, countering with equal expressive force their vehement views that the Stuarts had been rightly banished due to despotic sensibilities.

By 4 May 1787 Burns, during his first flush of literary fame in Edinburgh, had made Tytler's acquaintance, sending him on that date his 'Epistle to Mr Tytler'. As it addresses the historian, the poem pairs Mary's physical attractiveness with a respected, admirable, inner quality (or Stuart-ness) which should equally be respected:

> Revered Defender of beauteous Stuart,
> Of Stuart!—a Name once respected,
> A Name which to love was the mark of a true heart,
> But now 'tis despis'd and neglected.[18]

In stanza three, as elsewhere in his writings, Burns alludes to his own ancestry in support of the Stuart cause, and in stanza five he casts a sardonic eye upon the Hanoverian regime succeeding from 1688:

> But why of that Epocha make such a fuss,
> That brought us th' Electoral Stem?
> If bringing them over was lucky for us,
> I'm sure 'twas as lucky for them![19]

In this text, then, Burns restores the idea of honour (the possession of a 'true heart') to Stuart supporters and by extension to Mary herself, and suggests opportunism on the part of the Hanoverians (a quality often enough attributed by historians to Mary). It is this kind of utterance that sees Burns depicted by some after his death as a Tory as well as a Jacobite.[20] In the subsequent stanza, however, the poet affects a pulling back from the vicissitudes of changing ideological orthodoxy, expressing scepticism about absolute political rectitude while making a good Enlightenment point about the relativity of politics:

> But Politics, truce! We're on dangerous ground;
> Who knows how the fashions may alter:
> That doctrines today that are loyalty sound,
> Tomorrow may bring us a halter.[21]

---

[17] See especially Tytler's 'Introduction' to his *Inquiry* (London and Edinburgh, 1790), pp. 35–74.
[18] *The Poems and Songs of Robert Burns*, ed. James Kinsley, 3 vols (Oxford, 1968), Vol. 1, p. 332.
[19] *Poems and Songs of Robert Burns*, Vol. 1, p. 333.
[20] *Scotland and Scotsmen in the Eighteenth Century from the MSS of John Ramsay of Ochtertyre*, ed. Alexander Allardyce (Edinburgh and London, 1888), p. 554.
[21] *Poems and Songs of Robert Burns*, Vol. 1, p. 334.

Ideologically less committed than Tytler, Hume or Robertson, and operating as a creative writer rather than as a historian, Burns is overtly receptive to the romantic appeal of the Scottish queen. The signature quality of the text is emotion rather than rationality, denoted by Burn's statement that 'something like moisture conglobes in my eye'.[22] In the age of sentiment or sensibility, Mary was a prime subject in her beautiful, sublime and tragically maligned status.

We see Burns' sustained emotional fervour for Mary when, in April 1791, the Dumfriesshire Jacobite Lady Winifred Maxwell Constable (1736–1801) sent the poet a snuff-box inlaid with a miniature of the queen. In response, Burns wrote: 'I assure your Ladyship, I shall set it [the gift] apart: the symbols of Religion shall only be more sacred. – In the moment of Poetic composition, the Box shall be my inspiring Genius . . . when I would interest my fancy in the distresses incident to Humanity, I shall remember the unfortunate Mary.'[23] Here, somewhat chameleon-like, the cradle-Presbyterian poet appears in the guise of reverential Catholic as he writes to a Catholic woman. Burns also sent Lady Maxwell Constable his song 'Lament of Mary Queen of Scots on the Approach of Spring', which he had composed the year before. In this text, the resurgent beauty of nature in springtime is torment to the imprisoned Mary:

> Now blooms the lily by the bank,
> The primrose down the brae;
> The hawthorn's budding in the glen,
> And milk-white is the sale:
> The meanest hind in fair Scotland
> May rove their sweets amang;
> But I, the Queen of a' Scotland,
> Maun lie in prison strang.[24]

Mary's long confinement is a cornerstone of Burns's rendering of the queen; in the 'Lament', she is denied the free air of Scotland especially. He also follows some earlier and disputed historical accounts as he makes Mary a determinedly native figure speaking in Scots.[25] Picking up on one of the frequently observed ironies of Mary's history, Burns has her foresee her son James' reign (becoming the first king of a united British Isles in 1603) as being more successful than her

---

[22] *Poems and Songs of Robert Burns*, Vol. 1, p. 333.
[23] *Letters of Robert Burns*, Vol. II, pp. 88–89.
[24] *Poems and Songs of Robert Burns*, Vol. 2, p. 546.
[25] Interestingly, in the twenty-first century particularly, Mary's command of Scots has been a site of contention, with the nationalist Scots Language Centre and others sympathetic to the queen's facility in Scots so as to offset her 'French-ness' as emphasised elsewhere. See Jayne Lewis, who reflects on the long reputation of Mary: 'As reputations go, that of Mary Queen of Scots was never an especially Scottish one': (Lewis, 'The Reputations of Mary Queen of Scots').

own or that of her arch-nemesis, Queen Elizabeth. Taking into account, however, that the Stuart dynasty would not survive supplanting by the Hanoverians, Burns places Mary's fate within the cyclical time of poetic memory (to which he himself contributes, associating her even in her sorrow perennially with a spring that provides some kind of hope, perhaps of Stuart revival). Burns' Mary declaims in the final lines of the poem:

> ... in the narrow house o' death
> Let winter round me rave;
> And the next flowers, that deck the spring,
> Bloom on my peaceful grave.[26]

Calling on one of his favourite books of scripture, the Book of Job, for the 'house of death' reference,[27] Burns has Mary in suitably quiescent attitude to her fate, but 'spring' will 'bloom' for her again in some mysterious sense. This 'bloom', perhaps, was most apparent in the aesthetic sense, in the renewal of Mary's poetic image as the eighteenth century wore on, including in this example of Burns' song. We can therefore see its evolutionary process as Tytler provided the historical heft and the likes of Mickle, Boswell and Burns began to paint imaginatively the rehabilitation.

Mary's representational fortunes, clearly, had begun to change by the later eighteenth century, but it was a text early in the next that properly made her a literary, even a stage, icon. In a very general way too, this work might be seen against the backdrop of a Europe somewhat traumatised by the recent execution of another queen, Marie Antoinette of France, in 1793. *Mary Stuart* (1801) by Friedrich Schiller (1759–1805) combined good historical research with large-scale, sensual, poetic licence (most notoriously depicting a meeting between Mary and Elizabeth that never actually occurred).[28] In this fictional conversation, Mary, in line with the kind of artistic revisionism we have already

---

[26] *Poems and Songs of Robert Burns*, Vol. 2, p. 547.
[27] Job 30:23.
[28] The dramatic licence of bringing the two queens together, however, goes back at least as far as *The Island Queens, or, the Death of Mary, Queen of Scotland* (1684) by John Banks (1650–1706). Another drama, *Mary, Queen of Scots: An Historical Tragedy or Dramatic Poem* (London, 1792) by the English moral-writer and proto-feminist Mary Deverell (1731–1805), apparently never performed, might briefly be mentioned. This is a very static text narrating the canonical events around Mary's life, with little in the way of historical or psychological ambiguity. Nonetheless it too partakes in something of the recent literary temperature as its prologue speaks of 'injur'd Mary's heart/Faulty although in some degree she prove/Yet Pity prompts commiserating Love'. If the reader/audience is to 'pity' Mary and others through the affecting scenes of the drama, there is no potential for sophisticated analysis of personal volition. Deverell provides, essentially, opacity of character motivation, as opposed to the rich, ironic counterpointing of character and its expression via open emotion in Schiller. Deverell's straightforward didactic purposes are

been observing, declares to the English queen '[t]he worst of me is open to the world,/My highest virtue is as yet unknown'.[29] In one sense, this relates to Mary's self-conception as a martyr.[30] In the wider context of Schiller's drama, where both Mary and Elizabeth (and other characters) are driven as much by personal emotion as by historical circumstance or their own rationality, these words point potentially to an all too confident self-estimation by the Scottish queen. Schiller leads the way for subsequent fictional and dramatic representations of Mary to the present day in essaying an ambiguously interpretable individual. Indeed, all of the characters in *Mary Stuart* are open to being read as ironically lesser in their moral purpose than they pretend. This 'reduction' of character, however, or its projection within a context of relativity, has much to do with the fact that larger historical forces outwith the control of any one person are in operation, shaping individual fates. This depiction of history as not ours to command was to prove an influence particularly on the fictional practice of Sir Walter Scott, as he 'invented' the historical novel. Schiller's play is even-handed in dealing with history, most especially the characters of Mary and also Elizabeth, a figure as important, flawed, beleaguered and ultimately (to an extent) to be sympathised with as her cousin-queen. Indeed, working to present both queens in their heavy vulnerability, 'Schiller suggested that on stage Mary should appear about 25 and Elizabeth 30, whereas in fact Mary was 45 and Elizabeth 53 at the time of the execution'.[31] Mary, like Elizabeth, is arrestingly watchable as her character is in turn assured and vulnerable; at the beginning of Act III, Scene III, she falters as she anticipates meeting the English queen:

> I have spoken to her
> Over and over again, year after year,
> In my imagination, stirring words,
> Etching them on my mind in preparation.
> Now everything is on a sudden empty,

---

signalled in her choice of epigraph for her play, from Edward Young's 'The Complaint, or Night Thoughts' (1776):

> Through this opaque of nature and soul
> This double night, transmit one pitying ray,
> To lighten and to cheer. O lead my mind,
> (A mind that fain would wander from its woes,)
> Lead it through various scenes of life and death
> And from each scene the noblest truths inspire.

[29] Friedrich Schiller, *Don Carlos* and *Mary Stuart*, ed. and trans. Hilary Collier Sy-Quia and Peter Oswald (Oxford, 1999), p. 279.
[30] It is only in the later nineteenth century, we ought to note, that a case is seriously proposed for making Mary a saint. See Michael T. R. B. Turnbull, 'A Saint Too Far — the Canonisation of Mary Queen of Scots', unpublished paper: www.academia.edu/245325/The_canonisation_of_Mary_Queen_of_Scots, accessed 12 September 2023.
[31] Schiller, *Don Carlos* and *Mary Stuart*, introduction by Lesley Sharpe, p. xx.

And I remember only agony,
The death of every echo but its own.
My conscience is a mad-eyed animal,
And gentle thoughts escaping for their lives
Are changed to hailstones by my Gorgon hair.[32]

Here is one of many moments in the play when Mary becomes sublime spectacle, grand in her expression and in her plight. Her interiority as a human being is presented simultaneously with her undoubted historical importance for the audience, to consume as a kind of exquisite 'agony'. Mary's legendary deceitful charms are inflated as Schiller invents a hidden romantic intrigue between her and the earl of Leicester. The playwright also chooses his historical interpretation with ambidexterity, as Mary is seen certainly to be complicit with the earl of Bothwell in the murder of her second husband, Lord Darnley. On the other hand, the play holds her entirely innocent of the Babington plot to murder Elizabeth. Cleverly, this latter detail allows Elizabeth to assume the role of duplicitous monarch, as her subordinates carry out her wishes in executing Mary, leaving her supposedly not culpable. Had Schiller allowed Mary's knowledge of Babington, then the effect would have been less dramatically discordant, a simple evening of scores. His omission (or ignorance) of this detail allows Elizabeth to be painted as capricious and autocratic, but also humanly unsure to the end. She cavils at the death-warrant that she signs, which is passed through several hands and 'carried out,/ Rashly, before my final wish was known'.[33] In bringing both Mary and Elizabeth to the stage, Schiller's depictions of two historical characters full equally of duty and doubt and compromised by powerful political and religious interests is a treatment that becomes influential in popular perception across Europe. Schiller's Mary of course makes the more overtly tragic spectacle of the two and, indeed, enfolds Elizabeth's character in as much constraint as herself, as we see in one of the former's many compelling speeches:

Yes, I am weak and she is powerful,
And she can strengthen her position further
With ease through my destruction. But she should
Confess to that, and not describe as justice
Pure murder. It is not the sword of law
The Queen unsheathes to hush her opposition,
Nor can she hide the passion of this deed
In sacred robe – the world will not be fooled!
My death cannot be buried in the law!
There is no law that will support my death,

[32] Schiller, *Don Carlos* and *Mary Stuart*, p. 271.
[33] Schiller, *Don Carlos* and *Mary Stuart*, p. 337.

No matter what she does, Elizabeth
And she must end this pitiful attempt
To win the praise of angels for a crime.
Will lose her shine, the world will censure her,
She will appear in her true character![34]

Not only in its own day, but also down to very recently Schiller's *Mary Stuart* has helped embed enduring ambiguity over the situation of Mary and Elizabeth for a wide cultural audience. Emphasising this state of affairs, Robert Icke's version of 2017 at the Almeida Theatre in London, which then toured the United Kingdom, had its two leading actors specifically assigned the roles of Mary or Elizabeth only prior to each performance, on the tossing of a coin.[35] The rich theatrical history of the play could easily merit an essay in its own right on the modern reception of the two queens.

British Romantic writers became hugely interested in German drama at the end of the eighteenth and beginning of the nineteenth centuries, and though we have no direct evidence, Jane Austen (1775–1817) may have been influenced by Schiller in her preferential opinion of Mary. Around the turn of the century Austen produced a cod History of England, a product of her early youth that was not published in her lifetime.[36] Its animus is not to be missed; in writing of Elizabeth's rather sad relationship with Essex and his demise, Austen informs the reader 'Elizabeth did not long survive his loss, and died so miserable that were it not an injury to the memory of Mary I should pity her'. As Misty Krueger has suggested, Austen may also have had a partiality for martyred queens, shown in the treatment in her juvenile work of Henry VIII's fifth wife, Catherine Howard.[37] Whether or not a kind of proto-feminist predilection in Austen, Mary's appeal is to the fore under the male gaze of William Wordsworth (1770–1850). In 1817, the year Austen died, Wordsworth explicitly echoed Robert Burns with his own 'Lament of Mary Queen of Scots, on the Eve of a New Year'. Wordsworth has Mary begin her monologue:

Smile of the Moon – for so I name
That silent greeting from above,
A gentle flash of light that came
From her whom drooping captives love; . . .[38]

---

[34] Schiller, *Don Carlos* and *Mary Stuart*, p. 232.
[35] See www.standard.co.uk/culture/theatre/juliet-stevenson-says-she-still-finds-mary-stuart-coin-toss-absolutely-terrifying-a3750266.html, accessed 12 September 2023.
[36] See www.mollands.net/etexts/loveandfreindship/laf35.html, accessed 12 September 2023.
[37] Misty Krueger, 'From Marginalia to Juvenilia: Jane Austen's Vindication of the Stuarts', *The Eighteenth Century* 56 (2015) no. 2: 243–59. It might also be mentioned that, as a teenager, Austen transcribed two songs about the executed French queen, Marie Antoinette. See Joan Austen Leigh, 'Jane Austen: the French Connection', *Persuasions* 20 (1998): 106–18.
[38] *The Poems of William Wordsworth*, Vol. III, ed. Jared Curtis (Humanities-Ebooks, LLP, 2009), p. 109.

Mary, then, wryly reflects on her own captivity as greater than, and so bathetically compared to, the 'captivity' of being in love. In stanza three, the conceit of being in special communion with the cosmos, enabled by desire, continues:

> And yet, the soul-awakening gleam
> That struck perchance the farthest cone
> Of Scotland's rocky wilds, did seem
> To visit me, and me alone;
> Me unapproached by any Friend,
> But those who to my sorrows lend
> Tears due unto their own.[39]

Mary is special in her ability to feel and to generate heightened emotions, in captivity due to love of country and duty. The new year, in fact, means nothing to her as she – like the Moon – is timeless in her cold, benighted state. In stanza nine her permanent, earthly hopelessness is expressed as Wordsworth contributes to the image of Mary as martyr:

> Farewell forever human aid,
> Which abject Mortals vainly court!
> By friends deceived, by foes betrayed,
> Of fears the prey, of hopes the sport,
> Naught but the world-redeeming Cross
> Is able to supply my loss,
> My burthen to support.[40]

Like Burns earlier (especially when writing of Linlithgow Palace),[41] Wordsworth was a writer typical of his age in having his imagination fired by the geography of Mary's life. Alongside the similar cases of Charles I and Queen Elizabeth I, for Mary a topography of royal visitation has long been a phenomenon of popular fascination. Much later in his career, in 1833, Wordsworth the Cumbrian was inspired to write a sonnet on Mary landing at Siddick near Workington in 1568. In a technically well-executed text, Wordsworth brings forth Mary the full Romantic-age icon, at once breathtakingly beautiful and slaughtered by the world:

> Dear to the Loves, and to the Graces vowed,
> The Queen drew back the wimple that she wore;

---

[39] *Poems of William Wordsworth*, Vol. III, p. 109.
[40] *Poems of William Wordsworth*, Vol. III, pp. 110–11.
[41] In his *Journal of a Highland Tour* (1787), Burns reflects on the 'melancholy ruin' of Linlithgow Palace 'where the beautiful injured Mary Queen of Scots was born': Nigel Leask (ed.), *The Oxford Edition of the Works of Robert Burns*, Vol. I: *Commonplace books, Tour Journal and Miscellaneous Prose* (Oxford, 2014), p. 145.

And to the throng how touchingly she bowed
That hailed her landing on the Cumbrian shore;
Bright as a Star (that, from a sombre cloud
Of pine-tree foliage poised in air, forth darts,
When a soft summer gale at evening parts
The gloom that did its loveliness enshroud)
She smiled; but Time, the old Saturnian Seer,
Sighed on the wing as her foot pressed the strand,
With step prelusive to a long array
Of woes and degradations hand in hand,
Weeping captivity, and shuddering fear
Stilled by the ensanguined block of Fotheringay![42]

At Siddick, Mary had written to Elizabeth entreating the English queen's protection, but only a few days later she would begin nearly two decades of English captivity, staying briefly at Carlisle Castle before being sent further south. Wordsworth's text crushes the 'time' that crushes Mary, moving in short order from the 'Cumbrian shore' to Fotheringay in Northamptonshire where Mary was beheaded (and a place also associated with the demise of the Yorkist line, in the murder of Richard III). A familiar pattern is in place as Mary is 'hailed' by the people on the shore (a countermand, implicitly, to Elizabeth's legendary popularity) and bows graciously in return. In Cumbria, but also in futurity, her 'loveliness' is apparent 'like a star' 'enshrouded' by darkness. Wordsworth and his contemporaries, and writers in the previous seven or so decades, therefore rebuke Whig history in favour of minting a pristine image of Mary, Queen of Scots that still endures today.

Poets such as Wordsworth were no doubt influenced by the strong impression made on European culture by Schiller's popularisation of Mary, but we need next to turn to the fiction of Sir Walter Scott (1771–1832) for a more extensive treatment of Mary's 'personality'. Here, Scott in general follows most directly in the path of Schiller's character-treatment of Mary. David Hewitt sums up Scott's enthusiasm for German Romanticism from the early 1790s, during which decade he translated Burger, Goethe and Schiller, and its effect upon him:

'I was German-mad', said Scott in a letter of 13 December 1827 (*Letters*, 10.331). The new enthusiasm liberated [him] from the constrictions of eighteenth-century English poetry. But in the long run what was of far greater importance to Scott was the German interest in national identity, folk culture, and medieval literature.[43]

---

[42] *Poems of William Wordsworth*, Vol. III, pp. 492–93. Read dismissively as a piece of cloying sentimentality, Wordsworth's text features also in Brigid Brophy, Michael Levey and Charles Osborne (eds), *Fifty Works of English Literature We Could Do Without* (London, 1967).

[43] David Hewitt, 'Scott, Sir Walter (1771–1832)', *ODNB* (https://doi.org/10.1093/ref:odnb/24928).

It is a fairly obvious point, but one not always parsed in detail, that the historical dramas of Schiller, in particular, pave the way for the historical poetry and fiction of Scott. Scott's poetry provides our first encounter with the author's interest in Mary, quickened undoubtedly by the recent success of Schiller's hugely popular play.[44] In August 1802 he wrote to Lady Anne Hamilton (1766–1846), pleased that she had enjoyed his poem 'Cadzow Castle' (both one of the Hamilton houses and a text he had dedicated to her). The noble family of Hamilton had looked askance at Mary's marriage to Darnley, but came to support the queen when pressure was put on her to abdicate. In 'Cadzow Castle', Scott writes of 'haggard [Lord] Lindesay's iron eye,/That saw fair Mary weep in vain',[45] and explains who this person was in his letter to Lady Hamilton:

> Your Ladyship will recollect that this caitiff was the agent employed by Murray's faction as the most unrelenting of the party to force Mary when imprisoned in Lochleven Castle to sign a deed abdicating the throne: he executed his office with the most savage brutality and even pinched with his iron glove the arm of the weeping sovereign when she averted her eyes from the fatal parchment which she was compelld to sign.[46]

Previously associated with the murder of Rizzio, David Lindsay, tenth earl of Crawford, is for Scott a treacherous 'caitiff', or villain. Scott retained his strong emotional interest in Mary's narrative for the rest of his life, maintaining, perhaps, a kind of chivalrous attraction towards her while believing her to be grievously at fault in the conduct of many aspects of her life. She represented for him an intriguing mystery, because of both her legendary charisma and his own, self-acknowledged, ambivalence towards her. In 1822, Scott expressed delighted gratitude to Robert Pitcairn (1793–1855) for the gift of the latter's *Collections relative to the Funerals of Mary Queen of Scots* (1822), telling his correspondent about 'a painting in my possession, supposed to be original, of Queen Mary's head after decollation . . . if this painting was really executed the day after the murder, it is a first rate curiosity'.[47] Part of Scott's excitement about this painting is that Mary's likeness, he claims, resembles 'the testoon' or silver coin imprinted with her head from the period of her reign. Here, as in other

---

[44] Among an extensive collection of Schiller's works collected in his library at Abbotsford, Scott owned the first English translation of *Mary Stuart* (1801). See *Catalogue of the Library of Abbotsford* (Edinburgh, 1838), p. 212; when Scott obtained this copy is unknown, but there can be no doubt that he would have been aware of the English version shortly after publication.

[45] Sir Walter Scott, *The Shorter Poems*, ed. P. D. Garside and Gillian Hughes (Edinburgh, 2020), pp. 111–23, ll. 147–48.

[46] *The Letters of Sir Walter Scott*, ed. H. J. C. Grierson and others, centenary edn, 12 vols (London, 1932–79), vol. 1, p. 151.

[47] *Letters of Sir Walter Scott*, vol. 7, pp. 245–46.

instances, he seeks to come close to what he perceives as the idea of the real Mary; at some point, Scott had collected what he believed to be the mother of pearl crucifix that Mary had carried to her execution, this item remaining at his home at Abbotsford to this day.[48] The paradox of his irreconcilable attraction to, and censure of, the Scottish queen is summed up in a letter to his son-in-law John Gibson Lockhart of August 1828:

> I cannot think of any biography that I could easily do ex[c]epting Queen Mary and that I would decidedly not do because my opinion in point of fact is contrary both to the popular feeling and to my own.[49]

Scott provides a substantial depiction of Mary in his novel *The Abbot* (1820), having originally intended to treat her at length in its predecessor, *The Monastery* (1820). The latter, while set in the age of nascent Reformation strife between Catholics and Protestants in the 1550s, places its real historical figures largely in the background as it 'foregrounds some of the more localised events and practices in the Eastern part of the Scottish Border over which the centralised government had great difficulty maintaining control'.[50] Moving beyond this fascination with his home turf around Melrose and set around ten years later, *The Abbot* provided a more natural point to introduce his treatment of Mary, in the context of a pivotal moment in Scottish religious and dynastic history: her imprisonment and escape from Lochleven Castle in 1567. Mary appears for the first time in the second and much more substantially in the third volume of *The Abbot*, which was longer than usual as Scott did 'not like to cut the train of Queen Mary's vestment'.[51] What we witness yet again, then, is the continuously thoughtful intensity and difficulty that Mary posed in Scott's imaginative firmament. However, even in its ambivalent outcome, or perhaps because of it, Mary's character in *The Abbot* was to be significantly influential; as Jayne Lewis points out: 'The Abbot . . . was to inspire numerous nineteenth-century paintings of Mary and stage dramatizations of her life'.[52]

Scott's fictional avatar is the youth Roland Graeme, who has some similarity in his agency to Schiller's fictional protagonist Mortimer. Graeme encounters

---

[48] Scott's interest in Marian commemorative objects also extended to his sending to J. W. Croker (1780–1857) 'a snuff box made out [of] the wood of Queen Mary's celebrated Yew tree at Cruikston castle in Renfrewshire': *Letters of Sir Walter Scott*, vol. 5, p. 123.
[49] *Letters of Sir Walter Scott*, vol. 10, pp. 483–84.
[50] Sir Walter Scott, *The Monastery*, ed. Penny Fielding (Edinburgh, 2000), p. 436.
[51] Sir Walter Scott, *The Abbot*, ed. Christopher Johnson (Edinburgh, 2000), p. 386.
[52] Lewis, 'The Reputations of Mary Queen of Scots'. See also H. P. Bolton (ed.), *Scott Dramatised* (London, 1992), pp. 375–93; and Marian Gleason, 'Mary Stuart on the English and American Stage' (unpublished masters thesis, University of Massachusetts, Amherst, 1936), pp. 9–11.

and becomes an enthusiastic devotee to Mary during her captivity in Lochleven Castle. The queen is rapturously introduced:

> Her face, her form, have been so deeply impressed upon the imagination, that, even at the distance of nearly three centuries, it is unnecessary to remind the most ignorant and uninformed reader of the striking traits which characterize that remarkable countenance, which seems at once to combine our ideas of the majestic, the pleasing, and the brilliant, leaving us to doubt whether they express most happily the queen, the beauty, or the accomplished woman. Who is there, at the very mention of Mary Stuart's name, that has not her countenance before him, familiar as that of the mistress of his youth, or the favourite daughter of his advanced age? Even those who feel compelled to believe all, or much of what her enemies laid to her charge, cannot think without a sigh upon a countenance expressive of anything rather than the foul crimes with which she was charged when living, and which still continue to shade, if not to blacken her memory. That brow, so truly open and regal – these eyebrows, so regularly graceful, which yet were saved from the charge of regular insipidity by the beautiful effect of the hazel eyes, which they overarched, and which seem to utter a thousand histories – the nose, with all its Grecian precision of outline – the mouth, so well proportioned, so sweetly formed, as if to speak nothing but what was delightful to hear – the dimpled chin – the stately swanlike neck, form a countenance, the like of which we know not to have existed in any other character moving in that high class of life, where the actresses as well as the actors command general and undivided attention.[53]

It is fair to say that at this point Mary has bewitched Scott's attention. Ostensibly, the action (or, in fact, the picture) is at this point being brought into focus via Roland, but the narrator (or really Scott, the connoisseur antiquarian collector of historic portraits and pamphlets) has pushed his youthful character out of the way – not so much to have an audience with Mary, but to be a voyeur. It is 'unnecessary to remind the most ignorant and uninformed reader' of the queen's beauty and charisma, but Scott is going to expend considerable lyrical effort in doing so. He is obviously fascinated, like Mickle, Burns, Wordsworth and others, and the passage sharply confirms the history of the previous fifty-plus years down to *The Abbot* that had established Mary's iconography in artistic expression.

If Scott is beguiled by Mary, he also paints her with rounded personality, outwardly stately but with a rich interior emotional life (again we see a general debt to Schiller). Waspishly defiant, Mary maintains the rhetoric of courtliness as at one point she welcomes the decidedly unwelcome watchful mistress of her captivity, the Lady of Lochleven: 'our good hostess knows well she has at all times access to our presence, and need not observe the useless ceremony of

---

[53] Scott, *The Abbot*, p. 187.

requiring our permission'.[54] At Lochleven, she feels 'terror' in the presence of Lord Ruthven for his part in the murder of David Rizzio, but maintains a calm exterior.[55] The Rizzio detail is brought to Mary's mind at this point as Ruthven is in her presence to make obeisance and simultaneously demand that she sign a deed of abdication in favour of her infant son. Mary has been and is at the centre of tumultuous events, often beyond her control, and is eloquently silent; but anticipating Ruthven's business the queen asks whether she is to be returned to her throne. Ruthven tells her that as a Catholic she can no longer preside over a country constantly in internecine feuding (the losing Catholic interest to be simply shifted aside, clearly), but also acknowledges the circumstantial conflicts that have beleaguered Mary's life (in her infant years the English and French made Scotland their battlefield in their attempts to betrothe her to the respective princes in each nation). In spirited response, Mary provides a slightly different historical emphasis:

> 'My lord,' said Mary, 'it seems to me that you fling on my unhappy and devoted head those evils, which, with far more justice, I may impute to your own turbulent, wild, and untameable dispositions – the frantic violence with which you, the Magnates of Scotland, enter into feuds against each other, sticking at no cruelty to gratify your wrath, taking deep revenge for the slightest offences, and setting at defiance those wise laws which your ancestors made for the staunching of such cruelty, rebelling against the lawful authority, and bearing yourselves as if there were no king in the land, or rather as if each were king in his own premises. And now you throw the blame on me – on me, whose life has been embittered – whose sleep has been broken – whose happiness has been wrecked by your dissensions.
>
> Have I not myself been obliged to travise wilds and mountains, at the head of a few faithful followers, to maintain peace and to put down oppression? Have I not worn harness on my person, and carried pistols at my saddle; fain to lay the softness of a woman, and the dignity of a Queen, that I might show an example to my followers?'[56]

Here in Scott, unmistakeably, is a reading of Mary whose destiny was often shaped by muscular masculinist interests. Her gender, style and political significance as well as her iconic beauty have continued to fascinate both historians and creative artists since Scott's novel. This afterlife or memory of Mary in eighteenth- and nineteenth-century literature tells a story of deep attraction, though often one simultaneously tinged with censure and even some revulsion. The complexities and contradictions here arguably speak as much of those knowing only of her reputation as they do of the real-life history of the

---

[54] Scott, *The Abbot*, p. 188.
[55] Scott, *The Abbot*, p. 197
[56] Scott, *The Abbot*, pp. 201–02.

Scottish queen. The wide historical dimensions of Mary's reception, post-Stuart Britain and post-French Revolutionary Europe, are obviously enough in play here. However, the material disinterred in this chapter remains largely scattered and not as well known as it might be. Amid these texts, more nuance might be explored; for instance, with regard to gender and the body (including the theme of suffering amid femininity). There remains much to be explored in the minting of Mary's cultural reputation in the period of the long eighteenth century and Romanticism, as a route to deeper understanding of how we view and read her now. Here, we have barely begun to scratch the surface.

EIGHT

'A tracked and hunted creature': Mary, Queen of Scots and the Histories of David Hay Fleming, Andrew Lang, Gordon Donaldson and Antonia Fraser

Catriona M. M. Macdonald

There is no new manuscript, no new methodology, no new perspective that will charm the scraps of the past that we have *now* into the embodiment of Mary as she was, or indeed resolve contested visions of Mary Stuart. This does not mean that, in the absence of a singular narrative, we should abandon Mary, hollowed out by academic historians, to Romance (although one can think of worse fates). Rather, understanding how historiographical tensions emerged or were amplified at key moments of cultural development ought to be a principal influence on how Mary is researched today. We rely on the insights of past generations more than we acknowledge: it is best to know them better.

With this in mind, this essay addresses the influence of four historians as two contemporary pairs – David Hay Fleming (1849–1931) and Andrew Lang (1844–1912); Gordon Donaldson (1913–1993) and Antonia Fraser (1932 to date) – in an effort to examine the ways in which the Mary bequeathed to history exists at the interface of contested ways of knowing the past. More so than any other Scottish monarch Mary's historiographical legacy has been structured in terms of multiple binaries determined by opposing camps that rely on each other for meaning and purpose but regularly cut across each other: pro- and anti-Marian factions; Catholic and Protestant writers; Scots and English; manuscript scholars and novelists. Any pretence that history invariably follows a Whiggish progress – a linear sequence of generations each building logically and unproblematically on the work of shared and acknowledged forebears – is undermined by Mary's story. Her historicisation is a complex process and has been shaped as much by the environments in which writers execute their craft as by the character of life in Scotland in the sixteenth century. Hay Fleming and Lang wrote at a time when history as an academic discipline was only slowly emerging in Scottish universities, when the popular presses were encouraging a growing appetite for accessible histories, when unionist nationalism and Presbyterianism were markers of Scottish identity and when women's access to higher education was limited as were their rights as citizens. Donaldson and Fraser, by contrast, wrote in a period of heightened academic interest in Scottish history, increasing multi-media engagement in heritage, growing interest in the cause of Scottish devolution and independence, second wave feminism and accelerating secularisation. These influences did not necessarily determine the histories of these four historians but they shaped their motives, methodologies and theories, and contributed to the public reception of new historical insights in their times, not to mention the nature of the literary friendships brokered across intellectual divides.

David Hay Fleming and Andrew Lang

The late nineteenth century was an exhibiting age: the International Exhibition of Science, Art and Industry was held in Glasgow in 1888; London's New Gallery hosted the Exhibition of the Royal House of Stuart in 1889; that same year the Scottish National Portrait Gallery was founded in Edinburgh; and in 1891 the collections of the Society of Antiquaries of Scotland came to share the new Portrait Gallery. In Glasgow, two further international exhibitions were held, a decade apart, in 1901 and 1911: the profits of the second going some way to founding a chair of Scottish History and Literature at the University of Glasgow.

The title page of the catalogue for the 1889 Royal Stuart Exhibition bore the image of Mary Stuart, and those attending the event on Regent Street would have viewed nineteen portraits of Mary, seventeen miniatures, four engravings, manuscripts from her reign, seals, coins, medals and a wide variety of objects owned or worked by Mary – part of a dress, curtains, a tablecloth, a cabinet.[1] In like fashion, visitors to Glasgow in 1901 would have noticed that Mary was the only monarch's name to grace not one but two of the Scottish History galleries. There they could marvel at a wide range of Mary-related objects: cuffs from Darnley's gloves, time pieces, a tankard, a handbell.[2] It was much the same in 1911 when Scotland's 'national' history was celebrated: Mary slippers, Mary paintings, a book of hours and much more excited the visitors to the Glasgow exhibition.[3]

Only in the second half of the nineteenth century, when public exhibitions resting on loans from private collections became more common; when literacy

---

[1] Exhibition of the Royal House of Stuart, Catalogue (London, 1889).
[2] International Exhibition, Glasgow 1901, Official Catalogue of the Scottish History and Archaeology Section (Glasgow, 1901), pp. 42–55.
[3] Scottish National Exhibition of National History, Art and Industry, Palace of History: Catalogue of Exhibits, Vol. II (Glasgow, 1911).

became the norm (following compulsory education in Scotland from 1872); when the popular press exploded; and when photography transformed the art of illustration, did it become possible for the public to 'own' Mary, in part by seeing her and appreciating her through the senses as much as their intellect. Historians in this period could also aspire to a new way of writing Mary, if they wished. Historiographical debates in this period thus had an immediate and appreciable impact on the public: even more so when they were played out in the foremost literary presses of the day and in books which an expanding readership could afford or borrow from a growing number of public libraries.

In September 1894 Thomas Graves Law (1836–1904), secretary of the Scottish History Society and Keeper of the Signet Library in Edinburgh,[4] wrote to David Hay Fleming commending him on his recent *Bookman* articles on Mary, Queen of Scots, 'that very improper but unfortunate lady', and encouraging him to 'republish [the work] in a more desirable form'.[5] Three days later, Law wrote to Hay Fleming again, emphasising that '[t]he Mariolatry of the present day is becoming exasperating and before long she will be raised to the altars of the Roman Church as a model of virtue to be revered and imitated'.[6] Hay Fleming – a historian of the Reformation from St Andrews – shared Law's sceptical judgement of Mary Stuart, and of the contemporary Catholic church for that matter. Law, one should note, had been a Catholic priest, but left the communion of the church in 1878.[7] Hay Fleming, meanwhile, was a member of the original secession church, a devout Presbyterian, and a resolute defender of Reformation principles, leaders and institutions, historic and contemporary. Having already published two volumes for the Scottish History Society – editions of the registers of the ministers, elders and deacons of St Andrews[8] – it is perhaps not surprising that he appeared to take Law's advice, and after three years of exhaustive scholarship, in 1897 published in book form an account of the life of Mary Stuart, up to the point of her flight to England.[9] It cemented his reputation as the 'go to' expert should a London literary journal require a

---

[4] Hay Fleming applied for the librarianship of the Signet Library following the death of Graves Law. See *Testimonials in favour of D. Hay Fleming, LL.D. candidate for the Librarianship of the Signet Library, Edinburgh* (April 1904): it includes a testimonial in which Andrew Lang notes '[Hay Fleming's] work on Mary Queen of Scots is remarkable for accuracy, judicious treatment, and research', p. 13.
[5] St Andrews Special Collections, MS38977/1/L/8, Thomas G. Law to David Hay Fleming, 18 September 1894. Hay Fleming's series of articles in the *Bookman* began in May 1894 and continued monthly until April 1895.
[6] St Andrews Special Collections, MS38977/1/L/8, Law to Hay Fleming, 21 September 1894.
[7] Peter Hume Brown, 'Memoir', in *Collected Essays and Reviews of Thomas Graves Law, LL.D.* (Edinburgh, 1904), pp. vii–xx, at p. x.
[8] David Hay Fleming (ed.), *Register of the Minister, Elders and Deacons of the Christian Congregation of St Andrews* (Edinburgh, 1889), ser. 1, vols 4 and 7.
[9] David Hay Fleming, *Mary Queen of Scots from her Birth to her Flight into England* (London, 1897).

scholarly review of any volume relating to Mary, and Hay Fleming regularly obliged: he relished any opportunity to point to the errors of others.[10]

A frequent focus of Hay Fleming's ire, although they were good friends, was Andrew Lang, better known in the 1880s as an acclaimed classicist, folklorist, social anthropologist, literary editor (he edited Robert Burns, Sir Walter Scott and Robert Louis Stevenson, for example), a serious student of the supernatural and a writer of fairy tales.[11] Lang – a native of Selkirk – was by this stage (albeit reluctantly) a metropolitan Scot, having completed his education at Oxford, and settled into a literary life in Kensington.[12] He clashed first with Hay Fleming in 1893, when the younger man (an alumnus of St Andrews) published a history of Hay Fleming's home town,[13] but in the years that followed their principal battle-ground was the Reformation and, of course, in this regard, neither could avoid Mary Stuart.[14] Lang made it his principal aim to attack conventional, hagiographic treatments of the Reformation leaders, question the tenets of the movement, attack its legacy and seek justice for Mary.

By contrast, Hay Fleming believed that Mary had returned to Scotland seeking to 'trample down' the Reformation; that she had a 'criminal connection with the hated foreigner [David Rizzio]';[15] was deeply involved in Darnley's murder; had established an amoral alliance with Bothwell; and had placed in jeopardy the legacy of John Knox (*c.* 1514–72). Still, he admired aspects of her character: in 1900 he published two documents in the *Bookman* – one from the British Museum, the other from the Scottish National Portrait Gallery – that furnished 'fresh proof of [Mary's] indomitable courage [and] . . . her hopeful disposition'.[16]

For Lang, Mary's threat to the Reformation settlement was predictably of less significance. He deplored the intolerance of the Reformers and identified in their treatment of Mary abundant proof of their despotism and destructiveness. Lang had many reservations about Mary's role in Darnley's murder and her

---

[10] Examples from the *Bookman* include: David Hay Fleming, 'The Tragedy of Fotheringay', *Bookman*, June 1895; 'The Queen of Scots and Her Love Affairs', *Bookman*, October 1903; 'The Portraits of the Queen of Scots', *Bookman*, February 1904; 'The Queen's Quair', *Bookman*, August 1904; 'The Queen of Scots', *Bookman*, February 1906; 'The Girlhood of Mary Queen of Scots', *Bookman*, November 1908. See also David Hay Fleming, *Critical Reviews Relating Chiefly to Scotland* (London, 1912).

[11] Roger Lancelyn Green, *Andrew Lang* (Leicester, 1946).

[12] Catriona M. M. Macdonald, 'Andrew Lang and Scottish Historiography: Taking on Tradition', *SHR* 94 (2015): 207–36.

[13] Andrew Lang, *St Andrews* (London, 1893).

[14] Catriona M. M. Macdonald, 'Contesting the Reformation: Roger Mason's ("sufficiently plausible") Debt to David Hay Fleming and Andrew Lang', in *Re-Thinking the Renaissance and Reformation in Scotland: Essays in Honour of Roger A. Mason*, ed. S. Reid (Woodbridge, forthcoming), Chapter 2.

[15] *Bookman*, September 1894, p. 176; December 1894, p. 79.

[16] *Bookman*, April 1900, p. 11.

marriage to Bothwell, but the queen captivated him. In a letter to Sidney Lee (1859–1926), editor of the *Dictionary of National Biography*, an expert on the reign of England's Elizabeth I and an editor of Shakespeare, Lang compared the fates of the two queens:

> ... who would not rather have had a clean chop at Fotheringay, like a lady, than haunt and be haunted, like Elizabeth? I'd risk my soul with Mary rather than with Elizabeth.[17]

This was more than a clash of personalities. The methodologies each author deployed spoke to two contrasting views of history's purpose, two different attitudes to manuscript study and two different ideas about historical biography. Leaving to one side their books and articles on the Reformation, and reviews of each other's work and that of others on general Reformation themes, the literary dialogue between these two historians on all things Mary amounted to three books, three reviews and twenty-one articles concentrated in a period of fourteen years. Published by presses and in journals of national import at a time of cultural change, this represents a significant and yet neglected debate in Scottish history.

The story forms itself at the interface of romance and science, and at several crossing points where methodology, bias and judgement meet. Hay Fleming's intent was clear: he would destroy the myth of Mary by smothering it with facts. In the very act of historicising Mary he was confident her mystery would dissipate. For Lang, understanding the mystery was all. Facts were to be used to elucidate the mystery, to anchor it in reality: they were not mutually incompatible but mutually sustaining. And by pursuing Mary in material culture as well as manuscript study Lang aimed to make her real.

The approach that Hay Fleming would eventually take in his book-length treatment of Mary's life before her imprisonment was heralded in his *Bookman* articles of 1894–95 where he began as he meant to continue. He highlighted that even the dates of her birth and her father's death were contested from the very beginning;[18] he took issue both with contemporaries and with subsequent historians who showed insufficient care over matters relating to the minutiae of Mary's life; he disputed where she landed in France and when exactly she returned to Scotland.[19] This was more than pedantry: empiricism was to be the way that other opinions hiding just below the surface were to be proved. So, instead of a safe refuge for the infant queen, the French court, according to Hay Fleming, encouraged Mary to 'drynk of that liquor' that had brought

---

[17] Bodleian, MS Eng Misc.d.178, Andrew Lang to Sidney Lee, 11 February (no year given).
[18] Hay Fleming, 'Mary Queen of Scots I', *Bookman*, May 1894.
[19] Hay Fleming, 'Mary Queen of Scots II', *Bookman*, June 1894.

'plague to this realme' – namely Roman Catholicism.[20] Hay Fleming saw secret treaties signed by Mary at the time of her marriage to the *dauphin* as Mary making of Scotland a 'free gift' to the King of France should she die childless.[21] He extended no sympathy to the young queen on the breaking of candles by a mob during her first mass in Scotland, contrasting her inconvenience disparagingly with the trauma meted out to Protestants during the St Bartholomew's Day Massacre (1572).[22] Of all the authorities for whom Hay Fleming reserved particular criticism, Joseph Stevenson (1806–95) was to the fore. Stevenson – a Catholic convert, and ordained priest as well as a noted archivist and manuscript scholar – was referred to sarcastically as 'the learned Jesuit' who, according to Hay Fleming, glossed over the immoralities of the French court and in general acted as an apologist for Mary.

When Hay Fleming's *Mary Queen of Scots* appeared in 1897 his manifesto was fully developed: he would avoid 'fictitious facts' that had been passed uncritically down the years and 'ascertain truth'; he would 'state – fairly, briefly, and clearly – all the more interesting events in Mary's life . . . without attempting to suggest or sustain any theory'.[23] Again, Stevenson was attacked: Hay Fleming alleged he had 'dimmed his great reputation as an historical student by prejudice, partiality and perversion'.[24] What Hay Fleming offered instead was a narrative of 170 pages supplemented by 302 pages of notes and references, 23 further pages of hitherto unpublished documents, and a 28-page 'itinerary' showing Mary's movements on a day-to-day basis up to the point she crossed the border into England in 1568. It is a remarkable text for its structure if nothing else, but in that structure Hay Fleming's intent is clear and uncompromising. Mary would acquire mortal status by reducing her life to a series of facts – some of which, being contested, reduced her further and left few solid foundations on which to make meaning out of her life. Just a glimpse at Hay Fleming's 'itinerary' shows how effective this method could be. Mary's life is denied narrative coherence and becomes nothing more than the dated and tabulated traces left in the *Register of the Privy Seal*, the *Register of the Great Seal*, the *Register of the Privy Council* and various calendars, histories and epistolary and literary survivals. It is one of the most obvious attempts in Scottish history at having the last word (though, of course, Hay Fleming failed in this).

Lang's review of Hay Fleming's book saw behind the author's claims to impartiality: this was a man, after all, whose sympathies with the Regent Moray and John Knox were only too obvious. Lang also attacked Hay Fleming's polemics

---

[20] Ibid.
[21] Hay Fleming, 'Mary Queen of Scots IV', *Bookman*, August 1894.
[22] Hay Fleming, 'Mary Queen of Scots V', *Bookman*, September 1894.
[23] Hay Fleming, *Mary Queen of Scots*, pp. v–vi.
[24] Ibid., p. vi.

and defended Stevenson against his detractor.[25] Hay Fleming's footnotes Lang describes as 'copious, minute, and controversial', ideal for 'severe students'.[26] Echoing his literary hero, Sir Walter Scott, the reviewer admitted that Mary could not be absolved of Darnley's murder, but if Hay Fleming had hoped to destroy Mary's mystery, he was sadly mistaken. Lang countered Hay Fleming's reductionism by exploring, not avoiding, the contradictions and the unknowns that Hay Fleming thought would undermine the queen's allure, and he searched for Mary in types of evidence for which Hay Fleming had no answer.[27]

In 1900, Lang published his first study of the Casket Letters in *Blackwood's*, proposing that at least Letter II (the 'Glasgow letter') was a forgery. A year later, he published *The Mystery of Mary Stuart*, in which – *contra* Hay Fleming – he credits Father Pollen (1858-1925), a Jesuit priest, for his archival assistance. Even before one opens this volume, the centrality of material culture is writ large: the cover is embellished with an illustration of a coin from Mary's reign and the frontispiece is a portrait of Mary from the Earl of Morton's collection. In total there are fifteen illustrations and six photographic plates, including images of the casket in which the famous letters (printed in full) were alleged to have been found. Indeed, the very first paragraph places material culture front and centre:

> Mr Carlyle not unjustly described the tragedy of Mary Stuart as but a personal incident in the true national History of Scotland. He asked for other and more essential things than these revelations of high life. Yet he himself writes in great detail the story of the Diamond Necklace of Marie Antoinette. The diamonds of the French, the silver casket of the Scottish Queen, with all that turned on them, are of real historical interest, for these trifles brought to the surface the characters and principles of men living in an age of religious revolution.[28]

Hay Fleming haunts the first pages, where Lang eschews 'uninviting series of contradictory statements and of contested dates, and of disputable assertions':

> History is apt to be, and some think that it should be, a mere series of dry uncoloured statements. Such an event occurred, such a word was uttered, such a deed was done, at this date or the other. We give references to our authorities, to men who heard of the events or even saw them when they happened. But we the writer and the readers, *see* nothing: we only offer or accept bald and imperfect information. If we try to write

---

[25] Andrew Lang, 'Mary Queen of Scots', *Bookman*, October 1897.
[26] Ibid.
[27] Lang, a poet himself, also examined ballad evidence relating to the story of Mary Stuart: see 'The Mystery of "The Queen's Marie"', *Blackwood's Edinburgh Magazine*, September 1895.
[28] Andrew Lang, *Mystery of Mary Stuart* (London, 1901), p. v.

history on another method, we become 'picturesque': we are composing a novel, not striving painfully to attain the truth. Yet, when we know not the details; the aspect of dwellings now ruinous; the hue and cut of garments long wasted into dust; the passing frown, or smile, or tone of the actors and the speakers in these dramas of life long ago; ... then we know not the real history, the real truth.[29]

Lang sought to 'make mental pictures of the historic people who play their parts on what is now a dimly lighted stage', and dealt first with Mary:

> Her costumes when she would be queenly, have left their mark on the memory of men: the ruff from which rose the snowy neck; the brocaded bodice, with puffed and jewelled sleeves and stomacher; the diamonds enamelled with sacred scenes, or scenes from fable...[30]

The emphasis that Lang placed on 'seeing' Mary is crucial – in order to generate the type of history he valued he identified a need to go beyond manuscript scholarship and, in addition, to point to its limitations. Lang devoted over 170 pages of this volume to the Casket Letters: by doing so he laid out clearly that documents do not resolve historical mysteries, they are the very root and cause of debate; they do not undermine Romance, they are its very essence.

Hay Fleming, by contrast, considered Lang had offered in the *Mystery of Mary Stuart* 'a vivid, though occasionally overdrawn, presentation of the *dramatis personae*', and took issue with his analysis of the Casket Letters, pointing to dates that are 'out of joint', and accusing Lang of indulging in 'chronological impossibilities'. Yet he acknowledged Lang's 'fresh light and new theories'.[31]

Five years later, and a year after he published his *John Knox and the Reformation* (1905), Lang produced a second volume on Mary – *Portraits and Jewels of Mary Stuart*.[32] This book reproduced and expanded on essays in the *Scottish Historical Review* on the same subject, highlighting that Lang was now claiming academic as well as public audiences.[33] The book marks a shift in Lang's historical practice. Having identified material evidence as central to any appreciation of a historical figure, he highlighted here the dangers of 'false portraits', forgeries and – as he puts it – 'pseudo Maries'.[34] 'There lie before me', he writes, 'photographs

---

[29] Ibid., pp. 1–2. In the 1890s Lang reflected in a number of articles on the purpose of history and its status as a science and as literature. See, for example, 'History as She Ought to be Wrote', *Blackwood's Edinburgh Magazine*, August 1899.

[30] Ibid., p. 5.

[31] David Hay Fleming, 'The Mystery of Mary Stuart', *The Athenaeum*, 16 November 1901, as reproduced in Hay Fleming (ed.), *Critical Reviews Relating Chiefly to Scotland* (London, 1912), pp. 87–93, at pp. 87, 88, 93.

[32] See also Andrew Lang, 'Queen Mary's Jewels', *Good Works*, December 1895; 'Queen Mary in Art', *Bookman*, October 1907.

[33] Andrew Lang, 'Portraits and Jewels of Mary Stuart' *SHR* 3 (1906): 129–56, 273–300.

[34] Andrew Lang, *Portraits and Jewels of Mary Stuart* (Glasgow, 1906), p. 4.

of eighteen Maries, displayed at the Glasgow International Exhibition of 1901', but the real Mary 'in no way resembled 15 out of the 18 portraits exhibited for public edification at Glasgow'.[35] Mastering the history and provenance of a range of portraits, Lang may be credited with adding to scholarship in this area: no other Scottish historian writing at this time immersed themself quite as much in material culture. Lang concludes by pointing to thirteen authentic portraits or portraits related closely to other authentic or contemporary portraits.[36]

Lang's pursuit of authentic original portraits had much to do with 'seeing' Mary. He noted:

> Mary was either beautiful or she bewitched people into thinking her beautiful . . . Even Knox calls her face 'pleasing' . . . even Elizabeth recognized something 'divine' in her hated rival . . . the populace of Edinburgh cried: 'Heaven bless that sweet face', says Knox, as she rode by . . .[37]

By cross-referencing the portraits with the manuscript record and Mary's inventories of jewels, Lang attempts something extraordinary – to see *history* in the face of the queen. Writing of a drawing of the young queen in the Bibliothèque Nationale, he notes:

> The face has not the sly or foxy expression: Mary was not yet a tracked and hunted creature, but a candid girl. It is a pretty face, but the bald expanse of brow adds to the lifeless effect. Nobody could guess that this girl, so prim and staid, was a creature of infinitely changeful moods, flashing readily from laughter to tears. Yet that is what she undeniably was or became.[38]

Lang's last work on Mary appeared in 1907 when he retracted much of what he had written on Casket Letter II in 1901:[39] he announced in the *Scottish Historical*

---

[35] Ibid., p. 5.

[36] Lang lists these as follows: the Chantilly drawing of 1552; the bridal medal (1558); the drawing of about 1558–59 by 'the presumed Jehan de Court'; the Douce portrait in the Jones collection, South Kensington; the Probert portrait; the Florentine, Rijksmuseum, Medicean Book of Hours and Welbeck miniatures; the Breslau wax medallion; the miniature in the Royal Collection at Windsor; the Leven and Melville portrait, derived, at least, from some work of 1559–60; in first widowhood (1561), Janet's drawing of the 'Deuil Blanc'; as derivatives, Mrs Anstruther-Duncan's, Lord Leven's and the Powis miniatures, claiming to date from 1572; the Sheffield type of portrait, dating from 1578; the Lesley medallion, published in 1578; the Morton portrait (1577?); the Hilliard miniature of 1579 (?); Lady Orde's, the Rijksmuseum's, Lady Milford's and the Florentine later miniatures of c. 1584: *Portraits and Jewels*, pp. 105–06.

[37] Ibid., p. 13.

[38] Ibid., pp. 18–19.

[39] In 1911 Lang wrote to Hay Fleming sharing his doubts about again republishing *The Mystery of Mary Stuart*, as his analysis had moved on so dramatically: St Andrews, Special Collections, Lang to Hay Fleming, 30 November 1911.

Review that he had revised his earlier opinion and concluded that Mary had written the whole of Letter II or at least that the conclusions he had drawn from his earlier analysis pointed more convincingly towards Mary's guilt.[40] In response, T. F. Henderson (1844–1923), an author whose *Mary Queen of Scots* Lang had reviewed for the *Morning Post* in 1905 and with whom Lang had disagreed on the authorship of the Casket Letters, published a response to Lang's self-conversion (as Henderson styled it). He referred to Lang's *Mystery of Mary Stuart* as exhibiting the 'certainty of uncertainty', identifying in Lang 'a passionate predilection for his own pet "blood-thirsty" theory'. Henderson concluded:

> To render sufficiently plausible his version of the tragedy [Lang] had to crowd his piece with villains, to jumble their motives together, and to double-dye them in hues too deeply and monotonously dark.[41]

While Henderson suggested that Lang had sacrificed history for Romance, other historians then and since commended his forensic treatment of the evidence relating to Mary's alleged involvement in the death of Darnley, her second husband. In 1934 J. D. Mackie (1887–1978), Professor of Scottish History and Literature at the University of Glasgow, thought Lang was right to question the authenticity of Letter II; commended him for not overstating his case ('[a]ll [Lang] demanded was a suspension of judgement'); and suggested that Lang could have mounted a stronger defence against Henderson.[42] In 1949 John Bennett Black (1883–1964), Burnett-Fletcher Professor of History at the University of Aberdeen, having surveyed published works on the subject since Lang's death, concluded that

> Lang's suspicions, hypotheses, and affirmations, as he developed them in his 'unconverted state', were generally well-founded – better founded than he imagined: that his recantation in 1907 was premature and ill-advised; and furthermore, that his plea for a 'not proven' verdict was probably the right one in the circumstances.[43]

Lang was equivocal about Mary's innocence but a determined believer that her tragic fate had been sealed, no matter what she did. In the second volume of his *History of Scotland* (1902) Lang noted '[n]o conduct could have saved Mary from some "strange tragedy", but the passions that slept within her were to

---

[40] Andrew Lang, 'The Casket Letters', *SHR* 5 (1907): 1–12.
[41] T. F. Henderson, 'Mr Lang and the Casket Letters', *SHR* 5 (1908): 161–74, at pp. 166, 162, 174.
[42] J. D. Mackie, 'Andrew Lang and the House of Stuart', Andrew Lang Lecture, St Andrews, 21 November 1934 (Oxford, 1935), pp. 23–24.
[43] J. B. Black, 'Andrew Lang and the Casket Letter Controversy', Andrew Lang Lecture, St Andrews, 11 May 1949 (Edinburgh, 1951), p. 40.

add dishonour to her predestined fall'.[44] Similarly, in the *Mystery of Mary Stuart* Lang commented that 'destiny interwove the life-threads of Bothwell and Mary. They were fated to come together . . . In the phrase of Aristotle, "Nature *wishes*" to produce this or that result'.[45] While admitting that historical evidence may point in conflicting directions, opening up alternative routes through the past, Lang's belief in 'fate' trapped Mary as surely as the opinions of those who were convinced of her guilt. Ideas about destiny bequeathed to Lang's writing the air of Romance – something only enhanced by his recourse to visual and material evidence – but it was more than a narrator's ploy. Mary's execution foreclosed on an ending. The route to that final tragedy could be debated passionately, its meaning was the subject of academic disputations, but for Lang her story was inseparable from its ending. This was more than hindsight: it was a different vision of history itself. Lang read backwards while others, denying fate as an active power in the causal connections linking historical events or an explanation beyond reason for the consequences of actions, read forwards. In doing so, they kept open the prospect of choices not made, keeping alive the a-historical possibility of a different Mary. It is by no means clear which at times was the more honest approach, which the more 'professional'.

Gordon Donaldson and Antonia Fraser

In 1974, two years after the British release of Universal Pictures' film *Mary Queen of Scots*, which was nominated for five Academy Awards, Gordon Donaldson, Sir William Fraser Professor of Scottish History and Palaeography at the University of Edinburgh, published the biography *Mary Queen of Scots*. In the preface to Donaldson's biography, English historian and Elizabethan expert A. L. Rowse (1903–97) lamented the role of the amateur in the historiography of Mary:

> Mary Queen of Scots has been far too much written about by non-historians. Her romantic personality and tragic career have had a great appeal for poets, dramatists and general biographers; but it is time that the subject should be dealt with by a professional historian, particularly a Scottish historian.[46]

Neither Hay Fleming nor Lang were 'professional' historians; at least, neither occupied a university position, though Lang made a living as a writer across many genres, including history. Following the Second World War, however,

---

[44] Andrew Lang, *History of Scotland*, Vol. II (New York, 1902), p. 101. He also refers to Mary as the 'predestined victim of uncounted treasons, of unnumbered wrongs: wrongs that warped, maddened, and bewildered her noble nature, but never quenched her courage, never deadened her gratitude to a servant, never shook her loyalty to a friend' (p. 330).

[45] Lang, *Mystery of Mary Stuart*, p. 45.

[46] A. L. Rowse, 'Foreword' in Gordon Donaldson, *Mary Queen of Scots* (London, 1974), p. 5.

the expansion in higher education encouraged earlier trends of according university historians professional status while generally denying it to others whose relationship with the market was assumed to compromise their impartiality and rigour. And yet, while Donaldson had been flattered by being approached to contribute a Scottish volume to Rowse's 'Men and their Times' series, he admitted that his book contributed little that was new to the story of Mary, and considered it 'the least important book I have written'.[47] Elsewhere he reflected that

> ... any historian who wants to make a little money for a change will do well to turn his attention to Mary – at least there is that temptation to which I, among others, have succumbed. One might put it shortly – 'There's money in Mary'.[48]

Donaldson had already published *The First Trial of Mary Queen of Scots* in 1969, following in Lang's footsteps when it came to examining the manipulation of the Casket Letters (although he does not credit the earlier writer's influence). But the most lucrative publication on Mary in modern times, however, was Antonia Fraser's book of that year, *Mary Queen of Scots*, which was on the best seller list in the UK and USA for many weeks throughout 1969 and 1970.[49] Had she taken the advice of Sir James Fergusson of Kilkerran (1904–73), Keeper of the Records of Scotland, however, Fraser would have written instead on Mary's secretary, William Maitland of Lethington (1525–73).[50] Fraser's motivation, however, was not entirely financial, as her autobiography makes clear. In response to Kilkerran, Fraser 'wanted to cry out: "But I've not been obsessed since childhood by some Scottish civil servant!"'[51] Instead, ever since reading *Our Island Story* (1905) – a children's history of England – by Scotswoman H .E. Marshall (1867–1941) as a young girl, Fraser had identified with Mary, Queen of Scots.[52] In particular, she acknowledged the influence of A. S. Forrest's illustrations in that work.[53] Indeed, she has admitted to 'inserting' herself into Mary's story, in ways she has resisted in subsequent histories of other historical figures.[54]

---

[47] EUL, Research Collections, Gen1632/6/21, Gordon Donaldson to Antonia Fraser, 5 July 1974; James Kirk, *Her Majesty's Historiographer* (Edinburgh, 1926), pp. 61–62.

[48] EUL, Research Collections, Gen1635/9/39, Gordon Donaldson, 'Writers on Mary Queen of Scots' (typewritten MS, n.d.), p. 1.

[49] *Washington Post*, 31 May 1970; Antonia Fraser, *My History: a Memoir of Growing Up* (London, 2015), pp. 299–300.

[50] Antonia Fraser, 'Castles in the Air', *History Today*, 1 February 1999, pp. 62–63, at p. 63.

[51] Fraser, *My History*, pp. 294–95.

[52] Ibid., p. 41.

[53] When she designed her wedding trousseau, Fraser copied the peaked head-dress worn by the imprisoned Mary in Forrest's illustration.

[54] Fraser, *My History*, pp. 41–42, 301.

Fraser's personal motivation in writing about Mary, the literary lineage with which she identified in her quest for Mary, her gender, her confessional identity (she is a Roman Catholic) and her status outwith the academy, distinguished her from Donaldson (an Episcopalian) and most other university historians of this period. And yet, it was widely accepted (even by Donaldson) that Fraser's was one of the best studies of Mary, ever.[55] Fraser's exhaustively researched volume was more than 600 pages in length and was widely praised for its compelling narrative and engaging literary style. How is this to be reconciled? Did this prove, as Fraser suggested in a review of *The Crime of Mary Stuart* (1967) authored by the Scottish nationalist George Malcolm Thomson (1899-1996), that there was 'a reluctance in Scotland to face up to the subject of Mary, Queen of Scots', or were there deeper problems, unresolved tensions within Scottish history itself, despite an emerging historiographical renaissance in the 1960s, that fell to an amateur to resolve?[56]

In 1974 Donaldson and Fraser were 'angling in the same stream'[57] when both wrote on historiographical approaches to the life of Mary: the final chapter in Donaldson's *Mary Queen of Scots* lays out 'The Continuing Debate', while Fraser in February of that year delivered a lecture to the Royal Stuart Society on 'Mary Queen of Scots and the Historians'. Both covered much the same ground, tracing works on Mary by (among others) contemporaries John Knox, George Buchanan (1506-82) and John Leslie (1527-96), through the 'Enlightened' words of William Robertson (1721-93), David Hume (1711-76) and William Tytler (1711-92) and into the nineteenth century and beyond. When it came to Hay Fleming and Lang, it was clear where Donaldson's sympathies lay – he noted:

> [w]hile Lang was more a journalist than a scholar, Fleming was a scholar through and through, and everything he put down could be supported by documentary evidence . . . *The Life of Queen Mary* is less a book for the general reader than a quarry for scholars.[58]

Fraser, by contrast, pointed to Hay Fleming's religious prejudice in his 'so called biography', but credited him likewise with writing a book of inestimable

---

[55] R. G. Cant noted '[i]t is not merely the most comprehensive study of Queen Mary since the early days of this century but beyond doubt the best account of her career and personality yet produced': see 'Review', *SHR* 49 (1970): 204.
[56] Antonia Fraser, 'Misjudged Queen', *New Statesman*, 24 February 1967.
[57] EUL, Research Collections, Gen1632/6/21, Gordon Donaldson to Antonia Fraser, 5 July 1974.
[58] Donaldson, *Mary Queen of Scots*, p. 190.

value to later historians. When it came to Lang, she mounted a stout defence, although elsewhere she rejected his fatalism.[59] She noted:

> rereading their controversy today, I get the impression that Henderson was allowed to win the battle on points, simply because of Lang's lesser status as an amateur historian. Certainly Lang's logic is in nearly all cases superior to that of Henderson, yet in the end Lang surrendered to Henderson and allowed him to have the victory. Lang did not survive to see the day when no reputable historian would use them as unchallenged evidence.[60]

Donaldson and Fraser differed not only in their approach to a recognised literary lineage, but in the debts Fraser acknowledged to other scholars not credited in the accepted Marian canon. In addition to the male historians examined by Donaldson, Fraser acknowledged the influence (for good and ill) of Agnes Strickland (1796–1874):[61]

> Agnes Strickland worked hard and conscientiously from documents when this was extremely difficult to do . . . when the State Paper Office itself was first opened to the public even then women were debarred, and the Strickland sisters only secured entry after fearful struggles, wire-pulling and anguish.[62]

Fraser's mother, Elizabeth Pakenham, Countess of Longford (1906–2002) was herself an acclaimed biographer of royal women against whom Fraser in 1965 had to defend Mary as her own when it was suggested Longford write a biography of the Scottish queen. This galvanised Fraser, who until then had written only children's books, two books on toys and short articles about shooting parties.[63] Elsewhere, Fraser has also recorded her debt to romance novelist Barbara Cartland (1901–2000).[64]

Fraser's gender was an important influence that shaped the reception of her book, both positively and negatively. In 2000 historian Daniel Snowman (1938–) suggested that Fraser's biography of Mary, published a year before Germaine Greer's *Female Eunuch* (1970), 'helped raise an early standard for the

---

[59] Fraser notes '[i]t is far too easy in writing history to assume that the end is foreordained, and therefore to write it backwards with a doom-laden note of tragedy': 'Mary Queen of Scots and Marie Antoinette: Two Queens or One?' Royal Stuart Society, London, 2003, pp. 9, 11.

[60] Antonia Fraser, 'Mary Queen of Scots and the Historians', Royal Stuart Society, Ilford, 1974, p. 9.

[61] See Jane Margaret Strickland, *Life of Agnes Strickland* (Edinburgh, 1987). Among her many biographies of royal women, Agnes Strickland was the author of *Life of Mary Queen of Scots* (London, 1873).

[62] Fraser, 'Mary Queen of Scots and the Historians', p. 6.

[63] Fraser, *My History*, pp. 285–87.

[64] Ibid., p. 219.

sympathetic portrayal of women in history'.[65] But Fraser's gender also appeared to reinforce academic prejudices about its author's amateur status and women's contribution to Mary's narrative more generally.[66] Maurice Lee noted that some reviewers of Fraser's 'remarkably good' book

> dismissed it as the work of a non-academic amateur, one with a title, which was bad enough, and – still worse – one who looked like *that*. The stunning jacket photograph . . . helped make Fraser a celebrity but undoubtedly did great damage to her potential reputation as a scholar in the world at large.[67]

Donaldson himself, in what appears to be an early draft of the final historiographical chapter of his biography, noted that Fraser's book 'was launched with tremendous and most successful publicity', commenting: 'I suppose it was the combination of the glamour of the subject with the glamour of the authoress'.[68] In a reworked version of much of the same material, he goes further:

> I wonder if this, surely the most successful book about Mary if measured by its sales, owed its merits and its success to the fact that it was written by a woman who herself possessed considerable charm as well as literary ability and who – though we were not aware of this when the book was published – had problems in her own private life with some resemblance to those of Mary herself. It almost converts one to Sir John Neale's remark about the significance of Freud for the study of Mary.[69]

Donaldson here was referring to Fraser's much publicised affair with her future husband, Harold Pinter (1930–2008): it evidences an insensitivity born of Donaldson's embeddedness in the masculinities fostered in the profession in the first half of the twentieth century that survived the gender equality legislation of 1970 (Equal Pay Act) and 1975 (Sex Discrimination Act).[70] Donaldson followed up his biography with a prosopographical study, *All the Queen's Men* (1983), focusing on rivalries and divided loyalties in Mary's court.[71]

---

[65] Daniel Snowman, 'Antonia Fraser', *History Today*, 1 October 2000, pp. 26–28 at p. 27.
[66] In 1971 Ian B. Cowan disparaged 'Miss' Strickland ('the first to bring feminine intuition to bear on all these all too human problems') for introducing a 'fresh crop of myth and romanticism' into Mary's story: Ian B. Cowan, *The Enigma of Mary Stuart* (London, 1971), p. 24.
[67] Maurice Lee, 'The Daughter of Debate: Mary Queen of Scots after 400 years', *SHR* 68 (1989): 70–79, at p. 73.
[68] EUL, Research Collections, Gen1635/9/39, Donaldson, 'Writers on Mary Queen of Scots', p. 12.
[69] EUL, Research Collections, Gen1635/9/34, Gordon Donaldson, 'Mary Queen of Scots: the Historiography' (typewritten MS, n.d.), p. 7.
[70] Catriona M. M. Macdonald, 'Gordon Donaldson: Some Second Thoughts on a Private Public Intellectual', Scottish History Society, Presidential Lecture, 2021.
[71] Gordon Donaldson, *All the Queen's Men: Power and Politics in Mary Stewart's Scotland* (London, 1983).

Donaldson and Fraser met several times, exchanged published work, collaborated on a panel programme, and Fraser acknowledged in private and in public the influence Donaldson had on her approach to Mary.[72] Despite their denominational differences, unlike Hay Fleming and Lang they agreed on Mary's pragmatic approach to her Catholicism when she returned to Scotland. In 1987 Gordon Donaldson delivered an address in Westminster Abbey, commemorating the 400th anniversary of Mary's death: the royal family were conspicuous by their absence. He acknowledged that Mary had granted the reformed church both official recognition and financial support and had no intention of leading a Roman Catholic counter-revolution in Scotland; indeed, he claimed that Mary should be considered an ecumenical constitutional monarch, 'free from the bigotry predominant at the time'. The 'ostentatious piety' of her later years was opportunistic, he claimed, directed at her prospects of succeeding to the English throne: Mary was a martyr, not to religion, but to 'her place in the royal succession'.[73] Antonia Fraser, having read Donaldson's address, wrote to him: 'How right you are about MQS' real aim: the English throne, *not* a Catholic Scotland . . . may your views, so well expressed, prevail'.[74] Like Lang, Fraser did not claim that Mary was innocent of conspiring to kill her second husband or wishing her English cousin dead, but merely urged that the evidence against her should be critically assessed and Mary's motivations understood: in this she distanced herself from the 'furious pro-Marian apologists of the nineteenth century', like Strickland.[75]

Around this time, another Catholic female historian was writing on Mary: *Mary Queen of Scots: a Study in Failure* was published in 1988 by Jenny Wormald (1942–2015). Wormald bemoaned the Marian circus that had heralded the anniversary of Mary's death, and referred to herself and other historians 'trying to break through the legendary fog which envelops Mary and reach historical reality'.[76] In 1987 Liz Lochhead's play *Mary Queen of Scots got her Head Chopped Off* was performed for the first time; the Saltire Society published Ian B. Cowan's *Mary Queen of Scots*; the National Galleries of Scotland hosted an exhibition, produced a short educational guide on Mary and held workshops for children; the University of Sheffield produced a study of the English captivity of Mary; HMSO published an introduction to Scottish buildings associated with Mary; and in many Scottish localities links with Mary were commemorated.

---

[72] EUL, Research Collections, Gen1632/6/21, Antonia Fraser to Gordon Donaldson, 11 October 1970, 26 September 1970, 19 September 1974, 23 November 1974.

[73] Gordon Donaldson, 'Mary, Queen of Scots: an Address Delivered in Westminster Abbey on 6 October 1987', pp. 6–7.

[74] EUL, Research Collections, Gen1639/13/61, Antonia Fraser to Gordon Donaldson, 30 December 1987.

[75] Fraser, 'Mary Queen of Scots and the Historians', p. 10.

[76] Jenny Wormald, *Mary Queen of Scots: a Study in Failure* (London, 1988), p. 8.

Despite the clamour of competing commemorative practices and publications, Wormald credited Fraser with writing 'the most detailed and interesting portrait of Mary ever written', and grouped her with Gordon Donaldson and Ian B. Cowan as 'the new and sober school of historians of Mary Queen of Scots'.[77] But, according to Wormald, the time had arrived to move beyond the personality of Mary, and 'to ask about the success or failure of her rule'.[78]

A certain incomprehension in some reviews of Fraser's book, matched by the shrill and excitable tenor of others, suggest that need was real.[79] Poet and novelist Stevie Smith (1902–71) in the *Observer* lamented the fact that the short period of Mary's rule in Scotland was hard to follow, 'the Scottish nobility being so intermarried and inclined to murder, treachery and the fostering of illegitimate claimants'.[80] Roy Strong (1935–) in the *Spectator* acknowledged Fraser's achievement, but caricatured Mary as a 'dim and stupid woman': at the point of her death, '[l]ike a blue bottle in a jam jar, she was ready to be swatted'.[81] The review by A. S. Byatt (1936–) in the *New Statesman*, meanwhile, was dominated by its author's search for Elizabeth I in Fraser's biography of the Virgin Queen's cousin.[82]

Conclusion

Mary Stuart's posthumous reputation and history are fractured more than most because she lived at a time when Scotland, and indeed Europe, was divided. The Reformation demanded that people choose. Mary also ruled over an independent Scotland but had been queen of France and had a good claim to the English throne: not surprisingly irreconcilable camps were created and, in the years spanning the Union of the Crowns (1603), the Union of the Parliaments (1707) and beyond, irreconcilable histories were the result. Mary, more so than any other Scottish monarch, lived and has been remembered at the interface of multiple ways of knowing: she does not exist beyond this.

The passage of time has further complicated this state of affairs. Changes in religiosity and gender norms, shifting constitutional conventions and aspirations, dramatic social change, and revolutions in technology and the means of communication have all impacted historiographical practice, readerships and reception, and influenced those who have written Mary's story. Over the course

---

[77] Ibid., p. 16.
[78] Ibid., p. 18.
[79] Historian Dame Cicely Veronica (C. V.) Wedgwood (1910–97) agreed that Fraser was less successful in sketching the political forces in Europe that shaped Mary's life: *New York Times*, 23 November 1969.
[80] *Observer*, 18 May 1969.
[81] *Spectator*, 16 May 1969.
[82] *New Statesman*, 16 May 1969.

of the nineteenth and twentieth centuries, old prejudices had the appearance of waning: secularisation dulled the passions of those whose claims on the soul of the country once necessitated claiming its past. Scottish history became more secure than it had once been as a legitimate subject of inquiry, and more women than ever before were enrolled in history programmes in Scotland's universities.[83] And yet, prejudice remained that continued to refract Mary's historiographical legacy. The institutionalisation of Marian studies in universities perpetuated a bias against the unlettered amateur. The slow pace at which women entered the historical profession held back the re-gendering of her story. More menacingly, perhaps, embedded silently in the canon of works on Mary accepted as the greatest achievements of historians, there remained traces of a reductive snobbery which, masquerading as a defence of standards, fetishised bald fact to an extent the discipline in the modern age was ill-equipped to withstand, at least not without running the risk of losing its public and neglecting alternative approaches and sources.

---

[83] Robert Anderson, 'The Development of History Teaching in the Scottish Universities, 1894–1939', *Journal of Scottish Historical Studies* 32 (2012): 50–73.

NINE

Re-imagining Mary, Queen of Scots in Contemporary Scottish Women's Writing

Nia Clark

The publication of *Mary Queen of Scots Got Her Head Chopped Off* in 1987 marked the arrival of Liz Lochhead as a playwright. The play was first performed by Communicado Theatre Company at the Lyceum Theatre in Edinburgh in 1987 and it retells the story of Mary's life and undoing. This essay considers how Lochhead's portrayal of Mary both critiques and contributes to the wider fascination with Mary's life and, particularly, her death. Lochhead is conscious of the myths surrounding Mary and the impact of this mythology on Scotland's national story. In *Mary Queen of Scots Got Her Head Chopped Off*, there is a departure from one-dimensional depictions of the queen. Lochhead highlights the sectarian and misogynist nature of societal perceptions of Mary to ask what that might teach us about contemporary Scottish society: its religious, social and gendered divisions; ongoing political instability in Scotland and in Britain; and fundamental questions over Scotland's role and constitutional position in the United Kingdom. The essay examines Lochhead's depiction of Mary's relationships with John Knox and Elizabeth I and the challenges of being a woman and a queen, and closes with a study of the play's final scene, which jumps forward in time to a 1980s playground setting. Lochhead uses techniques such as character doubling to disrupt the binary narratives surrounding Mary, which portray her as either a martyr or a catalyst for women's wickedness, to expose issues of sectarianism and misogyny that persist in present-day Scotland. The play reveals a continued fascination with Mary, while manipulating well-worn myths to explore contemporary conflict and challenge the status quo in the context of the failed 1979 devolution referendum and the re-election of Margaret Thatcher's Conservative Party in 1987. Lochhead is often credited with paving the way for a new generation of writers in Scotland, and since her 1987 play, other Scottish women writers have used Mary to approach contemporary feminist issues. In addition to a review of the themes present in Lochhead's play, this essay considers dramatic and poetic responses to Mary's life by Linda McLean, Gerda Stevenson and Marion McCready, respectively. *Mary Queen of Scots Got*

Her Head Chopped Off is most effective in its use of historical events to comment on contemporary *malaise*. Meanwhile, McLean's 2017 play, *Glory on Earth*, is more sympathetic in its treatment and presentation of 18-year-old Mary. In their poetic re-imaginings, Stevenson and McCready also render a compassionate, and even sentimental, portrait of Mary the mother. By bringing Lochhead's play into conversation with the work of other contemporary female writers, this essay provides insight into their use of Mary's story to develop themes that speak to female agency, sectarianism and nationalism in Scotland. It demonstrates that the story of Mary's life and death continues to be a source of disputation and asks whether accepted narratives surrounding Mary might be challenged, and to what ends.

Lochhead began writing when she was studying at Glasgow School of Art from 1965 to 1970. Her first, bestselling collection *Memo for Spring* (1972) was published during a time when writing in Scotland was dominated by male writers. The gendered language employed by Robert Garioch, Stewart Conn and Alexander Scott in early reviews of the collection underlines the marginalisation of women's voices in Scotland at this time.[1] Alan Riach testifies to the male-dominated literary landscape in 'Scottish Poetry 1945–2010' with the inclusion of seven poets who 'have become iconic in Scottish poetry from the 1950s to the 1990s': Sorley MacLean, George Mackay Brown, Iain Crichton Smith, Robert Garioch, Sydney Goodsir Smith, Norman MacCaig and Edwin Morgan.[2] Emerging from this scene, the poems in *Memo for Spring* provided a new, Scottish, female voice. *Memo for Spring*'s focus on female experience established gender politics as a central concern in Lochhead's writing. Her work can be characterised by its formal transgression in its resistance to the categories of poetry *or* drama, its use of Scots language to render contemporary voices and its engagement with feminist politics.

In 1984, *Memo for Spring* was incorporated into a larger collection titled *Dreaming Frankenstein & Collected Poems*, where Lochhead's interest in representing the reality of female experience extends to a retelling of fairy tales, ballads and myth. The poetry and drama she published in the 1980s saw an increasing preoccupation with rewriting myth to undermine received images of women. In the 1981 collection *The Grimm Sisters*, Lochhead presents a contemporary female response to the Grimm brothers' *Children's and Household Tales* (1812); in *Dracula* (1985) she revisits Bram Stoker's classic novel (1898), placing a female protagonist at its centre; and in *Mary Queen of Scots Got Her Head Chopped Off* she provides a contemporary take on Mary and Elizabeth I in a play

---

[1] See Robert Garioch, 'Review of *Memo for Spring*', *Scottish International*, 5 (1972) no. 6: 35; Stewart Conn, 'New Verse, Loss and Love by Stewart Conn', *Glasgow Herald*, 19 August 1972; Alexander Scott, 'Scottish Poetry in 1972', *Studies in Scottish Literature* 11 (1973) no. 1: 20.

[2] Alan Riach, 'Scottish Poetry 1945–2010', in *The Cambridge Companion to British Poetry, 1945–2010*, ed. Edward Larissey (Cambridge, 2015), pp. 148–62, at p. 152.

that might best be described as 'a play with history rather than a history play',[3] because its focus is on Scotland's present more than its past. Lochhead explores Mary's story and the prejudices of sixteenth-century Scotland to show 'how those myths of the past have carried on into the present *malaise* of Scotland today'.[4] Similarly, in her revision of well-known fairy tales for a twentieth-century readership, Lochhead challenges received narratives to highlight the ways in which fairy tale and myth contribute to popular beliefs and binary views of women that filter into daily life and inform societal expectations of women. For example, in 'II: Beauty & the', Lochhead splices 'Sleeping Beauty', 'Cinderella' and 'Snow White' in a patchwork poem that exposes the gender inequality that these fairy tales promote:

> He was that old crocodile
> you had to kiss
> yes, Rosebud, I
> suppose you were right.
> Better than hanging around
> a hundred years for Someone
> to hack his way through the thorns
> for the shoe that fits
> for a chance to have you cough up
> the poisoned apple
> wodged in your gullet.
> So you (anything for a quiet
> life) embrace the beast, endure.[5]

Lochhead establishes a female narrative voice at the start of *The Grimm Sisters*, using the means by which myths about women are created in order to alter the 'ending we knew by heart'.[6] To the same end, she chooses not to deal with Mary, Queen of Scots' execution in the play, although she foregrounds the queen's death in the title, instead using the myth surrounding Mary to ask her audience whether history must repeat itself.

Since *Memo for Spring*, Lochhead has published seven major poetry collections and several plays, ranging from original plays to children's drama and adaptations, including *Shanghaied* (1983), *Tartuffe* (1985) and *Medea* (2000).

---

[3] Anne Varty, 'The Mirror and the Vamp', in *A History of Scottish Women's Writing*, ed. Douglas Gifford and Dorothy McMillan (Edinburgh, 1997), pp. 641–58, at p. 651.

[4] Rebecca Wilson, 'Liz Lochhead', in *Sleeping with Monsters: Conversations with Scottish and Irish Women Poets*, ed. Rebecca E. Wilson and Gillean Somerville-Arjat (Edinburgh, 1990), pp. 8–17, p. 9.

[5] Liz Lochhead, 'II: Beauty & the', in *The Grimm Sisters* in *Dreaming Frankenstein & Collected Poems* (Edinburgh, 1984), p. 90.

[6] Lochhead, 'I: Storyteller', in *The Grimm Sisters*, p. 79.

In 2011, she was appointed as Scots Makar, or the National Poet of Scotland, before being awarded the Queen's Gold Medal for Poetry in 2015, the ultimate recognition for her work as a public poet and her contribution to literature. She is celebrated for opening the door for a new generation of poets, including Jackie Kay, Carol Ann Duffy and Kathleen Jamie, but she is also heralded for her contribution to drama. Indeed, Gifford et al. argue that 'it was the arrival of Liz Lochhead and, in particular, her feminist revisioning of the history play in *Mary Queen of Scots Got Her Head Chopped Off* that seemed to usher in an era of new opportunities for women writers'.[7] The play demonstrates Lochhead's increasing interest in examining constitutional politics alongside gender politics. With *Mary Queen of Scots Got Her Head Chopped Off*, Lochhead initiated a literary interest in telling Mary's story from a feminist perspective, notably amongst other Scottish women writers, including Gerda Stevenson, Sarah MacGillivray, Marion McCready and Linda McLean.

In Lochhead's autobiographical prose essay 'A Protestant Girlhood' (1977), there are multiple references to visual art, as there so often is in her writing. For Lochhead, '[w]riting plays feels like making pictures'.[8] In the essay, she lovingly recalls her father taking her to the Scottish National Gallery:

> Remember the thrill of a *trompe l'oeil* picture of Mary Queen of Scots with a skull, a deathshead [sic] replacing her when you walked past at a slant. And a picture of a Minister on Skates, a black sober man on thin ice. You went to John Knox's house, up Scott monument, into the Camera Obscura.[9]

These early memories are indicative of her painter's eye and her interest in places of historic and national importance. Lochhead's description of a day out in Edinburgh foreshadows her interest in the people and locations that feature in subsequent writing, including what is her most critically acclaimed play, *Mary Queen of Scots Got Her Head Chopped Off*. In the play, the choric crow La Corbie compares herself to the iconic 'skating minister', believed to be the Reverend Robert Walker, adding 'or on the other fit, the parish priest, the durty beast?',[10] thereby establishing the conflict between Protestantism and Catholicism at the start of the play with a reference to a derogatory term, 'left footer', applied to Roman Catholics. In *Mary Queen of Scots Got Her Head Chopped Off*, Lochhead

---

[7] Douglas Gifford, Sarah Dunnigan and Alan MacGillivray, *Scottish Literature in English and Scots* (Edinburgh, 2002), p. 809.

[8] Alison Smith, 'Liz Lochhead: Speaking in her Own Voice', in *Liz Lochhead's Voices*, ed. Robert Crawford and Anne Varty (Edinburgh, 1993), pp. 1–16, p. 5.

[9] Liz Lochhead, 'A Protestant Girlhood', in *Jock Tamson's Bairns: Essays on a Scots Childhood*, ed. Trevor Royle (London, 1977), pp. 112–25, at p. 122.

[10] Liz Lochhead, *Mary Queen of Scots Got Her Head Chopped Off* (London, 2009), p. 6. This and all other references will be to the 2009 edition.

brings the historical figures Mary, Queen of Scots and John Knox together in a play that considers them in the context of 1980s politics and sectarianism. In her exploration of female and national experience, Lochhead takes on Scottish icons and myths in a conversation about Scotland, which questions accepted narratives perpetuated within Scotland.

The other painting that Lochhead refers to in 'A Protestant Girlhood' is *Anamorphosis, called Mary, Queen of Scots, 1542–1587. Reigned 1542–1567* (1580) (Figure 9.1). When viewed from left to right, the human head transforms into a skull. This *memento mori* acts as a reminder of the inevitability of death. Lochhead returns to a fascination with Mary's death in the *Mary Queen of Scots* play, which was written to commemorate the 400th anniversary of Mary's death rather than her birth. The author writes about working collaboratively

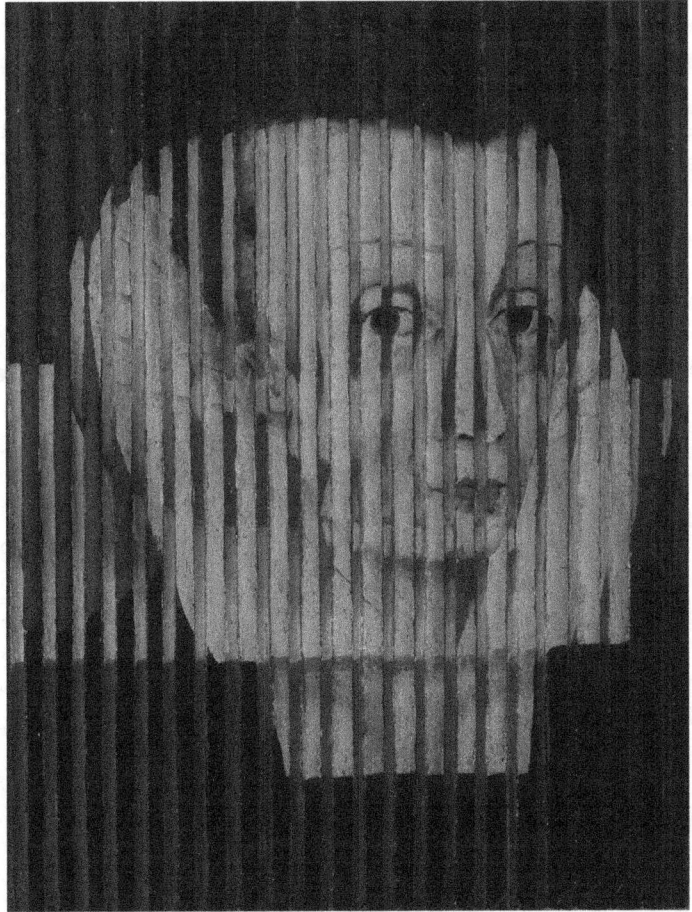

Figure 9.1 Unknown, *Anamorphosis, called Mary, Queen of Scots, 1542–1587. Reigned 1542–1567*, 1580 [Scottish National Portrait Gallery]
© National Galleries Scotland

with director Gerry Mulgrew, recalling that 'neither of us seemed to know much of anything of the history, except the blunt axe-man ending'.[11] Even though the play commemorates the anniversary of Mary's death, Lochhead considers Mary's life rather than the event of her death. Her death is foreshadowed in the play's title, highlighting the fact that we know that the queen is beheaded, but Lochhead rejects the fetishisation of her execution by choosing not to deal with it in the play. Perhaps for similar reasons, McLean's 2017 *Glory on Earth* opens with the line '[e]verybody knows about our death'.[12] The word 'our' establishes Mary's death as a shared national experience, evidencing McLean's awareness of the layers of mythology that popular culture has built around Mary. Many re-imagined narratives reveal the religious priorities of the storyteller first and foremost. As Lochhead has noted, she and Mulgrew 'had been brought up with totally different versions of the myth. The Catholic Mary is certainly a martyr and almost a saint.'[13] Meanwhile the Protestant version of Mary 'veers between limp victim and politically inept nymphomaniac devil-woman who almost scuppered Our Glorious Reformation.'[14] Traditionally, Mary is depicted either as saintly scapegoat, or as sex-obsessed and ineffective. Indeed, Sarah Dunnigan argues that 'the extensive poetic representations of Woman's fallen and redemptive status are linked to the debate about Mary Queen of Scots'.[15] In *Mary Queen of Scots Got Her Head Chopped Off*, Lochhead rejects one-dimensional portraits of Mary and presents her as a woman first and foremost. The playwright is acutely aware of the religious and sexual nature of the myth surrounding Mary and she uses it to highlight uglier aspects of contemporary Scottish society because, she argues, '[s]he was around when a lot of the things that rule Scotland today were forming and hardening, you know, misogyny, Calvinism, all sorts of stuff like that'.[16] Thus, some of the issues present in sixteenth-century Scotland are called upon to shed light on present-day issues of class division, sectarianism and antiquated patriarchal views.

Instead of placing Mary and her cousin Elizabeth I in opposition to one another, Lochhead asks her audience whether a woman can maintain a position of power in the sixteenth century and in twentieth-century politics. The play demonstrates the playwright's commitment to writing female experience from a woman's perspective, now at a national level rather than the personal perspective seen earlier in *Memo for Spring* and 'A Protestant Girlhood'. Events are narrated

---

[11] Liz Lochhead, 'Introduction', *Mary Queen of Scots Got Her Head Chopped Off*, p. vii.
[12] Linda McLean, *Glory on Earth* (London, 2017), p. 8. eBook: www.dramaonlinelibrary.com/plays/glory-on-earth-iid-183747, accessed 15 September 2023.
[13] Lochhead, 'Introduction', p. vii.
[14] Ibid.
[15] Sarah M. Dunnigan, *Eros and Poetry at the Courts of Mary, Queen of Scots and James VI* (Basingstoke, New York, 2002), pp. 10–11.
[16] Wilson, 'Liz Lochhead', p. 9.

by the talking crow, La Corbie, who introduces the two queens to the audience in a parade of circus animals with La Corbie as ringmaster. Although Lochhead dramatises the queens' shared experience as female monarchs who are expected to marry for political gain, the unreliable chorus La Corbie, Scotland's self-proclaimed 'national bird', places herself firmly *'On* MARY's, *not* ELIZABETH's *side'*.[17] Writing retrospectively about the play in 2009, Lochhead states that:

> When I look at it now it is clearly fundamentally about Mary and Elizabeth, the passion of these women to have sex and love and marriage – or not – for can they, without losing power? How do you have a full life as a woman and your full independence? All these things women are still struggling with.[18]

Lochhead's play centres on the commonality between female experience in the sixteenth century and in the present day. In her decision not to depict Mary and Elizabeth as opponents, Lochhead's play departs from traditional portrayals of the power dynamic between the two queens.

In Act One, Scene Two, titled 'The Suitors', Lochhead's stage directions highlight the queens' shared loneliness and although Mary and Elizabeth never met, this enables her to stage a meeting between them by sharing the space onstage. Rather than pitting the queens against each other – indeed, Elizabeth muses '[m]ethinks they do try to play me and my Scotch cousin off against each other'[19] – Lochhead invites us to contemplate their common humanity. La Corbie's speech in Act One, Scene Three, 'Queens and Maids', arguably reveals the play's central message:

> Ony queen has an army o ladies and maids
> That she juist snaps her fingers tae summon.
> And yet . . . I ask you, when's a queen a queen
> And when's a queen juist a wummin?[20]

The question, 'when's a queen a queen / And when's a queen juist a wummin?', is key to Lochhead's representation of Mary and Elizabeth as human beings and as women who struggle to reconcile their political power with their personal desires. Lochhead explores 'the dilemma of a woman being a queen and a queen being a woman',[21] and central to understanding Mary and Elizabeth as queens and as women is Lochhead's recognition that what they

---

[17] Lochhead, *Mary Queen of Scots Got Her Head Chopped Off*, pp. 5, 7.
[18] Lochhead, 'Introduction', p. xi.
[19] Lochhead, *Mary Queen of Scots Got Her Head Chopped Off*, p. 9.
[20] Ibid., p. 11.
[21] Jan McDonald, 'Liz Lochhead: Writer and Re-Writer: Stories, Ancient and Modern', in *A Companion to Modern British and Irish Drama, 1880–2005*, ed. Mary Luckhurst (Oxford, 2006), pp. 454–65, at p. 455.

have in common is their isolation and the battle to maintain power. In *Glory on Earth*, McLean presents Mary and Elizabeth as sister queens when Mary states that 'I will call her sister . . . And we shall talk about how dull and boring it is to be lectured by old men'.[22] Like Lochhead, McLean shows her audience that although the queens appear to have power, they are suppressed and marginalised by a patriarchal society and the decisions they make are subject to the interference and approval of men. Both are compelled to sacrifice personal happiness for political duty. Despite La Corbie's advice to 'show them wha's boss – / You're the Queen so mairry wha ye fancy',[23] Elizabeth must reject the man she loves, Robert Dudley, the earl of Leicester, because he is not deemed a suitable match. Mary and Elizabeth are portrayed as commodities; the search for a suitable husband is made on their behalf by others with political and national implications, made explicit when Elizabeth muses '[i]f we, the Queen, were to follow our own nature's inclinations it would be this: we would rather be a beggar woman and single than a queen and married'.[24] This indicates the lack of freedom that these women experience, despite their apparent positions of power. The plural pronouns 'we' and 'our' are reflective of Elizabeth's regal English but also implicitly bind the two women, while hinting at Mary's fate by contrasting the plural 'we' and the singular 'the Queen'. Mary and Elizabeth are opposed as rulers, but they are linked by their shared genealogy and socio-political positions, underlined in La Corbie's statement that the women are '[e]ach the other's nearest kinswoman on earth'.[25] Lochhead's depiction of the queens reflects her feminist project to encourage society to view women as complex, autonomous individuals. Her perceived enemy is another woman, but it is a patriarchal society that curtails Mary's reign.

One of the techniques that Lochhead uses to reject one-dimensional depictions of Mary and Elizabeth is character doubling, which allows women to shift roles in the play and provides another device that allows the queens to be onstage together without meeting. Through role fragmentation and by employing names that are variations of 'Mary' and 'Elizabeth', Lochhead highlights female stereotypes such as the virgin, the whore and the spinster, while emphasising the commonality of these female characters' experiences in a misogynistic society. The actor playing Mary also plays Elizabeth's handmaid, Marion; Mairn, a 'wee poor Scottish beggar lass';[26] and Maree, one of the children who feature in the final scene set in present-day Scotland. Meanwhile, Elizabeth is also

---

[22] McLean, *Glory on Earth*, p. 43.
[23] Lochhead, *Mary Queen of Scots Got Her Head Chopped Off*, p. 15.
[24] Ibid., p. 9.
[25] Ibid., p. 11.
[26] Ibid., p. 31.

transformed into Mary's handmaid, Bessie; Mairn's 'tarty wee companion',[27] Leezie; and Wee Betty, another of the present-day children. As highlighted by Anne Varty, the breakdown of the queens' roles into functions ascribed to them by a patriarchal society that they supposedly control underlines the gender politics that are central to the play.[28] The character doubling juxtaposes Mary and Elizabeth from the outset, as does La Corbie's fairy tale opening to the play: '[o]nce upon a time there were twa queens on the wan green island, and the wan green island was split intae twa kingdoms'.[29] These elements highlight that the queens are historically pitted against each other. With this familiar stock phrase, La Corbie not only splits the queens and their respective countries, but also draws attention to the unreliability of historical narratives and reminds the reader that Lochhead's play is a work of fiction.

Writing in the context of the failed Scottish devolution referendum in 1979 and the re-election of Margaret Thatcher as Prime Minister in 1987, La Corbie's opening speech juxtaposes Scotland's own divisions of religion and class – '[i]t's a tenement or a merchant's ha', a fistful o fish or a pickle o oatmeal'[30] – with a warring Scotland and England:

> Twa kingdoms. But no *equal* kingdoms, naebody in their richt mind would insist on that. For the northern kingdom was cauld and sma. And the people were low-statured and ignorant and feart o their lords and poor? They were starvin! . . . The other kingdom in the island was large, and prosperous . . . a glistening city that sucked all its wealth to its centre.[31]

Considering the unsuccessful referendum and the political tension within Britain, clear comparisons can be drawn between the political situation in sixteenth-century Scotland and 1980s Britain. The use of Scots and English language throughout the play highlights linguistic differences in addition to differing political opinion. By the 1979 election, Labour had a lead of 10.2% in Scotland whereas, in the rest of Britain, the Conservatives had an advantage of 9% over Labour.[32] In June 1987, Thatcher was elected for the third time and in the play Lochhead presents London, and more specifically Westminster, as the 'glistening city' sucking 'wealth to its centre'. The playwright has since

---

[27] Ibid.
[28] Varty, 'The Mirror and the Vamp', p. 653.
[29] Lochhead, *Mary Queen of Scots Got Her Head Chopped Off*, p. 6.
[30] Ibid., p. 5.
[31] Ibid., p. 6. For a clip of Lochhead performing this speech herself, see *Aye Talks* (2014), www.youtube.com/watch?v=7AHCoyIksR4, accessed 15 September 2023.
[32] John M. Bochel and David T. Denver, 'The 1983 General Election in Scotland', in *The Scottish Government Yearbook 1984*, ed. David McCrone (Edinburgh, 1984), pp. 1–15, at p. 4.

commented that, 'at the time of the first, failed, referendum I was, I remember, very anti any form of "nationalism" . . . I was much more interested in gender politics and identity, class, socialism and internationalism'.[33] However, she admits that '[a]fter the referendum I was ashamed and thought "What kind of country doesn't want to have more of a say in its own affairs?"'[34] Lochhead explores the Marian myth through the sense of political frustration felt in Scotland, what she describes as the 'need for us to tell our own stories and find our own language to tell it in'.[35] Lochhead thus revisits sixteenth-century power struggles to reflect on contemporary issues of nationhood, sectarianism and limitations on female autonomy.

For Lochhead, the story of Mary, Queen of Scots is the story of the tension between the two queens and a patriarchal society that is embodied by the characters of James Hepburn, fourth earl of Bothwell and Mary's third husband, and John Knox, Protestant opponent and antagonist to Mary. In *Glory on Earth*, McLean focuses less on the dynamic between Mary and Elizabeth and instead places emphasis on the relationship between Knox and Mary. McLean highlights Knox's misogyny through her use of two protagonists (Knox and Mary), supported by a chorus of six ladies-in-waiting all named Mary, in a play on the women historically known as the Four Marys: Mary Seton, Mary Beaton, Mary Fleming and Mary Livingston. Like Lochhead's play, McLean's was performed at a time of political division in Britain during the aftermath of the 2016 Brexit referendum. In a stark contrast with Knox's age and maleness, the seven female figures in McLean's play represent youthful defiance and a rejection of a stifling form of Presbyterianism.

In McLean's play, Mary is introduced to us as a striking yet nervous young woman who arrives in Leith and embarks on the journey to Holyrood. As she makes her way through the crowd, McLean's imagining of Mary is of a queen who displays a warmth and openness to her subjects:

> I am smiling already, the heady feeling of
> being loved by so many revives my sorry
> soul, as we trip along the Canongate I slow to
> let a woman touch my hem . . .

---

[33] Liz Lochhead, 'The Referendum Q&A: Liz Lochhead', *The Herald*, 11 April 2013, at www.heraldscotland.com/politics/13099816.the-referendum-q-a-liz-lochhead/, accessed 15 September 2023.
[34] Ibid.
[35] Liz Lochhead, *Penguin Plays: Mary Queen of Scots Got Her Head Chopped Off and Dracula* (London, 1989), p. 2.

I wait a moment too long as her fingers rub
over a small gem sewn into my dark skirt, her eyes
meet mine and I know in an instant that
she has no intention of theft, she has merely
been beguiled by the shine, I want to peel it out
of its socket and reward her with the stone, the
gift she gave me was worth so much more[36]

This moment of pause comes after a series of encouraging comments and remarks from the chorus who urge Mary not to be nervous:

// Mary look
    A crowd is coming to greet us
Cheering
Clapping . . .
// Wave then
Sit up
Straight back
You're never more alive than on a saddle
    // Smile[37]

Conversely, Knox's uncompromising religious beliefs and disgust at Mary's arrival are clearly expressed through the use of long passages of liturgical quotes, delivered with increasing venom, such as '[t]his city was clean . . . Antichrist are once again being chanted', until Knox and Mary finally meet: '[m]adam, I am instructed / by God in His Mercy to teach true knowledge'.[38] Although Mary's religious beliefs are steadfast, McLean posits the queen's humanity in opposition to Knox, who she describes as a 'fire-brandishing, punishing, wizened man with his sunken eyes and zealous words . . . This man below will suck the life and colour and joy from all of us, will punish us for laughter, bend us to him, he will never be subject to me.'[39] This is a comment on Knox's staunch Protestantism and there is a contrast between Mary's shining gemstones and Knox's colourlessness, linked to the limestone whitewash that obliterated religious paintings in Catholic churches and transformed them into stark places of Protestant worship during the Protestant Reformation. McLean's play is more sympathetic to Mary and arguably it overly portrays Mary as a victim exiled to

---

[36] McLean, *Glory on Earth*, p. 24.
[37] Ibid., pp. 20–21.
[38] Ibid., pp. 30, 33.
[39] Ibid., p. 35.

a country that did not welcome her rule. Lochhead's portrait of Knox is more sympathetic, and she emphasises the dangers of binary representations of Mary and Knox, Catholicism and Protestantism.

McLean's decision to place the relationship between Mary and Knox at the centre of *Glory on Earth* is an approach shared by Lochhead who self-consciously asserts Knox's prejudices, and what she termed 'his enduring anti-feminist, anti-feminine legacy in Scottish society',[40] as the starting point for *Mary Queen of Scots Got Her Head Chopped Off*. This is most evident in Act One, Scene Four where Knox's sectarianism is highlighted in the stage directions: '*KNOX, in bowler hat and with umbrella, marching. Two members of the COMPANY, stamping, sway a banner behind him, and all the COMPANY swagger with exaggerated Orangemen's gait.*'[41] Lochhead's reference to the Orange Order, named after King William of Orange (1650–1702), is familiar to a contemporary Scottish audience and underlines Knox as not only sectarian, but specifically masculinist. Both McLean and Lochhead make explicit reference to *The First Blast of the Trumpet Against the Monstrous Regiment of Women* (1558), in which Knox states that female rule is 'repugnant to Nature'.[42] Lochhead cites Knox's text in his opening statement in the play: 'I hae been commandit to blaw the first blast o the trumpet against the monstrous regiment o women, an abomination against nature and before God'.[43] The playwright acknowledges the fact that Knox's religious beliefs dictate that Mary is not eligible for rule as this contradicts God's will. When Knox claims that 'I am not master of myself but the mere instrument of Him wha commands me to speak plain and flatter no flesh upon the face of the earth',[44] he divorces himself from any responsibility for his actions. Knox's reformed religion interprets the Bible literally, and he truly believes that he is the mouthpiece of God. In this way, Lochhead contextualises Knox's behaviour. She uses religion to confront the human condition and to make her audience accountable for religious and gendered prejudices, which culminates in the play's final scene set in the present day.

Knox is portrayed most emphatically as a misogynist who undermines Mary's authority, manipulating and preventing her from acceding to the throne. He states that '[w]e, the people, should choose a husband fur a lassie raither than a silly wee furrin lassie should choose a king for a hale people'.[45] This is a loaded line and 'We Are The People' is a slogan and song sung by some Rangers football

---

[40] Lochhead, 'Introduction', p. vii.
[41] Lochhead, *Mary Queen of Scots Got Her Head Chopped Off*, p. 15.
[42] John Knox, *The First Blast of the Trumpet against the Monstrous Regiment of Women*, Project Gutenberg eBook (1558; 2003, 2020), p. v. www.gutenberg.org/files/9660/9660-h/9660-h.htm, accessed 15 September 2023.
[43] Lochhead, *Mary Queen of Scots Got Her Head Chopped Off*, pp. 15–16.
[44] Ibid., p. 16.
[45] Ibid., p. 34.

fans.[46] When Knox invokes 'we, the people', he does not mean all people, but rather his people, Protestant and male. His belittling comment that '[s]he's only a queen',[47] provides a link back to La Corbie's earlier question 'when's a queen juist a wummin?' Knox sees Mary as *only* a woman. For Knox, his religious beliefs justify the obstructions that prevent women from performing public and powerful roles. By saying he is 'the mere instrument' of God, Knox's views align with the Calvinist belief in predestination, that God has preordained the elect's salvation. For Knox, there is no openness to interpretation and his discourses with Mary are different due to their religious difference. This is further emphasised when Mary asks '[a]nd do ye no interpret as suits you?', to which Knox retorts 'I believe only what God plainly speaks in His word'.[48] The word 'His' emphasises that Knox's God represents the voice of male authority. Mary is aware that scripture can be misinterpreted, and she is portrayed as rational when she puts it to Knox that he is 'yin wha is convincit he be moved by love of God, but is in truth fired rather by hatred o mankind'.[49] Her prioritisation of love above politics and nation reveals the human core of Lochhead's play. Lochhead and McLean choose not to comment on Mary's success or failure as a monarch, instead seeking to depict her humanity. Mary stands up to Knox, arguing that 'because I am by nature douce, and queyet, dinna think I hae nae convictions or beliefs locked in my silent heart'.[50] Her words are an inversion of Elizabeth's famous Tilbury Speech (1588) where she allegedly stated 'I have the body but of a weak and feeble woman; but I have the heart and stomach of a king, and of a king of England too'.[51] Rather than depicting them as opponents, Lochhead binds the women together. The word 'douce' has connotations of a soft and sedate nature in both French and Scots, hinting at the patriarchal idea of women as the fairer sex. As queen, Mary does have a voice and, on the face of it at least, power to use Knox's words against him: 'I do not *trumpet* [my beliefs]'.[52] Lochhead encourages her audience to view Mary and Elizabeth as women first and foremost, facing the same issues of sex, love and marriage, as well as the forces of power and misogyny, that have persisted into the twenty-first century.

In addition to McLean's play, another recent dramatic representation is Sarah MacGillivray's one-woman play *Marie* (2019), loosely based on the life of Mary, Queen of Scots. In poetry, Mary features in the writer, actor and

---

[46] See Rangers Football Club, 'We Don't Do Walking Away', 17 February 2012, https://rangers.co.uk/news/headlines/we-dont-do-walking-away/, accessed November 2021.
[47] Lochhead, *Mary Queen of Scots Got Her Head Chopped Off*, p. 34.
[48] Ibid., p. 18.
[49] Ibid., p. 17.
[50] Ibid.
[51] *British Library*, 'Elizabeth's Tilbury Speech', www.bl.uk/learning/timeline/item102878.html, accessed 15 September 2023.
[52] Lochhead, *Mary Queen of Scots Got Her Head Chopped Off*, p. 17.

director Gerda Stevenson's 2018 collection *Quines: Poems in Tribute to Women of Scotland*, in the poem titled 'The Abdication of Mary Queen of Scots',[53] and in poet Marion McCready's 'Mary Stuart'. In *Quines*, Stevenson gives voice to fifty-seven women from Scotland's past to its present. 'The Abdication of Mary Queen of Scots' was first published in *The Hunterian Poems: An Anthology of Poems to Paintings from the collection of The Hunterian at the University of Glasgow* (2015), featuring poems written in response to, or inspired by, paintings held at the University of Glasgow. Stevenson's poem takes its title from the eighteenth-century painter Gavin Hamilton's *The Abdication of Mary Queen of Scots* (1765–73) (see Figure I.1). Hamilton's romanticised painting depicts the moment when the 24-year-old Mary is forced to give up her crown after reigning for only six years. Stevenson compares the painting, which was commissioned by James Boswell, to a scene from a play: Mary's crown lies on the table, a seated lawyer is writing something while a soldier grabs Mary's right arm and a woman presumed to be Mary Seton holds her other arm.[54] Like Lochhead's Mary, who speaks in fluent Scots with a French accent and not English, Stevenson attributes her Mary with Doric, the dialect of north-east Scotland:

> Tak ma croon, an dinna fash –
> aa yon wis ower fur me lang syne . . .
> an och, Mary, Mary Seton, last
> o ma fower leal ladies, dinna waste yer tears
> oan gien up a bittie gowd an glister; haud ma airm
> if it helps, but dinna, dinna greet fur *this*.[55]

Stevenson contextualises her poem with a biographical note that Mary miscarried twins while imprisoned in Loch Leven Castle in 1567 shortly before she was forced to abdicate in favour of her 1-year-old son James. The poet provides a poignant description of a woman who, following the trauma of the death of her twins who 'slippit cauld an stieve / intae the dowie air o' Leven's grey stane waas', is 'past carin noo'.[56] Instead of focusing on Mary's abdication, Stevenson re-imagines the moment Mary loses her political power, shifting the emphasis to prioritise the loss of her unborn children. Stevenson intimates that Mary's real sense of loss is that of her 'twa bairns',[57] not the relinquishing of her crown, which is just a bit of

---

[53] Stevenson performs 'The Abdication of Mary Queen of Scots' alongside other poems from *Quines* in Jackie Kay's *Makar to Makar* series. See *Makar to Makar*, ep. 3, on www.youtube.com/watch?v=rCXaklGWlso, accessed 15 September 2023.
[54] Stevenson, on *Makar to Makar*.
[55] Gerda Stevenson, 'The Abdication of Mary Queen of Scots', in *The Hunterian Poems: An Anthology of Poems to Paintings from the collection of The Hunterian at the University of Glasgow*, ed. Alan Riach (Glasgow, 2015), p. 75.
[56] Ibid.
[57] Ibid.

gold and glitter. The poet thereby moves away from Mary's reign to consider Mary the grieving mother, affording her dignity in the face of hardship.

Marion McCready follows Lochhead's, McLean's and Stevenson's feminist revisions in her poetic representation of Mary. In 'Mary Stuart', she re-imagines Mary's life from when the future queen was a young girl picking dandelions, to her execution. McCready traces key events, including the death of two husbands – King François II and Lord Darnley – the birth of James VI; and Mary's miscarriage. She also chooses to focus on Mary the mother, opening the poem with a prologue that refers to the twins 'who died before their feet touched the ground' and to her son who would become James VI and I.[58] There are numerous references to life and death, a theme that McCready continues to explore in subsequent writing in the triptych *Our Real Red Selves* (2015) and in the feminist and national perspectives that are central to *Madame Écosse* (2017). The exploration of life and death, and especially birth and warfare, is the focus of the triptych, the collection's title coming from a line in McCready's 'Poem for a Garden'. As Colin Waters notes, 'in birth we reveal our "real red selves"',[59] and McCready's work traverses the mysteries of birth and death. In 'Mary Stuart', the prologue gives way to a series of six groups of stanzas with repeated use of colour symbolism, firstly with red, '[i]n blood she came, in blood she will go', and white: snowdrops, a white veil, pearl buttons, 'fresh snow and milk' and 'the sacrificial lamb'.[60] The colours white and red allude to motherhood, while red also signifies Mary's death as well as being a colour closely associated with Catholic martyrdom.

The cycle of birth, death and rebirth is mirrored by the floral motif that is woven throughout the poem and which frames the narrative. The life cycle of a dandelion offers McCready a way to explore Mary's development from childhood, '[w]hen I find the tallest stalk / I know how much I'll grow',[61] to adulthood, marriage and childbirth:

I weave their sun bells
into my wedding bouquet. When I blow
seeds from the puffball
and three remain –
three children I will bear[62]

---

[58] Marion McCready, 'Mary Stuart', *Poetry* 208 (2016) no. 3: 270–78; at www.jstor.org/stable/44017294, accessed 15 September 2023, p. 270.
[59] Colin Waters, '"What words point to but cannot be" – an Introduction' in Harry Giles, Marion McCready and J. L. Williams, *Our Real Red Selves*, ed. Colin Waters (Glasgow, 2015), pp. 11–13, at p. 11.
[60] McCready, 'Mary Stuart', pp. 276–78.
[61] Ibid., p. 271.
[62] Ibid.

McCready describes here the prophetic children's game that Lochhead refers to in the final scene of *Mary Queen of Scots Got Her Head Chopped Off* – the play's title comes from 'flicking the heads off dandelions while chanting "Mary-Queen-of-Scots-Got-Her-Head-Chopped-Off"'[63] – and applies it to Mary's life as well as her death. The daffodils in McCready's poem, with their 'heads hung, necks / waiting to be snapped',[64] mirror Mary's fate. The reference to spring flowers such as daffodils and snowdrops that appear despite 'westerly gales' and 'the persistence of snowfall',[65] connote new life and resilience. In the shift from first-person to third-person perspective, '[w]hen they are ready / they send for her. . . . / men who must watch her die',[66] and back to the first person for the closing section of the poem, McCready's Mary reclaims her voice. In the poem's closing lines there is a recognition that Mary's life and death remain a source of fascination and that she lives on in national memory: 'I am a white horse ridden by Conquest; / you will remember my name'.[67] This is an explicit reference to the Vision of the Four Horsemen of the Apocalypse in the Book of Revelation, where the crowned first horseman rides a white horse, a colour associated with royal steeds.[68] The fact that Mary is ridden by Conquest, the act of military subjugation, is symbolic of her forced abdication and subsequent execution. It can also be read as a reference to sexual violence against her and to her seizure by Bothwell and then a group of her former noble subjects, all male. By referring to the apocalypse, McCready alludes to the words 'in my end is my beginning', in a cyclical return to the poem's epigraph. Rather than offering one version of Mary, McCready's poem, which is thick with symbolism, leaves space for multiple interpretations. These final lines warn against readily accepted narratives and highlight the conflict between a nation that rejected its queen's rule on the basis of gender, nationality and religion, and nostalgic or idealised portraits of Mary the martyr.

Vanda Zajko and Miriam Leonard contend that 'gender is the central preoccupation of myth', adding that 'the receptions of individual myths are not only linked to history but also to national identity'.[69] Lochhead's exploration of womanhood intersects with and relates to the themes of religion and national identity in the play. As well as exploring female stereotypes and gender politics in the play, Lochhead considers the ways in which popular culture has

---

[63] Lochhead, 'Introduction', pp. vi–vii.
[64] McCready, 'Mary Stuart', p. 274.
[65] Ibid., p. 273.
[66] Ibid., p. 276.
[67] Ibid., p. 278.
[68] Helmut Nickel, 'And Behold, a White Horse . . . Observations on the Colors of the Horses of the Four Horsemen of the Apocalypse', *Metropolitan Museum Journal*, 12 (1977): 179–83, at p. 179.
[69] Vanda Zajko and Miriam Leonard, 'Introduction', in *Laughing with Medusa: Classical Myth and Feminist Thought*, ed. Vanda Zajko and Miriam Leonard (Oxford, 2006), pp. 1–17, at pp. 11, 12.

constructed recognisable characterisations of Mary and Elizabeth and the impact that perpetuating these myths has on a nation's perception of itself. Her challenge to what Jan McDonald describes as a 'culturally constructed myth'[70] is underlined in the final scene set in a playground, which was later developed into a full-length play of the same title for the opening of Glasgow's year as European City of Culture in 1990. The title comes from the phrase 'we're all Jock Tamson's Bairns', meaning we are all the same. Although this may at first seem inclusive, there is a flippant tone to this stock phrase, especially when it surrounds such tales of perceived difference as those presented by Lochhead in these two plays. In *Jock Tamson's Bairns*, Lochhead provides a highly critical self-examination of divisions within Scotland and the desire to challenge accepted received narratives lies at the heart of both plays.

In *Mary Queen of Scots Got Her Head Chopped Off*, La Corbie comments on the ways in which history repeats itself when she introduces the final scene expressing her sadness that, '[m]air nor fower hunder years o Scotlan's historie . . . /An still we see Jock Tamson's bairns'.[71] Through La Corbie's narration of events, Lochhead instructs the audience that in the myth surrounding Mary there is a lesson to be learned. By revisiting the past, Elizabeth's and Mary's situations are transported to the 1980s and as such, the myth surrounding Mary bears new meaning. La Corbie's Scotland in the opening scene reminds the audience of Scotland's past while linking it to the contemporary imagination with references to 'Princes Street or Paddy's Merkit'.[72] The line '[a]h dinna ken whit *your* Scotland is. Here's mines',[73] warns the reader against the danger of readily accepting singular narratives, whether relating to Mary's fate or to Scotland's past. In an interview with James Blake reflecting on the play and on Scottishness, Lochhead warns that '[n]ationhood can limit as well as inspire'.[74] This theme of Scottish identity first introduced by La Corbie is returned to in the play's final scene where there is a shift to the present day, thus indicating that 1980s Scotland has not learned from what Lochhead describes as history's 'cultural biases'.[75] The playwright presents an alternative Scotland, an inclusive nation that takes responsibility for its past and for its future, but she emphasises that it is only one alternative. In the play, and particularly in the final scene, Lochhead questions the status quo not only for women, but for Scotland too.

In the 'Jock Tamson's Bairns' scene in *Mary Queen of Scots Got Her Head Chopped Off*, Lochhead returns to the roots of contemporary sectarianism in a

---

[70] Jan McDonald, 'Scottish Women Dramatists since 1945' in *A History of Scottish Women's Writing*, ed. Douglas Gifford and Dorothy McMillan (Edinburgh, 1997), pp. 494–513, at p. 499.
[71] Lochhead, *Mary Queen of Scots Got Her Head Chopped Off*, p. 72.
[72] Ibid., p. 5.
[73] Ibid.
[74] James Blake, 'Lessons Learned from a Tense Past', *The Scotsman*, 25 September 1995, p. 4.
[75] Lochhead, 'Introduction', p. vii.

playground setting to understand how the past dictates the future. This strand of her work can be traced back to the earlier essay 'A Protestant Girlhood'. Lochhead's experience of religion is entwined with her education at Dalziel High in Motherwell where '[e]ach day started off with the Lord's Prayer, half an hour or so of Bible'.[76] She writes about her school days through the lens of west coast of Scotland sectarianism, citing the landmarks of daily life – 'the school, the pub, the Tallies' Café, the Post Office and the Co-operative' – before returning to the wider setting of Motherwell and 'its steelworks, smoke, pubs, Orange Halls, Gospel Halls, Chapels, Churches, social clubs, shops and factories'.[77] The essay signals the emergence of themes that are key to *Mary Queen of Scots Got Her Head Chopped Off* and *Jock Tamson's Bairns*: a preoccupation with religious differences, gender, history and myth. In the BBC series *Growing up in Scotland: A Century of Childhood* (2017), Lochhead continued to tackle the subject of sectarianism. She described the segregation of Protestants and Catholics that took place after primary school when pupils attended denominational schools, a move that Lochhead describes as 'incredibly divisive'.[78] In 'A Protestant Girlhood', these perceived differences are explored in the context of the decline of traditional Scottish heavy industry and Clydeside shipbuilding and the resultant competition for jobs that Lochhead's family attributed to an influx of Irish Catholics to Glasgow: '[d]ivide and Rule . . . The words Catholic and Protestant. Raised voices.'[79]

In *Mary Queen of Scots Got Her Head Chopped Off*, Lochhead utilises Mary's story to comment on the sectarian divisions of the 1980s. The challenge Mary faces as a Catholic queen living in a Protestant country and a patriarchal society is echoed in the treatment of her present-day child counterpart, Maree, in the 'Jock Tamson's Bairns' scene. La Corbie watches on with frustration as children chant sectarian rhymes in the playground: '[h]ell, if we've got to play this bloody game again, then let's get on with it'.[80] The idea that 'we're all Jock Tamson's Bairns' is undermined by the children's hostility:

WEE BETTY. Maree?? Whit school do you go to?
JAMES HEPBURN. She means urr ye a left-fitter? Haw, stranger, d'you eat fish oan a Friday?[81]

---

[76] Lochhead, 'A Protestant Girlhood', p. 117.
[77] Ibid., pp. 115, 121.
[78] BBC Two Scotland, *Growing up in Scotland: A Century of Childhood*, ser. 1, ep. 1, 'Education', www.bbc.co.uk/iplayer/episode/b08gd0gc/growing-up-in-scotland-a-century-of-childhood-series-1-1-education, accessed 15 September 2023.
[79] Lochhead, 'A Protestant Girlhood', p. 113.
[80] Lochhead, *Mary Queen of Scots Got Her Head Chopped Off*, p. 73.
[81] Ibid., p. 74.

Lochhead shows her reader that the 'Jock Tamson's Bairns' myth is used as a way of diminishing issues of sectarianism and misogyny, and in this scene she invokes the phrase to highlight prejudice in Scotland. Indeed, James MacMillan argues that 'at the heart of this *malaise* is a very Scottish trait – a desire to narrow and to restrict the definition of what it means to be Scottish'.[82] The bairns' rhyming games and derogatory language-use – '[y]ou a Tim?', '[y]ou a Fenian?', '[a]re you a Pape?'[83] – draw attention to a Protestant–Catholic divide exacerbated by toxic masculinity, which still pervades Scottish society. Lochhead highlights the damaging effects of this identity myth that eradicates the potential for difference through its promotion of the idea that 'all men [sic] are created equal'.[84] Like the American dream, the Jock Tamson's Bairns myth is one of meritocracy, the idea that people can achieve a certain status according to their achievements, irrespective of their wealth, race, class or gender.

Lochhead recalls that the 'Jock Tamson's Bairns' ending for the Mary play came from the question: 'could we tell the whole story, do the whole play, as a set of contemporary children forced to re-enact a tragedy we didn't understand?'[85] Lochhead is highly critical of the way that things are, and the final scene also highlights adults' lack of understanding of the past, which is less forgivable. The children perform adult actions, and rather than making for a light-hearted conclusion, this only emphasises the deep-rooted sectarianism present in Scottish society. Like their adult counterparts Bothwell and Knox, James Hepburn and Smelly Wee Knoxxy display sexually aggressive behaviour resulting in an overriding sense of discomfort which is heightened by the fact that children are performing it. Wee Betty shouts at Maree 'Little Orphan Annie! Show us your fanny',[86] in a reference to the 1920s comic strip 'Little Orphan Annie', and the 1982 film *Annie*. This cruel allusion to Maree's dead mother further links Maree to queen Mary. Knox is also the target of the other children's jokes and the adult Knox's Calvinist beliefs are alluded to in Wee Knoxxy's repeated singing of 'I'm S.A.V.E.D / I'm S.A.V.E.D. / I know I am, I'm sure I am',[87] in a revision of the nursery rhyme 'I'm H-A-P-P-Y' and a reference to the doctrine of the elect. The scene culminates in Wee Knoxxy's head being shoved up Maree's skirt, while both are '*crying in real terror and distress*'.[88] Both are outsiders and Knox is told

---

[82] James MacMillan, 'Scotland's Shame?', in *Scotland's Shame? Bigotry and Sectarianism in Modern Scotland*, ed. T. M. Devine (Edinburgh and London, 2000) pp. 13–24, at p. 16.

[83] Lochhead, *Mary Queen of Scots Got Her Head Chopped Off*, p. 74.

[84] David McCrone, 'We're A' Jock Tamson's Bairns: Social Class in Twentieth-Century Scotland', in *Scotland in the Twentieth Century*, ed. T. M. Devine and R. J. Finlay (Edinburgh, 1996), pp. 102–21, at p. 114.

[85] Lochhead, 'Introduction', p. xii.

[86] Lochhead, *Mary Queen of Scots Got Her Head Chopped Off*, p. 74.

[87] Ibid., p. 75.

[88] Ibid.

'[g]et tae! Away an play wi yourself then, stinky!'[89] Lochhead does not display allegiance to either Protestantism or Catholicism, although our sympathies undoubtedly lie with Maree, who is left alone as a shamed victim. In the stage directions, Maree is depicted *'all by herself, very prominent, an outsider. She stands silent.'*[90] In the end, James Hepburn stands up for Maree and the children turn on the two of them, demonstrating how quickly they are willing to side with the majority to protect themselves.

The children's re-enactment of Mary's execution is violent, and it is notable that Lochhead chooses to describe the physical violence in the final scene, which is set in the present rather in the sixteenth century. Lochhead does not deal with the execution directly, thereby encouraging her audience to consider the events surrounding Mary's life and leading up to her death. She puts the execution in the hands of present-day children to show the damaging consequences of accepting inherited narratives without question. The description of the 'blood-red *blood*',[91] leaves no room for ambiguity and the '[s]*hriek of laughter from* WEE BETTY, *totally wild and hysterical, scaring herself as much as it does* MAREE',[92] provides a direct link to Elizabeth, further underlining the ongoing cycle of history. Lochhead demonstrates that both the adults and the children in the play have a deeply ingrained prejudice that seems to have been perpetuated by multiple generations.

The play ends with La Corbie playing with a flower on its stalk, plucking off its petals and eventually the head to represent Mary's undoing and resultant beheading while quietly chanting 'Mary Queen of Scots got her head chopped off.'[93] Lochhead's decision to open and close the play with the voice of La Corbie completes a cycle, yet the playwright emphasises that this cycle need not repeat itself. With reference to the final scene, Lochhead argues that 'this is a play that says, "This is who we are," "Do we have to always be like this?" Because I don't think we have to stay the way we are with the children.'[94] She explores tensions between Scotland and England, men and women, Catholicism and Protestantism, tensions that still exist in contemporary Scottish society. A bleaker reading of the play's ending might suggest that this cycle is inevitable and that the same tensions will continue to play out for another 400 years but, by forcing society to examine itself, Lochhead offers the possibility for change. Her adaptation of Mary's narrative asks us to confront the historical conditions that have shaped Scotland.

---

[89] Ibid.
[90] Ibid., p. 73.
[91] Ibid., p. 77.
[92] Ibid., p. 78.
[93] Ibid.
[94] Carla Rodríguez González, 'An Interview with Liz Lochhead', *Atlantis*, 1 (2004), pp. 101–10, at p. 105.

Lochhead liberates Mary and Elizabeth from the myths that have been attributed to them and considers them as both women and rulers. They are not one-dimensional characters but instead complex and flawed human beings. Lochhead allows the audience to judge the women for themselves, focusing on the challenges of being a woman in a patriarchal society, despite apparent privilege. This allows her to reveal their humanity, going beyond the problems of being a female monarch to consider the challenges that women face, both in the past and in the present. It is not just the struggles of being a woman, or of being Scottish, that the play explores, but the things that unite and divide society. As Neil Davidson argues in *The Origins of Scottish Nationhood* (2000), to dispel myths, they must first be understood.[95] He adds that 'to collude in the perpetuation of national myths . . . invites Scots not to concern themselves with historical truth, but to subscribe instead to whatever mythological version is most pleasing'.[96] Lochhead forces her audience to engage with the ugly reality of sectarianism and misogyny in Scotland.

In response to the conflict and controversy surrounding Mary, the works discussed in this essay choose to emphasise Mary's humanity. In doing so, Lochhead, McLean, Stevenson and McCready consider Mary as a woman as well as a monarch. The approach taken by these women writers not only re-imagines Mary as a complex and multi-layered woman, it also exposes the gendered nature of the debate around Mary's character since her death. By considering her through a feminist lens, they bring the divisions of the sixteenth century to a contemporary audience and, in doing so, they highlight the potential to forge alternative narratives around Mary and the need to question inherited prejudice. Lochhead in particular shows her reader that a thorough self-examination is essential in order to break the cycle of misogyny and sectarianism that she so skilfully depicts in the play's final scene. Though McLean's, Stevenson's and McCready's re-imaginings of Mary are more sentimental than Lochhead's depiction in *Mary Queen of Scots Got Her Head Chopped Off*, these poetic and dramatic responses to the Marian myth all work to encourage twenty-first-century Scotland to reconsider its past in order to change its future.

---

[95] Neil Davidson, *The Origins of Scottish Nationhood* (London, 2000), p. 208.
[96] Ibid.

Part Three

Collecting and Displaying Mary

TEN

Collecting and Exhibiting Marian Objects in Nineteenth-century Britain
Julie Holder

Marian objects were collected, exhibited and written about throughout the nineteenth century and held a fascination for scholars and the public alike. Yet due to their status as highly prized collectibles, very few of these Marian 'relics' were acquired for Scotland's national museum in Edinburgh.[1] So who was collecting Mary and why? Ruth Formanek's psychoanalytical study of collecting assessed the ways in which the act was (and is) intimately connected to the development of a person's sense of self within a matrix of relationships with other people across space and time.[2] Susan Pearce highlighted that the physical longevity of objects compared to humans, and the scope for them to embody a multiplicity of meanings, make them powerful tools for exploring the past: 'In our imaginations, collections make other times and other places open to us'.[3] Objects connected to Mary were prized items for families who could boast an ancestor who had met the queen, with their interpretation becoming a deeply personal part of a family's history and lineage. At the same time, these items were coveted by collectors who were eager to obtain objects touched by Mary's historical 'celebrity' status. In this way, the material and immaterial realms interacted to create meaning surrounding the collecting and exhibiting of Marian objects in both private and public spaces.[4]

---

[1] Society of Antiquaries of Scotland (SoAS), *Catalogue of the National Museum of Antiquities of Scotland* (Edinburgh, 1892) (from here, *Catalogue*, 1892); R. B. K. Stevenson, 'The Museum, its Beginnings and its Development', in *The Scottish Antiquarian Tradition*, ed. A. S. Bell (Edinburgh, 1981), pp. 31–85 and 142–211; J. Holder 'Collecting the Nation: Scottish History, Patriotism and Antiquarianism after Scott 1832-91' (unpublished PhD thesis, University of Glasgow, 2021).
[2] R. Formanek, 'Why they Collect: Collectors Reveal Their Motivations', in *Interpreting Objects and Collections*, ed. S. M. Pearce (London, 1994), pp. 327–35.
[3] S. M. Pearce, *Museums, Objects and Collections* (Leicester, 1992), p. 51.
[4] L. A. De Cunzo and C. Dann Roeber, 'Suitcases, Selfies, and the Global Environment: Material Culture, Materiality, and the New Materialism', in *The Cambridge Handbook of Material Culture Studies*, ed. L. A. De Cunzo and C. Dann Roeber (Cambridge, 2022), pp. 16–19.

The agency and influence of material culture within societies has been a subject of ongoing debate within and between the disciplines of archaeology, anthropology, social sciences, museum studies, history and literature.[5] One of these debates concerns the way objects can either embody a semiotic function by acting as a symbolic form of communication or be perceived as active agents in shaping human behaviour.[6] Manuel Charpy argues that 'objects are not mere witnesses of social and anthropological phenomena or arbitrary social indicators, they are instruments and tools through which individuals and groups define themselves on a daily basis'.[7] When considering the relationship between material culture and memory, Ivan Gaskell and Sarah Anne Carter maintain that the acts of 'choosing, making, and using material things . . . preserve and regulate knowledge of the past in order to shape the historical present'.[8] Material culture is an integral part of the construction and performance of historical memory. Nowhere is this more evident than during the process of interpreting and displaying historical objects in museums and temporary exhibitions.

But within public exhibition spaces the personal stories attached to Marian objects could be presented as part of very different interpretative frameworks. The meanings attached to Marian objects and the way they were physically placed in exhibition spaces reveals much about the concerns of nineteenth-century collectors and exhibitors. As James Coleman notes, the memorialisation of Mary in the nineteenth century was problematic because she did not align with Protestant grand narratives of Scottish (and by extension British) civil and religious liberty.[9] Much like her later, exiled Stuart descendants, she was representative of the losing side in Britain's national story, with Mary in particular being a historical figure dividing her sympathisers from her detractors.[10] However, an empathetic representation of Mary's life in the work of Robert Burns (1759–96) and Sir Walter Scott's (1771–1832) novel *The Abbot* (1820)

---

[5] Pearce, *Museums*; D. Hicks and M. Beaudry (eds), *The Oxford Handbook of Material Culture Studies* (Oxford, 2010); J. Sauttar, 'Thinking Objectively: An Overview of "Thing Theory" in Victorian Studies', *Victorian Literature and Culture*, 40 (2012): 347–57; C. B. Lake, *Artifacts: How We Think and Write about Found Objects* (Baltimore, MD, 2020); S. Dyer, 'State of the Field: Material Culture', *History*, 106 (2021): 282–92.

[6] S. M. Pearce (ed.), *Objects of Knowledge* (London, 1990); D. Miller, *Stuff* (Cambridge, 2010); A. Brower Stahl, 'Material Histories', in Hicks and Beaudry (eds), *The Oxford Handbook of Material Culture Studies*, pp. 150–72.

[7] M. Charpy, 'How Things Shape Us: Material Culture and Identity in the Industrial Age', in *Writing Material Culture History*, ed. A. Gerritsen and G. Riello (London, 2015), p. 199.

[8] I. Gaskell and S. A. Carter, 'Introduction: Why History and Material Culture?' in *The Oxford Handbook of History and Material Culture*, ed. I. Gaskell and S. A. Carter (Oxford, 2020), p. 10.

[9] J. J. Coleman, *Remembering the Past in Nineteenth-Century Scotland: Commemoration, Nationality and Memory* (Edinburgh, 2014), pp. 165–75.

[10] Ibid., pp. 165–66.

allowed people to sympathise with her story, even if they were opposed to the political and religious stances that she represented.[11] As a contested figure in British history, the interpretation of Marian objects in the late nineteenth century was diverse, with popular and scholarly perceptions of Mary influencing the meanings attached to items. The following discussion explores some of the meanings attached to Marian objects held by the National Museum of Antiquities of Scotland (from here on, NMAS) and within private collections in late nineteenth century Britain.[12] This will be accomplished through a quantitative analysis and qualitative discussion of the Marian objects displayed at the 1887 Mary Queen of Scots Exhibition in Peterborough, the Bishop's Castle display at the 1888 International Exhibition in Glasgow, the 1889 Exhibition of the Royal House of Stuart in London and within the permanent galleries of NMAS in 1892.[13]

Marian objects in the National Museum of Antiquities of Scotland

NMAS was formed from the historical and archaeological collection of the Society of Antiquaries of Scotland (SoAS), which became state property in 1851.[14] The Society retained curatorial control of the collection after it was transferred to public ownership and Fellows of the SoAS often discussed items acquired by the museum in papers published in the *Proceedings of the Society of Antiquaries of Scotland*. A number of Marian objects were exhibited at the Society's meetings throughout the nineteenth century; for example, on 30 May 1848 the Society held an evening *conversazione* at which portraits and relics of Mary and her contemporaries were exhibited.[15] Various items with Marian connections had entered the collection during the late eighteenth and early nineteenth century, with nine acquired by NMAS by either purchase or

---

[11] Sir Walter Scott, *The Abbot* (Edinburgh, 1820); G. Carruthers, 'The Reception and Transmission of Mary Queen of Scots by Robert Burns and Walter Scott', https://mqs.glasgow.ac.uk/index.php/2020/11/24/the-reception-and-transmission-of-mary-queen-of-scots-by-robert-burns-and-walter-scott/, accessed 16 September 2023.

[12] The museum had various titles throughout the nineteenth century and was eventually named the National Museum of Antiquities of Scotland in 1891.

[13] The quantitative analysis is based on data collected from the exhibition catalogues for Peterborough, Glasgow and London, and included 260 objects with Marian connections. Information on items with alleged Marian connections acquired by NMAS between 1832 and 1891 was obtained from the Society's minute books, museum accession registers, *Archaeologia Scotica*, *Proceedings of the Society of Antiquaries of Scotland* (*PSAS*) and the National Museums Scotland (NMS) collections database.

[14] Stevenson, 'The Museum', pp. 80–82; NMS, Edinburgh, SAS.MB.1840–1853, Council Meeting, 6 November 1851, pp. 409–15.

[15] NMS, SAS.MB.1840–1853, Evening *conversazione*, 30 May 1848, pp. 234–38.

Figure 10.1 Queen Mary harp, National Museums Scotland, H.LT 1
Image © National Museums Scotland

donation between 1832 and 1891.[16] Of these nine items, an iron chisel and a drinking glass found in Queen Mary's room at Edinburgh Castle (acquired in 1848) had very loose connections to Mary through the location of their discovery.[17] Another item, donated in 1888, was a pin-cushion alleged by the donor to have been owned by the queen, but declared by the Society to not be of sixteenth-century date.[18] A more direct relic of Mary's history was represented by the sword donated by Baroness Sempill (1790–1884) in the year of her death, which had been carried by her ancestor Lord Sempill (c. 1505–76) who fought

---

[16] In addition to the items discussed, there were three casts of medals (object numbers unknown) and a silver medal commemorating her marriage to François II in 1558, possibly NMS, medal H.R 2; SoAS, 'List of Donations 1830–51', *Archaeologia Scotica*, 5 (1890), Appendix, p. 42; SoAS, 'Monday 2nd July 1860', *PSAS*, 3 (1862): 481–82.

[17] SoAS, 'List of Donations 1830–51', pp. 60–62; NMS, iron chisel W.QU 2; drinking glass object number unknown.

[18] SoAS, 'Monday 13th February 1888', *PSAS*, 22 (1888): 109–10; NMS, pin-cushion H.RHE 4.

in the opposing army at the Battle of Langside.[19] But two items in the museum were more intimately related to Mary's story: the harp that was deposited on loan in 1880 and some keys found in Loch Leven, acquired in 1860.[20]

Since the early nineteenth century, the Queen Mary harp had been associated with an oral tradition that during a hunting trip to Atholl in *c.* 1563 Mary had judged a harp-playing competition, after which the queen had presented the harp as the prize to Beatrix Gardyn of Banchory.[21]

This story was retold by Agnes Strickland (1796–1874) in *Lives of the Queens of Scotland* (1850) and by Robert Chambers (1802–71) in *Domestic Annals of Scotland* (1858).[22] In these retellings the harp symbolised Mary's good-natured personality and assimilation into Scottish culture – as Strickland claimed, '[Mary] had the good policy to visit in turn every district in Scotland, by which she made herself thoroughly acquainted with the condition of her people, and rendered herself admired and beloved'.[23] Beatrix's descendants, the Robertsons of Lude, were in possession of the harp in 1805 when it came to the attention of the Highland Society in Edinburgh. It was then inherited by John Steuart of Dalguise (1799–1881), who deposited it in NMAS on loan in 1880.[24] By 1880, the story of the harp-playing contest was a well-known narrative and was indicative of the romantic Celticisation of Mary that had been established in the poetry of Robert Burns and in James Hogg's (*c.* 1770–1835) *The Queen's Wake* (1813).[25] However, for Fellows of the Society, who were at the forefront of systematising historical and archaeological research practices, speculative stories needed to be proven through primary source research to be accepted as authentic.

By the late nineteenth century, the SoAS had established itself as the main historical and archaeological body in Scotland.[26] Its members were therefore concerned with demonstrating their academic rigour in interpreting and

---

[19] H. Dryden, 'Notice of the Sempill Sword, now presented to the Museum by the Baroness Sempill', *PSAS*, 18 (1884): 226–28; NMS, sword H.LA 45.

[20] NMS, keys H.MJ 57; harp H.LT 1. The Queen Mary harp was not acquired until 1904 but was on display from 1880.

[21] J. Gunn, *An Historical Enquiry Respecting the Performance on the Harp in the Highlands of Scotland* (Edinburgh, 1807).

[22] A. Strickland, *Lives of the Queens of Scotland: and English Princesses Connected with the Regal Succession of Great Britain*, 8 vols (Edinburgh, 1850–59), vol. 4, pp. 53–54; R. Chambers, *Domestic Annals of Scotland*, 2 vols (Edinburgh, 1858), vol. 1, pp. 30–32.

[23] Strickland, *Lives of the Queens*, vol. 4, p. 53.

[24] C. D. Bell, 'Notice of the Harp said to have been given to Beatrix Gardyn of Banchory by Queen Mary, and of the Harp called the "Lamont Harp", both formerly possessed by the family of Robertsons of Lude, and now deposited for exhibition in the Museum, along with two Ancient Highland Targets, by John Steuart, Esq. of Dalguise', *PSAS*, 15 (1881): 10–33; K. Sanger, 'LUDE: The Robertson Family and their Harps', *WireStrungharp*, www.wirestrungharp.com/harps/lude/lude_robertson_tarlochson.html, accessed 16 September 2023.

[25] J. Hogg, *The Queen's Wake* (Edinburgh, 1813).

[26] D. V. Clarke, 'Scottish Archaeology in the Second Half of the Nineteenth Century', in Bell (ed.), *The Scottish Antiquarian Tradition*, pp. 114–41.

authenticating the histories of the objects displayed in the museum. For the harp, there was scant evidence that a musical contest had ever occurred and there was debate over whether it had any connection to Mary at all, with Charles Bell (1813–82) proposing that it may have been a gift by Mary of Guise (1515–60) rather than Mary, Queen of Scots.[27] Instead, after 1880 the harp's traditional story was abandoned by Fellows of the Society in favour of presenting it as a unique survival of medieval west Highland craftsmanship.[28] By examining and describing the harp's construction and decoration, Fellows such as Robert Armstrong (1838–1913) argued that there was much to be learned about the musical, cultural and artistic history of Scotland.[29] This material approach to studying the harp reflected the museum's long-term aspirations to investigate and display what the Society termed 'the unwritten story of Scotland and her people'.[30] The harp's association with Mary was presented as an interesting, but dubious, aside to its primary significance as an archaeological relic of medieval and early modern Scottish society and craft practices. The emphasis on the harp's cultural history was indicative of wider collecting and interpretation practices within the Society during this period, with Fellows increasingly focused on identifying evidence of Scotland's broader history of society, culture and civilised progress.[31]

The Society's concern with encouraging more systematic approaches to investigating historical objects was equally relevant to the interpretation of a set of keys that were donated to the museum in 1860. The story of Queen Mary's escape from Loch Leven Castle was popularised through Scott's novel *The Abbot*, with a set of keys found in the loch in 1805 taking a central role in the narrative.[32] There were several keys in nineteenth-century collections that laid claim to being linked to Mary's imprisonment and subsequent escape. By 1860, there was a set of three at Abbotsford; the set of five discovered in 1805 were in the possession of the earls of Morton; and a single key was held by Liberal MP William

---

[27] C. D. Bell, 'Harp', pp. 31–32. The connection to Mary, Queen of Scots has since been re-established. See K. Sanger and A. Kinnaird, *Tree of Strings – Crann nan Teud: a History of the Harp in Scotland* (London, 2016), pp. 75–77; K. Sanger, 'The "Queen Mary" Harp', *WireStrungharp*, https://www.wirestrungharp.com/harps/lude/queen_mary_details/, accessed 16 September 2023.

[28] C. D. Bell, 'Harp'; J. Drummond and J. Anderson, *Ancient Scottish Weapons* (Edinburgh, 1881), pp. 25–26. Recent research dates the harp as mid-fourteenth to early-fifteenth century: K. Loomis et al., 'The Lamont and Queen Mary Harps', *Galpin Society Journal*, 65 (2012): 113–67.

[29] R. B. Armstrong, *Musical Instruments: The Irish and the Highland Harps* (Edinburgh, 1904), pp. 168–83.

[30] SoAS, 'Monday 11th April 1881', *PSAS*, 15 (1881): 188.

[31] J. Holder, 'Collecting the Nation in the Museum of the Society of Antiquaries of Scotland 1832–91', *Journal of the History of Collections*, fhad008 (2023), https://doi.org/10.1093/jhc/fhad008.

[32] A. Lang (ed.), *The Abbot by Sir Walter Scott, Bart., with introductory essay and notes by Andrew Lang* (London, 1914), pp. 553–72 and 661–65; L. Linforth, 'Fragments of the Past: Walter Scott, Material Antiquarianism, and Writing as Preservation' (unpublished PhD thesis, University of Edinburgh, 2016), pp. 182–84.

Figure 10.2 Sixteenth-century cabinet keys, National Museums Scotland, H.MJ 57
Image © National Museums Scotland

Adam (1823–81) at Blair-Adam.[33] In addition, jeweller William Forrest donated a key found in Loch Leven to NMAS in 1829.[34] In 1860, surgeon Robert Annan presented a paper to the Society alongside yet another set of eight keys that had been found in the loch in 1831.[35] Annan interpreted all the keys found in Loch Leven as important historical sources from which the location of Mary's landing on the shores of the loch could be determined, which he noted was 'a question on which writers of this subject differ not a little'.[36] By examining their sizes and forms, he concluded that it was not impossible that all the keys found in the loch over the years were connected to different buildings in the castle grounds. Annan paid particular attention to the location where the 1805 keys were discovered by

---

[33] R. Annan, 'Notes on the Antiquities of Kinross-shire', *PSAS*, 3 (1862): 375–82; W. S. Crockett, *Abbotsford* (London, 1905), p. 194.

[34] D. Laing and S. Hibbert, 'Account of the Institution and Progress of the Society of the Antiquaries of Scotland', *Archaeologia Scotica*, 3 (1831), Appendix III, p. 133, possibly NMS, key H.MJ 56, which is listed as donated by Annan in 1860; but this may be incorrect due to fragmented acquisition data. NMS object record states that this key may have been donated by Forrest in 1829.

[35] Annan was not a Fellow of the Society but had been asked by Fellows Professor James Young Simpson (1811–70) and James Drummond (1816–77) to present this paper.

[36] Annan, 'Antiquities', p. 376.

questioning William Honeyman, the person who had discovered them as a boy. By examining the loch's topography and assessing areas where a landing would not have been detected, Annan refuted the traditional story that a site named 'Mary's Knowe' was where Mary had disembarked.[37] The keys discovered in 1831 were found in a similar location to the 1805 set but were small cabinet keys, so could not have been used in Mary's escape. Instead, Annan proposed that their site of discovery gave weight to the theory that these smaller keys were from Mary's personal wardrobe and perhaps had been dropped by her lady-in-waiting during the escape.[38]

Even though Annan endeavoured to provide a scholarly analysis of all the evidence he had to hand, it was quite an imaginative leap to claim the cabinet keys had belonged to Mary. Annan was not a Fellow of the Society, but his methods show that his antiquarianism was influenced by the systematic approaches developing in the SoAS during this period, through which observation and material-culture analysis were key. Annan's argument concerning the landing site of Mary's boat and the function of the keys followed a logical path of enquiry, and yet the assertion that the cabinet keys were connected to Mary was personal speculation. The fact that the museum's catalogue merely related that the keys had been found in Loch Leven, with no reference to Mary at all, demonstrates that Annan's suggested attribution was not adopted by NMAS.[39] In contrast, the museum catalogue did retain the Marian connection to the harp, but put the name in inverted commas, stating it was '*called* "Queen Mary Harp"'.[40] When the harp was eventually purchased by NMAS in 1904, the Society did not believe the harp's association with Mary was authentic since they stated that '[t]he price was unfortunately enhanced by the quite mythical attribution to Queen Mary'.[41] All the Marian objects discussed thus far were exhibited throughout the museum's galleries within material-themed sections titled 'Locks, Keys, Etc.', 'Musical Instruments', 'Arms and Armour', and 'Tools, Implements, Etc.'[42] NMAS did not display the historic collection as illustrative of a chronological narrative or group objects by historical period.[43] Instead, objects with links to historical figures and events were subsumed within the museum's core display strategy of presenting a material history of Scottish

---

[37] Ibid., pp. 376–78.
[38] Ibid., pp. 378–80.
[39] SoAS, *Catalogue of Antiquities in the National Museum of the Society of Antiquaries of Scotland* (Edinburgh, 1876), p. 147; SoAS, *Catalogue* (1892), p. 338.
[40] SoAS, *Catalogue* (1892), p. 317, my emphasis.
[41] SoAS, 'Anniversary Meeting 30th November 1904', *PSAS*, 39 (1905): 9.
[42] SoAS, *Catalogue* (1892), pp. 282–374.
[43] This differed to the prehistoric gallery that was divided into Stone, Bronze, Roman and Viking periods.

Figure 10.3 National Museum of Antiquities of Scotland, c. 1900, Historic Environment Scotland, SC 684147
Image © Courtesy of HES (Bedford Lemere and Company Collection)

social and cultural progress and references to well-known figures in Scotland's national past, such as Mary, were noticeably absent.

Marian objects at Peterborough, Glasgow and London

Compared to NMAS, there were more items with connections to Mary displayed at the temporary exhibitions held in Peterborough in 1887, Glasgow in 1888 and London in 1889. These fell within a broad range of categories and included painted portraits, miniatures, engravings, manuscripts, books and objects. The following discussion focuses on Marian objects, rather than artworks, manuscripts or books. Accordingly, it includes material culture that would commonly be displayed in a museum, rather than an art gallery or library. Miniatures have been included in this definition due to their size and tactile quality, making them more of an object than an artwork. Objects linked to historical figures other than Mary are not included in the following quantitative analysis but form part of the discussion on how Mary was placed within the three different exhibition spaces.[44]

---

[44] The information from the catalogues was collated into Excel spreadsheets noting lender names, whether lenders were peers or an item was an heirloom, type of object, at which exhibition(s) it was exhibited, whether the lender was an institution or private individual and any relevant notes on each item.

If the 1892 catalogue of NMAS is compared with those published for these three exhibitions, it becomes evident that the collecting of Marian objects primarily occurred within the private sphere rather than in public museums.[45] Out of the 260 Marian objects that were included in this study's quantitative analysis, only 24 were lent by institutions rather than private lenders. The relationships that individual collectors had with Marian objects were more explicit in temporary exhibition spaces, which were constructed with a greater emphasis on popular appeal and history as entertainment. The exhibition at Peterborough marked the tercentenary of Mary's death and the location was chosen due to her being originally buried at Peterborough Cathedral in 1587.[46] Some of the collection then travelled to Glasgow in 1888 to feature within its own dedicated section in the Scottish History display at the recreated Bishop's Castle at the Glasgow International Exhibition.[47] A small number of these relics then appeared in 1889 in the Exhibition of the Royal House of Stuart held in London. In larger temporary exhibitions there was more freedom to present Marian objects in a more subjective and narrative fashion than was possible in the archaeological and material-focussed galleries of NMAS. In addition, since most Marian objects were in private hands, it was only through loan exhibitions that such items could be brought together and exhibited in the same space.

A detailed inventory of objects and names of lenders appeared in the catalogues published for each separate exhibition. A comparison of Marian objects in the three exhibitions shows that only seventeen items travelled between all of them, with most only appearing in one or two of the exhibitions (as shown in Table 10.1). Lenders included Queen Victoria (1819–1901), members of noble families, antiquarian societies, churches, museums and the public. In Peterborough and Glasgow there was an even spread of objects from noble families compared to those contributed by other lenders. This suggests that Marian objects were popular with a wide variety of collectors from different social backgrounds. In contrast, 88 per cent of the objects in the London exhibition were from noble families (see Table 10.2). The bias towards noble

---

[45] SoAS, *Catalogue* (1892); *Catalogue of the Tercentenary of Mary Queen of Scots Exhibition, Peterborough* (Peterborough, 1887); J. Paton, ed., *Scottish National Memorials: a Record of the Historical and Archaeological Collection in the Bishop's Castle, Glasgow, 1888* (Glasgow, 1890); *The Book of the Bishop's Castle and Handbook of the Archaeological Collection*, 2nd edn, exhibition catalogue (Glasgow, 1888); *Exhibition of the Royal House of Stuart*, catalogue, The New Gallery, Regent Street (London, 1889).

[46] Coleman, *Remembering the Past*, p. 170. Mary's body was moved to Westminster Abbey by her son James VI and I in 1612.

[47] Ibid., pp. 170–71; P. Kinchin, J. Kinchin and N. Baxter, *Glasgow's Great Exhibitions 1888.1901. 1911.1938.1988* (Bicester, 1988), pp. 17–53; anon., 'Glasgow International Exhibition: The Bishop's Palace', *Glasgow Herald*, 16 January 1888, Issue 13; anon., 'Glasgow International Exhibition: Opening of the Bishop's Palace', *The Scotsman*, 26 May 1888.

Table 10.1 Number of Marian objects exhibited at the temporary exhibitions in Peterborough, Glasgow and London

Exhibition locations	Number of objects
Peterborough only	95
Glasgow only	33
London only	86
Peterborough and Glasgow	10
Peterborough and London	4
Glasgow and London	15
Peterborough, Glasgow and London	17

Sources: *Catalogue of the Tercentenary of Mary Queen of Scots Exhibition, Peterborough*, Exhibition Catalogue (Peterborough, 1887); *The Book of the Bishop's Castle and Handbook of the Archaeological Collection*, 2nd edition, Exhibition Catalogue (Glasgow: T. & A. Constable, 1888); *Exhibition of the Royal House of Stuart*, Exhibition Catalogue, The New Gallery Regent Street (London, 1889). Data based on the 260 Marian objects that were included in this study.

Table 10.2 Status of lenders of Marian objects exhibited at the temporary exhibitions in Peterborough, Glasgow and London

Exhibition locations	Quantity and percentage of objects from noble families	Quantity and percentage of objects from other lenders	Total
Peterborough	55 (44%)	71 (56%)	126
Glasgow	44 (59%)	31 (41%)	75
London	107 (88%)	15 (12%)	122

Sources: As for Table 10.1

lenders for the London exhibition correlates with the fact that the exhibition was organised through members of the Order of the White Rose, which had several nobles among its membership.[48] In addition, the London location may have encouraged more nobles to lend objects from their family collections if they had a residence in the city.

Marian objects were labelled as 'relics' in all three temporary exhibitions. As Pearce noted, objects with connections to historical figures held by museums and private collections were often labelled as 'historic relics', venerated much like those of Catholic saints, and were a form of 'community souvenir' for a society.[49] The religious element of Mary's story, as a practising Catholic fighting against Protestant rivals and then suffering martyrdom via execution, brought Marian objects even closer to traditional definitions of religious relics. George Dalgleish argues that due to the religious nature of the Jacobite opposition,

---

[48] M. Pittock, 'The Jacobite Cult', in *Scottish History: The Power of the Past*, ed. E. J. Cowan and R. J. Finlay (Edinburgh, 2002), p. 200; N. Guthrie, *Material Culture of the Jacobites* (Cambridge, 2013), pp. 155-56. The Order of the White Rose was a Jacobite society established in Britain in 1886 by Bertram Ashburnham, fifth earl of Ashburnham (1840-1913).

[49] Pearce, *Museums*, pp. 197-202.

Jacobite objects were also treated like religious relics by many collectors, with their meanings combining historical and religious sentiment.[50] However, even though there were undoubtedly collectors who attached religious meaning to Marian objects, particularly within the Catholic communities of Britain, these items also represented other associations that went beyond the idea of Mary as a Catholic martyr.

Many of the items exhibited at Peterborough, Glasgow and London were related to tragic episodes in Mary's life and popular fascination with her dramatic story was a common way of emotionally engaging with these objects. For example, there were several items exhibited from the years when Mary was imprisoned, such as embroidery worked by the queen and her ladies at Fotheringhay Castle, as well as items associated with her execution, including the veil she allegedly wore at the scaffold.[51] The ability of objects to survive longer than their human makers meant that Marian relics could be perceived as physically 'witnessing' historic events, linking nineteenth-century collectors to Mary's story through ownership.[52] Possession of these items allowed collectors to physically touch items that had been held in Mary's hands, creating a tangible (but illusory) connection across time to Mary's life and experiences. The imprisonment and execution of Mary was a major part of her story and ownership of an object that was part of that story undoubtedly contributed to its value for collectors. Reflection on the final years of Mary's life also provoked the strongest feelings of pity, affinity or condemnation from her sympathisers and detractors, resulting in an inherently emotional engagement with Marian objects from this period.

All three exhibitions contained items that were stated to be family heirlooms, although only a few had continuous provenance linking a lender's family to Mary. Of the 260 items displayed at these exhibitions, 32 were described as heirlooms in their object descriptions.[53] The importance of demonstrating that an ancestor had met the queen and received her favour was clearly important for many individuals. This was evident in descriptions detailing the long history of an item within a family, such as the watch lent by Captain Anstruther Thomson (1818–1904) that had been in his family since Mary allegedly gifted it to his ancestor Margaret, marchioness of Hamilton (*d*. 1625).[54] However, there

---

[50] G. Dalgleish, 'Objects as Icons: Myths and Realities of Jacobite Relics', in *Heritage and Museums: Shaping National Identity*, ed. J. M. Fladmark (Abingdon, 2014), pp. 91–102.

[51] *Tercentenary of Mary Queen of Scots*, pp. 28–29. It is well documented that the clothes Mary wore at the scaffold were burned to prevent them becoming religious relics, so this attribution is unlikely.

[52] Pearce, *Museums*, pp. 203–07.

[53] *Tercentenary of Mary Queen of Scots*; *Book of the Bishop's Castle*; *Exhibition of the Royal House of Stuart*.

[54] *Tercentenary of Mary Queen of Scots*, pp. 16–7.

Figure 10.4 Cabinet, seventeenth century, RCIN 26305
Royal Collection Trust/© His Majesty King Charles III, 2022

were many heirlooms in the exhibitions that had been acquired by families in the eighteenth and nineteenth centuries, with unverified oral traditions playing a significant role in claiming a Marian connection. The emotional appeal of objects as material links to Mary's life perhaps explains why unsubstantiated Marian connections were often accepted with scant evidence; collectors wanted them to be true. Even Queen Victoria was willing to accept the validity of such associations with the person she described as the 'poor Queen Mary'.[55]

At Peterborough, Glasgow and London Queen Victoria lent a cabinet, an embroidered purse and a lock of Mary's hair, which had been bequeathed to the royal collection by Robert Hamilton, eighth baron Belhaven and Stenton

---

[55] A. Helps (ed.) and Queen Victoria, *Leaves from the Journal of Our Life in the Highlands, from 1848 to 1861* (London, 1868), p. 17.

(1793–1868).⁵⁶ It was claimed that the cabinet containing the purse and hair had been brought from France by Mary, given to the regent, Lord Mar (*d.* 1572) and inherited by the Belhaven family. The lock of hair is particularly interesting since it was believed to have been a physical part of Mary, much like traditional saints' relics. The lock of hair was brown, and this was deemed of antiquarian interest since there was disagreement about the true colour of the queen's hair, a question that was much debated and fed into wider historical arguments about her supposed beauty.⁵⁷ Even though family tradition was the only evidence that the cabinet, purse and hair had been gifts from Mary to Lord Mar, and the cabinet has since been identified as being of seventeenth century date, all these items were accepted by Queen Victoria as genuine Marian relics. A Marian connection enhanced the value of any object, regardless of the corroboration of such claims, and these Marian associations were perpetually self-validated by the retelling of traditions within a family and the acceptance of these stories by other collectors.

While many objects claimed a connection to Mary, at the same time some of these items represented tangible links to the historical actors that surrounded her during the political and religious upheavals of the sixteenth century. Such items included a workbox given to Mary's chancellor Lord Forrester and a *memento mori* timepiece given to the queen's lady-in-waiting Mary Seton (*c.* 1541–*c.*1615); both items were still held by the descendants of these historical figures.⁵⁸ Another collection of Marian objects had been gifted to Sir James Balfour (*c.* 1525–83), deputy governor of Edinburgh Castle under the earl Bothwell (*c.* 1535–78), and inherited by Lord Balfour of Burleigh, Alexander Hugh Bruce (1849–1921). This collection consisted of a handbell, a tankard, a fan handle, a necklace, a *ciborium* (small vessel for holding consecrated bread) and four silver teaspoons.⁵⁹ At all three exhibitions, Sir Balfour was described as Mary's 'faithful partisan'⁶⁰ or 'faithful adherent',⁶¹ although his history of loyalty to Mary was somewhat chequered.⁶² Sir Balfour's descendant Alexander Bruce was a staunch Presbyterian and Conservative peer but he excused Marian

---

⁵⁶ Paton (ed.), *Scottish National Memorials*, pp. 43–44; Royal Collection Trust, purse RCIN 43820; cabinet RCIN 26305; www.rct.uk/collection/26305/cabinet, accessed 16 September 2023.

⁵⁷ Paton (ed.) *Scottish National Memorials*, pp. 44–5; A. Lang, *Portraits and Jewels of Mary Stuart* (Glasgow, 1906).

⁵⁸ *Book of the Bishop's Castle*, pp. 61 and 56–7. James Walter Grimston, second earl of Verulam, baron Forrester (1809–95), owned the workbox and Sir Thomas North Dick-Lauder (1846–1919) owned the timepiece.

⁵⁹ *Book of the Bishop's Castle*, pp. 50–56.

⁶⁰ *Tercentenary of Mary Queen of Scots*, p. 19.

⁶¹ *Book of the Bishop's Castle*, p. 51; *Exhibition of the Royal House of Stuart*, p. 78.

⁶² Balfour frequently switched sides between Mary and the Protestant lords and was accused of being involved in the murder of Lord Darnley. However, by his death he had regained possession of his lands and was an Elder at the General Assembly of the Church of Scotland.

supporters who were also Protestant reformers by stating that '[c]hivalry and diplomacy drew to Mary's side some men who were stout anti-Romanists'.[63] To claim an ancestor of the Marian period was to assert a family's prime place in Britain's national story and demonstrated a lender's own important lineage. Possession of Marian objects was physical evidence that the current owner was descended from an important historical figure who had been at the forefront of one of the best-known episodes in Scottish and English history and displaying these items was a matter of personal prestige.

Marian objects within broader exhibition frameworks

This final section considers the broader context in which Marian objects were displayed at Glasgow, Peterborough and London in comparison to the galleries at NMAS. As was noted earlier in this chapter, historical figures and events were marginalised in the permanent galleries of NMAS, with the Scottish historical collection categorised by material themes to demonstrate social and cultural progress and the development of civilisation in Scotland. Mary did not contribute to this material-focused narrative, nor was she a historical figure considered to reflect rational modern progress due to her Catholic religion. Therefore, although NMAS held a few objects with connections to Mary in its collection, these items were not prominent within the museum's overall display strategy. In contrast, at Peterborough, Glasgow and London Marian objects occupied significant space in the displays.

The main way that the temporary exhibitions at Peterborough, Glasgow and London differed from NMAS was the way they exhibited Marian objects as illustrating a narrative of Mary's life. In all three exhibition catalogues there was a clear sense of storytelling in the way visitors could follow a chronology of events through the placement of the objects, with each object's description allowing readers to make connections with her history.[64] For example, exhibited at the Bishop's Castle in Glasgow were Mary's own carved oak cradle, a jewel given to Mary by the *dauphin* of France (1544–60) just before their marriage, two silver cups used at the wedding of Mary and Lord Darnley (1546–67), various objects linked to her residence at Holyrood such as a tapestry and some needlework, the leading-strings (an early form of toddler harness) she made for her son James VI and I (1566–1625), the watch that Mary gave to John Knox (c. 1514–72), three bronze cannons used at the Battle of Langside and numerous

---

[63] A. H. Bruce, Lord Balfour of Burleigh, *An Historical Account of the Rise and Development of Presbyterianism in Scotland* (Cambridge, 1911), p. 58.
[64] *Tercentenary of Mary Queen of Scots*; *Book of the Bishop's Castle*; *Exhibition of the Royal House of Stuart*.

items linked to her years of imprisonment.[65] Fellow of the Society Alexander James Steele Brook (1842–1908) argued that all the items in the Mary Stuart section at the Bishop's Castle were 'evidence of the refinement of her own tastes . . . The occupation of her leisure hours . . . cover[ing] the whole period of the Queen's life and reign, and help to bring us in touch with it alike at the happiest and most tragic parts of her history'.[66] The representation of Marian objects as 'illustrated narrative' brought the symbolic and tangible qualities of such objects into conjunction, allowing visitors to follow the story of Mary's life through the material remains that had survived. Although exhibition visitors could not touch Marian objects in the same way as the individual lenders who had contributed these items, the physicality of objects that had been there at the time was a key part of the overall experience, allowing visitors to connect with Mary's story through the objects on display. However, although the narrative approach was evident in the exhibitions at Peterborough, Glasgow and London, there were noticeable differences in the way this narrative was presented within each exhibition's overarching interpretative strategy.

The commemoration and memorialisation of Mary lay at the heart of the way in which Mary's life was represented in Peterborough in 1887, emphasised by the fact that this exhibition marked the tercentenary of her death. The original plan had been to hold a procession from Fotheringhay where she was executed to Peterborough Cathedral where she was first buried.[67] By early 1887, the plan had been changed from a procession to putting together an exhibition of historical relics to be displayed in the precincts of Peterborough Cathedral.[68] The Peterborough exhibition was wholly built around a sentimental engagement with Mary's plight and sympathy with the troubles she had endured during her life. There was a small section of portraits and miniatures of Mary's Stuart descendants and other historical figures of the sixteenth century, but the personal story of Mary's life took centre stage.[69] The organisers maintained that the commemoration of Mary in 1887 was 'not as a matter of partisan vindication of her conduct, but of general concern for her unhappy fate'.[70] However, it is worth noting that around the same time that the exhibition was being organised, the Roman Catholic Archbishop of Edinburgh was attempting to get Mary canonised, so the perception of Mary as a persecuted Catholic martyr was still

[65] Paton (ed.), *Scottish National Memorials*, pp. 40–76.
[66] Ibid., p. 43.
[67] Coleman, *Remembering the Past*, p. 170.
[68] Ibid.
[69] *Tercentenary of Mary Queen of Scots*, pp. 42–46.
[70] Anon., 'From our London Correspondent', *Manchester Guardian*, 2 December 1886, p. 5. This display was organised by the Peterborough National History, Scientific and Archaeological Society.

an important way in which nineteenth-century Catholics likely engaged with this exhibition.[71] Indeed, it was prominent Scottish Catholic and great-granddaughter of Sir Walter Scott, Mary Maxwell-Scott (1852–1920), who started a committee to mount a similar display of Marian relics in Edinburgh after the Peterborough exhibition ended.[72] However, arrangements had already been made for the Marian collection to form part of the International Exhibition at Glasgow in 1888, within which Mary's story was presented very differently to the personal, emotional representation of her at Peterborough.

Rather than focusing only on Mary, the committee organising the Bishop's Castle exhibition aimed to represent the whole of the history of Scotland, with a specialised display of Glasgow's regional history and another of Mary and her Stuart descendants.[73] When the Bishop's Castle opened, the Glasgow section was on the ground floor, the prehistoric to modern history of Scotland section was on the first floor, and the Mary and Stuart collection was on the top floor, alongside a small display of items linked to Robert the Bruce (1274–1329) and early Scottish monarchs.[74] The first floor display of Scotland's national history exhibited prehistoric to modern objects, covering Scottish social, agricultural, industrial, burghal and cultural history.[75] In many ways this floor was similar to the material-themed galleries at NMAS with their focus on telling the story of the development of civilisation in Scotland and presenting objects as tangible illustrations of the progress of Scottish arts, technology and society. Alongside these material-themed displays were historical sections covering the Covenanters and the Royalists and a Scottish literature section containing items linked to authors such as Burns and Scott.[76] However, the Bruce, Marian and Jacobite collections were elevated above the Scottish national history displays both figuratively and physically through their placement in the grand gallery on the top floor of the Bishop's Castle.[77]

Robert the Bruce, Mary, Queen of Scots and the Jacobites epitomised the stereotypical popular version of Scottish history that would have been most

---

[71] Coleman, *Remembering the Past*, p. 168; anon., *Aberdeen Journal*, issue 9983, 19 February 1887. See also E. Vickers, 'Memorialising Mary as Martyr', https://mqs.glasgow.ac.uk/index.php/2021/05/11/memorialising-mary-as-martyr/, accessed 16 September 2023.

[72] Coleman, *Remembering the Past*, p. 171.

[73] Anon., 'Glasgow International Exhibition', *Glasgow Herald*. The organising committee were mainly members of the Glasgow Archaeological Society.

[74] J. Honeyman, 'Archaeology at the Glasgow Exhibition', *The British Architect*, 29 (1888) no. 25: 457–58.

[75] *Book of the Bishop's Castle*, pp. 19–44 and 171–262; Paton (ed.), *Scottish National Memorials*, pp. 1–39 and 197–344.

[76] *Book of the Bishop's Castle*, pp. 79–101 and 133–44; Paton (ed.), *Scottish National Memorials*, pp. 87–126 and 169–94.

[77] Honeyman, 'Glasgow Exhibition', p. 457.

familiar to nineteenth-century visitors.[78] The elevation of their stories fed into the theatricality of the recreated Bishop's Castle, transporting visitors back in time as they were surrounded by richly decorated interiors mimicking a fifteenth-century bishop's residence.[79] As one contemporary commentator enthused, '[w]hat visions of brave men and fair women we can conjure up as we wander through the Bishop's Castle! what memories do we see on every side of knaves and heroes, what suggestions of romance and chivalry'.[80] But although the Marian collection was exhibited in pride of place in the grand gallery, there were fewer items on display than at Peterborough and the space was shared with the equally prominent Jacobite collection.[81] Out of the 126 Marian objects that had been displayed in Peterborough, only 27 were then exhibited in Glasgow (see Table 10.1). In total, only 75 Marian objects were displayed at the Bishop's Castle (see Table 10.2).[82] Therefore, two-thirds of the collection was different to that seen in Peterborough. In the grand gallery, Mary's story competed with that of Robert the Bruce and the Stuart royal house, with the Jacobite narrative placed on a par with Mary's turbulent history. Overall, Mary's presence was not as prominent in Glasgow as at Peterborough because she represented only one period of Scotland's national history. Despite this, she remained a significant presence in the Bishop's Castle displays, reflecting the extent to which she was considered a key figure in public perceptions of Scotland's national story.

Whereas the Peterborough exhibition focused on a deeply personal commemoration of Mary, and the Glasgow exhibition displayed Mary as part of the Scottish national story, in London the 1889 Exhibition of the Royal House of Stuart placed Mary within a British historical framework. The underlying motivation for mounting the Stuart exhibition was to commemorate the Revolution of 1688 when James VII and II (1633–1701) was deposed.[83] The organising committee put forward the argument that 'the Revolution of 1688 may be commemorated in the proposed exhibition both by those who approve of it and by those whose sympathies are rather with the family whose chief then ceased to reign'.[84] But as Murray Pittock and Neil Guthrie note, the exhibition cannot

---

[78] M. Ash, *The Strange Death of Scottish History* (Edinburgh, 1980), pp. 10–11. Ash saw this preoccupation with select historical figures as representing Scottish history descending into meaningless nostalgia by the late nineteenth century.

[79] Kinchin, Kinchin and Baxter, *Glasgow's Great Exhibitions*, p. 45; anon., 'The Bishop's Castle', *Art Journal* (1888) December, pp. 28–32.

[80] Anon., 'The Bishop's Castle', p. 30.

[81] *Book of the Bishop's Castle*, pp. 103–32; Paton (ed.), *Scottish National Memorials*, pp. 127–54.

[82] *Book of the Bishop's Castle*, pp. 45–78; Paton (ed.), *Scottish National Memorials*, pp. 40–86. This number excludes portraits, books and manuscripts, which were also exhibited in both exhibitions.

[83] Anon., 'Proposed Stuart Exhibition', *The Scotsman*, 4 April 1888, p. 9; anon., 'The Stuart Exhibition in London', *Manchester Guardian*, 31 December 1888, p. 5. The exhibition ran from 31 December 1888 until 31 March 1889.

[84] Anon, 'Proposed Stuart Exhibition'.

be disconnected from the wider neo-Jacobite movement and the influence of the Order of the White Rose, with the post-1688 titles of exiled Stuarts put in parentheses in the catalogue.[85] A similar number of Marian objects was displayed at London as there had been at Peterborough (122 and 126 respectively; see Table 10.2). But again, a significant number of items were only exhibited at London, 86 out of 122 items. Although the Marian collection was larger at London than in Glasgow, the London exhibition also contained sizeable collections connected to other famous Stuarts, particularly Charles I (1600–49) and Prince Charles Edward Stuart (1720–88).[86] The Stuart Exhibition, as its name suggests, displayed objects connected to the whole of the royal house of Stuart, with Mary just one figure within her family's long and important influence on the history of the British Isles. Indeed, as Guthrie argues, Mary's claim to the throne of England was part of the narrative legitimising Jacobitism in the 1889 exhibition.[87] Mary's life was thus part of English, Scottish and British history. In London, Mary's tangible remains could be exhibited as part of a completely different Jacobite interpretative framework in 1889, compared to the Scottish history display in Glasgow in 1888 and the exhibition commemorating Mary at Peterborough in 1887.

Conclusion

Ivan Gaskell and Sarah Anne Carter propose that '[m]aterial things may shape understandings of chronology and time, transform a wide range of historical practices and, crucially, complicate distinctions between memory and history'.[88] Mary was a complicated historical figure in her own time, and the collecting and interpretation of Marian objects in the nineteenth century and their relationship to historical memory was equally complex. A comparison of the exhibitions at NMAS, Peterborough, Glasgow and London has revealed that the collecting of Marian objects primarily occurred in the private sphere, with the meanings attached to these items often based on the scope for them to function as tangible connections to people and events of the past. This form of meaning-making entangled memory and history, imagination and reality, resulting in a combination of fact and myth surrounding these items. The physical and symbolic properties of Marian 'relics' facilitated an imagined relationship between Mary, nineteenth-century collectors and exhibition visitors, allowing these objects to illustrate a narrative of her life within very different

---

[85] M. Pittock, *The Invention of Scotland: The Stuart Myth and the Scottish Identity, 1638 to the Present* (London, 1991), p. 122; Pittock, 'Jacobite Cult', p. 200; *Exhibition of the Royal House of Stuart*, pp. 7–8; Guthrie, *Material Culture*, p. 157.
[86] *Exhibition of the Royal House of Stuart*, pp. 86–98 and 103–15.
[87] Guthrie, *Material Culture*, p. 155.
[88] Gaskell and Carter, 'Introduction', p. 10.

exhibition frameworks. Susan Pearce identified that the veneration of historical relics as community souvenirs transforms them into romantic, almost mythological, foci for an illusory connection between people in the present and those of the past.[89] Mary's story belongs to Scotland, England and Britain, and the multiple identities of the queen allowed (and still allow) objects connected to her to be interpreted and re-interpreted as community souvenirs of Scottish, English and British history, drawing on different aspects of her life and story.

Many of the meanings attached to Marian objects discussed in this chapter continue to resonate with collectors, researchers and museum visitors today. Mary still appeals to the public imagination in the twenty-first century, with the story of her life drawing audiences to blockbuster exhibitions and enticing collectors to purchase Marian relics from auctions and antique shops. The physicality of Marian objects, as with all historic survivals, mean that they continue to act as a tangible medium to the past. Serena Dyer noted that the inherently sensory quality of objects exerts a powerful influence over human thought and experiences, particularly historic artefacts.[90] When displayed in public museum spaces, people can stand in close physical proximity to items that illustrate a narrative of Mary's life, providing an illusory connection between the past and the present through objects that were material witnesses of historic events. These Marian relics still evoke emotional responses of fascination, sympathy or condemnation in modern audiences, particularly those from her final years.[91] Private collectors can experience a physical connection to Mary by being able to touch objects that she may have touched, while family heirlooms continue to represent a relationship across time to ancestors who met the queen and received gifts from her hand or were important historical actors in the upheavals of the sixteenth century. For current scholars, these objects are subject to rigorous analytical research for investigating not only Mary, but the histories of the objects themselves and the sixteenth-century world which the queen inhabited.[92] And so, the collecting of Marian objects continues, and their re-interpretation broadens our understanding of not only her life and sixteenth-century society, but also of our own society through the values we impose on our interpretation of her.

---

[89] Pearce, *Museums*, pp. 196–98.
[90] Dyer, 'State of the Field', pp. 288–90.
[91] D. Forsyth, 'Exhibiting Mary: Challenges and Opportunities', https://mqs.glasgow.ac.uk/index.php/2020/08/13/exhibiting-mary-challenges-and-opportunities/, accessed 16 September 2023.
[92] Loomis et al., 'The Lamont and Queen Mary Harps'.

ELEVEN

'The most interesting apartment in Scotland': The History and Presentation of Mary, Queen of Scots' Chambers at the Palace of Holyroodhouse

Deborah Clarke

Introduction

The historic apartments at the Palace of Holyroodhouse, which Mary, Queen of Scots occupied between 1561 and 1567, have exerted a powerful fascination for royalty, residents and visitors alike over the centuries. The apartments, which were the location of some of the most dramatic events of Mary's life – in particular the murder of her Italian secretary David Rizzio – have played a significant role in Mary's memorialisation and commemoration. This chapter will look at Mary's association with Holyroodhouse and the development of Marian tourism at the palace, the various changes in the presentation of her apartments and the experience and reaction of visitors, many of whom wrote fulsomely about what they saw. It will examine how the apartments in the eighteenth century, full of shabby and decaying furnishings, were presented as unchanged since Mary's day to a largely uncritical audience entranced and enthralled by the romantic story of Mary. The opening up of the palace to the public on a more formal basis will be explored, following visits by George IV and Queen Victoria, when fascination with Mary's story increased. With their faded tapestries, tattered hangings and dilapidated four-poster bed, these rooms became 'the most interesting apartment in Scotland'.[1] The change in attitudes and expectations in the twentieth century will be analysed, as awareness grew of the need for truth and authenticity in historical interiors. This led to several alterations in presentation throughout the century as Mary's apartments took on a less prominent role in the palace. From stripped-back, empty spaces in the 1970s to a recreation in the 1990s of the romantic atmosphere of the rooms, presenting

---

[1] Robert McBean, *The Palace and Abbey of Holyrood* (Edinburgh, 1849), p. 168.

these apartments in an authentic way has remained a continual challenge in the twentieth and twenty-first centuries.

The early palace as a royal residence

The Palace of Holyroodhouse, which stands at the foot of the Royal Mile in Edinburgh and in the shadow of Arthur's Seat, was begun in 1502 by Mary's grandfather James IV. It lay next to the magnificent Holyrood Abbey, founded in 1128, which had provided royal lodgings until these were converted into the palace. Much of James IV's palace was rebuilt by Mary's father James V between 1528 and 1542.[2] When Mary returned to Scotland from France in 1561, after the death of her husband, the French king François II, she established herself and her court at Holyroodhouse for the next six years. The palace remained a fully functioning royal residence during the reign of James VI, until his departure in 1603. Following the removal of the court to London, Holyroodhouse was never again to be occupied regularly by the monarch and its importance faded. Mary's apartments remained intact, although stripped of their original furnishings, and were to be preserved from any further alterations that took place in the palace during the seventeenth century and later.

Mary occupied the queen's apartments on the second floor of the north-west tower, where her mother Mary of Guise had lived between 1538 and 1560. The tower had been constructed by James V between 1528 and 1532 and contained the king's apartments on the first floor and the queen's apartments on the second floor.[3] Both sets of apartments comprised an outer chamber, a bedchamber and two closets, and the queen's apartments had wardrobes on the floor above. The rest of James V's newly built palace was used by Mary and her court and included state apartments in the west range behind an impressive renaissance façade, the council chamber in the north range and the chapel in the south range.

Inventories of Mary's possessions during her residence document a large number of furnishings, including cloths of state, tapestries, carpets and cushions, many of which were brought by the queen from France.[4] In 1561, three months after Mary's arrival, forty-five beds, five canopies and around twenty

---

[2] T. Dickens et al. (eds), *Accounts of the (Lord High) Treasurer of Scotland*, 13 vols (Edinburgh, 1877–1978), vol. 2, pp. 87, 269.

[3] Henry M. Paton, John Imrie and John G. Dunbar, *Accounts of the Masters of Works for Building and Repairing Royal Residences and Castles* (Edinburgh, 1957–82), vol. 1, pp. 1–55; John G. Dunbar, *Scottish Royal Palaces. The Architecture of the Royal Residences during the Late Medieval and Early Renaissance Periods* (East Linton, 1999), pp. 63–64; G. Ewart and D. Gallagher, *Monastery and Palace: Archaeological Investigations at Holyroodhouse 1996–2009* (Edinburgh, 2013), pp. 50–56.

[4] Joseph Robertson (ed.), *Inventaires de la Royne Decosse Douairier De France. Catalogues of the Jewels, Dresses, Furniture, Books and Paintings of Mary, Queen of Scots 1556–1569* (Edinburgh, 1863), p. xx.

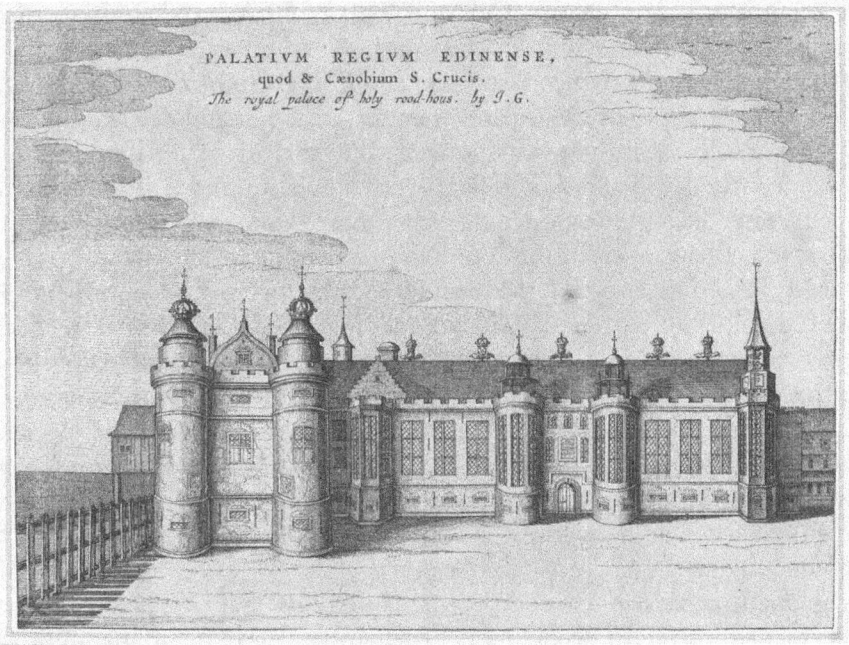

Figure 11.1 The Palace of Holyroodhouse in the 1560s. James Gordon (1615?–86), *Palatium Regium Edinense, West front of Palace*, c. 1649; RCIN 702909
Royal Collection Trust/© His Majesty King Charles III, 2023

coverings or 'cloths going about the bed for warmth' were recorded in the palace. More than twenty sets of tapestries were noted and these included the *Triumphe of Veritie*, the *Judgement of Paris*, the *Sailing of Aeneas*, the '*Huntis of the Sangleir*', as well as tapestries of trees, holly branches and flowers.[5] There is little evidence relating to specific moveable furniture for these rooms and none of the original furniture, furnishings, tapestries or other objects noted within Mary's apartments survive in the Royal Collection.

Mary's outer chamber, a large room with windows looking on one side south over the façade of the palace, and on the other side north to the entrance of Holyrood Abbey, was accessed through a spiral staircase in the north-east turret of the tower. During Mary of Guise's residence carved and painted heraldic decoration, to celebrate the marriage of Mary, Queen of Scots to the *dauphin* of France in 1558, was added to the wooden ceiling of the outer chamber. There is little evidence of specific furniture or furnishings used in this room, although it is documented that on one occasion it was hung with black velvet.[6] Mary used the outer chamber as an audience room and it was here that she met the

[5] Ibid., pp. 28–48.
[6] Ibid., pp. 9. lxi, 126.

indomitable Protestant reformer and theologian John Knox, on four occasions. Their lively and argumentative discussions often reduced her to tears.[7]

Mary's bedchamber, which faces west and in the 1560s overlooked the gate house and forecourt of the palace, was her private chamber. Like the outer chamber, its timber ceiling was adorned with heraldry. The elaborate *grisaille* frieze, decorated with flowers, foliage, cornucopia and grotesques to imitate three-dimensional plasterwork, may have been painted before her arrival.[8] A bed would have been in the room and dresses, cloth, plate and jewels are recorded in coffers, probably within her bedchamber.[9] An inventory of 1564 reveals that a cloth of state of gold and red, furnished with three valances and entirely fringed with gold and red silk, was taken apart to 'cover the flure about the Quenis bed'.[10] Few people apart from close members of Mary's household would have been allowed into the bedchamber but in February 1563, the French poet Pierre de Bocosel de Chastelard was discovered lying under the royal bed as Mary retired for the night. He was found by her grooms, who every night routinely checked behind the tapestries and beneath the bed, and was subsequently reprimanded.[11]

The apartments also included two small closets that occupied the north-west and south-west turrets of Mary's bedchamber. The closet in the south-west turret was probably Mary's dressing room, although it could have had other functions and may have been used as a study.[12] That in the north-west turret, which had a window overlooking the privy garden, was used as an intimate supper room. Mary is known to have favoured the colour green and her closets were furnished with green hangings and fabrics. In September 1561, 26½ ells of 'Pareis grene' were delivered to the *tapissier* for a closet in the queen's chambers at Holyroodhouse, together with another 24 ells of 'Inglis grene' cloth.[13] In June 1565 a further 2 ells of green fabric were ordered for the queen's closet.[14]

When Mary married Henry Stuart, Lord Darnley in 1565 in the private chapel of the palace, he was accommodated in the king's apartments on the first floor, previously occupied by James V. These were directly below Mary's second-floor apartments and had the same layout as the queen's apartments. Access between the two sets of bedchambers was by a straight private or privy stair or a turnpike stair.

---

[7] Jane E. A. Dawson, 'Knox, John (*c.* 1514–1572), Religious Reformer', *ODNB* (https://doi.org/10.1093/ref:odnb/15781).

[8] M. Bath, *Renaissance Decorative Painting in Scotland* (Edinburgh, 2003), p. 243.

[9] Robertson, *Inventaires*, p. lix (n. 4).

[10] Ibid., p. 58.

[11] *Treasurers Accounts*, vol. 11, pp. xxiv; when he repeated the offence at Rossend Castle, Burntisland in 1563 he was executed.

[12] Ewart and Gallagher, *Monastery and Palace*, p. 56.

[13] *Treasurers Accounts*, vol. 11, p. 66. The first payment was for £47.14s. and the second payment for £33. One ell measured approximately 0.94metres.

[14] *Treasurers Accounts*, vol. 11, p. 368. Payment for £7.10s.

One of the most dramatic events in Mary's reign took place at Holyroodhouse, when her secretary David Rizzio was brutally murdered in her private apartments. The long association of this shocking and violent event with Mary's chambers has fascinated and thrilled visitors and writers ever since and has influenced the way the apartments have been presented. The murder took place on Saturday 9 March 1566 when Mary, who was pregnant at the time, was dining in the small supper room in the north-west turret. Rizzio was with her, and others present included the countess of Argyll, Mary's half-sister and confidante; Arthur Erskine, Mary's favourite equerry; and Robert Stewart, Mary's half-brother. Darnley entered the tiny room first, having come up the privy staircase directly from his bedchamber below. He was closely followed by an armour-clad Lord Ruthven, and others entered the apartments, probably from the main turnpike stair. At the same time around 160 men took control of the palace and prevented anyone from leaving. Fighting broke out as a terrified Rizzio clung to Mary's skirts, and food and candles were strewn across the supper room. Mary herself described the brutal scene, where Ruthven and his accomplices 'cast down our table upon ourself, put violent hands on him [Rizzio], [and] struck him over our shoulder with whinyards [short swords]'.[15] Rizzio was dragged to the outer chamber and stabbed repeatedly, between fifty-two and sixty times, with both daggers and swords. His body was left bleeding in the outer chamber before being thrown down the main turnpike stair and tossed into the porter's lodge. Mary and Darnley had remained in the supper room, and when the provost of Edinburgh appeared outside, alerted to events by the ringing of a bell, Darnley went to the window and assured them that the queen was safe. A terrified Mary was kept captive in her chambers until she escaped the following day. The story of the violent murder of Rizzio was to be firmly associated with Mary and her apartments and indelibly connected to future presentations of the rooms. Alleged traces of the ill-fated Rizzio's blood, supposedly visible on the floor of the outer chamber, were consistently woven into the story and proved particularly memorable to future visitors.

Mary stayed at the palace only intermittently following this shocking event. After Darnley's death in February 1567, Mary married James Hepburn, earl of Bothwell in the palace. Bothwell took over the king's apartments, previously Darnley's rooms, just below the queen's apartments. Mary spent little time in the palace and only a few weeks later left for the last time, when she was forced to abdicate in favour of her young son who became James VI of Scotland.

James VI, who was brought up at Stirling Castle, began to move his court to Holyroodhouse in 1579, aged 13, and resided in the king's apartments. Mary's chambers remained empty until James brought his bride Anne of Denmark to the palace in 1590. By this time a large court was in residence but the queen's

---

[15] Labanoff (ed.), *Lettres*, vol. 1, p. 342.

apartments, which Anne occupied, were probably little altered in appearance since Mary had left in 1567. On her arrival, Anne expressed a desire for more privacy and requested restrictions to the customary free access to the king's bedchamber on the first floor, directly below her own apartments.[16] In 1603, when James succeeded to the English throne as James I, the king, queen and court moved to London. Nearly all the furniture, tapestries, paintings, jewellery, clothing and plate left the palace with the royal court. Holyroodhouse, bare of furnishings and empty of a court, would enjoy only intermittent visits by royalty over the following centuries.

The rebuilding of the palace and the growth of Marian tourism in the seventeenth and eighteenth centuries

The formal life of Holyroodhouse as a royal residence effectively ended with the removal of the court, but during the rebuilding of the palace in the seventeenth century, the north-west tower that contained Mary's apartments was preserved from any major alteration. A location for Marian tourism, having a very close association with Mary, was created and the process of the memorialisation of the queen at the palace commenced. Furnishings and objects within the palace, with their history gently exaggerated or manipulated, were used to make the apartments more appealing. The response of visitors captivated by Mary was generally full of enthusiasm and wonder and largely uncritical. This was a trend that would continue until the modern period.

During the 1670s the palace was almost completely rebuilt for Charles II by the Scottish architect Sir William Bruce but the historic, sixteenth-century north-west tower containing the old king's and queen's apartments was retained. This decision dictated the form of the entire project as Bruce designed a new, matching, south-west tower, giving a symmetrical and balanced appearance to the façade of the palace and maintaining the look of a Scottish castle. The new building included apartments for the king on the east side of the palace and the old king's apartments, which had been occupied by Darnley, Bothwell and James VI, were reconfigured as the queen's apartments.[17] The rooms formerly occupied by Mary were little changed and the timber ceilings were retained, preserving the character and significance of the earlier Stuart residence and celebrating the 'antiquated Stuart style' as a valuable legacy.[18]

---

[16] *CSP Scot*, vol. 10, pp. 298–99.
[17] They were occupied by Mary of Modena as duchess of York when James, duke of York resided in the palace at various times between 1679 and 1682.
[18] Aonghus MacKechnie, 'Birth-stool of Scottish Romanticism? Holyrood and Sir William Bruce, Surveyor-General and Overseer of the King's Buildings in Scotland', *Architectural Heritage* 23 (2012): 148.

In 1646 Charles I had nominated William Hamilton, second duke of Hamilton, premier peer and former secretary of state for Scotland, as hereditary keeper of the Palace of Holyroodhouse. This appointment required the duke to take care of the palace and its rooms, together with the gardens.[19] In return, the duke and his heirs were granted accommodation within the palace.[20] Around 1684 the duke and duchess of Hamilton began to occupy the rooms in the north-west tower. They moved their furnishings into the newly appointed queen's apartments on the first floor of the tower (the former king's apartments) as well as rooms along the west front, and lived in great style. The duchess of Hamilton took over the chambers that had been Darnley's, including his outer chamber, bedchamber and closets. A small extension was built to the north which contained the duchess's bedchamber. In 1740-41, the Scottish architect William Adam undertook an ambitious refurbishment of the apartments for the fifth duke of Hamilton, creating one of the most fashionable residences in Edinburgh. These rooms were occupied by Prince Charles Edward Stuart in 1745 when he held court in the palace for six weeks. The prince used Darnley's outer chamber as his public dining room and Darnley's bedchamber as his drawing room.

Mary's bedchamber and outer chamber, located directly above the rooms used by the duchess of Hamilton, were of little importance in the new scheme and began to be utilised by the Hamilton's household as a storage area for old and outmoded furniture and unwanted items. Despite this there was much interest in these rooms in the oldest part of the palace, particularly due to their close association with the story of Mary. During the eighteenth century Holyroodhouse attracted many travellers who were interested in visiting picturesque sites and ruins. Although the palace was not officially open to visitors at this time, those interested could write directly to the duke of Hamilton, using their own connections or letters of introduction as a means of admittance. Others gained entry simply by knocking on the door of the palace. Sightseers were then shown around by the duke of Hamilton's housekeeper, who took upon the role of guide to the rooms and their contents. This led to many erroneous attributions of furniture, especially the supposed identification of the original bed that Mary had slept in, creating a narrative that was to last for around two centuries.

Most people were particularly captivated by Mary, Queen of Scots' apartments, together with the dramatic story of the queen's life at Holyroodhouse and, above all, the brutal murder of Rizzio. Visitors could see the location of the murder, which made a great impression, and the exact spot where the body

---

[19] J. Harrison, *The History of the Monastery of the Holy-Rood and the Palace of Holyrood House* (Edinburgh and London, 1919), p. 94.
[20] The office of hereditary keeper is still held by the dukes of Hamilton.

had been left, indelibly marked by red stains that were supposedly traces of the unfortunate Rizzio's blood. These stains were frequently commented on with fascination and awe by visitors during the eighteenth and early nineteenth centuries but later in the Victorian period some doubt began to creep into observations about the marks on the floor.

One of the earliest accounts of a visit to Mary, Queen of Scots' chambers was in 1723 by the politician Sir John Evelyn, of Wotton, Surrey, grandson of the diarist. He described in some detail what he saw:

> Last week my wife and I had the curiosity to see Duke of Hamilton's lodgings in Holyroodhouse, which are very handsome, and have some good pictures . . . But the chief sight was the little room in a corner tower, the remains of the old palace, where David Rizzio was at supper with Queen Mary, when he was murdered; and there are still some marks of blood, said to be his, in the passage beyond the outer room, to which place he was dragged.[21]

In 1760, Elizabeth, duchess of Northumberland, later lady of the bedchamber to Queen Charlotte, recorded in her diary a walk round Holyroodhouse:

> I went also to see Mary Q of Scots Bedchamber (a very small one it is) from whence David Rizzio was drag'd out and stab'd in the ante room where is some of his Blood which they can't get wash'd out.[22]

The Welsh antiquary and naturalist Thomas Pennant wrote about his visit in 1769 and again in 1772, described in numerous editions of his *Tours in Scotland*. Samuel Johnson and James Boswell toured Holyroodhouse in 1773 and Boswell wrote of their visit in his life of Johnson, noting '[w]e surveyed that part of the palace appropriated to the Duke of Hamilton, as keeper, in which our beautiful Queen Mary lived, and in which David Rizzio was murdered'.[23]

Many pieces of furniture, furnishings and objects left or stored in the apartments took on prominent roles in Mary's story, and often the more worn or dilapidated the better. Over time, an interior was created essentially for inspection by tourists. The events of Mary's life at the palace were embellished by the duke of Hamilton's housekeeper using the items in the rooms, the story exaggerated in expectation of a more appreciative audience and therefore a more profitable gratuity at the end of the tour. This is probably the earliest example

---

[21] Letter from Sir John Evelyn, of Wotton in Surrey, to Mr Nicholas of Horsley Place near Guildford, 24 October 1723, *The Gentleman's Magazine*, vol. 57, part I, p. 476.

[22] J. Greig (ed.), *The Diaries of a Duchess: Extracts from the Diaries of the First Duchess of Northumberland* (New York, 1926), p. 20.

[23] James Boswell, *The Life of Samuel Johnson, LL.D* (London, 1835), p. 19.

Figure 11.2 Samuel Dukinfield Swarbreck, *Mary, Queen of Scots' Bedchamber*, 1861, RCIN 403228
Royal Collection Trust/© His Majesty King Charles III, 2023

of Marian tourism in Scotland in which the exploitation of Mary's story and surroundings led to greater financial reward. This manipulation of the contents of the apartments to fit in with Mary's story can be seen with a piece of furniture that had a long association with these rooms, although no links at all to Mary, Queen of Scots. This was the large and handsome seventeenth-century tester bed, with ornate carved and pierced cresting and hung with rich red damask embellished with silk fringe, the appearance of which in the chambers was completely accidental.[24]

The bed was probably commissioned in the 1670s by the first duke of Hamilton's daughter Anne, who was duchess of Hamilton in her own right, for use by her husband, the third duke of Hamilton. It is first recorded in an inventory of the Hamilton apartments in 1684 as a 'bed with reid Damas courtines & feather bed, in my lord's Bedchamber' and noted in successive inventories.[25] When the duchess's apartments were renovated in the 1740s a new and fashionable bed was ordered and another large tester bed, hung with yellow and red velvet, was moved into the duke's bedchamber.[26] By 1761 the unfashion-

---

[24] Royal Collection Trust RCIN 27918.
[25] Margaret Swain, 'The State Beds at Holyroodhouse', *Furniture History* 14 (1978): 58–60, at p. 59.
[26] Ibid.

able red damask bed had been moved upstairs and out of the way to Mary's bedchamber, described as 'Lady Susan Stewart's Room'.[27] The transformation into Mary's bed was complete when the inventory of 1784, made by the house steward William Kinnaivie, described the same room correctly as 'Queen Mary's Room' but erroneously documents the 'Queen's bedstead red damask curtains' in the chamber.[28]

The beginnings of tourism in Scotland after the 1745 Jacobite uprising and an interest in the country's past led to an increased number of travellers, tourists and writers who came to view Mary's apartments in the late eighteenth and early nineteenth centuries. Fascinated by antiquarianism and a sense of Romanticism, many of those who viewed Mary's chambers wrote accounts of their visits. Stories told by the housekeeper about the dramatic events that had taken place in the rooms and the supposed provenance of many of the objects, together with the almost theatrical display, left many writers full of wonder and with a sense of reverence for the interior, putting aside any doubts about what they saw. The writer and advocate Hugo Arnot wrote an influential account of his visit to Holyroodhouse in his *History of Edinburgh* of 1779. Although he described the palace as 'magnificent', he noted '[t]he only apartments which are worth viewing, are those possessed by the Duke of Hamilton, heritable keeper of the palace. These occupy all that remains of the old palace'.[29] He went on to describe the bed that was the centrepiece of Mary's bedchamber and by then clearly associated with her:

> In the second floor are Queen Mary's apartments, in one of which her own bed still remains, It is of crimson damask, bordered with green silk tassels and fringes, and is now almost in tatters. The cornice of the bed is of open figured work, in the present taste; but more light in the execution than any modern one we have seen.[30]

Its shabby and threadbare state lent the bed an aura of authenticity and Arnot's description was to be repeated by many other visitors. Arnot was also fascinated by the murder of Rizzio, relating it in detail. He described how 'Rizzio was pushed out of the closet, dragged through the bed-chamber, into the chamber of presence where, being pierced with redoubled wounds, he expired'.[31]

Europeans also visited and another admirer of Mary's apartments was the 18-year-old Frenchman Alexandre de La Rochefoucauld, who travelled around Scotland in 1786 accompanied by his mentor Maximillien de Lazowski, and

---

[27] Ibid., p. 60; NRAS332/M/4/46.
[28] Ibid.
[29] Hugo Arnot, *The History of Edinburgh* (Edinburgh and London, 1779), p. 305.
[30] Ibid.
[31] Ibid., p. 306.

visited the Palace of Holyroodhouse during his sojourn in Edinburgh. In his journal he carefully noted the contents of Mary's chambers:

> The duke of Hamilton, by virtue of an hereditary office, occupies the ancient apartment of Mary, Queen of Scots, in which they keep, with reverence, various furnishings from her time; such as her damask bed with fringes, etc., in silk; her armchairs, and some of her embroidery.[32]

He too was fascinated to see the site of Rizzio's murder and the bloodstains on the floor.

Another writer, the Banffshire clergyman and naturalist Charles Cordiner, chronicled his visit to Holyroodhouse in 1788, no doubt reiterating the information given on his tour: 'The embroidery on the bed and chairs is said to be chiefly the work of Mary's own fingers'.[33] He also commented favourably on the state of the furniture: 'Considering the age of the furniture, it is astonishing to see it so little decayed. The Keeper of the palace has great merit for the excellent repair in which these apartments are preserved.'[34] After seeing the bloodstains alleged to be those of Rizzio, he noted that some doubts had been expressed: 'Many tales are handed down concerning them, which have no claim to probability. But the tradition of the fact has been so uniform that there can be no doubt of its truth.'[35]

Not all visitors were completely enthralled and, in 1803, Charles Dibdin commented '[t]he whole suite of apartments made but a miserable appearance'.[36] Despite this there were still visitors in awe of what they saw, such as the English barrister and travel writer Sir John Carr, who 'inspected this venerable seat of royalty' in 1807. He remarked,

> The interesting history of Queen Mary of Scotland naturally hastens the steps of the traveller to visit the place where she resided, in which to this day so many vestiges illustrative of her habits and life, leniently touched by the hand of time, still remain.[37]

He was moved to see the Scottish queen's chambers and observed that they 'cannot fail of exciting the deepest interest, and of awakening many tender

---

[32] Norman Scarfe, *To the Highlands in 1786: The Inquisitive Journey of a Young French Aristocrat* (Woodbridge, 2001), p. xx.

[33] Charles Cordiner, *Romantic Ruins, and Romantic Prospects, of North Britain. With Ancient Monuments, and Singular Subjects of Natural History* (London, 1788). No pagination.

[34] Ibid.

[35] Ibid.

[36] Charles Dibdin, *Observations on a Tour Through Almost the Whole of England, and a Considerable Part of Scotland, in a Series of Letters, Addressed to a large number of intelligent and respectable Friends* (London 1801–02), pp. 207–08.

[37] Sir John Carr, *Caledonian Sketches, or, A Tour Through Scotland in 1807 . . .* (London, 1809), p. 58.

emotions'.[38] In an increasingly Romantic age the story of Mary as exemplified in her own apartments, presented as unchanged since her last sojourn, visitors were able to put any misgivings aside to record their sentimental and passionate feelings and responses.

Visitors in the nineteenth century

The nineteenth century saw a rise in more visible and eventually more formal tourism at the palace and this led to its eventual opening to the public in 1854. At the same time visits from royalty, such as George IV and Queen Victoria, drew further attention to Holyroodhouse and its history. Both monarchs made private visits to Mary's chambers and official events and presentations also endeavoured to maintain the romantic and dramatic feel of the palace. The earliest visual images of Mary's apartments were published in the 1830s, adding to interest in the rooms, their contents and the sense of antiquity they presented.

In order to cater for additional visitors, the first guidebook to the palace and abbey was published in 1818, written by Charles Mackie, author of guides to several historical sites, including Linlithgow Palace. Holyroodhouse was described in detail, including Mary's apartments and the 'large dusky spots said to have been occasioned by Rizzio's blood staining the floor, which no washing of the boards has been able to deface'.[39] Although there are no visual depictions of the rooms at this date, the descriptions give a better idea of the contents. 'The armour of Henry Darnley, and James VI is shewn in the room from which Rizzio was dragged out to be murdered. The queen's dressing-box is also shewn.'[40] By the time a new edition was published in 1832 Mackie perhaps reflected an increasing scepticism that was becoming apparent among less gullible visitors when he changed what he had written to 'a dark stain said to have been the blood of the unfortunate Rizzio, is pointed out by the house-keeper upon the floor; the boards, however, are far too modern to bear testimony to this traditionary absurdity'.[41] The walls were hung with tapestries depicting the story of Phaeton.[42]

Further attention was drawn to Holyroodhouse and Mary's apartments in 1822 when George IV visited Scotland, amidst extraordinary scenes of celebration and jubilation. It was an occasion imbued with great significance, as this was the first visit by a monarch to Scotland since that of Charles II in 1650 for

---

[38] Ibid.
[39] C. Mackie, *The Original Historical Description of the Monastery and Chapel Royal of Holyroodhouse* (Edinburgh, 1819), p. 95.
[40] Ibid.
[41] C. Mackie, *The Original Historical Description of the Monastery and Chapel Royal of Holyroodhouse* (Edinburgh, 1832), p. 113.
[42] These four tapestries are still in the Royal Collection, RCIN 28218-21.

his Scottish coronation. Although Holyroodhouse was not considered in good enough repair for the king to take up residence and he stayed at Dalkeith Palace instead, the palace burst into life when the flamboyant monarch used it as the setting for many royal events. Amidst the rapturous welcome and extravagant occasions, George paid a private visit to the old royal apartments. The king was greeted by the duke of Hamilton and led around Mary's chambers by the duke's housekeeper. The king was enthralled when he was shown the large and ornate tester bed in the centre of Mary's bedchamber, described as the very bed in which Mary had slept. He 'caught hold of the blanket, and remarked how wonderful it was, that it had been kept so long in a state of preservation'.[43] The visit made a deep impression on the king and he declared 'in repairing the palace these apartments should be preserved from every alteration'.[44] George's visit drew further attention to the appeal of the palace as a focus for early Scottish history. Interest in Holyroodhouse escalated and the number of sightseers, tourists and visitors swelled after the king's departure.

The Scottish writer Sir Walter Scott, who had stage-managed George IV's highly successful visit, was particularly fascinated by Holyroodhouse and valued its antiquarian appeal. The neglected and decaying palace, which he described as a 'venerable pile', featured in several of his novels, including *Waverley*, *The Fair Maid of Perth* and *The Antiquary*. In the second series of the *Chronicles of the Canongate* (which forms the introduction to *The Fair Maid of Perth*), Chrystal Croftangry, the fictitious author of the volume, is involved in a long discussion about the murder of Rizzio and, in particular, the durability of the bloodstains. Croftangry contemplates spending the night in Mary's bedchamber on the 'couch of the rose of Scotland' as the red damask bed is poetically described by Scott, moved by the thought of 'what dreams might be produced by a mansion of so many memories'.[45] Scott, the prolific and popular writer of Romantic novels, thus perpetuated the romantic story of Mary and her memorialisation within the chambers at Holyroodhouse.

The bibliographer Thomas Frognall Dibdin could hardly contain his interest in Mary's apartments and his reverence for the objects and furnishings within when he visited with his daughter in 1838.[46] He was particularly fascinated to see Mary's bedchamber and wrote '[o]f all the rooms ever visited by me, THIS was the room of the most intense interest'.[47] Wanting the full experience and to get as close to Mary as possible he records how he

---

[43] Robert Mudie, *A Historical Account of His Majesty's Visit to Scotland* (Edinburgh, 1822), p. 252.
[44] Ibid.
[45] Sir Walter Scott, *Chronicles of the Canongate, Second Series* (Edinburgh and London, 1828), vol. 1, p. 11.
[46] Thomas F. Dibdin, *A Bibliographical, Antiquarian and Picturesque Tour in the Northern Counties of England and in Scotland*, 2 vols (London, 1838), vol. 2, pp. 522–23.
[47] Ibid., p. 522.

attempted, very delicately, with the end of my fore-finger, to touch the bed furniture of red velvet. The guide was quite alarmed, saying 'it would fall to pieces if I touched it'. Indeed, it seemed to shake as my finger came in contact with it.[48]

He was less impressed by the remaining contents of the room, noting that 'the relics of her *toilette* were of secondary interest; and the pictures and portraits, third-rate. An air of falsification pervades the whole.'[49] Despite this awareness of the possible artificiality of the contents, Dibdin still engaged with the original setting of the dramatic events of Mary's reign. Like many other visitors he was drawn to the location of the murder of Rizzio and on viewing it he could imagine in detail the full drama and tragedy of the occasion, envisaging the moment '. . . when Rizzio was torn away for destruction, midst the agonizing shrieks and thrilling entreaties of his royal patroness'.[50]

In 1839 some of the earliest visual images that record the appearance of the bedchamber and the two turret rooms were published by Samuel Dukinfield Swarbreck in *Sketches in Scotland*. Swarbreck's later oil painting of the bedchamber (see Figure 11.2) was based on the lithograph in this publication. The heraldic oak ceiling can be seen clearly in a room dominated by the imposing red damask bed and hung with the Phaeton tapestries. Mary's 'workbox' is displayed on a large table in the window. The two turret rooms, closely associated with the story of Mary, were filled with what was thought to be original furniture and tapestries.

The supper room contained pieces of armour including a breast plate, a helmet and a pair of gauntlets, described as the armour worn by Darnley on the night of Rizzio's murder.[51] Swarbreck's depiction of the closet shows a timber-panelled ceiling and tapestries hung on at least two of its walls. In addition two seventeenth-century gilt candlestands are present.[52] The settee was a piece of Hamilton furniture.[53]

Holyroodhouse became the focus of royal interest again in 1850 when Queen Victoria, Prince Albert and their growing family stayed at the palace for the first time, after initially visiting Scotland in 1842.[54] The Scots viewed Victoria's return to the palace of her Stuart ancestors as an event of profound significance. The queen herself was aware of this, and later wrote of her deep connection to Scotland's past, commenting '[f]or Stewart blood is in my veins and I am

[48] Ibid.
[49] Ibid., p. 523.
[50] Ibid., p. 524.
[51] Samuel Dukinfield Swarbreck, *Sketches in Scotland: Drawn from Nature and Stone* (London, 1839), p. xx. The armour dates from the 1660s and is still in the Royal Collection, RCIN 28137.
[52] RCIN 27938 and RCIN 27939.
[53] Whereabouts unknown. This also appears in later images of the outer chamber.
[54] They had visited Edinburgh in 1842 but had been unable to visit the palace owing to an outbreak of smallpox.

Figure 11.3 From Samuel Dukinfield Swarbreck's Sketches in Scotland (1839), Queen Mary's closet (right) and Queen Mary's dressing room (left), RCIN 1070498
Royal Collection Trust/© His Majesty King Charles III, 2023

now their representative'.[55] While viewing the ruins of Holyrood Abbey, Victoria reflected on the life of Mary, Queen of Scots, who she called 'my unfortunate ancestress'.[56] She took a great interest in visiting Mary's apartments, paying particular attention to 'the dressing room, into which the murderers, who killed Rizzio, had entered, & the spot where he fell'.[57] She was shown the bloodstained floorboards by the housekeeper who instructed her 'that if the lady would stand on this side, she would see that the boards were discoloured with blood'.[58] Queen Victoria's visits to the palace and the publication of Swarbreck's lithographs prompted further interest in the red damask bed and copies were made for several country houses during the early part of the queen's reign.[59]

Queen Victoria's travels around Scotland engendered a deep love of the country and the purchase of Balmoral Castle in Aberdeenshire. Her enthusiasm for her Highland home led to a huge focus on Scottish culture and an international

---

[55] *Queen Victoria's Journals*, 12 September 1873, www.queenvictoriasjournals.org, accessed 18 September 2023.
[56] Ibid., 29 August 1850.
[57] Ibid.
[58] Ibid.
[59] A replica was made for the duke of Portland at Welbeck Abbey. The room became known as 'Queen Mary's Room', though Mary, Queen of Scots never stayed at Welbeck. Swain, 'The State Beds at Holyroodhouse', p. 58.

interest in tourism. The queen's visits to Holyroodhouse on her journeys to and from Balmoral drew attention to the palace and led to a growing interest from the public to visit. Although Mary, Queen of Scots' apartments had developed as a tourist attraction in the eighteenth century, in 1852 the Lord Provost of Edinburgh petitioned the queen with a request that Holyroodhouse might be opened more formally, in a similar manner to Hampton Court Palace, which had been on view to the public since 1838 and received a large number of visitors.[60] Nevertheless, shortly after the queen's visit, a writer in *The Scotsman* was not impressed when he showed a visitor the palace: 'I must say I blushed with shame to show an intelligent stranger – in a corner of the same palace where her Majesty had been lodged only a week or two before – a beggarly array of spurious and tawdry relics'.[61] Despite the interest in opening the apartments to the public, there seemed a growing awareness from some of the paucity of what was on display.

Agreement was reached with the Office of Works to open the apartments in James V's tower (the former Mary, Queen of Scots and Darnley apartments) and arrangements were brought under the management of architect Robert Matheson, clerk of works for HM's Office of Works in Scotland, who had been responsible for the recent renovations of the Royal Apartments in preparation for Queen Victoria's visits. Alexander, tenth duke of Hamilton, relinquished his apartments in James V's tower to allow them to be opened to visitors.[62] He was provided with alternative accommodation on the second floor of the palace. Existing arrangements, which allowed people to be shown round Mary, Queen of Scots' apartments by the duke of Hamilton's housekeeper in return for a personal gratuity, were dropped. The current incumbent, 83-year-old Mrs Quinet, who had begun her service in the Hamilton apartments in around 1825, was persuaded to retire. Instead, Matheson made a more professional arrangement and male staff were appointed to show the apartments on a regular basis. William Ross was engaged to look after Mary, Queen of Scots' rooms and Peter Gray oversaw the 'Darnley Rooms'.[63]

The Historic Apartments, as they became known, consisting of Mary, Queen of Scots' chambers on the second floor and the former Darnley apartments on the first floor, opened in January 1854 for the first time under this arrangement; tickets cost sixpence during the week but on Saturday entry was free of charge.[64] The opening to the public proved very successful and *The Scotsman* reported that in 1854, the first full year of opening, just under 67,000 people

---

[60] NRS MW2/68; NRS MW2/12.
[61] *The Scotsman*, 18 December 1850.
[62] NRS MW2/12.
[63] NRS MW2/68; Ian Gow, *The Scottish Interior* (Edinburgh, 1992), pp. 80–81.
[64] *The Scotsman*, 4 January 1854.

visited, although it also noted that a high proportion came on Saturday, when admittance was free of charge.[65] The publication of guidebooks increased to satisfy visitors and they give some idea of the additional contents in the rooms. Paintings listed in the bedchamber included portraits of Henry VIII, Queen Elizabeth and Elizabeth of York, Henry VII's consort.[66] The combined effect of the magnificent bed complete with dilapidated hangings, heraldic ceilings, ancient tapestries and paintings gave a sense of theatrical display to the rooms which made them increasingly popular and a source of inspiration throughout the nineteenth century.

The large number of visitors meant that steps were taken to prevent the public from getting too close to items on display, particularly the red damask bed, and elaborate and unsightly barriers were introduced which must have destroyed some of the atmosphere of the rooms. By 1863 Matheson was aware that repairs needed to be carried out to the apartments and work proceeded with a complete overhaul of the panelling, the oak ceilings were repaired and the existing stone-coloured paint was replaced with a coat of graining 'in imitation of old oak' to add to the antiquarian effect.[67] Matheson therefore deliberately manipulated the appearance of the rooms to an imagined sixteenth-century ideal, to make them seem more authentic and therefore appealing. The first-floor rooms, which had become known as the Darnley apartments, had been emptied of most furnishings when the duke of Hamilton vacated them. To rectify this, in 1864 furniture and tapestries were purchased from Adam Gibb Ellis, an Edinburgh lawyer, in order to create a 'museum' collection at the palace. Ellis had spent a number of years assembling a collection from 'the Royal Palaces of Scotland', including Falkland, Dunfermline, Linlithgow and Holyroodhouse. Matheson, who was aware of the importance and significance of acquiring such pieces to give a real sense of authenticity to the spaces, realised that 'the opportunity of making such a collection is one that very rarely occurs'.[68]

Queen Victoria herself visited Mary, Queen of Scots' rooms again in 1872, finding them 'deeply interesting', and she wrote in her journal about the 'dark winding staircase at the top of which poor Rizzio was foully murdered . . . then into poor Queen Mary's bedroom with the old faded bed she used . . . The room is all hung with Tapestry!'[69] She went into Mary's outer chamber and noted '[h]ere stands the original bed made for Charles I^{rst}'.[70] This comment relates

---

[65] *The Scotsman*, 5 September 1855.
[66] Robert McBean, *The Palace and Abbey of Holyrood* (Edinburgh, 1849), p. 168.
[67] NRS MW2/51.
[68] NRS MW2/6; letter from Robert Matheson to Alfred Austin, Office of Works, 26 January 1863; A. G. Ellis died before the sale could be progressed and it was completed with his inheritor, his brother Robert Ellis.
[69] *Queen Victoria's Journals*, 14 August 1872.
[70] Ibid.

to another seventeenth-century Hamilton bed which had been moved to this room but had erroneously been connected to Charles I. Robert Chambers' *Walks in Edinburgh* of 1825 describes this bed as 'brought from another part of the Palace, and placed here, for the convenience of exhibition'.[71] He goes on to explain the bed's connection with both Prince Charles Edward Stuart and the Duke of Cumberland, who reputedly had both slept in this bed within a few weeks of each other. He states that 'it has the appearance of great antiquity; being now in a very infirm condition, [it] is encircled with a line of low screens, in order to protect it from the contact of the spectators'.[72] The bed, of crimson and gold velvet and lined with yellow satin, was supplied for the duchess of Hamilton's bedchamber at Holyroodhouse and is recorded in inventories as being in her room until 1741. At that date the duchess acquired a new bed and the crimson and gold bed (along with added footposts) was moved to the duke of Hamilton's bedchamber in the west range. The bed made its way up to Mary's outer chamber in the early nineteenth century and became known as

Figure 11.4 Alexander Fraser, *Mary, Queen of Scots Outer Chamber, Holyroodhouse*, c. 1884, RCIN 403239 Royal Collection Trust/© His Majesty King Charles III, 2023

---

[71] Robert Chambers, *Walks in Edinburgh* (Edinburgh, 1825), p. 156.
[72] Ibid.

Charles I's bed.[73] This was perhaps another romantic exaggeration developed by the housekeeper as she showed visitors round, another bed connected to a monarch who had met a tragic end and linked to a prince with a failed claim to the crown.

Fascination with Mary continued throughout the nineteenth century and numerous books were published about her, including Agnes Strickland's *Life of Mary, Queen of Scots* in 1844, which proved very popular with female readers, and historical novels, such as that by Charlotte Mary Yonge in 1882, *Unknown to History*.[74] In 1887, to mark the tercentenary of her execution, an exhibition of 200 relics relating to Mary was held in Peterborough, and many of the items were also shown at the Glasgow International Exhibition of 1888.[75] All of this added to the interest in Mary as visitors to Holyroodhouse were swept up in the romance of her life. Despite some growing unease expressed by more learned visitors, most tourists were happy to suspend belief as each item on show was woven intricately into the Scottish queen's story.

Re-presenting the apartments in the twentieth and twenty-first centuries

The early twentieth century saw the development of a greater interest in the seventeenth-century palace and its architecture, and an awareness of its importance. At this time major renovations took place in the palace to allow Holyroodhouse to be used as the official royal residence in Scotland. The state apartments created for Charles II, with their baroque interiors and ornate plasterwork ceilings, were opened to the public in 1925. Although much thought was given to the display of Mary's apartments, there was a growing belief that Mary's story should not be the main narrative in the palace and greater emphasis should be given to other areas. Critical expectations of historical accuracy rose during the twentieth and the twenty-first centuries and ideas changed concerning the importance and authenticity of the objects on display.

Appreciation of the aesthetic qualities of Holyroodhouse was stimulated when Sir Robert Rowand Anderson, architect of the Scottish National Portrait Gallery and founder of the Edinburgh School of Applied Art, included the palace in the National Art Survey, a record of all buildings in Scotland dating to before the eighteenth century, which was begun in 1893.[76] Appreciation of historical buildings and recognition of the importance of study and scholarship developed in the late nineteenth century. The Society of Antiquaries of Scotland (SoAS) played a key role and a significant figure was Joseph Anderson, assistant

---

[73] Swain, 'The State Beds at Holyroodhouse', pp. 58–60.
[74] Jayne Lewis, *Mary Queen of Scots: Romance and Nation* (London, 1998), pp. 213–14.
[75] Ibid., p. 173. See Chapter 10 for discussion.
[76] I. Gow, 'Sir Rowand Anderson's Art Survey of Scotland', *Architectural History*, 27 (1984): 543–54.

secretary of SoAS, editor of their *Proceedings* and keeper of the Antiquities Museum, the collection of the Society, from 1869–1913. He expanded and studied the historical collection, focusing on primary source analysis and cultural history.[77] The study of furniture increased and seminal works, such as those by Percy MacQuoid and Ralph Edwards, allowed for further examination of the items within the palace.[78]

In 1903 Sir Herbert Maxwell, president of SoAS, who was aware of Anderson's work and was mindful of the growing need to present the interior with greater accuracy, was asked to evaluate the historic apartments and advise on their presentation. Attempts were made to clarify the display, particularly in Mary's outer chamber, where some of the duke of Hamilton's furniture was dispersed and the remainder was cleaned and repaired.[79] Maxwell wrote the most up-to-date guidebook for the palace, first published in 1906, which ran into many editions up until 1937 and which reflects the changes made in the rooms. The bed known as Charles I's bed, described by Maxwell in his guidebook as 'incongruous with the original purpose of the chamber', was moved in 1911 down to Lord Darnley's former bedchamber.[80] Despite the realisation that this bed was not appropriate for Mary's chambers, confusion as to its origins continued as, implausibly, it soon became known as the 'Darnley bed' purely due to its location in Darnley's apartments. Maxwell was also responsible for the installation of a brass plaque that marked where Rizzio's body was left, to allow the story of the murder to be told effectively and reliably. According to his guidebook, the reputed blood stain on the floor had been hacked at by 'the knives of unscrupulous curiosity hunters' although traces of the marks remained.[81] Around this time tempera friezes were discovered beneath the wooden panelling in both the bedchamber and the outer chamber.

The large bed hung with decaying red damask was still the centrepiece of Mary's bedchamber. Early in the twentieth century the Edinburgh-born artist James Pryde painted a series of dark and brooding studies of the bedchamber, *The Human Comedy*, in which the towering red damask tester bed is the focal point of each composition. These were inspired by the painter's childhood memory of visiting Mary's bedchamber and seeing the bed in which she supposedly slept. Pryde, a theatrical set and poster designer and one of the

---

[77] Julie Holder, 'Joseph Anderson (1832–1916) and the Scottish Historical Collection at the Antiquities Museum, 1869 to 1892', *Proceeding of the Society of Antiquities of Scotland* 151 (2022): 257–75; and see Chapter 10.

[78] Percy Macquoid, *A History of English Furniture*, 4 vols (London, 1904–08); Percy Macquoid and Ralph Edwards, *A Dictionary of English Furniture*, 3 vols (London, 1924).

[79] The seventeenth-century chair to the left of the fireplace, made for the third Duke of Hamilton between 1682 and 1695, is now in the National Museums Scotland (K.2006.160.1).

[80] Sir Herbert Maxwell, *Official Guide Palace Abbey-church And Environs of Holyroodhouse* (Edinburgh, 1906), p. 24.

[81] Ibid.

Beggarstaff Brothers, imbues each scene with melodramatic lighting and additional props as the magnificent bed dominates each scene.

In 1911 King George V and Queen Mary stayed at Holyroodhouse for the first time and used it as a royal palace. To commemorate their visit *Country Life* published two articles on the palace in that year, leading to further admiration for the baroque palace. Although the first article was devoted to Mary, Queen of Scots and the 'doomed Stuart line', the second, by Lawrence Weaver the architectural editor of the magazine, focused on Sir William Bruce and the sumptuous seventeenth-century interiors, acknowledging Holyroodhouse as one of the most significant buildings of the period.[82] Over the following years the focus of attention and interest inside shifted from the apartments of Mary and her dramatic story to the baroque palace of Charles II and the importance and significance of the architecture and interior, much of which had survived intact. In 1925 the seventeenth-century state apartments created for Charles II were opened to the public for the first time. Mary's chambers remained open to visitors but, as knowledge of the history of furniture improved, it became apparent that many items in the room were not from the sixteenth century and the dilapidated furnishings began to look decidedly neglected. In particular, the red damask bed, supposedly slept in by Mary, Queen of Scots, was shown to date from the seventeenth century. Although in the 1919 version of his guidebook Maxwell identified the bed hangings as seventeenth century, it was not until 1929 that he notes that 'the bed is wrongly alleged to have been that once occupied by Queen Mary'.[83] It was also felt that the cleaning of the bed and other furniture had led to a loss of the atmosphere and visual appeal of the rooms. Nevertheless, the bed, such a focal point of the bedchamber, was to remain in place until the 1970s.

The opening of the state apartments led to the setting up of the Holyrood Amenity Trust in 1926 under the chairmanship of the duke of Atholl, to administer a proportion of the income received and to use it in a beneficial way. The aim was to purchase or receive articles of historical or aesthetic value for display in the palace. One of the earliest acquisitions made by the Trust was a stained-glass window, presented by the duke of Atholl in June 1927.[84] The panel, by the English arts and crafts stained-glass artist Louis Davis, represents Queen Margaret, mother of David I, king of Scotland and founder of Holyrood Abbey. It was installed at the east end of Mary's outer chamber, in the small niche that was probably Mary's oratory. The Trust was particularly interested in acquiring

---

[82] Lawrence Weaver, 'Holyrood Palace II: the Scottish Palace of His Majesty King George V', *Country Life*, 22 July 1911, pp. 132–38.
[83] Sir Herbert Maxwell, *Official Guide Palace Abbey-church And Environs of Holyroodhouse* (Edinburgh, 1929), p. 25.
[84] Royal Collection Trust RCIN 39198.

objects associated with Mary to increase the display of authentic items in the rooms. In 1951 it accepted a silver-gilt pomander, said to have belonged to Mary, and in 1953 it was presented with a portrait of David Rizzio.[85] The Trust purchased three embroideries in 1957, two created by Mary, Queen of Scots when she was kept in captivity in England after her departure from Scotland, and one by Elizabeth of Shrewsbury (Bess of Hardwick), the wife of her jailor.[86] These three pieces were originally part of a large corpus of Marian embroidered panels known as the Oxburgh hangings. Their acquisition showed a wish by the Trust to procure genuine articles to enhance the historic interior, particularly for an area of the palace where, it was by now recognised, objects often had a spurious provenance.

In the 1970s serious consideration was given again to the presentation of the Mary and Darnley apartments. It was agreed that the historical interpretation of the palace should place less emphasis on the story of Mary and that the seventeenth-century palace should be given more prominence. The first-floor rooms in the James V tower (the former Darnley apartments) were renamed the queens' apartments to show other queens had occupied these rooms. In Mary's apartments the tapestries remained but the red damask bed was conserved and finally and appropriately moved down to the king's bedchamber in the seventeenth-century part of the palace, and other furniture and furnishings were stripped out. The panelling was painted white, the floors were covered in brown carpet and in the outer chamber the Marian embroideries were displayed, together with the Darnley Jewel, in a purpose-built display case.

The Darnley Jewel, commissioned by Margaret Lennox, mother of Lord Darnley, had been acquired by Queen Victoria and was moved up from Windsor Castle.[87] On the wall was hung the painting, *The Memorial of Lord Darnley* by Livinus de Vogelaare, showing Darnley being mourned by his family.[88] The *grisaille* frieze was finally uncovered and conserved.

By the 1990s it was felt that much of the appeal and sense of history that had imbued Mary's chambers and proved such an attraction to visitors had been stripped away and lost. In 1994 the artist and decorator Alec Cobbe was commissioned to devise a re-presentation of these rooms. The intention was to enhance the handful of objects that had a genuine association with Mary, such as the Darnley Jewel and the embroideries, while restoring the visual impact and picturesque resonance of the apartments, so restoring something of the antiquarian mood that had been removed during the preceding decades.

---

[85] Royal Collection Trust RCIN 28121 and RCIN 401172.
[86] Royal Collection Trust RCIN 28223, 28224, 28225.
[87] Royal Collection Trust RCIN 28181.
[88] Royal Collection Trust RCIN 401230.

Figure 11.5 Mary, Queen of Scots' outer chamber, c. 1981
Royal Collection Trust/© His Majesty King Charles III, 2023

In the bedchamber a bed was recreated with seventeenth-century crewelwork hangings.[89]

Mary's supper room was filled with objects, many of which had featured in Swarbreck's view, including 'Darnley's armour'. In the outer chamber additional pictures were hung and much of the collection of Stuart memorabilia formed largely by Queen Mary, consort of George V, was brought to Holyroodhouse from Windsor Castle and put on display. It was shown in purpose-built display cases based on designs of Scottish funerary monuments; the Darnley Jewel was displayed in its own cabinet. Every other case was completely filled with objects and works of art, each with its own hand-written label.

Between 2016 and 2018 Mary's rooms were examined again in the light of increased visitor expectation of improvements in interpretation and consideration was given as to how to show through displays and narratives the story of Mary and the ongoing history of her rooms. Displays were clarified to concentrate on objects with a close association with Mary and included the three embroideries, the Darnley Jewel and the pomander, as well as other renaissance jewellery with links to Mary, such as a gold pendant decorated with a

---

[89] Royal Collection Trust RCIN 26810.

Figure 11.6 Alec Cobbe, *Design for Mary, Queen of Scots' bedchamber*, 1994
Royal Collection Trust/© His Majesty King Charles III, 2023

Figure 11.7 Mary, Queen of Scots' outer chamber, 1995–2019
Royal Collection Trust/© His Majesty King Charles III, 2023

serpent coiled round a tree.⁹⁰ Paintings were hung densely over the tapestries and included a large early seventeenth-century portrait of Mary (a copy of the Blairs Portrait).⁹¹ Work was carried out in Mary, Queen of Scots' closet and further research led to the identification of two of the tapestries illustrated by Swarbreck as *Tobias and the Angel* and *Tobit before Shalmanezer*, from the Flemish series, *The Story of Tobit*, c. 1625.⁹² The tapestries had been recorded in the palace before 1700, hanging in the marquess of Breadalbane's apartments before

Figure 11.8 Mary Queen of Scots' closet, 2019
Royal Collection Trust/© His Majesty King Charles III, 2023

⁹⁰ Royal Collection Trust RCIN 51008.
⁹¹ Royal Collection Trust RCIN 404408; and see Chapter 2.
⁹² Margaret Swain, *Tapestries and Textiles at the Palace of Holyroodhouse* (London, 1988), p. 47 (RCIN 96591); p. 45 (RCIN 95203).

being moved to the closet during the eighteenth century.[93] The tapestries had been altered and cut to fit a room at some point and after conservation the two of them fitted perfectly within the architectural features of the closet when they were rehung in 2019. Following this work the room was opened up to visitors. The apartments at Holyroodhouse have played a key role in the memorialisation of Mary and their presentation and visitor history can be seen to mark several major shifts in the way the queen has been commemorated at the palace. As has been noted, early visitors were full of reverence for Mary and were largely uncritical, carried away by the romance of her story and the presentation of her rooms as untouched by time, a sentiment that peaked in the mid-nineteenth century when Queen Victoria popularised all things Scottish. As Holyroodhouse developed as a venerated tourist attraction it was also used as a source of income. This can be seen clearly as housekeepers acting as tour guides hoped to further line their pockets by exaggeration of Mary's story and embellishment of the contents of her rooms, which developed into a more formal presentation that involved moving furniture, and some misleading identification to add to the drama and mystery. Although, as has been shown, interest in the apartments began to shift in the twentieth century as more emphasis was put on truth and authenticity, the end of the century saw a change in ideas with the recreation of the antiquarian and romantic mood of the rooms.

It is evident that there are clear emotional links between visitor experiences across the centuries, particularly in relation to the murder of Rizzio. Many tourists, awed by the narrow staircase and the tiny supper room, have found these apartments highly imaginative spaces. The murder can be clearly visualised and visitors can almost feel themselves present, as Thomas Dibdin remarked in 1838: 'Methought I saw them again in advance, with their flashing eyes and clenched daggers'.[94] Although there may have been an awareness at one level of the spuriousness of the bloodstain and the artificiality of the whole, visitors were (and are) prepared to put this to one side to embrace the romanticism and drama of the apartments and the compelling story of Mary, Queen of Scots.

---

[93] The marquess of Breadalbane had grace-and-favour apartments within the palace. The tapestries were purchased from the marquess when he relinquished his apartments in 1860.

[94] Dibdin, *A Bibliographical, Antiquarian and Picturesque Tour*, vol. 2, p. 519.

TWELVE

Materialising Mary in a Museum: Marian Objects and Authenticity
Anna Groundwater

There are few verified bodily relics pertaining to Mary, and certainly not any resulting from her execution. A fire was burning at the behest of the Elizabethan government even before her head left her body, and her blood-stained clothing was consigned immediately to it. However, over the longer term these measures proved ineffective against the perpetuation of her memory through other types of object associated with her, which have achieved relic status even though they are not her physical remains:[1] her jewellery and embroidery-work, the beds she slept in, the gifts she made, the things she might have touched, a piece of the yew tree under which she supposedly met Henry, Lord Darnley at Crookston; and mementoes, particularly jewellery, created to memorialise her. In this process Mary herself was active: throughout her life she gave objects to seal alliances in the royal tradition of gift-giving, which often carried her own image, intended to act as physical representations of Mary in her bodily absence. As she approached death, these gifts were made consciously to project her presence beyond her mortal life, and to secure for her a lasting reputation as a royal Catholic martyr. Over the long years since, these objects have been invested with deep meaning by their owners and those who see them, a meaning derived from their alleged association with Mary. However, many of these objects survive with only limited, often dubious, provenance.

In a museum context, this leaves us with several challenges in interpreting the objects that relate to the queen. Mary, Queen of Scots is one of the most recognised and iconic figures in Scottish history. She remains a huge draw for public audiences, in fiction and drama, and at heritage sites. The exhibition, *Mary, Queen of Scots*, held at the National Museum of Scotland in 2013, was one of the

---

[1] Matthew Martin, for instance, ranks bodily relics as higher in significance than touched or owned objects: Martin, 'Infinite Bodies: The Baroque, the Counter-Reformation Relic, and the Body of James II' in *Emotion and the Seduction of the Senses, Baroque to Neo-Baroque*, ed. L. Beavan and A. Ndalianis (Kalamazoo, MI, 2018), pp. 165–85.

most popular exhibitions ever held in the Chambers Street museum. Inevitably, visitors apply their own, often firmly held, assumptions and previous knowledge to framing the Marian objects they see on display, as do the guides that give tours, and the museum professionals that collect, curate, conserve and classify them.[2] All of us, academics and administrators alike, inescapably operate within incomplete understandings of the many-faceted Mary and her Scottish, British and European historical contexts, and any version of Mary presented cannot capture the significance of all those multiple stories and perspectives. While museum curators can shape narratives informed by the latest research, and influence the perception of Mary in the twenty-first century, they cannot control the reception and re-interpretation of Marian-related objects by their visitors. As a result, no object used within the telling of Mary's life has only one meaning, and there can never be only one authoritative narrative. This chapter considers the multiplicity of meanings of objects related to Mary on display at the National Museum of Scotland, and the authority these might give to multiple narratives of her life and times.

Recent research in material culture and public history has foregrounded the socially constructed and historically contingent nature of an object's meaning. Marian objects thus have multiple meanings dependent on who is seeing them, when and within what contexts.[3] It follows therefore that the meanings of objects associated with Mary, and the nature of the association itself, are as Marian as we each understand them to be, whether their provenance is 'authentic' or more ambiguous. As each of us invest our own meanings in the objects we view, those objects are given meaning in relation to Mary, no matter how dubious such connections might be. How then should a museum engage with the multiplicity of these understandings of Mary in the curation of these Marian objects to narrate her mortal life and cultural afterlives? How should tensions between audience expectations and assumptions, and current scholarship be negotiated alongside due acknowledgement of the ambiguities of ownership and provenance? Finally, how important is authenticity in the presentation of these objects in a museum, and how might changing cultural and historical contexts affect understandings of authenticity, of the authentic object, of its historical 'truth'?

Putting this theory into practice, if we acknowledge the ambivalence that frames these objects, this chapter asks: what methods could be deployed to provide more nuanced narratives in museum spaces, which make explicit the objects' multi-faceted ambiguities, while making them relatable and relevant

---

[2] Ethan W. Lasser, 'The Return of the *Wunderkammer*: Material Culture in the Museum', in *Writing Material Culture History*, ed. Anne Gerritsen and Giorgio Riello (London, 2015), pp. 225–39.

[3] Chris Fowler, 'From Identity and Material Culture to Personhood and Materiality', in *The Oxford Handbook of Material Culture Studies*, ed. Dan Hicks and Mary C. Beaudry (Oxford, 2010), pp. 352–85, at p. 362; Viccy Coltman, 'Material Culture and the History of Art(efacts)', in *Writing Material Culture History*, ed. Gerritsen and Riello, pp. 17–41.

to today's museum visitors? How might the complexities of Mary's own life be suggested, given the fluctuating and multiple meanings invested in objects associated with her, and the entanglement of the objects' own itineraries with the histories of Mary herself, and those that remember her? Finally, if establishing authenticity has been a defining rationale for museum collections in the past, how might embracing ambiguity in the present affect the role of the museum in its engagement with Mary and those interested in her?[4] It will be argued here that the role of the viewer should become more integral to collecting, curating, narrating and display practices, to re-present the multiple Marys in our minds – no matter how non-specialist that understanding may be, it is authentic within its own terms.

Multiple meanings

National Museums Scotland holds around ninety objects associated with Mary, Queen of Scots. Despite having a well developed catalogue of our holdings, the hesitation over precise numbers lies in the imprecise strengths of attribution and provenance. However, if it is accepted that even an alleged association with Mary constitutes in itself a meaningful relationship between object, dead queen and present viewer, then we can begin to understand all these objects within a Marian framework, to some degree at least. In the centuries following Mary's death, these objects came to provide a tangible link between those seeing or handling them, both specialist and public, and this iconic historical figure. This section evaluates a few of the museum's Marian objects within this overarching perspective, focusing on three objects, two of which, the Penicuik Jewels, have an accepted and direct Marian provenance, and the other, the Craigmillar crucifix, has a linkage to Mary that is much more tenuous.[5] It will be suggested that we should engage more creatively with the ambiguities of these objects' provenance in considering the value of the supposed Marian associations embedded in them by successive generations.

Let us turn first to the objects with the closest links to Mary that NMS hold, the Penicuik Jewels. These are a set of fourteen intricately worked, filigree gold, pomander beads, of about a centimetre in size each, with thirteen smaller gold spacer beads between them; and a jewelled pendant locket containing miniature portraits (probably) of Mary and her youthful son James VI, which may have

---

[4] Ole Marius Hylland, 'Even Better than the Real Thing? Digital Copies and Digital Museums in a Digital Cultural Policy', *Culture Unbound: Journal of Current Cultural Research*, 9 (2017) no. 1: 62–84, at pp. 62, 62, 74, 80; Siân Jones, 'Negotiating Authentic Objects and Authentic Selves. Beyond the Deconstruction of Authenticity', *Journal of Material Culture*, 15 (2010) no. 2: 181–203 at pp. 181, 182, 192–93, 200.

[5] The Penicuik Jewels: pomander beads, NMS H.NA 421 and locket, NMS H.NA 422; the Craigmillar Crucifix, NMS, H.KE 16.

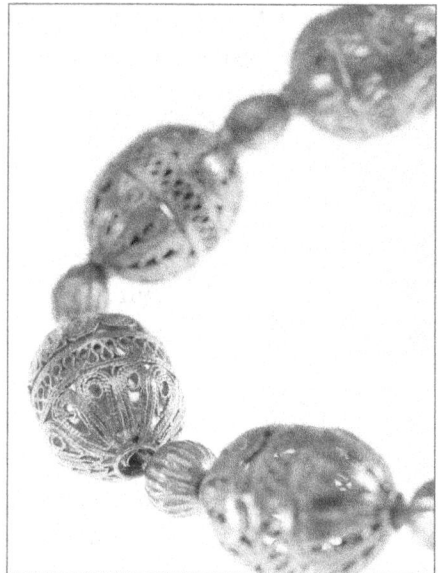 

Figure 12.1 Penicuik Jewels: necklace, H.NA 421
Image © National Museums Scotland

Figure 12.2 Penicuik Jewels: locket, H.NA 422
Image © National Museums Scotland

hung at one time from the beads. The locket is framed by a coiled string of tiny pearls on a gold wire. It is a suitably impressive set of jewellery, of a type similar to examples in the inventories made of Mary's possessions at various stages in her life, and often seen in contemporary portraits of elite women. The pomander beads will have carried perfume, valued for its therapeutic properties in warding off disease as much as noxious odours, and scientific analysis has shown the residue of an organic resin in one of the beads, thought to be ambergris. The function of the beads, though, was various, and changing; it is likely that the beads that now form the necklace were known too as paternoster beads, and possibly part of one of the several gold and silver rosaries also listed in Mary's inventories.[6]

These exquisite objects are said to have been given by Mary to Gilles Mowbray, one of her lady attendants, before her execution. A descendant of Gilles married into the Clerks of Penicuik family, prosperous merchants in seventeenth-century Edinburgh. The jewels were in the possession of this family and regarded by them as relics of Mary until they were acquired by the museum's forerunner, the National Museum of Antiquities, in 1923, following a public subscription

---

[6] For instance, she intended the gift of '*Une tours garny de xxxvj patenostre dor a jour plaines de parfum garnies de petis grains dor a jour entredeux*' to her sister-in-law Agnes, countess of Moray in her will of 1566. Joseph Robertson (ed.), *Inventaires de la Royne Descosse Douairiere de France Inventaires de la Royne Decosse Douairier De France. Catalogues of the Jewels, Dresses, Furniture, Books and Paintings of Mary, Queen of Scots 1556–1569* (Edinburgh, 1863), pp. 104–05.

campaign.⁷ This attribution is acknowledged in the text accompanying their display. This stated provenance links the museum visitor and curator alike, via their viewing of the object in the present, directly to Mary in the past, facilitated by a belief in the authority of the provenance.

The assumptions that follow, that she owned these jewels and might have worn them against her skin, are wholly dependent on that 'authorised' version. As one visitor to the exhibition of 2013 said, they liked 'the thought that she had touched things or had them in her possession'.⁸ That sense of touch, the haptic, seems to resonate deeply with viewers (even though they cannot touch an object themselves) and helps to make a connection that bridges centuries feel more intimate. Given the presence of the perfumed resin, just how much closer (or otherwise) might that take a viewer to Mary's physical presence? Equally, the jewels' qualities and components, the high quality of the craftsmanship, the gold and pearls used in their construction, and the remnants of an expensive resin all suggest the person that owned these jewels had high social status. Mary used the high monetary value of jewels like this to demonstrate her own self-worth, as part of her crafted 'performance' of monarchy.⁹ For us in later centuries, the glittering materialities of the Penicuik Jewels appear monarchical, and as viewers we are consequently persuaded that they are Marian. Concomitantly, if Mary did indeed wear these jewels, she bestowed an extra level of meaning upon them simply by doing so that adds a value to them beyond the richness of their making. In their combination of Marian provenance and elite materiality, the jewels are what Sherry Turkle describes as 'evocative objects', communicating a sense of what Mary may have been like, and the messages she was broadcasting in wearing and gifting them.¹⁰ But even given a relatively well-established provenance, and the princely attributes of the jewels, it is only our informed assumption, provided by the testimony of the Clerks of Penicuik, that gives these objects their full meaning.

In contrast, the attribution of the Craigmillar Crucifix to Mary is much weaker. This silver crucifix from the fifteenth or sixteenth century, decorated with black *niello*, was mounted on a plain ebony cross in the nineteenth century. It was found around 1815 in a bedroom allegedly once occupied by Mary, Queen of Scots at Craigmillar Castle in the hills above Edinburgh, which offered space

---

[7] *Proceedings of the Society of Antiquaries of Scotland* (*PSAS*), 58 (1923–4): 17.
[8] Mary, Queen of Scots: Visitors' Views, posted by NMS, 10 November 2014: www.youtube.com/watch?v=DssIcNmGqgc, accessed 19 September 2023.
[9] Anna Groundwater, 'Afterword: What Now?', in Jenny Wormald, *Mary Queen of Scots: A Study in Failure* (Edinburgh, 2017 edn), pp. 207–38, at pp. 226–32; Kevin Sharpe, 'Representations and Negotiations: Texts, Images and Authority in Early Modern England', *The Historical Journal*, 42 (1999) no. 3: 853–81, at pp. 853, 854, 878.
[10] Sherry Turkle, 'Introduction: The Things that Matter', and 'What Makes an Object Evocative', in *Evocative Objects: Things We Think With* (Cambridge, MA, 2007), pp. 3–10, 307–27.

Figure 12.3 Craigmillar Crucifix, H.KE 16
Image © National Museums Scotland

and hunting while being not too far from Holyrood. It is well known that Mary stayed there several times. Her most notorious visit to the castle occurred in December 1566, when the Craigmillar Bond was signed by the conspirators planning Lord Darnley's death. Craigmillar thus plays a significant part in the narrative of Mary's personal reign and subsequent downfall. The chain of association between location, person and object for the Craigmillar Crucifix is therefore: Mary visits Craigmillar; Mary is Catholic; Mary is seen wearing such items in her portraits, and they feature in her inventories; therefore it might be one of her crucifixes. The crucifix also potentially *feels* authentic, albeit in a highly subjective way: we know Mary was an avowed Catholic, that she liked the paraphernalia of Catholicism, and that she continued to uphold Catholic practices in the face of Presbyterian disapproval and political and religious dissent. However, by any standards this linkage is tenuous – a retrofitting of attribution shaped by past desires for it to be so, for it to be 'true'. Currently the interpretation's text allows for this ambiguity over its provenance.

However, the historical significance given to what is otherwise a fairly ordinary crucifix for its time wholly depends on the association with Mary. Its meaning derives from its treatment historically as a relic of Mary, even if that provenance is questionable and its claims of authenticity suspect. It is a Marian object chiefly because people who have subsequently encountered it have given it that meaning. Yet their belief is no less 'real' for them than the belief in the more provable provenance for the Penicuik Jewels. In determining the significance of the crucifix and its history, that meaning is authentic in its own terms within the present, as something historically associated with the unfortunate queen, even if Mary never went anywhere near the object in the past. Given the current public location of the crucifix in a museum, acknowledging this meaning is crucial, since such objects (as Murray Pittock says of later Jacobite objects) 'are public memory: they create and inform cultural memory and they compose what is remembered and how it is remembered by individuals'.[11] Any rendering of the crucifix's biography is inescapably imbued with its associations with Mary if we are to make this as representative and comprehensive as possible.

In the years following the crucifix's discovery, there was increasingly widespread academic, and more popular, romantic interest in Mary's fortunes, as various chapters in this volume attest. The meanings now attached to the crucifix were made in these contexts: what this object meant to those who saw and handled it was thus historically contingent, and changed following new academic research, the wider cultural contexts of the Victorian era that included the historical novels of Sir Walter Scott, antiquarian and collecting practices and early public museum exhibitions, and the development of museum science. As academic history and curatorship was consciously professionalised through the nineteenth century, the authenticity of 'Marian' objects became increasingly subjected to more rigorous evaluation, and different interpretation. For instance, as Julie Holder has shown, the interpretation of the so-called Queen Mary Harp, exhibited at the Glasgow International Exhibition in 1888 as a gift from Mary to Beatrix Gardyn of Banchory, was subsequently recast by such as Joseph Anderson (in 1881, keeper of the museum) as an excellent example of late medieval Celtic workmanship in which the significance of any association with Mary was diluted, and ultimately rebutted.[12] Seen in these historical contexts, a more critical, 'professional' evaluation of the crucifix's provenance would downplay the likelihood of such an object disappearing for more than 200 years and turning up in a room that Mary may have stayed in, highlighting instead its physical characteristics and similarities to other historical objects. The crucifix's text in the online database notes: 'This silver rosary crucifix dates from the 15th or 16th century. It is possibly a copy of a 12th-century cross

---

[11] Murray Pittock, *Material Culture and Sedition 1688–1760: Treacherous Objects, Secret Places* (Basingstoke, 2013), pp. 13–14; see also, Pittock, 'Treacherous Objects: Towards a Theory of Jacobite Material Culture', *Journal for Eighteenth-Century Studies*, 34 (2011) no. 1: 39–63.

[12] See Julie Holder, Chapter 10; C. D. Bell, 'Notice of the Harp said to have been given . . . by Queen Mary, and of the Harp called the "Lamont Harp", by John Steuart Esq. of Dalguise', *PSAS*, 15 (1881): 10–33; J. Drummond and J. Anderson, *Ancient Scottish Weapons* (Edinburgh, 1881).

bought by a pilgrim as a souvenir', before it states the claimed association to Mary.¹³ However, this association with Mary still determines the crucifix's positioning in the National Museum of Scotland, displayed amongst other Marian objects, and it appears in the crucifix's interpretation text. That association is acknowledged as tenuous, but it is also recognised as part of this object's history, and rightly so.

Both examples discussed above, though having very different levels of confidence in terms of provenance, are intrinsically interrelated by the various people that invest them with such meaning. These meanings are necessarily shaped by the social, religious or political communities in which those individuals act, and with which they identify. Thus, as each person brings their own beliefs to their interaction with the object, their identity becomes bound up with that object's meaning. Personal identity and material culture are, as Fowler observes, 'mutually constitutive within the cultural, political, social, and material conditions in which they historically occur'. Understanding this, he says, is a prerequisite for any 'sophisticated analysis of material culture and identity'.¹⁴ Since such conditions are endlessly subject to change, an object's meaning and the identity it expresses are similarly dynamic; inescapably, meanings invested in Mary's possessions change over time.¹⁵ Initially, they recalled a living, or recently deceased, person; subsequently, and dependent on personal ideologies, these objects commemorated a religious martyr or political victim, or alternatively a less comfortable reminder of a manipulative tyrant. Over time, as the rawness of the execution faded, and ownership of these objects went beyond those for whom Mary was a living memory, they became an expression of loyalty to the Stuart dynasty; as such, in the early to mid-eighteenth century, they became potentially treasonous objects during the Jacobite rebellions. In the nineteenth century their meanings were affected by romanticised notions of Mary's life, propagated by novelists such as Sir Walter Scott in *The Abbot*, countless etchings and paintings, and a spirited debate over her guilt or innocence. These multi-layered and ever-changing meanings (wholly dependent on audience and ownership) collectively map the 'non-linear journey' of these 'itinerant' objects, their lives entangled with ever-mobile cultural contexts and their associated fluid, complex identities.¹⁶

---

¹³ SCRAN, Online ID 000-100-000-333-C: http://nms.scran.ac.uk/database/results.php?QUICK-SEARCH=1&search_term=craigmillar+crucifix, accessed 19 September 2023.
¹⁴ Fowler, 'Identity and Material Culture', p. 360.
¹⁵ Ibid., pp. 360–62, 376.
¹⁶ Alexander A. Bauer, 'Itinerant Objects', *Annual Review of Anthropology*, 48 (2019): 335–52, at pp. 335–6, 342–3, 343, 345, quotations at pp. 335, 343.

Authenticity, empathetic connections, narratives

Both the Penicuik Jewels and the crucifix should therefore be understood within the frameworks of each individual's historical knowledge, and their assumptions about Mary's life. For twenty-first-century visitors, the crucifix variously symbolises the dangerous threat she was thought to present to the nascent Protestant Reformation, and the polarisation of Scottish society in the ensuing Marian wars (1567–73); or her Catholic martyrdom in the face of Presbyterian intolerance, scheming Scottish nobles and English councillors bent on subjugating Scotland. The crucifix can signify victimhood, guilt, innocence, societal disruption, martyrdom, Scottish defiance of English oppression, or any combination of these. Which framework an individual chooses is shaped by their knowledge, education and politics – and by their reception of Mary in the present via representations of her in film, fiction and heritage. This section considers empathetic connections, made through objects between current viewers and the historical figure, the significance of authenticity (or otherwise) in establishing these connections and the narratives that result.[17]

Current understandings of Mary are strongly shaped by Mary's cultural afterlife in the past, which will have helped to determine what 'Marian' objects were collected and preserved by individuals and museums alike, and the narratives used today by specialists and non-specialists to classify, interpret and present them. These narrative frameworks are conditioned too by the varying levels of the viewers' interests in historical peoples, objects and places. Writing about the Rhondda Heritage Park, Bella Dicks notes that 'visitors' experiences of the site are informed by their different degrees of personal investment in, and cultural proximity to the history presented'. This is significant 'because these factors impact on their ability to make connections and situate themselves in relation to the narratives they encounter'.[18] Taken further, this engagement (or lack of it) greatly impacts on the historical narratives visitors create for themselves, and in which they situate the objects. These narratives may equally be affected by personal prejudices. One striking example of the political construction of such narratives was calls by some Scottish Nationalists in the early 2000s for the repatriation of Mary's remains from Westminster Abbey to Scotland. The rationale given was that since Mary had been killed by the English state, she would not have wanted to live permanently there.[19] Mary as an English victim clearly fits with some current political opinions. Twenty-first-century Scottish nationalism

---

[17] On engaging with empathy in the museum, Geerte M. Savenije and Pieter de Bruijn, 'Historical Empathy in a Museum: Uniting Contextualisation and Emotional Engagement', *International Journal of Heritage Studies*, 23 (2017) no. 9: 832–45.

[18] Bella Dicks (2000) paraphrased by Jones, 'Negotiating Authentic Objects', p. 190.

[19] BBC News, 12 October 2008: http://news.bbc.co.uk/1/hi/scotland/south_of_scotland/7666291.stm: accessed 2 October 2023.

is just one material context for Marian objects, as was Anglo-Scottish hostility in the sixteenth century, the subterfuge of Jacobite rebellion in the eighteenth century and the romanticisation of the Scottish Highlands in the nineteenth century.

Additionally, in the case of Marian objects, a sense of personal connection between the human and the iconic historical figure is as important as the cultural circumstances in determining the interaction between human and object. Where audiences sympathise with Mary and her predicaments, they view those objects within a different narrative to those who see her less positively. In *The Abbot*, Scott describes Mary appearing in a room, 'advancing with an air of peculiar grace and majesty' in a modest black velvet dress which 'gave a full view of her beautifully formed chin and neck, but veiled the bosom'. 'She wore a cross of gold around her neck, and had her rosary of gold and ebony hanging from her girdle. Even Lord Lindesay . . . was surprised into something like respect by the unconcerned and majestic *mien* of her.'[20] Here the appurtenances of Catholicism, the crucifix and the rosary, are presented as objects suggesting Mary's dignified majesty, modesty and piety. Scott's partiality to Mary is voiced repeatedly in *The Abbot*, revealing his sense of personal and sympathetic connection to this divisive historical figure. But of particular interest here is the prominence that Scott, the antiquarian and collector, gives to objects in his fiction to help him make that connection and to suggest to his readers where their sympathies should lie.[21]

This sense of personal connection is no less true of some of Mary's current students. In 2017, in an interview with *The Scotsman*, David Greig, the director of *Glory on Earth*, a play about Mary's confrontations with John Knox (see Chapter 9), described it as 'a single act of empathetic imagination to take us back to the reality of this woman and this place and this time'. Maintaining that sense of empathy, the playwright Linda McLean recalled how 'it really shocked me, that she was so young' when she returned to Scotland. For McLean, Mary was an 18-year-old given a daunting job for which she was too young. In empathising with the teenage queen, the playwright was reflecting her own, twenty-first-century, cultural logic and upbringing back into the 1560s, and onto very different social and cultural contexts. Average life expectancy was half what it is now, children were treated as adults earlier, and Mary had been brought up from birth, as a monarch, to rule. She had also spent just over a year being queen consort in France, one of the most sophisticated courts in Europe. She was used to court intrigue and the machinations of competitive nobles.

---

[20] Sir Walter Scott, *The Abbot* (1820; 1886 edn), pp. 231–32.
[21] Viccy Coltman calls Scott a notably 'pictorial' writer, in his use of visual and material culture: Coltman, 'Borders Bard: "The Exactness of the Resemblance": Sir Walter Scott and the Physiognomy of Romanticism', in *Art and Identity in Scotland* (Cambridge, 2019), pp. 220–52, at pp. 221, 250.

Perceptively, *The Scotsman*'s journalist concluded that '[e]very generation of theatre-makers finds in the story of Mary reflections of their own concerns'.[22] Mary is as malleable as we want her to be. As a result, her story is endlessly rewritten, with each generation applying their own cultural assumptions to a life that was lived in completely different circumstances. Historical distance is thus shrunk by the personal parallels established, no matter how misleading those assumed or empathetic connections are.

That sense of such personal connection to Mary, imagined as a living person despite the intervening centuries, was much in evidence in the comments made by visitors to the National Museum's exhibition in 2013, recorded in qualitative post-visit interviews. Some comments showed an awareness of the historical distance, one visitor observing of the sixteenth century that it was a 'life that one cannot imagine these days'. Asked how they felt about Mary, visitors' responses included:

> I think she was a victim.
> I guess I would say she was a martyr.

Alternatively, less sympathetically,

> [s]he played the game.
> Devious.

Others however claimed an understanding of how Mary herself would have felt:

> how unhappy her life had been.
> I think what happened to Mary was very sad, and extreme but she did live on. Mary would be innately proud of the legacy she left.[23]

Such comments repeatedly revealed the personal connections being made to a historical figure, which were directly facilitated by the objects on display.

This exhibition was an opportunity to bring together a large number of objects related in some way to Mary. Arguably, that massing of objects and the space to tell more complex stories may have helped to accentuate a sense of proximity to the long-dead queen. The Penicuik Jewels and the Craigmillar crucifix were on display, alongside other Marian objects including a reliquary holding a piece of Holy Thorn given to Mary by Henri II, her father-in-law,

---

[22] *The Scotsman*, Sunday 14 May 2017: www.scotsman.com/arts-and-culture/theatre-and-stage/theatre-preview-behind-scenes-lyceums-mary-queen-scots-play-856451, accessed 19 September 2023; on 'cultural logic', Mark S. R. Jenner, 'The Great Dog Massacre', in *Fear in Early Modern Society*, ed. William Naphy and Penny Roberts (Manchester, 1997), pp. 44–61.

[23] Mary, Queen of Scots: Visitors' Views.

documents written or signed by Mary, and a locket with a depiction of the crucifixion ('The Mary, Queen of Scots Jewel') that she gave to the sheriff of Northampton before her execution. These were intimate items, many of which could demonstrably be proven to have been owned or held or written by Mary. For museum visitors, it appears that these objects helped to fuel a sense of intimacy in which touch appeared important. Even though they could not touch the jewellery or embroidery exhibited, it was enough that they believed that Mary had. The frisson of being so close to objects held by such a famous figure moved them: that she 'had read the books . . . and written the letters, I loved that,' said one. Similarly, one of the conservation staff preparing the letters and books for display said '[s]he sat there with this piece of paper, touched it, signed it; it's amazing to work on them', while David Forsyth, the exhibition's curator, noted '[i]t's a once-in-a-lifetime opportunity. Objects have a resonance, the thorn, the prayer book, jewels. People in the past touched them and that's what's important [for visitors].'[24]

Siân Jones' work with the local community of Hilton of Cadboll in 2001, during the excavation of its ancient stone cross, recorded similar responses that linked the viewer through their understanding of the touched object to the historical person: 'to know that my people were here and that stone is there, just to touch it, you know they must have seen it, they must have touched it, you know, going back these years, it was like something holy, I just, I just needed to touch it'.[25] Jones noted 'the object seemed to possess a magical, almost numinous, aura, which was produced through their own and others' relationships with it'. She noted the 'ineffable sense of connection with the people who had erected it in that place and touched it in the past'. Their desire to touch it seemed to promise to 'achieve some magical communion with the past'.[26]

Back in the museum, that sense of connection is predicated on the belief that these are authentically Marian objects. But, as Jones observes, 'authenticity is not inherent in the object. Rather it is a quality that is culturally constructed and varies according to who is observing the object and in what context'.[27] As she has more recently written with Sally Foster, '[a]uthenticity is not an intrinsic, material quality of a thing, but a socially mediated experience'.[28] If an exhibition is held within a national museum, audiences are potentially conditioned to accept that the museum's authority and expertise give these objects a stamp of authenticity. Work by Jones, and others such as Ole Marius Hylland, highlights

[24] Janet Christie, 'Exhibition Reveals the Real Mary, Queen of Scots', *The Scotsman*, 23 June 2013.
[25] Jones, 'Negotiating Authentic Objects', quoted at p. 199.
[26] Ibid., p. 193.
[27] Ibid., p. 182.
[28] Sally Foster, Siân Jones et al., 'New Futures for Replicas: Principles and Guidance for Museums and Heritage' (University of Stirling, 2020): https://replicas.stir.ac.uk/principles-and-guidance/, accessed 19 September 2023, p. 5.

the role (for Hylland, the problematic legitimating rationale) of museums as 'guardians of authenticity': 'authenticity is a core value for museums'.[29] But like the meaning invested in objects by those viewers, authenticity is socially constructed in a dialogue between them, the museum's curators and conservators, other viewers and owners, that helps to validate provenance, and the object and its physical and cultural contexts (both in the past and the present).

We have already seen that it is not possible to guarantee the provenance of some of these objects. In the later nineteenth century, Queen Mary's harp's relationship with Mary became 'inauthentic', though its function as an excellent exemplar of late medieval Scottish craftsmanship did not. The same may be said of the crucifix. However, the meaning invested in these objects as Marian in the past still resonates in their histories today. In those terms, that social construction of meaning is authentic since it has been felt or understood by visitors, in the same way a reader can take a message from a text that may not correspond with what the author intended.[30] One visitor in 2013 concluded of what they had seen that 'I thought she really came to life. I could imagine who she could be and I got a real sense of her personality'.[31] For such visitors, the exhibition felt like an authentic experience, a representation of Mary that felt legitimate. Further, this was an authenticity implicitly guaranteed by the authority of the museum in which the objects were displayed. To deny that authenticity would be to deny that this personal response is authentic.

In the case of the Penicuik Jewels, establishing authenticity seems easier given their long provenance, and their high-status materiality. The viewer's response to and framing of these jewels seems more securely anchored in an object where there is a greater likelihood of Mary having touched it, than the dubiously provenanced Craigmillar crucifix. That said, some ambiguity clouds even the Penicuik Jewels' links to Mary: Mary's gift to Gilles Mowbray is listed only as a pair of gold bracelets, nor does the queen appear in any portraits wearing the Jewels.[32] Much of what we believe of the Jewels, which has shaped their classification, interpretation and reception, is still assumption, a probability built on what the Clerks of Penicuik have historically claimed. For all that, they *feel* authentic. They possess, to use Jones' fine words, that 'magical, almost numinous, aura' of association with Mary, an iconic historical figure.[33] They help to bridge the historical distance between viewer and previous owner (and indeed

---

[29] Hylland, 'Even Better than the Real Thing?', pp. 63, 80; Jones, 'Negotiating Authentic Objects', p. 192.

[30] Jane Rickard, *Authorship and Authority: The Writings of James VI and I* (Manchester, 2007), pp. 1–2, 6–8, 13, 16–17; Roger Chartier, 'Texts, Printing, Readings', in *A New Cultural History*, ed. Lynn Hunt (London, 1989), pp. 154–75.

[31] Mary, Queen of Scots: Visitors' Views.

[32] Labanoff (ed.), *Lettres*, vol. 7, p. 259.

[33] Jones, 'Negotiating Authentic Objects', p. 193.

social disparity given her monarchical status), and function as an aid in creating a sense of connection, of communion, with the past.

The meanings invested in these jewels are socially constructed and historically contingent, but this is true too of the less well provenanced crucifix. What all these objects mean is built in a dialogue between the cultural and historical contexts of the past and the present, and the people that have created, owned, disposed of, abandoned, lost, passed on, classified, interpreted, curated and viewed them. In the accretion of those meanings, and their intersection with the personal histories of all these people, we arrive at a multiplicity of meanings in which no one meaning should be privileged over another, because all are ultimately intangible mental constructions, perpetually in conversation with fluctuating contexts, and thus fluid and subject to constant change. They are equally authentic within their own terms, as constructed by that person in that moment in a dialogue with the object's past and the present. Ambiguous provenance therefore does not mean that these objects are less meaningful. They embody the fluid and changing meanings given to them over centuries, and the empathetic connections of successive generations of people to a historical figure. They are *felt*, and that feeling in itself is authentic. They help to make Mary who we each want her to be, and they help shape individually constructed narratives.

Memorialising Mary

The value of the Penicuik Jewels and the Craigmillar crucifix lies directly in their claimed association with Mary. In contrast, this section considers two of the many objects created in her memory in the centuries following her death, rather than those claiming bodily association. The significance of these later objects is in the function of memorialisation instead of the haptic and empathetic connections found in objects Mary is alleged to have touched. This class of object is particularly compelling when it is composite in nature, that is, a piece that changes over time to incorporate different elements and create a new whole. The National Collection holds several such composite pieces created in commemoration, two of which contain cameo portraits of Mary: one is embedded in a late-eighteenth-century ring, the other in an ornate, gold and enamelled locket that is probably nineteenth century.[34]

The images of Mary depicted correspond to a painting by François Clouet of a young Mary at the French court.[35] While the cameos themselves may have been

---

[34] Gold finger ring set with a sixteenth-century cameo of Mary, Queen of Scots, lent by Mr and Mrs Geoffrey Munn, NMS, IL.2001.208; gold and enamel pendant locket containing a sixteenth-century cameo of Mary, NMS, H.NF 33.

[35] *Mary, Queen of Scots*, by François Clouet, c. 1558, Royal Collection Trust RCIN 401229: see also Figure 2.15.

produced during her lifetime, and may even have been commissioned by Mary in the 1570s, they do not claim a physical connection to her (as yet). Instead, these jewels embody Mary in her physical absence after her execution, extending the function of cameos she is known to have given in her lifetime, including those she gave to perpetuate her memory after death.[36]

Over their long lifetimes, from commission to their current location in a national museum, the meaning and function of these jewels, as they were made and re-made, has fluctuated through changing cultural and political contexts, and the type of commemoration intended. Such composite pieces are an overt manifestation of what is integral to all objects: complex histories composed of the intertwining of the object's own trajectory from its components' origins, to maker, to user to museum, and the lives of the people that encountered and invested meaning in them. These are 'itinerant objects' in the cultural afterlife of Mary, their journeys entangled in dynamic sets of relationships with other material culture, different networks of people, and through different temporalities. And into the present, as Alexander Bauer observes, their current meanings 'as heritage objects, as items of political struggle or sovereignty' are 'fully intertwined with how we understand [their] past meanings, since arguments about the past are still and unavoidably made in the present'.[37]

They are 'evocative objects' too, to use Turkle's phrase, in that their materialities suggest the reasons for their composition and preservation, the richness of their decoration echoing the majesty of the person they are purposed to remember.[38] In constructing their meaning, as Marius Kwint observes, their evocativeness indicates 'an open dialogue between the object, the maker and the consumer'.[39] Their meanings are, like those of the Penicuik Jewels and the crucifix, socially constructed, historically contingent and built in a dialogue with the memories of a dead queen. While not authentic in terms of a direct association with Mary, in the meanings they evoke they are authentic representations of Mary's memorialisation. They are thus as much part of the story of Mary's afterlife as the objects she touched in her mortal one.

One, a heart-shaped locket on display in the museum, frames a sixteenth-century cameo of Mary; the locket was originally thought to have been created in her lifetime, or shortly after it. It is an extravagantly fashioned, intricately worked jewel, studded with diamonds, and a large ruby sits at the kick-point of the heart. The same attention has been paid to its reverse, with very fine foliate enamelwork around a central classical-shaped vase. If sixteenth century, this

---

[36] Mary to Archbishop Beaton, 9 January 1575: Labanoff (ed.), *Lettres*, vol. 4, pp. 256–57.
[37] Bauer, 'Itinerant Objects', pp. 336, 341–46, quotes at 345.
[38] Turkle, *Evocative Objects*, pp. 3–10, 307–27.
[39] Marius Kwint, 'Introduction: The Physical Past', in *Material Memories*, ed. Marius Kwint, Christopher Breward and Jeremy Aynsley (Oxford, 1999), pp. 1–16, at p. 3.

Figure 12.4 Cameo heart-shaped locket, H.NF 33
Image © National Museums Scotland

Figure 12.5 Cameo ring, IL.2001.208. Lent by Mr and Mrs Geoffrey Munn
Image © National Museums Scotland

ornate setting could have been made in either Paris or Edinburgh, with recent research showing the capacity of the latter's goldsmiths to work at this level. However, recent research by Lyndsay McGill has uncovered in Paris a similarly shaped locket mould from the nineteenth century, and it seems likely that this setting is a later reimagining of a renaissance-style jewel. The mould itself may have reproduced the original setting.[40] At over 5 centimetres in diameter, and a centimetre deep, the locket has a striking presence. Whether sixteenth or nineteenth century, it was designed to impress those who saw it, and to communicate the majestic persona of the person it commemorated. As Fowler observes, 'worldly things ... can convey personal qualities' because qualities are 'invested in material things as well as [being] the key metaphors for personhood'.[41] The locket's material attributes, the virtuosity of its craftsmanship and the opulence of its decoration were intended to evoke Mary's own queenly characteristics (in the eyes of those that commissioned or wore it) of good rule, virtue and elite status. It was commissioned and crafted to recall in its very composition those personal characteristics over subsequent centuries.

A less flamboyant Mary is commemorated in the setting of a similar sixteenth-century cameo, this one in a late eighteenth-century ring. Stylistically the cameo's high-ruffed dress and braided hair echoes that of the locket although the etching differs in detail. However, unlike the distractions of the bejewelled heart, the focus of interest in the ring is the person depicted in the cameo, here simply framed by beaded gold. Mary remains regal, but the ring's function is somewhat different. It is an object designed less to impress, but instead perhaps as a daily reminder of the woman it portrays. In its simplicity it suggests the intimacy of an affective connection, and more frequent contact, given that (unlike the grander locket) it could be worn more often. It conveys an interest in Mary that is deeply personal, and personalised, the ring now bearing the evidence of its wearing. We can imagine perhaps its owner, touching it, twisting it, in an everyday remembrance of a queen then fading into historical distance.

Both locket and ring were intended to establish and maintain emotional bonds between the wearer and the person they commemorated. Their affective affordances will have been intrinsic to the commissioning of the original cameos as well, as much as their subsequent settings. These were objects deliberately made 'to stimulate emotion and memorization'.[42] They helped to perpetuate her memory long after she had gone, to pass on that memory to successive

---

[40] *PSAS*, 93 (1959–60): 244–5, at p. 257; Lyndsay McGill, 'Scottish Renaissance Jewels in the National Collection', in *Decoding the Jewels: Renaissance Jewellery in Scotland*, ed. Anna Groundwater (Leiden/Edinburgh, 2024), pp. 105–25.

[41] Fowler, 'Identity and Material Culture', pp. 371, 374.

[42] Kwint, 'Introduction: The Physical Past', p. 13; Pittock, *Treacherous Objects*, p. 13; Christoph Breither, 'Capture the Feeling: Memory Practices in Between the Emotional Affordances of Heritage Sites and Digital Media', *Memory Studies*, 14 (2021) no. 3: 578–91.

generations. They were intended to be things that were 'good-to-think-with' (to use another of Turkle's phrases), to prompt in the wearer or viewer a recollection of Mary.[43] They were also to record in physical form a suitably regal version of Mary, the image in the cameos almost certainly authorised by the queen herself. As Kwint has observed, 'objects serve memory', they 'furnish recollection; they constitute our picture of the past'; they 'form records: analogues to living memory, storing information beyond individual experience', in this case a record of a queenly Mary.[44] These cameos were, to use Jeffrey Olick's term, a 'technology of memory', their central purpose being to perpetuate the memory of the queen. However, their individual casings suggest a particular Mary: in the locket, one of magnificence and not pathos.[45] Whether constructed in the sixteenth or the nineteenth century, this jewel seeks to erase the diminished status of the queen's forced abdication, and the brutality of her ending; this celebrates Mary at the height of her reign.

But while the locket may have been created to evoke one particular version of Mary, the meanings of such memorial objects and the memories they evoked were not set in stone. Given the multiple individuals, communities of interest and temporalities that have built the queen's memory, there is no one version of it. Individuals and groups have always chosen how they remember her, and what to occlude. Memory, as R. I. Moore has observed, is 'learned, borrowed and inherited – in part, and part of, a common stock, constructed, sustained, and transmitted by the families, communities, and culture to which we belong'; it is formed out of an interplay between individual and collective memories. Memory 'is an artefact and a trickster, and an active trickster at that, not merely a relic of the past, but the past shaped and adapted to the uses of the present'.[46] So the memory of Mary has always been fluid, dynamic and varying in political and cultural impact as successive generations negotiated their own relationships with the controversial queen. Some did this through objects, and the meanings of those objects were as fluid and capricious as the memories they facilitated, affected by the personal agendas of that present. Read alternatively, from the perspective of the Presbyterian John Knox the locket would have told of the idle extravagance of a woman prone to uncontrollable passions, so undesirable in someone born to govern.[47]

---

[43] Turkle, 'Introduction: The Things that Matter', p. 4.
[44] Kwint, 'Introduction: The Physical Past', p. 2.
[45] Jeffrey K. Olick, *The Politics of Regret: Collective Memory in the Age of Atrocity* (Abingdon, 2007), pp. 14, 29.
[46] R. I. Moore, 'Editor's Preface', to James Fentress and Chris Wickham, *Social Memory* (Oxford, 1992), p. viii.
[47] John Knox, *The First Blast of the Trumpet Against the Monstruous Regiment of Women* (1558).

However, from the perspective of a supporter of Mary, both cameos demonstrated, in their ownership or wearing, a personal loyalty to the queen.[48] If worn in the aftermath of Mary's execution, they would have been a significant political and religious statement of loyalty to a murdered queen, and possibly to Catholicism, though not necessarily since not all Marian supporters were Catholic. Such objects were therefore pieces of 'communication technology' in expressing support for, and in perpetuating a visual reminder of, the dead queen.[49] In the early to mid-eighteenth century, in the context of the Hanoverian succession and the Jacobite rebellions in support of the exiled Stuart kings, such cameos were also potentially 'treacherous objects', and dangerous to wear. Their messaging was more explicit than the medallions struck to indicate support for the deposed Stuart kings which sometimes carried more loyalist Hanoverian slogans on the other side to obfuscate their meaning; or conversely, where such tokens were overtly Jacobite, they could be worn secretly under outer garments.[50]

But as the temporal proximity to the Jacobite challenge grew more distant, and the risk of prosecution for loyalty to Mary's descendants diminished, both cameos would have become less dangerous objects to own, wear or display. From treacherous objects of 'oppositional memorialisation', the political and emotional trajectory of Jacobite tokens moved towards ahistorical sentimentality and kitsch; so too did the meaning of those created in memory of Mary change.[51] This is especially true of those created from the later eighteenth century onwards, when the hopes of restoring the deposed and defeated Stuart dynasty were finally over. The wearing of mementoes, such as these two cameos, was no longer a dangerous business; the caution necessarily applied to earlier eighteenth-century Jacobite objects was replaced with overt expressions of loyalty. The ring in particular, given its relative simplicity, could have been worn more or less daily. Its open portrayal of devotion to Mary suggests, to use Pittock again, 'the more explicit statements characteristic of a movement whose growing freedom of expression existed in an inverse ratio to its fading force'; 'the marked change in language and presentation [of Jacobite objects] evidences the declining status and threat posed by the Jacobite cause'.[52]

---

[48] See Leith Davis on objects relating to the later Stuart monarchs: *Mediating Cultural Memory in Britain and Ireland: From the 1688 Revolution to the 1745 Jacobite Rising* (Cambridge, 2022), pp. 14–20.
[49] Sam Alberti et al., 'The Art and Science of Replication: Copies and Copying in the Multidisciplinary Museum', *Museums as Cultures of Copies: The Crafting of Artefacts and Authenticity*, ed. Brita Brenna et al. (Routledge, 2018), pp. 13–26, at p. 18.
[50] Pittock, *Treacherous Objects*, pp. 128, 130.
[51] Ibid., p. 151.
[52] Ibid., pp. 135–36.

From around the 1780s onwards, the ending of this challenge was reflected in the translation of overtly political and for some, religious, sentiments expressed through pro-Jacobite objects, to more affective connections. The cameos of Mary, and objects more closely associated with her person (like the Penicuik Jewels), should be seen within this broader material context, and the increasingly de-politicised and sentimentalised affordances they carried. Combined, this body of Stuart-related memorabilia was to perpetuate a cultural memory of the Stuarts into the nineteenth century that was no longer politically threatening; and which was to frame the romanticisation of Mary's memorialisation, in tandem with that of the Scottish Highlands.[53] The focus of interest in Stuart-related objects changed too, embraced in a 'cult of Romantic celebrity', where the individual personality was the attraction and not the politics. Such was the framing of the Stuart relics exhibited at the 1888 Exhibition of the Royal House of Stuart.[54]

This interest stimulated a proliferation of Stuart memorabilia, which in its turn conditioned the 'public memory of Jacobitism' in a newly sentimentalised manner.[55] Popular demand for such objects outstripped supply, generating the fanciful claims made of many fake 'Jacobite' items, and the production of new objects of commemoration. It was probably prompted by such desires that André, the French goldsmith, created the mould for his extravagant setting for Mary's cameo, a material expression of the queen as an iconic historical figure. At the museum today, it is Mary as celebrity (rather than a subject of religious or political devotion or hatred) that continues to fascinate. This engagement is facilitated through objects on display created to remember her, and those preserved since the sixteenth century thanks to their association with her. Given the relatively rare survival of jewellery from this period, much melted down for its monetary value or repurposed into newer fashions, the preservation of such as the Penicuik Jewels attests to the reverence in which they have been held. Memorialising Mary in the past continues to perpetuate that memory into the future.

Marian objects and interpretation in the twenty-first-century museum

History, in Raphael Samuel's trumpet call for the democratisation of the subject, 'is not the prerogative of the historian . . . It is rather, a social form of knowledge; the work in a given instance, of a thousand different hands.' In this final section, it is argued that in the construction of Mary's narrative in the museum these 'hands' are not just those of scholarly historians, but also, as Samuel suggested, those of the 'people'.

---

[53] Davis, *Mediating Cultural Memory*, pp. 14–20, 249–51.
[54] Pittock, *Treacherous Objects*, pp. 148, 150; and see Chapter 10.
[55] Ibid., p. 148.

For Samuel, history was a 'hybrid form of knowledge, syncretizing past and present, memory and myth, the written record and the spoken word'.[56] In his telling there would be no artificial division between history, memory and heritage; heritage should help to democratise history in the 'history from below' of country houses and industrial museums. For him, such a holistic and collaborative approach to history offered a more authentic connection to the past through the aggregation of multiple types of source and voice, specialist and non-specialist, and including that of material culture.[57] In a similar vein, Michael Frisch's influential *A Shared Authority* argued for a similarly democratising recognition of the voice of the non-professional in creating shared authorings of history using oral and public history methods.[58] These perspectives inform recent work in public history and cultural heritage that demonstrate collaborative, inclusive and participatory practices in research and outcomes, that include the non-specialist in an interplay of scholarly and popular narratives. Key to this is the recognition of the 'ordinary' voice in creating narratives in public spaces and institutions such as museums. This conclusion considers how such practices might offer new methods in creating narratives of Mary in public or institutional spaces and, in so doing, give her life, cultural afterlives and the objects associated with her a fresh relevance in the twenty-first century.[59]

Currently, the National Museum's Marian objects in the Renaissance Gallery are displayed within contexts chosen by curators, in collaboration with display, conservation and collection services teams. Each department's specific concerns – whether research-led, environmental, aesthetic, financial or logistical – will have influenced the resultant display. Inevitably, this approach imposes museum-authored meanings on these objects. Likewise, their current interpretation situates these objects within the curators' choices of intersecting historical contexts: the reign of Mary, Queen of Scots and sixteenth-century Scotland, Scotland in the wider European cultural landscapes of the Renaissance and Reformation, and the longer-term fortunes of the Stuart monarchs. These are the sort of research themes that interest us as historians, and give Mary what we have determined to be her significant contemporary contexts.

Further, in situating them within the lifetime of the person they narrate, the museum also fixes them in one specific temporal period, that of mid-sixteenth

---

[56] Raphael Samuel, *Theatres of Memory*, Vol. 1: *Past and Present in Contemporary Culture* (London, 1994), pp. 8, 15, 443; Kyrin Gentry, '"The Pathos of Conservation": Raphael Samuel and the Politics of Heritage', *International Journal of Heritage Studies*, 21 (2015) no. 6: 561–76, at pp. 569–70.

[57] Samuel, *Theatres of Memory*, vol. 1, p. 8; Gentry, 'The Pathos of Conservation', pp. 564, 568–69, 570.

[58] Michael Frisch, *A Shared Authority: Essays on the Craft and Meaning of Oral and Public History* (Albany, NY, 1990).

[59] David Dean (ed.), *A Companion to Public History* (Oxford, 2018); Paul Ashton and Meg Foster, 'Public Histories', in *New Directions in Social and Cultural History*, ed. Sasha Handley, Rohan McWilliam and Lucy Noakes (London, 2018), pp. 151–70.

Figure 12.6 The Renaissance Gallery, Kingdom of the Scots, National Museums Scotland
Image © National Museums Scotland

century Scotland. Decorative wood panels and carved furniture provide the physical surroundings for our Marian objects, and overwhelmingly, these objects date from the time they are intended by the museum to evoke. For Siân Jones, writing of a Pictish stone cross also on display in the museum, this is the curators privileging the object's 'original form, meaning and use', which obscures its subsequent repurposing and concomitant changes in its interpretation. That said, Jones observes that while it is 'divorced from its subsequent biography . . . the networks of relationships it embodies refuse to be entirely silenced'.[60] Similarly, Mary's objects are narrated in their original form, as sixteenth-century artefacts, stripped of the multiplicity of their afterlives and unencumbered by the fluidity of their subsequent meanings. However, despite being 'masked by modes of classification and display', is there something that speaks covertly but irresistibly of richer histories of the many people that have interacted with the jewels over subsequent centuries, their repurposing and new meanings that, like those of the Pictish cross, cannot be suppressed?[61]

On the surface, the institution holding the most significant collection of Marian objects in public ownership in Scotland does not seem to have accepted

---

[60] Jones, 'Negotiating Authentic Objects', p. 192.
[61] Ibid., p. 193.

much input from the non-specialist voice in creating Marian narratives. It is the museum communicating its research in a chronologically constrained narrative, as the objects' custodian and with the implicit authority of that role. Its interpretation strives for neutrality and objectivity (inevitably unachievable given the instability both of language and meaning), in which professional expertise is privileged over popular experience. After all, establishing their authority over what is accepted as the authentic version of what their objects are, has been the mission of museums since their inception.[62] So currently, in our Marian displays, it is not the museum in dialogue with its audience: it seeks to transmit, not converse.

However, perhaps not all is as it first seems, given that not all the objects on display were contemporaneous with Mary. Significantly, some were created to commemorate the queen after she had died: the plaster cast from 1928 of the magnificent tomb at Westminster that James VI commissioned to commemorate his mother (itself created twenty-five years after her death); the late eighteenth-century cameo ring; a small Victorian pendant framing the Scottish Stuart arms. Whilst the accompanying interpretative texts have only recently been altered to acknowledge this process of memorialisation, in including these later objects within its displays relating to Mary's lifetime the museum is implicitly acknowledging the cultural significance of the popular commemoration of the queen. Memorial objects like these embody how successive generations have chosen to remember Mary, and the affective connections they have historically made with her. Paradoxically, Mary's viewers, rather than being excluded or ignored, are integral to the materiality and afterlives of these objects.

We can take this further. The very survival over four centuries of the objects made in Mary's lifetime, as exemplified by the Penicuik Jewels, is a testament to the people that preserved them as relics of Mary. Ambiguities over provenance similarly encapsulate the faith that some, outside the heritage profession and academia, have had in these objects' function in remembering Mary. If we accept that the multiple meanings of these objects have been invested in them by the people who have produced, circulated, owned, given, preserved or simply viewed them, then the writing of that object's history intrinsically includes those people too. The non-specialist's involvement, as one of the 'thousand different hands' in a multi-authored history of Mary, is already in the museum, whether consciously included by the professionals or not.

Non-specialist interaction continues to be built into Mary's story into the twenty-first century. If we accept that an object's meaning is created in its interaction with the person that views it, that meaning must be specific to each visitor's own imagining of Mary's history and the object's part in it. Visitors' responses are shaped by their own historical knowledge, Marian objects elsewhere and

[62] Hylland, 'Even Better than the Real Thing?', pp. 63, 80.

heritage sites related to her; they understand these objects in relation to the films they have watched, and the books they have read, as much as by the museum's interpretation. A visitor, fresh from binge-watching CW's *Reign* (previously on Netflix), will have a glittering French context for Mary that many others, more steeped in her Scottish experience from the books of Alison Weir, John Guy and Nigel Tranter, may not. Still others, with their ears ringing from the visceral encounter between John Knox and Mary in Linda McLean's *Glory on Earth*, will bring a deeper understanding of the impact of a confessional divide to the objects they view. It is from here that I would suggest that a more collaborative narration of Mary might evolve, in which the museum acknowledges the authority of the non-specialist in creating new narratives that bring those popular understandings of the queen into the telling of her cultural afterlives.

Our visitors live in a completely different set of cultural, social and political contexts to Mary; they can never replicate her experience or feel exactly as she would have felt. They cannot re-make her decisions 'authentically' in their minds, since they cannot be exposed to the cultural pressures that conditioned her. Their experience of these objects in a museum context today is not 'authentic' in terms of replicating the manner in which the objects would have been experienced in the sixteenth century. That said, the visitors' reception of the museum's interpretation, their affective responses to objects she is thought to have touched, and for some, what feel like empathetic connections to her, are meaningful in understanding what Mary means today. That response is authentic within its own terms. It should be part of the story we tell, and it needs to be told in collaboration with those visitors, creating a shared authoring of Mary's life in what she meant and means today. In so doing, we would materialise a history of Mary that encompasses the multiple and changing perceptions of a controversial queen, and that reflects the continued relevance of her memory perpetuated through objects associated with her.

Part Four

Mary in Media

THIRTEEN

Minstrels of Maelstroms: Mary's Musical Afterlives

Tim Duguid

In 2008, Lisa Simeone of US National Public Radio (NPR) discussed a controversy surrounding the popular band, the Dixie Chicks (now known as The Chicks), which was an early manifestation of cancel culture. The group's lead singer, Natalie Maines, had proclaimed to a London audience in 2003: 'we're ashamed the President of the United States is from Texas'. These comments about then-President George W. Bush (*b.* 1946), when American (and British) troops were about to be sent to Iraq, led to a boycott of the group both from fans and radio stations.[1] Ultimately, the Dixie Chicks' popularity would survive the controversy, which NPR's Simeone argued provided the connection to Gaetano Donizetti's (1797–1848) opera, *Maria Stuarda*. The opera was originally to be premiered in Naples, but during the dress rehearsal a row broke out between the singers portraying Elizabeth I and Mary, Queen of Scots after the latter gave the opera's famous insult:

> Impure daughter of Boleyn,
> Do you speak of dishonour?
> Unworthy and obscene whore,
> I blush for you.
> The English throne is profaned,
> vile bastard, by your foot![2]

---

[1] Andrew Dansby, 'Fans Turn on Dixie Chicks: Natalie Maines Apologizes for Bush Comment', *Rolling Stone*, 17 March 2003, www.rollingstone.com/music/music-news/fans-turn-on-dixie-chicks-251772/, accessed 20 September 2023.

[2] Original Italian:

> Figlia impura di Bolena,
> parli tu di disonore?
> Meretrice indegna e oscena,
> in te cada il mio rossore.
> Profanato è il soglio inglese,
> vil bastarda, dal tuo piè!

The two singers were separated and the one playing Mary had to be carried away because she fainted during the exchange. The incident caught the attention of Ferdinand II, King of Naples, and he quickly banned the opera. An undaunted Donizetti tried again to have the opera performed, in Milan, thinking that revising Mary's diatribe would make it more palatable. However, his female lead refused to perform the corrections and instead sang the original text, and the opera was banned yet again.[3] As with the Dixie Chicks, Simeone argued that the controversies surrounding *Maria Stuarda* only cemented Donizetti's popularity as a composer. For Simeone, then, the impudence of the Dixie Chicks and of Donizetti parallel that of Mary, which points to the enduring popularity of all three.[4]

Simeone's analysis is characteristic of a broader movement in musical culture that aligns contemporary events and political thought with Mary's story. For instance, the group Grave Digger released a song called 'Ballad of Mary (Queen of Scots)' in 1996, which described Mary's thoughts as she was being held against her will in Fotheringhay Castle. Interspersed amongst its verses lies a refrain that attaches broader significance to Mary's imprisonment: 'Scotland cries; her queen is lost./Agony's her friend again'. According to Grave Digger, England had imprisoned Scotland resulting in 'silence everywhere'.[5] Considering that this song was released at the height of the Campaign for a Scottish Assembly and one year before Scotland would overwhelmingly approve the Scottish devolution referendum, Grave Digger's song painted Mary's imprisonment as an analogue to Scotland's political standing within the United Kingdom.[6]

In many ways, the themes of political succession, national sovereignty and religious purity that were central to Mary's life and more broadly to sixteenth-century Britain continue to occupy significant places in public discourse and consciousness four centuries later. It is no wonder that the events of her life continue to be conscripted to various ends. In contrast, scholarly

---

[3] The opera only received six performances in Milan, and some of those were only of the first act. There were a few other Italian productions during the nineteenth century, with a couple in Spain and Portugal. It would not start to gain widespread recognition until the 1960s with productions in London and New York. Charles Osborne, *The Bel Canto Operas of Rossini, Donizetti, and Bellini* (London, 1994), pp. 231–32.

[4] Lisa Simeone, 'Quarreling Queens: Donizetti's *Maria Stuarda*', NPR, 28 May 2008, www.npr.org/2008/05/28/90891928/quarreling-queens-donizettis-maria-stuarda, accessed 20 September 2023.

[5] Grave Digger, 'The Ballad of Mary (Queen of Scots)', on *Tunes of War (Remastered 2006)*, GUN Records GmbH, 1996.

[6] Mary's story would be used again five years later, in 2001, by Dougie MacLean (b. 1954). Much like the Dixie Chicks, MacLean opposed political violence, so he used Mary's story to decry political violence in his song 'Mary Queen of Scots'. He equates the violence done to Mary with war and political violence: 'We give our might to men who take it as their own;/And in our name destroy with every thrown stone': Dougie MacLean, 'Mary Queen of Scots', on *Who Am I*, Dunkeld Records, 2001.

attention to musical expressions of it has not been as profuse. There has been only one attempt to list the musical works related to her life,[7] and none have directed their energies towards analysing these settings across time, media and genre. Instead, music historians have focused their attentions on single works or on comparing multiple works within single musical genres.[8] The following discussion, therefore, is an initial effort to consider musical works across time and genre that are related to Mary, identifying some of their overarching trends and characteristics. It will begin by surveying some of the more commonly known works before engaging in a more detailed comparison of one of the better-established large-scale pieces within the canon of western classical music, Gaetano Donizetti's 1835 *opera seria* (dramatic opera) *Maria Stuarda*, with the soundtrack for Josie Rourke's (*b.* 1976) 2018 film *Mary Queen of Scots* by Max Richter (*b.* 1966).

Overview of historical settings

The pervasiveness of Mary's story can be observed across musical genres, from childhood nursery rhymes such as 'Mary, Mary quite contrary' to complex art music. Some examples from popular balladry include 'Earl Bothwell' and 'The Battle of Corrichie'. 'Earl Bothwell' laments many of Scotland's woes, including the death of the queen's favourite David Riccio and the suspected involvement of Bothwell in the assassination of Scotland's king consort Lord Darnley. Rather uniquely, however, this ballad casts Riccio, Darnley and even Bothwell in positive lights: Riccio 'was as wel beloued as euer was he', Darnley is styled as the 'worthy king' and Bothwell was the avenger for beloved Riccio's death. Lord James Stewart, earl of Moray, on the other hand, is the only person presented in a negative light. Despite the fact that he did not become regent until after Mary's removal in 1567, the ballad describes him as the 'gouernor of Scottland' who '. . . hath banished the queene soe bitterlye/That in Scottland shee dare not remain'.[9] Moray is again targeted in the ballad 'The Battle of Corrichie'. This one recounts the battle in which George Gordon, fourth earl of Huntly

---

[7] Samuel A. Tannenbaum and Dorothy R. Tannenbaum, *Marie Stuart, Queen of Scots: A Concise Bibliography*, 3 vols (New York, 1944–46). In particular, Vol. 3, *Marie Stuart: In Her Relations to the Arts* references nearly 2,000 works including ballads, ballets, operas and songs that are either attributed to or inspired by the Scottish queen.

[8] For instance, see Federico Ghisi, '*Il lamento in morte di Maria Starda* di Carissimi', *Rassegna Musicale* 21 (1951): 43–47; Jon W. Finson, 'At the Interstice between "Popular" and "Classical": Schumann's *Poems of Queen Mary Stuart* and European Sentimentality at Midcentury', in *Rethinking Schumann*, ed. Roe-Min Kok and Laura Tunbridge (Oxford, 2011), pp. 69–87; and Alexander Weatherson, 'Queen of Dissent: Mary Stuart and the Opera in her Honour by Carlo Coccia', *Donizetti Society Newsletter* (2005), www.donizettisociety.com/Articles/articlemarystuart.htm, accessed 20 September 2023.

[9] *The Percy Folio*, British Library, MS: Add. 27879, p. 272.

(1514–1562) was killed after his family staged a brief and confused insurrection against Mary. The ballad, supposedly written in 1772 by a schoolmaster with the surname Forbes from Kirkton of Maryculter, looks favourably on Mary and even praises Huntly despite his sedition. Moray, who led Mary's forces in the battle, is repeatedly criticised, being caricatured as 'fause Murry' who is responsible for many of Scotland's ills as described in the concluding quatrain:

> I wis our quine had better frinds,
> I wis our countrie better peice;
> I wis our lords wid na discord,
> I wis our weirs at hame may ceise![10]

Beyond anglophone balladry and folk music, Giacomo Carissimi's (c. 1605–1674) *Il lamento di Maria Stuarda* (1650) is among the earliest musical settings still performed today.[11] Using the poem 'Ferma, lascia ch'io parli', a text likely written by Giovanni Filippo Apolloni (c. 1620–1688),[12] Carissimi's setting was indicative of the Italian outrage over Mary's death in 1587 that continued into the mid-seventeenth century.[13] The text begins with Mary's parting words as she is led to the execution block. Between the thrice-repeated refrain 'A morire!' (To die!), she asserts her innocence and decries injustice. She also expresses her love and appreciation for her ladies-in-waiting whilst decrying worldly London and its ruler Elizabeth, who she describes as the second Jezebel.[14] Most of the text is set in the first person, but the concluding section switches to the third person, recasting the performer as an omniscient angelic bard who seemingly asserts with divine authority that the unconquered Scottish queen safely arrived at her heavenly destiny.

Carissimi sets this emotionally charged text using the typical tripartite cantata form: an extended *arioso* recitative set in 4/4 time, an *adagio* aria set in 3/4 time and finally a 4/4 *da capo* recitative.[15] As noted by Charles Burney, Carissimi's general approach to the recitative was an improvement upon those of his predecessors; he aligned the music of his recitatives more closely with speech and natural

---

[10] Forbes, 'The Battle of Corrichie', *Scots Weekly Magazine* (July 1772).
[11] Margaret Murata, 'Image and Eloquence: Secular Song', in *The Cambridge History of Seventeenth-Century Music*, ed. Tim Carter and John Butt (Cambridge, 2008), p. 419.
[12] The poem is attributed to Apollini in a manuscript held by the Biblioteca Angelica in Rome: Ang. 2479, c. 12r.
[13] For a bibliography of Italian responses in literature and music, see Stefano Villani, 'From Mary Queen of Scots to the Scottish Capuchins: Scotland as a Symbol of Protestant Persecution in Seventeenth-century Italian Literature', *The Innes Review*, 64 (2013) no. 2: 100–119.
[14] The first Jezebel was the infamous wife of King Ahab of Israel, described in the books 1 Kings and 2 Kings. The name itself means 'unmarried', which is one further reason for its association with Elizabeth. Ironically, the English tended to view Mary as Jezebel. Anne McLaren, 'Gender, Religion, and Early Modern Nationalism: Elizabeth I, Mary Queen of Scots, and the Genesis of English Anti-Catholicism', *American History Review* 107 (2002) no. 3: 759.
[15] Ghisi, '*Il lamento*', pp. 43–47.

declamation, rendering them '... more expressive, articulate, and intelligible...'[16] In *Il lamento*, Carissimi's recitatives are paired with melodies that closely parallel the text's meaning by employing repeated melodic intervals in sequences or chained modulations.[17] Federico Ghisi observed that the proliferation of modulations found throughout the two recitative sections contrast the more stable aria section in the middle. This pattern, he argues, parallels the multifarious thoughts and subjects covered in *Il lamento*. The churning modulations are balanced by a largely syllabic treatment of the text (that is, one note per syllable), atypical of Carissimi's tendencies to include gratuitous melismas (series of notes sung on the same syllable of text).[18] Apart from some *appoggiaturas* (two notes assigned to a single syllable with the second note acting as the 'main' note), the handful of melismas in *Il lamento* follow an arc that climaxes with Mary's lament in the aria section: 'Per serbar giustiziae fede/più non vaglion le corone' (To preserve justice and faith/the crown has no longer any worth). The longest melisma is paired with 'vaglion' (no longer). The second longest melisma then appears on the word 'serbar' (preserve), highlighting Mary's realisation that her political standing cannot save her. Carissimi, like his contemporaries, viewed Mary's death as religiously motivated persecution, but his setting also emphasises the political injustice she endured at the hands of an envious Elizabeth.

As Scotland's rugged landscapes inspired nineteenth-century European artists including Felix Mendelssohn (1809–47) to compose Scottish-themed works such as the *Hebridean Overture*, Op. 26 and his *Third Symphony* (Scottish), Op. 56, Mary's story continued to feature in musical works. One noteworthy example is Robert Schumann's (1810–56) song cycle *Gedichte der Königin Maria Stuart*, Op. 135. Completed in 1852, the cycle was a Christmas present for his wife Clara (1819–96). It employs translations of five poems that Schumann presumed to have been written by Mary herself, which recount important events of her life: her departure from France ('Abschied von Frankreich'), the birth of her son James ('Nach der Geburt ihres Sohnes'), a letter to Elizabeth ('An die Königin Elisabeth'), her parting words before execution ('Abschied von der Welt') and a final prayer ('Gebet').

---

[16] Charles Burney, *A General History of Music*, ed. Frank Mercer, 2 vols (New York, 1935), vol. 2, pp. 607–10.

[17] '... vi si riconosce il robusto respiro melodico del Carissimi, caratterizzato da tipici intervalli di note, che si ripetono spesso in sequenze, secondo un ordine di modulazioni concatenate in stretta relazione con il significato espressivo del testo': Ghisi, '*Il lamento*', p. 45.

[18] One example is his *Domine, Deus meus* cantata, discussed by Andrew Jones: Andrew V. Jones, 'Carissimi, Giacomo [Jacomo]', *Grove Music Online* (2001), www.oxfordmusiconline.com/grove-music/view/10.1093/gmo/9781561592630.001.0001/omo-9781561592630-e-0000004932, accessed 20 September 2023.

Considering that further literary investigation has attributed the first two poems and the concluding prayer to male authors,[19] scholars such as Ruth Solie have characterised the cycle as a male 'impersonation of female voices'.[20] However, the third person 'Gebet' would support Laura Tunbridge's conclusion that Schumann, much like Carissimi, did not intend the work as a type of role play, but rather the singer has '. . . a reduced agency – they need not engage with the characters as intimately as might be expected of singing as Maria Stuart'.[21] Beyond this, scholars have investigated *Gedichte* because its songs were some of the last composed by Schumann before he was admitted to the asylum at Endenich, where he would eventually die from pneumonia.[22] Jon Finson observes that the songs in *Gedichte* bear some resemblances to Schumann's other songs. For instance, the watery waves depicted in the accompaniment of 'Abschied von Frankreich' can also be observed in 'Loreley' from Schumann's *Romanzen & Balladen*, Op. 53.[23] Beyond these parallels, it is striking that Schumann used E-minor throughout *Gedichte*. While this key may be an appropriate framework for the sorrow and nostalgia expressed as Mary leaves her beloved France in 'Abschied von Frankreich', it is less convincing for 'Nach der Geburt ihres Sohnes', in which she expresses joy at the birth of her son James. That second song adopts a sombre, chorale-like accompaniment complete with closing 'Amen'-like plagal cadence whilst invoking the merciful, once thorn-crowned Jesus to preserve the baby:

> Lord Jesus Christ who was crowned with thorns,
> preserve the life of the boy born here,
> And if it be thy will, let his succession,
> long rule in this realm.
> And whatever is done in his name,
> be to your glory and honour.[24]

---

[19] 'Abscheid von Frankreich' was probably by Anne-Gabriel Meunier de Querlon, and 'Nach der Geburt ihres Sohnes' is an anonymous graffito in Edinburgh Castle. 'An die Königin Elisabeth' and 'Abschied von der Welt' were both likely written by Mary, but the concluding 'Gebet' was a Latin poem written by Henry Harrington. See Hans-Joachim Zimmerman, 'Die Gedichte der Königin Maria Stuart: Gisbert Vincke, Robert Schumann, und eine sentimentale Tradition', *Archiv für das Studium der neueren Sprachen und Literaturen* 214 (1977): 294–324. Schumann is not the only musician to set these texts to music. Joseph Joachim Raff (1822–82) also set them in his *Maria Stuart: Ein Cyclus von Gesängen* für eine Singstimme mit Begleitung des Pianoforte, Op. 172: Molly J. Johnson, '*Maria Stuart*, Opus 172: A Song Cycle by Joseph Joachim Raff Based on the Poetry of Mary Queen of Scots', DMA diss. (Louisiana State University, 1997).

[20] Ruth M. Solie, 'Whose Life? The Gendered Self in Schumann's *Frauenliebe* Songs', in *Music and Text: Critical Inquiries*, ed. Steven Paul Scher (Cambridge, 1992), pp. 219–40, 220.

[21] Laura Tunbridge, 'Robert Schumann's *Frauenleben*', in *Life as an Aesthetic Idea of Music*, ed. Manos Perrakis (Vienna, 2019), pp. 45–62, 59.

[22] For example, see Finson, 'Interstice', pp. 69–87.

[23] Finson, 'Interstice'.

[24] Original German:

> Herr Jesu Christ, den sie gekrönt mit Dornen,

The final song of the cycle, 'Gebet', employs a similar harmonic approach and prayer-like quality. Paired with 'Nach der Geburt ihres Sohnes', the two songs provide a religious tone for the song cycle that, according to Finson, appealed to nineteenth-century middle-class traditions of sentimentality.[25] In this setting, then, Schumann has cast Mary as a victim of circumstance who turned to her faith in times of blessing (that is, the birth of James) and tribulation (that is, her imprisonment and execution).

Nineteenth-century sympathies for Mary were also captured in larger-scale works. As a romantic symbol of oppression and resistance, she became the subject of operatic works by François-Joseph Fétis (1784–1871), Charles-François Gounod (1818–93), Louis Niedermeyer (1802–61) and others. The complexities of European confessional politics at the time, however, dictated that composers deal carefully with Mary's story. By far, the most successful and well-known operatic setting has come to be Donizetti's *Maria Stuarda*.

Donizetti's Mary

Maria Stuarda now occupies a firm place in the canon of modern western opera, but it was not initially well received. In fact, it was one of many operas to be banned in Italy due to its story focusing on Mary, Queen of Scots. Donizetti and his contemporaries had to navigate a labyrinth of censorship that prized political congruity particularly in the wake of the Neapolitan War and the new uniting of the kingdoms of Naples and Sicily. The ruling class viewed conspiracy as one of the most heinous crimes, and even though Mary had been Roman Catholic, her story was tainted due to the conspiracy charges that she faced and because ultimately she was beheaded. The Italian opera-supporting elite would not allow anything that might be seen to promote conspiracy or regicide.[26]

Arguably, Pietro Casella (1769–1843) wrote the earliest Italian opera based on the Scottish queen, and another more politically charged version would follow from the pen of Pasquale Sogner (1793–1842). Neither was particularly successful, and Luigi Carlini's (1785–187?) *Maria Stuarda, Regina di Scozia* (1818) was doomed to a similar fate despite being focused solely on Mary's Scottish reign rather than her imprisonment and execution. Other operatic

---

Beschütze die Geburt des hier Gebor'nen.
Und sei's dein Will', lass sein Geschlecht zugleich
Lang herrschen noch in diesem Königreich.
Und alles, was geschieht in seinem Namen,
Sei dir zu Ruhm und Preis und Ehre, Amen.

The original Scots text for the poem was scribed on the walls of Edinburgh Castle: A. J. Youngson, *The Companion Guide to Edinburgh and the Borders* (Edinburgh, 2001), p. 10.

[25] Finson, 'Interstice'.
[26] Weatherson, 'Queen of Dissent'.

attempts would follow, including those by Saverio Mercadante (1795–1870)[27] and Fétis, neither of which gained any significant traction. When Carlo Coccia (1782–1872) tried his hand at a setting whilst living away from the Bourbons' influence in London, it seemed there would finally be a successful opera on Mary, Queen of Scots. Though Coccia and his librettist Pietro Giannone (1792–1872) may have been freed to a certain extent, they still had to exercise caution in aligning their text with nineteenth-century London's perceptions of Mary. Sadly, the care they exercised in writing was not reflected in the opera's performances. Beyond the opera's considerable length, performances suffered from undisciplined singers, poor costuming and an under-rehearsed orchestra.[28] As a result, it received only four performances. Despite this unfortunate fate, Coccia's impact was remarkable insofar as his opera seems to have directed Donizetti's efforts in writing *Maria Stuarda*.[29] Crucially for the present discussion, Mary's afterlife in the hands of Coccia and Giannone was prototypically English: Mary was not a martyr but rather a politically inept ruler whose death was justified due to her involvement in a conspiracy to assassinate Elizabeth.

Despite many similarities with the Coccia/Giannone version, Donizetti's presentation of Mary, via a libretto by Giuseppe Bardari (1817–61), aligned more closely with typical Italian and Roman Catholic portrayals that painted her as a victim of Elizabeth's insecurities (whether they be romantic, political or religious). Bardari's libretto was based on a translation of Friedrich Schiller's (1759–1805) play *Maria Stuart* from 1800, and the opera was first performed in 1835. The work is one of several Donizetti operas focused on English and Scottish narratives: *Anna Bolena* (1830), *Lucia di Lammermoor* (1835), *Robert Devereux* (1837) and *Maria Stuarda*. As discussed at the beginning of the chapter, Donizetti struggled to navigate the same turbulent politics that had doomed the operatic settings of his contemporaries. Between the work being banned in Naples and Milan, he also tried adapting its music to fit a different story in an opera entitled *Buodelmonte*. However, even this modified version would ultimately receive only six performances in Naples.

Although originally written in two acts, the three-act version of *Maria Stuarda*, dividing the first act in two, is most common today. The first act is set in the Palace of Whitehall, where Elizabeth is considering what to do with the imprisoned Queen of Scots. During her deliberations, it is revealed that Elizabeth's favourite, Leicester (Robert Dudley), has fallen in love with Mary. The jilted

---

[27] Few recordings have been made of these early operas, but Mercadante's *Maria Stuarda regina di Scozia* is one exception: Servio Mercadante, *Maria Stuarda regina di Scozia (highlights)*, Opera Rara ORR241, Judith Howarth, Jennifer Larmore, Colin Lee, Manuela Custer, Pauls Putnins, Philharmonia Orchestra, cond. Antonello Allemandi, 2007, streaming audio, accessed 23 March 2023, Spotify.

[28] Weatherson, 'Queen of Dissent'.

[29] Weatherson completes a detailed comparison between the two operas in 'Queen of Dissent'.

Elizabeth agrees to meet Mary at Fotheringhay Castle. Mary finally appears at the start of Act 2, wandering the forests and reminiscing about France. A duet with Leicester prepares Mary for her encounter with Elizabeth, but when the queens do meet, Elizabeth's derisive comments eventually innervate Mary to exclaim that the English queen is a 'vile bastard'. Elizabeth vows that Mary will pay for her words and storms off the stage. The packed third act depicts Elizabeth signing the execution order followed by a confessional scene in which Mary discusses her actions with friend Talbot (presumably George Talbot, sixth earl of Shrewsbury) before eventually being led to the execution block surrounded by throngs of people decrying her execution.

Bardari's portrayal of Mary's demise uses the interactions of Mary and Leicester to bookend significant moments in her acquiescence to her fate. She first appears onstage with an aria that presents her as a woman who enjoys nature and who would love to return to her home in France. This idyllic moment is shattered when hunting horns ring through the forest. Leicester suddenly appears, and the ensuing duet between him and Mary follows *la solita forma* (see Table 13.1), a common Italian form in the operas of Donizetti as well as Bellini, Verdi and Rossini.[30] *La solita forma* typically consists of four sections: (1) an initial dialogue in which the characters outline their concerns; (2) a section of reflection in which characters consider the information they have just received; (3) a section presenting information about the situation; and (4) a section in which the characters reach a shared solution. In typical fashion, Mary and Leicester outline their current situations in the section labelled *tempo di primo*: Mary loves Leicester but is afraid of her imprisoner Elizabeth, and Leicester has been working to arrange a meeting between the two queens so that Mary can be freed and she and Leicester can finally be together. This flows into the reflective *cantabile* section, in which Mary begins with a solo stanza outlining her fears about Elizabeth. Typically, Leicester would have been given a full stanza to respond, but Mary frequently interrupts his assurances that Elizabeth will be kind and grant the Scottish queen her freedom. The two then conclude the section in typical fashion in parallel thirds: Mary sings *'può i mali miei calmar'* (can I calm myself) against Leicester's *'vedrai tutu cangiar'* (everything will change). Notably, the passage features the two singing corresponding vowel sounds whilst modulating to F-major.[31] The hunting horns sound again to begin the

---

[30] Philip Gossett, 'Verdi, Ghislanzoni, and *Aida*: The Uses of Convention', *Critical Inquiry* 1 (1974) no. 2: 291–334; Harold Powers, '"La solita forma" and "The Uses of Convention"', *Acta Musicologica* 59 (1987) fasc. 1: 65–90.

[31] For Donizetti, keys were critical to the dramatic flow of his works. For instance, specific characters are associated with certain keys: Elizabeth is E♭ major, Mary is C major and D♭ major, and Leicester is E major. See Karen Brookens, 'A Comparative Study of Thea Musgrave's *Mary, Queen of Scots*, and Gaetano Donizetti's *Maria Stuarda*', Doctor of Musical Arts dissertation, Arizona State University, 1997, pp. 97–107.

third section, marked *tempo di mezzo*, and Mary's fears are renewed. Instead of trying to console her, Leicester vows to take revenge if Elizabeth harms her, and the music returns to D♭ major. Mary argues he should not sacrifice himself for her: he is supposed to save her from her misery, not add to it by dying himself. The duet then ends with a *cabaletta* section that uniquely remains in the original key of D♭ major instead of returning to the key of F major from the *cantabile*: a tonal stagnation indicating that the two have been unable to devise a suitable solution. In the final section, Mary reiterates that Leicester should not sacrifice himself and Leicester assures Mary that she will be freed. This time Mary does not interrupt Leicester, and the two conclude together. However, the repeated phrases at the end foreshadow Mary's ultimate fate: Mary repeats *'no cosi'* (not like that) and Leicester *'che le tue prigioni aprì'* (your prison is opened). Her prison would indeed be opened, not by Elizabeth's kindness but by Mary's death.

Elizabeth appears onstage at the conclusion of the duet, commencing the exchange that would cement her perception of Mary.[32] Initially Mary begs Elizabeth for mercy, but Elizabeth responds with repeated insults. Having had enough of the ill-treatment, Mary finally blurts out her famous invective (*vile bastarda*, etc.). This sends Elizabeth into a rage and she and Cecil temporarily storm off. The rest of the cast remain: Mary, Anna, Leicester and Talbot reflect on the encounter along with the chorus. Elizabeth and Cecil then return, building to the full-cast second-act finale.[33] Cutting through the other voices, Elizabeth exclaims *'nella scure che ti aspetta troverai la mia vendetta'* (in the axe that awaits you, you will find my revenge). Mary, on the other hand, has been emboldened by the exchange and is heard exclaiming:

> Now lead me to death:
> I will challenge the extreme fate.
> A single moment of triumph,
> compensated for every pain.[34]

Mary is next seen in a prison at Fotheringhay Castle in Act 3, Scene 2, after Elizabeth has signed the execution order. Cecil informs her that the order has been signed, and contrary to Mary's brave comments at the end of Act 2, she

---

[32] The musical forms utilised by Donizetti in this dialogue are discussed in detail by Ashbrook: William Ashbrook, *Donizetti and his Operas* (Cambridge, 1982), pp. 276–79.

[33] Although ensemble finales are typical in operas, Donizetti's treatment of the form is unique. See Ashbrook, *Donizetti*, p. 276.

[34] The original Italian is:

> Or guidatemi alla morte:
> sfiderò l'estrema sorte.
> Di trionfo un sol momento
> ogni affanno compensò.

Table 13.1 Schema for duet between Mary and Leicester, *Maria Stuarda*, Act 2, Scene 2

Section	Key	Description
1. *Tempo di primo* 'Ah! non m'inganna la gioia!'	D♭ major	Back-and-forth discussion about the current situation. A lot of new information is presented: Mary's love for Leicester, her fear of Elizabeth, Leicester's requiting love and the belief that he will be able to engineer Mary's release.
2. *Cantabile* 'Da tutti abbandonata'	D♭ > F major	Mary gives full stanza on her fears. She then repeatedly interrupts Leicester's stanza, which tries to reassure her. The two conclude with a passage in parallel thirds, with parallel vowel sounds.
3. *Tempo di mezzo* 'Del suo core'	F > D♭ major	The two trade lines: Mary overshadows the English throne and cannot receive mercy; Leicester will take revenge if Elizabeth hurts Mary.
4. *Cabaletta* 'Ah! Se il mio cor tremò giammai'	D♭ major	Mary sings a stanza reasserting that Leicester should not sacrifice himself for her, and Leicester responds with a stanza wishing he could give her a kingdom but will be contented with setting her free from prison. The two finish in parallel thirds this time with contrasting vowel sounds.

now feels the weight of her impending death. She asks Talbot to remain, and the scene proceeds with two episodes that walk the line between duet and aria.[35] This combination allows Donizetti to generate a musical confessional in which Mary bares her soul, or at least some of it. In the first of the episodes, the queen describes the spirits of Darnley and Rizzio who accuse her of wrongdoing, and she laments that her desire for love led to both their deaths. When Talbot presses her about her interactions with Babington (*'unita eri a Babington'*), she initially seems to admit her guilt, stating that it was a mistake (*'fu error fatale!'*). Talbot follows with a stern reminder that she cannot hide her guilt from God, and she ironically adopts more ambiguous language:

> Oh my trust! A dense veil
> has so far covered the truth.
> Yes, a heart that languishes,
> asks for mercy from God.[36]

---

[35] Ashbrook, *Donizetti*, p. 361.
[36] The original Italian is:

> Ah mio fido! Un denso velo
> ha finor coperto il vero.
> Sì, lo giura un cor che langue,
> che da dio chiede pietà.

It is unclear what this 'truth' is. Did she simply put her hopes in Babington to manage her release from prison? Did she see this freedom as an opportunity to seize the throne from Elizabeth? Did she participate in schemes to kill Elizabeth? Whatever the circumstances, she does acknowledge her sorrowful heart and begs God for mercy. Talbot responds that she is forgiven, and the two conclude in a duet confirming her spiritual pardon.

Leicester again appears on stage with Mary in the *scena ultima*. This time the couple is not alone: Mary is accompanied by Cecil, Talbot, her stalwart attendant Anna and crowds protesting her execution. When Leicester storms onto the scene, Mary has just finished her aria promising that she will pray for the good of England despite her ill-treatment at the hands of Elizabeth. Leicester exclaims that all should tremble in the presence of a God who avenges the innocent, and Mary's response in B-minor asks Leicester to give her strength for what faces her and to trust that her shed blood will satisfy heaven's wrath against England. The music modulates to D-major before the finale in which Cecil states that peace will now come to England, the chorus proclaims Mary's innocence and Mary repeats that God is vengeful.

Donizetti's Mary is presented as a contrast to Elizabeth. Though Donizetti infamously disparaged them both: 'those two queens were whores',[37] he also seems to have been sympathetic to both.[38] On the temporal level, Mary's death signals that she has been defeated: losing her lover, crown and life. Elizabeth, on the other hand, is the victor, having secured her throne and kingdom (Cecil proclaims as much after Elizabeth signs the execution order and again as Mary is led to her execution).[39] However, Donizetti perceived some redeeming qualities in Mary, and he shaped the opera to contrast this superficial assessment. His Mary moves upward from sin to glorification,[40] while Elizabeth moves in the opposite direction, from exaltation to condemnation. One of the many manifestations of this contrasting motion can be observed in Donizetti's staging of the opera. The audience first encounters Mary alone – or at least with just

---

[37] In a letter to his Roman librettist Ferretti dated 7 October 1834, Donizetti wrote, 'ma p . . . erano quelle due': Guido Zavidine (ed.), *Gaetano Donizetti: Vita, Musiche, Epistolario* (Bergamo, 1948), p. 362. Quoted and translated in Ashbrook, *Donizetti*, p. 85.

[38] John Stewart Allitt, *Donizetti in Light of Romanticism and the Teaching of Johann Simon Mayr* (Shaftesbury, 1991), p. 154.

[39] Cecil proclaims 'Your Majesty, serenely turn your face/back towards peace and joyfulness! This will be the most beautiful day/for your throne and for England!' (*Ah, Regina, serena il tuo volto/ alla pace, alla gioia ritorni./Questo il piú bello del giorni/pel tuo soglio, per Anglia sarà*). Though he is barely heard amidst the remainder of the cast as Mary is led to the block at the end of Act 3, he exclaims, 'Now England's peace is secure;/the enemy of the kingdom dies!' (*Or dell'Anglia la pace è sicura;/la nemica del regno già muor*).

[40] Morello writes '[a]d una maggiore linearità di Maria nel suo itinerario di peccato, sacrificio, espiazione corrisponde la tortuosità . . .': Riccardo Morello, 'Da Schiller a Donizetti: Maria Stuarda', in *Auguri Schiller! Atti del convegno perugino in occasione del 250° anniversario della nascita di Friedrich Schiller*, ed. Hermann Dorowin and Uta Treder (Perugia, 2011), pp. 185–86.

her handmaiden Anna – but she is ultimately led to the execution block surrounded by crowds of people supporting her and decrying her unjust sentence. Elizabeth, on the other hand, first appears surrounded by her subjects who are praising her and her glorious reign, but she is last seen on stage in Act 3 by herself. Donizetti (with the help of Bardari) thus creates a Mary who undergoes triumphant transformation. She evolves from a lonely, fearful, sinful lover in Act 2 to an Act 3 victim of jealous love, a martyr and heroine of the Catholic faith, and a beloved and perhaps even saintly intercessor for an apostate England.[41]

Rourke's Mary

Josie Rourke's film *Mary Queen of Scots* takes a somewhat different approach to the queen's biography. Beau Willimon's (*b*. 1977) screenplay was adapted from the work of historian John Guy (*b*. 1949), giving a historically grounded framework that Schiller's play lacks.[42] Even so, many have been quick to note the historical inaccuracies that persist in Willimon's account.[43] Instead of focusing on these, the present discussion considers Rourke's portrayal of Mary, particularly through the soundtrack composed by Max Richter. In a story that presents contemporaneous events in the lives of Mary and Elizabeth, Richter constructs overarching musical motifs that draw the events together. The central and most familiar-sounding of these motifs is distilled from George Frideric Handel's (1685–1759) *Zadok the Priest*, HWV 258, an anthem that was composed for the coronation of King George II in 1727 and that has been used for every subsequent British coronation. Despite the prominence of this motif throughout the film, it will be temporarily set aside to explore two other motifs that are crucial to the narrative and to Richter's musical portrayal of the tensions in Mary's life and death. For the purposes of this discussion, they are called the Peril motif and the Usurper's motif.

---

[41] Allitt argues that this transformation aligns with Donizetti's views of Roman Catholic martyrdom: John Stewart Allitt, introduction to *Maria Stuarda* by Gaetano Donizetti (London, 1973), p. 1.

[42] Guy, *My Heart is My Own*.

[43] For examples, see Maria Puente, '*Mary Queen of Scots*: Off with her Head and to Hell with the Facts (Spoilers)!' *USA Today*, 10 December 2018, www.usatoday.com/story/life/movies/2018/12/10/mary-queen-scots-fact-check-how-accurate-film-spoilers/1909270002/; Clarisse Loughrey, '*Mary Queen of Scots*: How Historically Accurate is it?', *The Independent*, 15 January 2019, www.independent.co.uk/arts-entertainment/films/news/mary-queen-of-scots-historical-accuracy-meet-queen-elizabeth-margot-robbie-saoirse-ronan-a8666266.html; John Orquiola, 'Mary Queen of Scots True Story: What the Movie Gets Right & Changes', *Screenrant*, 22 September 2019, https://screenrant.com/mary-queen-scots-movie-true-story-historical-accuracy/; and Alex Barasch, 'What's Fact and What's Fiction in *Mary Queen of Scots*', *Slate*, 7 December 2018, https://slate.com/culture/2018/12/mary-queen-of-scots-movie-fact-vs-fiction-historical-accuracy.html, all accessed 20 September 2023.

Figure 13.1 'Peril motif'
Max Richter, *Mary Queen of Scots* (2018)

The Peril motif features two successive melodic cross-figures that begin with an upward leap followed by a syncopated, scalar downward progression to the original pitch (Figure 13.1). This motif first sounds twenty-eight minutes into the film, after Mary has learned that Elizabeth is sick with smallpox. Initially, the Zadok motif is heard as Mary quickly gets dressed and begins to dictate a letter to Elizabeth. Mary concludes the letter by agreeing to marry Lord Dudley on condition that she is named heir to the English throne. Upon making this stipulation, the Peril motif breaks out in the strings, buttressed by ominous war-like drums along with a countermelody in the winds. The scene immediately shifts to Elizabeth and her response to the letter. In this moment of peril, Elizabeth fears that her life and reign are crumbling in her hands: smallpox is threatening her health and Mary is positioning herself to take Elizabeth's 'special friend' (Robert Dudley) along with the English throne. Crying, Elizabeth runs out of her bedchamber, and Richter increases the musical intensity by doubling the melody an octave higher. Elizabeth's attendants are then seen scrambling to clear a room of male members of court practising their fencing before the veiled, sickly Elizabeth bursts into the room and into Dudley's arms. Her relief is made more palpable by Richter's reduction of the orchestration to violins and violas in a simple, unadorned, harmonised setting of the motif, and Dudley – in a moment reminiscent of a wedding – lifts her veil and assures her 'I am yours, forever yours'.[44]

The Peril motif appears three more times in the film but is adapted to suit the level of peril being expressed along with the political standing of the person in peril. The most subtle iteration involves the strings playing the motif's harmonic progression without the actual melody while Rizzio begs forgiveness from Mary for his relations with her husband Darnley. It is also heard as Mary is packing to flee Holyrood Palace and is counselled that she must leave her son James behind. In a similar manifestation to that of Rizzo's pleas, Richter's simple, strings-only setting of the motif allows James' cries for his mother to fill the emotional space, and the motif continues into the depths of the low strings as Mary is transported to Bothwell's estate. It is heard for the last time when Mary and Bothwell marry and as John Knox preaches against her. Just as at the first iteration, the pulsing drums are heard, but this time the melody is played

---

[44] *Mary Queen of Scots*, directed by Josie Rourke (Universal Pictures, 2018), 0:01:25. https://www.amazon.co.uk/gp/video/detail/B07NSTXZ2B/ref=atv_dp_share_cu_r, accessed 20 September 2023.

Figure 13.2 'Usurper's motif'
Max Richter, *Mary Queen of Scots* (2018)

by the violins with an almost ethereal, organ-like quality. Mary's political future is now in peril: she has married the man accused of killing her husband, and Knox is stirring the populace against her.

The second motif, the Usurper's motif, is built upon a simple, repeated note progression played in the contrabass violins (Figure 13.2, Line 1), and it is usually accompanied by a drum cadence. Its most extensive manifestation occurs at the beginning of the film, as Mary is first seen praying in a dark room.[45] Here the motif starts with the basses slowly walking through the progression alongside drums and ethereal treble vocals. When Mary rises off her knees

---

[45] *Mary Queen of Scots*, 0:29:47.

and is led to her execution chamber, the violins and violas enter (lines 3 and 4, respectively). In this ominous sequence, one in which everyone is wearing black (including both Mary and Elizabeth) and nobody speaks apart from Mary muttering prayers at the execution block, there is a noticeable sense of tension and momentum: the portrayal of Mary's final moments is emotionally distant, yet laden with significance. This sequence presents the traditional Elizabethan portrayal of Mary: a conspirator who is punished for attempting to usurp the English throne.

The Usurper's motif is not heard again until after Rizzio's death, when Darnley is trying to endear himself to Mary.[46] Here, an arpeggiated *clarsach* line is accompanied by voices and drums. The basses enter (line 1), followed by the duple-rhythm (line 2) in strings when Darnley begins to speak to Moray, Lennox and Maitland. Violas playing line 4 are added as the conversation turns, with Darnley demanding 'Am I not the king to whom you promised fealty before you carried out your violence [referring to the Chase-about Raids]?' The triplet strings (line 3) are then added with Darnley's parting statement that '... this king shall go where he pleases with his wife when it pleases him'. Darnley and Mary are next seen riding in the Scottish hills along with their entourage, presumably to Dunbar Castle. He hopes that Mary will finally acknowledge him as king now that he has saved her from the scheming Moray, Lennox and Maitland. Darnley even goes so far as to enter Dunbar ahead of his queen. However, it is the queen who is announced as she enters and not Darnley, and Bothwell confirms that the troops gathered there are part of the queen's army, not his. Darnley's hopes for control have been quickly extinguished, and the Usurper's motif unravels along with it.

The third iteration of the motif occurs right after Mary abdicates the throne.[47] The drums and bass line (line 1) undergird atmospheric vocals that form the background as Mary talks with her gentlewoman about her loyalty to Scotland, while simultaneously Elizabeth speaks with Dudley about her loyalty to her 'sister' Mary. With Elizabeth's words 'How cruel men are', chords of high strings ring out over the looming bass and drums, and the duple-rhythms in the middle strings (lines 2 and 4) are added. A new usurper has arisen in Moray, and he is seen taking the oath of regency for his nephew James. The motif continues as Mary looks upon England for the first time and is told by a fisherman that England and Scotland are 'sisters'. However, Moray is not the only usurper in the montage. The triplet strings (line 3) that are added when the scene cuts to Elizabeth racing her horse through the woods identify Mary as another usurper who is threatening the English throne.

---

[46] *Mary Queen of Scots*, 1:15:32.
[47] *Mary Queen of Scots*, 1:38:30.

These themes accompany some of the most dramatic portions of the film, highlighting Rourke's interest in the political circumstances that surrounded Mary. This political bent is arguably confirmed by the central musical motif for the entire film, the Coronation or Zadok motif mentioned earlier. It is heard seven times during the film and always at times of political significance (see Table 13.2). Each iteration is different, depending on the characters involved: Mary's version employs a countermelody by the cor anglais, Elizabeth's features oboes and a triumphant version features brass (that is, trumpets, horns and trombones). The first use of the motif starts with the bass and strings and develops into the triumphant version with brass as Mary's train makes its way through the Scottish landscapes. Mary's cor anglais countermelody then sounds with its characteristically frequent suspensions when the group reaches Edinburgh and Holyrood Palace. By contrast, the brass and cor anglais are absent in the second iteration of the theme, which instead serves as the background for Elizabeth's palace and the discussions between Cecil and Dudley about the English royal succession. Here the oboes provide another countermelody that refers to Elizabeth throughout the rest of the film.

While the iterations of the Zadok motif could warrant a significant discussion on their own, the motif's final manifestation is worthy of note for the present discussion. It is heard as the meeting between Mary and Elizabeth begins to deteriorate. Elizabeth removes both her crown and wig, revealing the hair-loss she suffered after many bouts with smallpox, and remarks 'I had this made because I wanted to present the best version of myself'. With this line, lower strings begin to be heard playing a version of the Zadok theme that has been dramatically transformed into a simple chord progression accompanying a new countermelody played by the cellos. Similar to Mary's countermelody, the syncopations of this new cello melody illustrate the multifarious tensions manifested in the meeting. Notably, these include Elizabeth's views of Mary ('you seem to surpass me in every way' versus 'your gifts are your downfall') along with the difference between what Mary wants from Elizabeth (an army) and what Elizabeth can provide (safe asylum). Richter's skilful instrumentation naturally smooths and merges melodic lines, lending warmth to Elizabeth's benevolent yet firm response 'you will still have my protection under my terms'. The motif continues despite the fact that Mary adds more tension to the situation by insisting Elizabeth will have her killed just as Henry VIII killed Elizabeth's mother. Musically, higher strings emerge, paralleling the walking bass that has been supporting the cello melody. Yet Elizabeth remains undaunted in her offer of asylum '. . . as long as you do not provoke my enemies . . .'.[48]

Mary pushes again, justifying any potential conspiracies and charging that if Elizabeth executes her, 'you murder your queen!' With these statements,

---

[48] *Mary Queen of Scots*, 1:48:38–1:49:47.

310   TIM DUGUID

Table 13.2 Instances of the 'Zadok' motif in *Mary Queen of Scots* (2018)

	Time	Description
1	0:03:30	Strings start with the Zadok harmonic progression; the broken chords are heard on top as a girl runs alongside Mary on her horse, newly returned to Scotland; brass and woodwinds are added as Mary and her entourage make their way through the Scottish landscapes; solo cor anglais enters with a countermelody as Mary arrives at Holyrood Palace and is greeted by Lord James Stuart.
2	0:09:30	Strings take Zadok progression, with oboe countermelody as we see Elizabeth's palace. The strings continue, muted, while Cecil and Dudley discuss succession to the throne of England.
3	0:22:30	Strings with *clarsach* and oboes sound as Elizabeth sends Dudley to Scotland as a suitor for Mary.
4	0:28:00	Strings play the Zadok progression with oboes since the topic of conversation is initially Elizabeth and her illness. The oboes fade as Mary writes a letter to Elizabeth, agreeing to wed Dudley if she is named heir.
5	0:40:45	Full Zadok progression as in number 1: Elizabeth storms out of the Privy Council after hearing about Darnley's advances towards Mary. Mary and Darnley ride horses with the trumpets and horns punctuating the landscapes. Darnley finally comments 'How it must feel ruling all you can see' and the cor anglais takes over when Mary takes centre stage and Darnley proposes marriage to her.
6	1:21:45	Drums are heard with strings carrying Zadok progression, accented by flutes and oboes, as Mary writes to Elizabeth asking her to be James' godmother and Elizabeth works on quilling. Treble vocals are punctuated briefly by horns as Mary gives birth to James, and a solo voice breaks out on his first appearance. There is no cor anglais countermelody since James, not Mary, is at the heart of this sequence.
7	1:51:50	Starts with strings taking Zadok progression in chordal form, and oboes playing on the offbeats at a slow pace. Elizabeth sends Mary to Fotheringhay and 'speaks' to Mary about the unfortunate situation. Drums sound as Elizabeth signs the execution, and the strings enter with arpeggios on the Zadok progression as Elizabeth sits on the throne and Mary is led from her cell towards the execution chamber. Brasses are added when the two queens are called to their respective destinies. Mary enters the chamber and all attention in the chamber shifts to her, the cor anglais then sounds with Mary's countermelody one final time. Horns punctuate Mary's disrobing and ascending chords replace the arpeggios as the Scottish queen speaks to James.

Elizabeth's oboe countermelody is added, and the cello countermelody begins to disintegrate, giving way to the plain chords of Elizabeth's version of the Zadok motif (that is, featuring the oboes playing the offbeats without any supporting arpeggios), and the English queen storms out, giving instructions for Mary to be well guarded.[49] This plodding form of Elizabeth's Zadok motif provides the backdrop for her words of apology to Mary (both of defence and regret). Drums sound as Elizabeth signs the execution order and the Zadok theme continues

---

[49] *Mary Queen of Scots*, 1:49:47–1:51:10.

whilst she sits on the throne, now with the arpeggios in the strings. The film rehearses the visuals from the beginning, but its stark and harsh realities are now laden with complexity for both Elizabeth and Mary. Musically, the visual montage is now accompanied by the Zadok motif instead of the Usurper's motif. The triumphant version of the Zadok motif with brasses sounds as the two queens are simultaneously addressed as 'Your Grace'. Whereas the first iteration of this version of the motif was heard as Mary made her way from Leith to Edinburgh, this time she is making her way through Fotheringhay Castle up to the execution block. Mary's cor anglais countermelody is heard as she enters the execution chamber, but the triumphant version again comes to the fore when her red garments are revealed. Mary directs her parting words to James, who is pictured walking into the English Privy Council chamber and sitting on the English throne, and the Zadok motif is transformed into a rising chordal progression that simultaneously represents Mary's soul leaving the earth and James' ascent.

Much like Donizetti's Mary, Rourke's Mary is presented in relation to Elizabeth. Musically this is evident in the different versions of the Zadok motif that Richter employs for the two queens. Elizabeth's version with oboes playing on the downbeats illustrates that the English queen is content to align with the advice of her counsellors and the demands of the English throne. On the other hand, Mary's version with the similarly double-reeded cor anglais frequently utilises suspensions to generate syncopations that illustrate the frequent clashes she has with her advisors and their expectations. She is trying to rule as a British monarch, but her French upbringing and Catholic beliefs are among the impediments to her rule. In Rourke's hands (aided by Richter), Mary is given an afterlife in which she is metamorphosed from an embattled Scottish queen and suspected usurper of the English throne into a triumphant political martyr who gives her life for the unification of England and Scotland under her son's rule.

Enduring influence

The Metropolitan Opera first performed Donizetti's *Maria Stuarda* in 2012, and leading up to that performance, director Sir David McVicar (b. 1966) and mezzo-soprano Joyce DiDonato (b. 1969) – playing the lead role of Mary – captured the tension that exists in contemporary performances depicting the important events of the queen's life. Commenting on his realisation of the opera, McVicar stated:

> This time we have gone for something which is freer – more romantic – but still honours the period of history in which these people lived. I think this is important because . . . Mary Queen of Scots and Elizabeth I are such familiar historical figures, so they have to be located within that period: I don't understand the society that these women live

in and are governing unless it is about the sixteenth century. But, it's also an early nineteenth-century Italian, Romantic treatment of history.[50]

DiDonato was willing to go a step further, commenting '. . . it's such an important story and historical figure . . . there are so many parallels still today with what's going on in the world. So, [it is a privilege] to bring her to life and try to help humanity keep learning.'[51] Indeed, there is a tension in storytelling between originalism that prioritises the original work and events, and an audience's need to connect with and learn from the events that are portrayed. While this tension has resulted in musicological debates surrounding performance practice, it has also resulted in a modern-day metamorphosis of Mary as her story is translated for new audiences.

One avenue for this translation has been to cast Mary's story using a present-day lens of feminist critique. This is particularly relevant given sixteenth-century debates surrounding female sovereigns. John Knox famously wrote his treatise *The First Blast of the Trumpet Against the Monstrous Regiment of Women* in 1558, and though it was directed towards the English queen Mary I, Elizabeth remained sceptical of Knox and all things related to Geneva (from where he wrote the treatise) throughout the rest of her life.[52] Knox tried (unsuccessfully) to ingratiate himself with Elizabeth,[53] but he was more actively antagonistic towards Mary and particularly her continuation of Roman Catholic worship services in the Chapel Royal. Many of Mary's musical afterlives, therefore, present her response to the unique pressures she experienced as a female ruler. Entire articles could be devoted just to feminist critiques of Donizetti's *Maria Stuarda* and Rourke's *Mary Queen of Scots*, but detailed discussions are outside the scope of the present chapter. Nevertheless, Donizetti's Mary is characteristic of a western opera tradition that is replete with strong female characters. Both Mary and Elizabeth are depicted as strong leaders, but their relationships to male influence determine their ultimate fate. Elizabeth is first seen considering a possible suiter from France, and her ultimate acquiescence to Cecil's demands aligns her with the traditional view of rulers and ultimately to a lonely end.

---

[50] Sir David McVicar, '*Maria Stuarda*: Joyce DiDonato in Rehearsal (Met Opera)', Metropolitan Opera, 8 December 2012, rehearsal and interview, 6:20 to 7:20, https://youtu.be/Jrt2olaTq_A, accessed 20 September 2023.

[51] Joyce DiDonato, '*Maria Stuarda*: Joyce DiDonato in Rehearsal (Met Opera)', Metropolitan Opera, 8 December 2012, rehearsal and interview, 4:20 to 4:55, https://youtu.be/Jrt2olaTq_A, accessed 20 September 2023.

[52] In addition to Knox's treatise, Christopher Goodman's Geneva-printed *How Superior Powers Ought to be Obeyd of Their Subjects* became a significant treatise on resistance theory. See Jane E. A. Dawson, 'Trumpeting the Resistance: Christopher Goodman and John Knox', in *John Knox and the British Reformations*, ed. Roger A. Mason (Aldershot, 1998), pp. 131–53.

[53] Jane E. A. Dawson, 'Knox, Goodman, and the "Example of Geneva"', in *The Reception of Continental Reformation in Britain*, ed. Polly Ha and Patrick Collinson (Oxford, 2010), p. 108.

Mary, on the other hand, appears as the love interest of Leicester, but she eventually eschews that earthly love for a higher calling.

Feminist critiques of Rourke's Mary would also prove fruitful, considering it was released as the #metoo movement was gaining significant traction in the public discourse.[54] In the film, Mary is surrounded by a half-brother, advisers and husband who are all intent on usurping her power. Most commonly, Richter employs repeated drum cadences to highlight the scheming men (Table 13.3). At the same time, however, the cadences accompany iterations of the Zadok motif that do not portray masculine scheming. In these instances, one might understand these cadences as part of traditional views of a masculine ruler to which one queen's countermelody aligns (Elizabeth's oboe theme) and which the other queen's syncopates (Mary's cor anglais theme).

In addition to feminist critiques, the opera and film would prove fruitful grounds for martyrology and related discussions of the nature of martyrdom and reasons for which one might give one's life. David Rebhun's English translations for the Metropolitan Opera's 2012 performance provide one example. In the closing moments of Act 2 (Act 1, by the Met production), discussed above, Rebhun took some liberties with the original language (Table 13.4). Donizetti's text highlights his view of the spiritual blessings to be lavished upon martyrs for the faith. However, Rebhun's translation uses the word 'throne' instead of 'crown', which effectively transforms Mary's comments into a political statement that her death would ultimately lead to a victorious reign. In this context, 'crown' could have been a reference to the Christian view that Christ's people receive the crown of life, but 'throne' assumes an earthly reign since only God sits on the heavenly throne (unless Rebhun is asserting that Mary would be privileged to be among the twenty-four elders who sit around God's heavenly throne in Revelation 4:4). Therefore, for Rebhun, Mary would be victorious through the rule of her son, James VI and I.

Table 13.3 Drum beat patterns in *Mary Queen of Scots*

Pattern	Associated motifs/tracks
[4/4 rhythmic pattern]	• Usurper's motif • Zadok motif
[6/8 rhythmic pattern]	• Peril motif
[4/4 rhythmic pattern]	• 'The Wedding,' track 8

---

[54] For introductions, see Laurie Collier Hillstrom, *The #MeToo Movement* (Santa Barbara, CA, 2019); and Ann M. Noel and David Benjamin Oppenheimer (eds), *The Global #metoo Movement: How Social Media Propelled a Historic Movement and the Law Responded* (Englewood Cliffs, NJ, 2020).

Table 13.4 Translations of Maria's words, *Maria Stuarda*, Act 2

Original Italian	Literal English	Rebhun[981]
Or guidatemi alla morte: sfiderò l'estrema sorte. Di trionfo un sol momento ogni affanno compensò.	Now lead me to death: I will challenge the extreme fate A single moment of triumph compensated for every pain.	Lead me to death! I defy my fate to the end! Death is my victory and my throne!

This parallels Rourke's Mary as a martyr who endeavoured to unite the kingdoms of England and Scotland. After all, Mary herself pleads with her brother upon abdicating the Scottish throne, '[a]ll I have done is try to unify this land'.[55] Though she is presumably speaking of Scotland in this instance, her other actions during the film reveal that her aspirations lie beyond Scotland. In addition to her preoccupation with being named heir to the English throne, her exhortation to her son as she is led to the block indicates that Rourke's Mary envisions a greater unity that includes England. Mary comments 'I pray . . . that you will succeed where I could not . . . I shall be watching you from heaven as your crown one day unites two kingdoms, and we shall have peace'.[56] Rourke's Mary therefore carries unionist tones: she died so that James could bring unity and peace. In this way, the film's timing is ironic considering the context of the evolving Scottish and British political landscape. Filming was supposed to have begun in 2007, just before the Scottish National Party started an active campaign for an independence referendum. However, casting challenges and other delays pushed filming back to 2017 – three years after that referendum failed, one year after Brexit was approved (despite a majority of the Scottish populace voting against it) and after the SNP had started to push for a second referendum.[57]

On the other hand, a June 2022 staging of Donizetti's *Maria Stuarda* produced by Tom Creed and performed by the Irish National Opera adopted a much more nationalistic lens.[58] This was the first Irish performance of the opera, and it eschewed many of McVicar's quasi-originalist realisations of the work. One of the most striking modernisations is the Irish Opera's choice of costuming under Katie Davenport. Elizabeth is first seen in a skirt suit clad with a Union

---

[55] *Mary Queen of Scots*, 1:37:45.
[56] *Mary Queen of Scots*, 1:55:46–1:56:20.
[57] Similar parallels to the 2018 British political landscape have been identified by Jo Livingstone and Alison Rowat: Jo Livingstone, '*Mary Queen of Scots* in the Age of Brexit', *The New Republic*, 12 December 2018, https://newrepublic.com/article/152625/mary-queen-scots-age-brexit; Alison Rowat, 'Film Review: *Mary Queen of Scots*', *The Herald*, 15 January 2019, www.heraldscotland.com/news/17357001.film-review-mary-queen-scots/, both accessed 20 September 2023.
[58] OperaVision, '*Maria Stuarda* Donizetti – Irish National Opera', live performance stream, 8 July 2022, https://operavision.eu/performance/maria-stuarda, accessed 20 September 2023.

Jack. She then wears a riding suit for her encounter with Mary and a black skirt for her final scene when she signs Mary's execution order. Mary, on the other hand, appears throughout the opera in a floral-print dress, a visual representation of innocence and the love of nature that she expresses in her first aria. Her costume only changes once. In the final section of the final act, the *scena ultima*, she appears wearing the Scottish St Andrews flag as a shawl. She finally unfurls the flag in triumph as she turns her back to the audience and walks to the back of the stage, towards the execution block. Creed's Mary, therefore, is cast as an analogue for Scotland, with its hopes and future ultimately resting in the hands of an autocracy operating under the guise of the United Kingdom.

The limited examples provided here illustrate a few of the more significant threads of influence that Mary, Queen of Scots has exerted on varying genres of musical culture over the past four centuries. Some settings such as 'Earl Bothwell' and 'The Battle of Corrichie' mention Mary but their focus and critique is on the persons that surrounded her. Of the works that focus more intently on the queen of Scots, some – like those by Donizetti and Rourke/Richter – cast Mary in terms of her relationship with Elizabeth, while others – like those by Carissimi and Schumann – allow Mary and the tumultuous events of her life to stand on their own merit. Yet, interestingly, all these settings adopt sympathetic views towards Mary. Indeed, Carissimi, Schumann, Donizetti and Rourke, along with their subsequent manifestations (particularly in the case of Donizetti's opera), align in their portrayal of her literal afterlife. In each example, Mary's death results in a significant transformation. Once she has laid aside her life and the accompanying preoccupations with love interests and royal rights, she takes on a new heavenly reality. Mary assumes a triumphant, beneficent afterlife in heaven to the welfare of those who remain on earth.

Surrounded by the romantic, political and religious intrigue that characterised her life from her birth and the period of Henry VIII's 'Rough Wooing' to her execution, Mary was a polarising figure, and this continues today. As we view the musical retellings of Mary's story as part of a larger tapestry of cultural history, the personalities of the storytellers begin to take shape whilst the actual historical figures begin to fade into the background. More work is therefore warranted in exploring the musical portrayals of Mary's life, both to identify commonalities across time and to analyse the lenses of cultural bias that have shaped each retelling. In addition to the examples discussed here, in 1946 Samuel and Dorothy Tannenbaum identified 97 'Operas, Songs, Cantatas, Ballets, Overtures, etc.' relating to Mary,[59] and we could potentially add many of the Tannenbaums' list of 294 'Poems & Ballads' that may have been written with particular melodies in mind.[60] While there are some duplicates within

---

[59] Tannenbaum, *Marie Stuart*, pp. 16–20.
[60] Tannenbaum, *Marie Stuart*, pp. 34–49.

these lists, several musical works (such as those by Grave Digger) have been written since 1946. This vast musical corpus is a veritable treasure chest of artefacts ideal for tracing cultural trends over the past four centuries. For instance, it could help to identify when it became fashionable to portray aspects of Mary's story (e.g. her flight to France as a child, the birth of James, the fictitious meeting with Elizabeth, etc.). Moreover, while the examples here are unanimously sympathetic towards Mary, it is unclear to what extent the queen has enjoyed such a positive reception. To the extent that any critical and negative views may be represented in other works, it is similarly unclear whether there are any historical trends that can be related to the cultural priorities that may have triggered the creation of those works. Continued research therefore promises to provide society with ongoing opportunities for self-reflection as its musicians persist in breathing life into Mary and her story.

FOURTEEN

The Transformations of Mary, Queen of Scots in Early Cinema, 1895–1923

Ian Goode and Stephen McBurney

Introduction

'Mary, Queen of Scots', by H. G. Bell
1. It was a stately convent, with its old and lofty walls
2. And there five Noble Maidens sat, beneath the Orchard Tree
3. It was the Court – the Gay Court of Bourbon
4. And on its deck a Lady sat, who gazed with tearful eyes
5. Sat Mary listening to the rain, and sighing with the winds
6. And summoned Rizzio with his lute, and bade the Minstrel play
7. The ruffian steel in his heart – the faithful Rizzio's slain
8. She wrote the words, she stood erect – a Queen without a Crown!
9. She stayed her steed upon a hill – she saw them marching by
10. Away! Away! Thy gallant steed must act no Laggard's part
11. Beside the block a sullen headsman stood
12. Laps the warm blood that trickling falls unheeded to the floor

Extra Special Illustrated Catalogue of Magic Lanterns, Slides and Apparatus, c. 1890s, p. 64.

These titles for H. G. Bell's slide set *Mary, Queen of Scots* have more in common with a nursery rhyme than historical literature. Mary is caricatured with a cartoon-esque, listless and introspective disposition, and the description of 'warm blood that trickling falls unheeded to the floor' evokes the morbid morality tales of the Brothers Grimm. This slide set is one of countless examples of a historical account that has lost its polemical and partisan nature – the fall of Mary Stuart has transcended academic debate, to become popular myth and folklore. Film has engaged and challenged these myths and tropes in disparate ways, to an extent unseating the ubiquitous caricature exemplified above. This chapter will illustrate how the early filmic versions of Mary evolved over time, from the *Execution of Mary, Queen of Scots* (1895) to *The Loves of Mary,*

Queen of Scots (1923). We argue that each production grapples the past with a brazen malleability, reinvigorating this popular folklore for polemical purposes, but in each case for divergent ideological ends.

The historian Cairns Craig argues that the demise of Mary Stuart forms part of an overarching constellation of loss and destruction that shaped the bedrock of the national character of Scotland within the United Kingdom:

> Scotland's historical conflicts do not develop the nation; they abolish it. Rather than being the story of the nation's struggle towards freedom, the national narrative is the story of the destruction of its virtues, whether the feminine virtue of Mary or the masculine virtue discredited at Culloden.[1]

For Craig, this impoverishment of Scotland's historiography leads to an abundance of overtly nostalgic and romantic tropes, and a fundamental divorce of the past from present-day reality: what he describes as a 'fictionalising of the past which leaves the present trapped in a fog of illusion'.[2] Craig's examples focus predominantly on literature, and whilst film undoubtedly does perpetuate nostalgic and romantic images of Scotland, it also does more than this.

This chapter will demonstrate that across the earliest filmic iterations of Mary, Queen of Scots, the 'fog of illusion' derided by Craig has more subtlety of form than hitherto acknowledged. The opening section of this chapter contextualises *Execution of Mary Queen of Scots* (1895) within the apogee of the British Empire. We argue that this text forms part of a variety of Marian representations across disparate media, which collectively offer a base caricature of Mary Stuart in keeping with the lantern-slide set referenced at the opening of this chapter. The second section discusses two further productions released during the silent era, and foregrounds how markedly the characterisation of Mary and Scotland can shift amidst conflicting national agendas. It concludes with a case study on an unfinished version of a Mary film by an English filmmaker named Walter West, which was billed as a super-production that would elevate the British film industry as a whole. The third and final section focuses on a rhetorical shift towards historicity and British nationalism, as embodied in *Mary, Queen of Scots* (1922) and *The Loves of Mary, Queen of Scots* (1923). Commandeered by The British National Film League, these films were used as a platform to quell the anxieties of a crumbling British Empire. Film was grasped as a means of shoring up a diminishing British identity under a wave of American cultural imperialism, which by the 1920s was being perpetuated across cinema screens worldwide. Our overarching argument is twofold: firstly, the early filmic incarnations

---

[1] Cairns Craig, *The Modern Scottish Novel: Narrative and the National Imagination* (Edinburgh, 1999), p. 125.
[2] Ibid., p. 14.

of Mary Stuart creatively reflect and reinforce an evolving imperial identity; and secondly, a film-specific historiography is integral to understanding the ongoing relevance of Mary, Queen of Scots in present-day society.

The Execution of Mary Queen of Scots (1895)

Extant footage of *The Execution of Mary Queen of Scots* remains largely unrestored, but has been digitised and is widely available. It consists of an 18-second stationary medium shot, which opens with Mary standing beside the executioner's block in an outdoor setting. Besides the executioner, Mary is joined by what appear to be two handmaidens, seven guards holding spears and two members of the English court. The scene opens with Mary looking onto the block, and gesturing with the sign of the cross. She is hurriedly comforted by a handmaiden, before dropping to her knees to lean over the block. As the masked executioner raises a large axe, Mary extends her arms outwards, hands clasped in prayer. The axe rises in tandem with the arms of the two court representatives, who ready themselves to give the signal. In counterbalance to these upward motions, Mary withdraws her outstretched arms and brings them down to her side, whilst extending her neck in quiet submission. With the executioner at full stretch, the axe is brought down swiftly and with full force, cleanly severing the head from the body. Mary's servants raise their hands in fright, as the guards and court representatives lean forward to witness the macabre spectacle. The head rolls off the block towards one of the servants, and Mary's body falls limp to the floor. Using the axe for balance, the executioner stretches over to lift Mary's head, and holds it up triumphantly in direct address to the camera.

In a retrospective article printed in the British trade journal *Kinematograph Weekly* in 1938, *The Execution of Mary Queen of Scots* is heralded as the first ever 'short-story' film.[3] Yet the film clearly adopts a presentational format, with no inherent storyline or narrative. The direct address of the executioner to the camera invites a response from the viewer; we are asked to celebrate, mock or recoil from the shocking and morbid spectacle before us. In its designation of *The Execution of Mary Queen of Scots* as the first 'short-story' film, *Kinematograph Weekly* unconsciously assimilates it into a tapestry of narratives and plotlines with Mary Stuart at the centre, which have evolved across the world stage over centuries.

Produced towards the end of the Victorian era and at the apogee of the British Empire, the ideological drive of *Execution of Mary Queen of Scots* is symptomatic of its socio-political context. Mary falls at the hands of her English counterpart Elizabeth, and by association Scotland is subjugated by England. Albeit not focusing on Mary Stuart or Scotland *per se*, Edward Said's discussion of a

---

[3] 'An American Jubilee: Edison's Earliest Experiments', *Kinematograph Weekly*, 19 May 1938, p. 43.

'strategic formation' becomes apt here. Said defines this as 'the relationship between texts and the way in which groups of texts, types of texts, even textual genres, acquire mass, density, and referential power among themselves and thereafter in the culture at large'.[4] Such a phenomenon occurs with the cultural depictions of Mary Stuart in the late 1890s. Lantern-slide sets of Mary Stuart were produced by multiple manufacturers, including W. C. Hughes, York & Son, G. W. Wilson, Alfred Pumphrey and Newton & Company, each one culminating with the execution scene (see Figures 14.1 and 14.2 for examples).[5] In 1896, Madame Tussaud's in London exhibited a wax tableau entitled *Execution of Mary, Queen of Scots*, which featured heavily in newspaper advertisement columns.[6] *Execution of Mary, Queen of Scots* was also a popular scene for *tableaux vivant*, taken up by myriad professionals and amateurs; for example, in 1896 the *Norwich Mercury* commended the inclusion of just such a spectacle in a floral fete in the small town of Gorleston-on-Sea in England.[7] In 1895, *The Pall Mall Gazette* heralded *Trial and Execution of Mary Queen of Scots* by Mary Monica Maxwell-Scott as its 'book of the week', whilst the subject was also a popular choice for public-facing lectures.[8] Also in 1895, the *Dundee Courier* described an automaton of the macabre event, which formed part of a local fundraising event in the city:

> Besides the Refreshment Stall, which is prettily draped in coral and white, there are three other stalls, hung respectively with heliotrope and terracotta, pale blue and primrose, and orange and green. The centre of the hall is occupied by a miniature representation of a jail, where by putting a penny in the slot you may enjoy the spectacle of Deeming's execution or Mary Queen of Scots' beheadal.[9]

Thus, the film *Execution of Mary Queen of Scots* formed part of a network of texts in the 1890s, encompassing lantern slides, waxworks, *tableaux vivant*, books, lectures, comedy sketches and automata. Each of these texts naturalised the gruesome spectacle, and subtly legitimised and celebrated the overarching

---

[4] Edward Said, *Culture and Imperialism* (London, 1994), p. 20.
[5] LUCERNA – the Magic Lantern Web Resource, http://lucerna.exeter.ac.uk, accessed 20 September 2023.
[6] 'Madame Tussaud's Exhibition', *London Evening Standard*, 23 May 1896, p. 1.
[7] 'Gorleston Floral Fete and Bazaar', *Norwich Mercury*, 6 June 1896, p. 6.
[8] 'The Weekly Sun', *Pall Mall Gazette*, 1 June 1895, p. 6; 'Buchan News', *Buchan Observer and East Aberdeenshire Advertiser*, 18 January 1898, p. 4.
[9] Frederick Bailey Deeming was convicted and executed for the gruesome murder of his wife, Emily Lydia Deeming (*née* Mather) in 1892. He gained further notoriety as a prime suspect behind the Jack the Ripper murders. 'Thistle Harriers Sale of Work', *Dundee Courier*, 27 April 1895, p. 3.

Figure 14.1 Slide 21 of 24, *Mary Queen of Scots* (York & Son, 1885)
From the author's private collection

imperialist ethos of its age – a Scottish Catholic queen falling at the hands of her English Protestant counterpart.

The synchronicity between the texts can be gleaned from a comparison of the extant film *Execution of Mary Queen of Scots* and the closing lantern slides from *Mary Queen of Scots* (Figures 14.1 and 14.2). As with the film, the slides reference the religious context of the beheading, with Mary holding a cross as she makes her way to the executioner's block. In both versions, Mary approaches the block from left to right, with two handmaidens in attendance who raise their hands in grief and shock at the point of severance of head from body. Several guards stand by in both versions, steadfastly holding spears as the spectacle unfolds. Furthermore, Mary wears a coloured dress with white cuffs in both the film and the lantern slides; notably, in the hand-painted lantern slide the colour is blue,

Figure 14.2 Slide 23 of 24, *Mary Queen of Scots* (York & Son, 1885)
From the author's private collection

rather than the red of martyrdom that features so prominently in later filmic versions, such as *Mary Queen of Scots* (2018). The parallels between these texts are not happenchance and are instead indicative of a coherent collection of tropes and icons that span across multiple media in the late nineteenth century. The scope and uniformity of this depiction naturalises it, and its ubiquity shrouds any underlying ideological motivation.[10]

The imperial and colonial connotations of *Execution of Mary Queen of Scots* can be seen more clearly when considering the film catalogues and exhibition programmes of which it was part. Film historian Ian Christie points out that, like any other primary artefact, film catalogues are not neutral or objective

---

[10] 'Argyle Theatre of Varieties', *Birkenhead News*, 25 November 1896, p. 2.

documents.¹¹ Tom Gunning builds on this assertion, stating that early film 'followed global pathways opened up by worldwide capitalism, colonialism, and imperialism', which is reflected in the discourse of early film catalogues.¹² An imperial and colonial agenda is clear in the film catalogues that advertised *Execution of Mary Queen of Scots*, with the film listed alongside titles such as *Young Savages at Dinner* (1897) and *Egyptian Dance* (1897).¹³ These connotations were evident across the exhibition itself; for example, the *tableau vivant Britannia and Her Children* often marked the close of film exhibitions.¹⁴ *Execution of Mary Queen of Scots* is symptomatic of a wider colonial and imperial cultural programme, with (a version of) Scotland and Catholicism suppressed under the identity of the British Empire.

The pervasiveness of jingoist and imperialist sentiment transcended the Victorian era, and remained a defining characteristic of Great Britain into the period between the world wars.¹⁵ Nevertheless, by the 1910s the British Empire was contracting, and its colonial and moral legitimacy was increasingly questioned. In subsequent filmic incarnations of Mary Stuart, the recognisable tropes of this well-trodden narrative are more nuanced, with rhetoric about national identity, gender and historiography brought more to the fore.

Marie Stuart (1908), *Mary Stuart* (1913) and *Mary Queen of Scots* (1921, unfinished)

Marie Stuart deviates from its precursor *Execution of Mary Queen of Scots* to reflect a national identity that is at odds with the British Empire. Produced by Pathé Frères in France, the film foregrounds Mary's religious martyrdom, and questions the moral integrity of Elizabeth and England. Upon its release, the trade press enthused that 'this beautifully colored picture shows us the principal events in the life of Mary Queen of Scots'.¹⁶ The synopsis describes Mary as a 'devout Roman Catholic', whose 'great beauty and charm of manners won for her the hearts of Scots'. The film opens with her time in France, and marriage to François II. Upon François' death, Mary returns to Scotland, only to be unjustly

---

[11] Ian Christie, 'Comparing Catalogues', in *Networks of Entertainment: Early Film Distribution 1895–1915*, ed. Frank Kessler and Nanna Verhoff (Herts, 2007), p. 209.

[12] Tom Gunning, 'Early Cinema as Global Cinema: the Encyclopaedic Ambition', in *Early Cinema and the National*, ed. Richard Abel, Giogio Bertellini and Rob King (Herts, 2016), pp. 6 and 11.

[13] *Film Catalogue 1897* (London and New York, 1897), p. 11.

[14] 'Forgue', *Aberdeen Press and Journal*, 27 December 1898, p. 6; 'Peckham Pupil Teachers' Social Society', *South London Mail*, 25 January 1896, p. 15.

[15] John Mackenzie, 'Introduction', in *Imperialism and Popular Culture*, ed. John Mackenzie (Manchester, 1986), pp. 1–16.

[16] 'Films of the Week', *The Film Index*, no. 136 (28 November 1908): 8–9.

Figure 14.3 A still from Pathé Frères' *Marie Stuart* (1908)
Courtesy of the Media History Digital Library

imprisoned by her Protestant noblemen. She completes a daring escape, and in good faith seeks the assistance of her English cousin and counterpart Elizabeth, only to be betrayed and imprisoned once again. One further escape is made with the help of a brave maid, but Mary is recaptured on the road and, enraged by her impudence, Elizabeth orders her death. The religious martyrdom of Mary is confirmed in the closing scene, which is described in saint-like terms:

> Then comes the walk to the death chamber, where she goes with unfaltering steps, showering blessings upon her enemies, and as she kneels before the block her peaceful countenance bears the same sweet smile that never left her through all her trials, and, kissing the cross for the last time, lay[s] her head calmly on the block and immediately all is over.[17]

The queen of Scots is charming, faithful, brave and just, whilst queen Elizabeth is vilified and rendered treacherous. Through these divergent characterisations, *Marie Stuart* undermines the jingoism of late-Victorian Britain, to promote the Catholic cause and thereby France's moral and spiritual superiority.

---

[17] Ibid.

Film historian Richard Abel discusses the xenophobic rejection of Pathé Frères films by exhibitors in America, who cited fears that they undermined a sense of American national identity and unity.[18] Pathé Frères were synonymous with stencil-painted films, which were often deemed foreign, artificial and superficial by American nationalist exhibitors. Thus, whilst *The Film Weekly* praises *Marie Stuart* for its colouring, to certain exhibitors and distributors it is indicative of an unwelcome subversiveness. Although Abel was writing in an American context, many of these ideas are directly transferable to Britain, especially as the sovereignty and legitimacy of the British Empire came to falter in the period before the Second World War.

To mitigate the perceived corrupting connotations of foreign productions, local exhibitors in Britain acted as cultural intermediaries, repackaging films to shape or limit their ideological effect. In the advertising columns for second-hand reels in *Kinematograph Weekly*, versions of *Marie Stuart* were listed at 750ft, 780ft and 800ft, indicating that local exhibitors had edited and censored the film.[19] The wider exhibition programme could also curb a film's polemical nature. For example, at a screening in Edinburgh *Marie Stuart* was in the same programme as lantern slides representing Mary's life, giving the exhibitor a further means to shape audience reception. Although *Marie Stuart* is a Pathé Frères film at odds with the populist imperialist sentiment of the time, British exhibitors could still draw audiences in with its beautiful colouring, whilst quelling its critical and subversive message.

Thomas A. Edison Ltd's *Mary Stuart* (1913) marked the most ambitious production to date, and at approximately 3,000ft was more than triple the length of *Marie Stuart*. The film deviates from *Marie Stuart* to offer several aesthetic and ideological parallels with *Execution of Mary Queen of Scots*. For example, once again the execution scene is sensationalised – a full-page advertisement depicts Mary in silhouette beneath the executioner's axe (Figure 14.4). The *mise-en-scène* of the execution scene parallels that of the studio's original production, *Execution of Mary Queen of Scots* (1895). The main actors are arranged in a presentational format, with Mary surrounded by representatives of the court, sympathetic onlookers and an array of guards holding weapons (Figure 14.5). The film is in black and white, and this absence of applied colouring distinguishes it from its French counterpart, *Marie Stuart*. *Mary Stuart* thus builds upon *Execution of Mary Queen of Scots*, mirroring its fetishisation of the execution scene and aesthetic strategies.

---

[18] Richard Abel, *The Red Rooster Scare: Making Cinema American, 1900–1910* (Berkeley, CA, Los Angeles and London, 1999).

[19] 'Walturdaw', *Kinematograph Weekly*, 5 May 1910, p. 1487; 'Walturdaw', *Kinematograph Weekly*, 19 January 1911, p. 744; 'Walturdaw', *Kinematograph Weekly*, 28 April 1910, p. 1427.

Figure 14.4 Full-page advertisement for Edison's *Mary Stuart,* printed in *Kinematograph Weekly*
With thanks to The British Newspaper Archive[20]

Whilst[20] there are notable parallels between *The Execution of Mary Queen of Scots* and *Mary Stuart,* there are important innovations too. In the former, Mary is a pantomime-esque figure, whereas in *Mary Stuart* she embodies a femininity

---

[20] Supplement to the *Kinematograph and Lantern Weekly,* 4 September 1913, p. xliv (www.britishnewspaperarchive.co.uk).

MARY STUART
At the place of execution. Leicester asks forgiveness from Mary.

Figure 14.5 Production still from Edison's *Mary Stuart*, which parallels the *mise-en-scène* of *Execution of Mary Queen of Scots*
Courtesy of the Media History Digital Library[21]

that threatens patriarchal society.[22] This is most evident in a sub-plot involving a warden at Fotheringay Castle, who 'has fallen in love with Mary's picture', and who ultimately stabs himself in despair at the queen's demise.[23] Similarly, the earl of Leicester is described as being 'divided between two loves and two ambitions', as he wrestles between choosing the beautiful Mary or the formidable Elizabeth – he is thus torn between heart and mind, and marks an inconsolable figure at the close of the film.[24] Mary's femininity is strengthened by contrast with Elizabeth; for example, a fabricated encounter between the two is described as a 'stormy one with Mary at first suppliant and later angry, and

---

[21] *The Moving Picture News* VII, no. 20 (17 May 1913): 12.
[22] This idea – of Mary bewitching her captors, especially her English ones – is found in dramatic retellings of her story by Friedrich Schiller and Donizetti, as well as in Sir Walter Scott's *The Abbot*.
[23] '*Mary Stuart*', *The Moving Picture News* VII, no. 20: 12.
[24] Ibid.

MARY STUART
Mary denouncing Elizabeth.

Figure 14.6 Production still from Edison's *Mary Stuart*, illustrating Mary publicly denouncing Elizabeth
Courtesy of the Media History Digital Library[27]

Elizabeth cold and scornful throughout'.[25] Mary is feminine, tempestuous and impudent, whilst Elizabeth is masculine, distant and calm. Reviews of the film further strengthened a gendered divide, with Mary Fuller (as Mary) praised for her 'natural loveliness' and 'grace', whilst Miriam Nesbitt (as Elizabeth) is gently decried for being 'too beautiful' and thus giving Elizabeth 'too much grace . . . and not enough severe intellectuality'.[26] In *Mary Stuart*, Mary embodies a femininity that is dangerous to the men who succumb to it, and by proxy the wider nation over which she governs.

Mary Stuart foregrounds Mary's purported culpability in her own downfall, thereby absolving Elizabeth and the English monarchy of any guilt. Mary publicly denounces Elizabeth (Figure 14.6), and the synopsis stresses that her imprisonment is the result of fabricated 'pretensions to the English throne'.[27] Elizabeth only reluctantly signs Mary's death warrant, following a botched

---

[25] Ibid.
[26] 'Mary Stuart', *The Moving Picture World* 16, no. 9 (31 May 1913): 904.
[27] Ibid.

attempt on her life involving a dagger in the hand of one of Mary's supporters. Thus, whilst *Marie Stuart* characterises Mary as a saint and a martyr, *Mary Stuart* portrays her as overly ambitious and dangerous, and ultimately responsible for her own beheading.

Mary Stuart was praised for its aesthetics and purported educational value. Production stills indicate on-location shooting, rather than fabricated sets. Advertisements described the film in absolute terms, as 'vividly picturing the life and death of Mary Queen of Scots', and reviews commended it for its 'exhaustive attention to details'.[29] Actors were chosen for their resemblance to historical characters, as illustrated in a discussion of *Mary Stuart* in *The Telegraph*:

> As 'make-up' in picture plays is extremely difficult, it becomes essential that the actors who impersonate these notable people shall resemble them in face and form. The picture producers are, in consequence, searching far and wide for 'doubles', who can perform before the camera. Actors of this kind are very hard to find, and those who bear a strong resemblance to notable personages soon obtain good positions.[30]

Historical authenticity is equated with aesthetics, rather than any rigorous assessment of primary artefacts or historiographies, and neither is there any transparent consideration of ideological motivations.

A focus on visual authenticity continued to grow throughout the 1910s and 1920s, in tandem with wider social and political changes as embodied in the 1918 Education Act. The Act instigated practical changes, such as raising the age for leaving school and improving working conditions for teachers, but it was also a catalyst for pedagogical reflection and triggered a reassessment of the potential of cinema. Writing to *Kinematograph Weekly* in 1919, a correspondent named W. MacCormack opined:

> The New Education Act has brought in its train new methods of teaching. Much ink has been wasted on attempts to prove that history could be taught more readily by the kinema than by the most readable handbook yet published . . . yet here we are [in the UK] still waiting on our first accurately historic film play.[31]

MacCormack goes on to highlight D. W. Griffith's *Birth of a Nation* (1915) as an exemplar of historical film, claiming 'the Americans have the knack of seizing the salient features of their own brief national history', before citing the promise of a British-produced feature of Mary, Queen of Scots in preparation.[32]

---

[28] *The Moving Picture News* VII, no. 20: 12.
[29] 'Mary Stuart', Supplement to the *Kinematograph and Lantern Weekly*, 21 August 1913, pp. xxxii and xxxiii; 'Mary Stuart', *The Moving Picture World* 16, no. 9 (31 May 1913): 904.
[30] Untitled excerpt from the *Telegraph*, reprinted in *Kinematograph Weekly*, 19 June 1913, p. 834.
[31] W. MacCormack, 'A Jacobite Film Wanted', *Kinematograph Weekly*, 13 November 1919, p. 116.
[32] Ibid.

Mary, Queen of Scots was announced by the English filmmaker Walter West in 1919, with the assurance that 'no expense will be spared' in its creation.[33] Promotional materials focused on the production's visual authenticity, educational value, nationalism and unprecedented scale. For example, early reports stated that 'British Museum Officials are actively engaged in helping the producer [Walter West] in his work of getting everything historically correct, while the art director, S. T. Hosken, is scouring the country for articles of furniture and the correct draperies of the period'.[34] This exacting approach was extended to costuming, with *Kinematograph Weekly* printing:

> [s]ketches from originals, to be found only after long searches in the British and Oxford Museums, have been made of gowns and jewels worn by Queen Mary on the noted occasions which form the outstanding incidents in her career . . . these will be carefully copied for Miss Hopson [the leading actor] to wear during the making of the film.[35]

West reputedly engaged an historian as part of the production crew, who was an 'expert authority on the customs and dressing of the Elizabethan period', whilst care was also taken to recruit actors who bore 'close resemblance to the historical characters as represented in available pen and ink sketches'.[36] What were described as 'lavish' reconstructions of interiors were also planned, including a full-scale sixteenth-century version of Holyrood Palace.[37] Walter West was promising a definitive account of Mary Stuart, with a scrupulous attention to aesthetic verisimilitude.

West's *Mary, Queen of Scots* sought to gain comparison with American productions such as *Birth of a Nation*, and was billed as a 'British super-production', and 'one of the biggest ever attempted in this country'. The value of the gowns for Violet Hopson alone (set to play Mary Stuart), were said to 'run easily into four figures'.[38] The trade press enthused that West had even overcome the unfavourable British climate, to compete toe-to-toe with the output of American producers:

> Other great drawbacks to the English producer are fog and cold – in cases where the studios are not properly heated, it is impossible to film on cold days owing to the fact that the player's breath is visible. But Walter West had provided against these emergencies . . . and no matter how cold it may be, with the excellent heating system which is installed, work goes on as usual. Mr West is one of the few British producers who does not allow the grass to grow under his feet.[39]

---

[33] 'Walter West to Produce *Mary, Queen of Scots*', *Kinematograph Weekly*, 23 October 1919, pp. 110–11.
[34] '*Mary Queen of Scots*', *Kinematograph Weekly*, 22 January 1920, p. 124.
[35] 'Walter West to Produce *Mary, Queen of Scots*', pp. 110–11.
[36] Ibid.
[37] Ibid.
[38] '*Mary Queen of Scots*', *Kinematograph Weekly*, p. 124.
[39] 'Warm Studios', *Kinematograph Weekly*, 13 November 1919, p. 111.

West's version of *Mary, Queen of Scots* was to put the British film industry on the front foot, on a par with productions from any country worldwide. With a degree of jingoism, the British press eulogised

> Mr West has undertaken a task which no other Britisher has dared to attempt . . . an all-British production which will not only set a very high standard of art in kinematography, but one that should find a place in every country where humans congregate to view the motion picture.[40]

Less than two years after these rapturous early reports, newspapers conceded such ambitions would remain unfulfilled:

> A paragraph has been going the rounds of the Scottish newspapers that a British producer has met the disappointment of his like in not being able to screen *Mary Queen of Scots*. According to the story, people in all parts of the country had offered him antique furniture, valuable heirlooms and personal relics of the ill-fated Mary, and the production would have proceeded, but he could not find an actress suitable for the principal part [presumably meaning Violet Hopson]. To add to this British producer's chagrin, he has learned that an American producer is about to screen *Mary Queen of Scots*.[41]

The British press were careful to distance this failure from economic and logistical issues, reframing it as an intentional withdrawal by a perfectionist filmmaker.

The American producer referred to is William Fox of Fox Film Corporation, who was visiting England and Scotland to shoot *Mary Queen of Scots* – billed in preliminary marketing materials as 'the first Fox masterpiece to be produced in Great Britain'.[42] Fox had engaged the renowned film director James Gordon Edwards for the production, along with the film star Betty Blythe, an unnamed assistant director and unnamed camera-men. With trepidation, the visit was described by the British trade press as a 'further extension of the American desire . . . to strengthen their hold on the international market by using locations in European countries for the purpose of expanding the universality of their productions'.[43] Although a full production crew had travelled to Britain, and several scenes were reputedly completed in America prior to this, there is no known extant footage – it appears that the production was never fully realised or released.[44] Subsequent reports state that Betty Blythe pulled out of the production due to a pay dispute, whilst Edwards was impeded by red tape when

---

[40] 'Mary Queen of Scots', *Kinematograph Weekly*, p. 124.
[41] Untitled, *Kinematograph Weekly*, 5 May 1921, p. 75.
[42] 'Special Announcement', *Kinematograph Weekly*, 28 April 1921.
[43] 'Fox to Produce Here', *Kinematograph Weekly*, 24 March 1921, p. 54.
[44] 'Fox's European Plans', *Kinematograph Weekly*, 12 May 1921, p. 63.

attempting to film at Holyroodhouse.[45] Nevertheless, the American interest in yet another filmic version of Mary Stuart raised insecurities about an increasingly impotent British film industry, unable to express its own national history or identity.

The increasing stress on visual authenticity in the late 1910s strengthened and naturalised the ideological function of historical film in Britain, which became bestowed with aesthetic and educational values that marked them as distinctly British productions. As will be presently illustrated, films such as *Mary, Queen of Scots* (1922) and *The Loves of Mary, Queen of Scots* (1923) were lauded by British lobbyists as being superior to the output of other countries. Such parties believed that the 'right' sort of film would transform British cinema and its standing on the world stage, and reinstate the crumbling superiority of Britain and the British Empire in the popular imagination. *The Loves of Mary, Queen of Scots* incorporated schizophrenic tendencies though, as it sought to embody 'British' values whilst vying for a commercial mass audience. The film was competing against more technically advanced and overtly populist American offerings, and is indicative of a British Empire struggling to come to terms with its diminishing status in the modern world. By the 1920s, the waning influence of the British Empire was being superseded by an emerging and unprecedented American cultural imperialism, effected through the mass media.

Mary, Queen of Scots (1922) and *The Loves of Mary, Queen of Scots* (1923)

In *Orientalism* (1978), Edward Said traces a shifting in world power from Britain and France to America, citing the Second World War as the threshold between these two eras. Said's thesis traces an old world order of British and French imperialism 'broken into many parts', and a network of knowledge structures 'dissolved and released into new forms' by the mid-twentieth century.[46] In the period between the world wars, we see the beginnings of this shift to an American *imperium*, encapsulated in the power relations of the international film industry. Lobbyists, politicians, film producers and other interest groups voiced anxieties over how the cinema could shape national identity and imperialism in the popular imagination. This tension between a fading British imperialism and an emerging American one is epitomised by *Mary, Queen of Scots* (1922) and *The Loves of Mary, Queen of Scots* (1923), and their relationship with the newly formed British National Film League (BNFL).

---

[45] 'Exploiting Historical Backgrounds', *Kinematograph Weekly*, 21 April 1921, p. 57; 'Fox's British Productions', *Kinematograph Weekly*, 21 April 1921, p. 46.
[46] Edward Said, *Orientalism* (London, 2003 edn), pp. 284–85.

The BNFL was founded in 1921 by a consortium of producers and renters, and headed by Lieutenant Colonel A. C. Bromhead. Film historian Olly Gruner argues that Bromhead 'saw cinema as an ideological weapon', and that 'fears were rife that Hollywood's dominance meant British identity and values had been eroded in favour of a vulgar "Americanised" national culture'.[47] There is a clear overtone of jingoism and imperialism in reports of the League's activities and objectives; for example, *Kinematograph Weekly* wrote that the BNFL 'had a profound belief in British films for British screens. They felt they had the right to a certain proportion of the programme in the kinemas of this country and the colonies'.[48] The BNFL was established to counter a growing cultural imperialism from across the Atlantic, and to place pressure on British exhibitors to prioritise indigenous productions.[49]

One of the earliest projects the BNFL were involved with was the Romance of History series in 1922, which provides an important context for *The Loves of Mary, Queen of Scots* (released the following year). The programme consisted of twelve short films, produced by the British & Colonial Film Company and distributed by Incorporated British Renters, Ltd under the auspices of the BNFL (Figure 14.7).[50] In a sentiment reminiscent of MacCormack's coveting of *Birth of a Nation*, *The Times* reported 'this series deals with events mostly drawn from English history and comprises episodes which prove to be epoch-making for the Countries in which they occurred'.[51] The trade press elaborated further on the historical aims of the project:

> Following upon the recent discussions in the Press concerning the possibility of representing authentic historical events on the screen, the B. and C. Kine. Co., Ltd. [British & Colonial Film Company], has decided to produce a series of one- and two-reel historical episodes. These, it is claimed, will be reconstructed from the actual records of the period, and every effort is to be made to ensure accuracy and to avoid irrelevance, while attention will be centred upon moving incident and story appeal, rather than spectacular embellishment.[52]

---

[47] Olly Gruner, '"Good Business, Good Policy, Good Patriotism": The British Film Weeks of 1924', *Historical Journal of Film, Radio and Television* 32 (2012) no. 1: 43.
[48] 'Plans of the League', *Kinematograph Weekly*, 17 November 1921, p. 52.
[49] This involved a rejection of the blind- and block-booking system. To book a single high-wprofile American production, British exhibitors were typically forced to blind-book an entire programme of American films from the distributor. Many of the other films in the programme were of questionable merit or were older productions, but nevertheless helped to solidify the American film industry's grasp on foreign markets.
[50] 'Co-operative Renting', *Kinematograph Weekly*, 28 September 1922, p. 74.
[51] Untitled, *The Times*, 29 June 1922 (quoted in *Kinematograph Weekly*, 5 October 1922, p. 32).
[52] 'The Romance of History', *Kinematograph Weekly*, 23 March 1922, p. 50.

This focus on authenticity echoes the rhetoric surrounding Walter West's failed production of *Mary Queen of Scots*. Unlike West though, the producers did not attempt to compete with their American counterparts in terms of scale, opting instead to express a subtle disdain of 'spectacular embellishment'.

With the Romance of History series, we see the beginnings of an essentialist 'British' film, one that is distinct from its American counterparts. The opening film of the series was *Mary, Queen of Scots* (1922), produced by George Ridgwell and Edwin Greenwood, and starring Kathleen Nesbit and Reginald Bach (see Figure 14.8).[53] The national press noted with approval its 'devotion to fact' and 'simplicity'.[54] This focus on historical accuracy strengthens the purported educational and national value of the series, whilst the reference to romance expands the breadth of appeal. The *Dundee Courier* exploits these qualities to build a dichotomy between British and American productions:

> British pictures have set out to raise the taste of their public, and in the majority of them is to be found that vein of romanticism which makes a welcome change from the cynical materialism characteristic of Uncle Sam's products.[55]

The producers of the Romance of History series learned from Walter West's failure, and instead of competing toe-to-toe with high-profile American productions, a supposedly superior, essentially British product was crafted – one with a perceived authenticity and moral uplift, where epic scale (or 'cynical materialism') was discarded. The one-reel *Mary, Queen of Scots* was endorsed precisely for these qualities, and in many ways set the blueprint for the eight-reel 7,684ft production of *The Loves of Mary, Queen of Scots*.[56]

The BNFL's British Film Weeks were on a much larger scale than the Romance of History series. As well as lobbying for economic changes to the rental system, the project sought to reinstate an imperial spirit in cinema screens across Britain and the British Empire. A high-profile luncheon was organised in the Banqueting Hall of the Hotel Victoria to inaugurate the programme. The guest of honour was the Prince of Wales, who was reportedly joined by 'five hundred representatives of the Trade, famous statesmen, novelists, artists, journalists, actors, and actresses'.[57] Other speakers included J. Ramsay MacDonald, MP (Leader of the Opposition) and Reginald Victor Wilson (a senator from

---

[53] 'Ye Owners and Controllers Incorporated British Renters Ltd', *Kinematograph Weekly*, 5 October 1922, p. 34.
[54] Untitled, *Daily Mail*, 30 March 1922 (quoted in *Kinematograph Weekly*, 5 October 1922, p. 32).
[55] 'British Films on their Mettle', *Dundee Courier*, 6 February 1924, p. 4.
[56] 'Films Passed by Censor', *Kinematograph Weekly*, 13 December 1923, p. 74; 'Trade Show Offers of the Past Month', *Kinematograph Weekly*, 6 December 1923, p. 77.
[57] 'Great Send Off for British Film Week', *Kinematograph Weekly*, 15 November 1923, pp. 2–5.

Figure 14.7 Full-page advertisement for the Romance of History series, printed by *Kinematograph Weekly* in 1922 (5 October 1922, p. 31). The one-reel *Mary Queen of Scots* is included in the programme (represented by the thistle to the right), and stars Kathleen Nesbit and Reginald Bach
Reproduced by kind permission of the Syndics of Cambridge University Library (classmark NPR.B.415)

South Australia). In his opening address, the Prince of Wales made the ideological and imperial ambitions of the programme abundantly clear:

> Film was an important factor in modern life, it was an instrument which played on the heart of the world. Its wealth, nobly used, was incalculable and limitless. Millions daily were amused and impressed by films. Millions of people who could not even read were affected or disaffected by films, all colours and creeds throughout the universe were affected. There was no other power which had such a universal pull . . . A nation with no films of its own at the present day was inarticulate in the world's sense. This simple entertainment of the people had much to do with the destiny of the Empire.[58]

[58] Ibid.

Figure 14.8 Film still from *Mary, Queen of Scots* (1922) (*Kinematograph Weekly*, 5 October 1922, p. 32) Reproduced by kind permission of the Syndics of Cambridge University Library

The film chosen to inaugurate the British Film Weeks was *The Loves of Mary, Queen of Scots*, produced by Denison Clift, under contract with Ideal Films, Ltd (Figure 14.9). The trade press enthused that 'no better film could have been chosen to inaugurate the British Film Week series'.[59] The *Western Daily Press* claimed 'in its story, as well as in its employment of the finest resources of the British studios, it is . . . a representative national picture'.[60] Press reports were keen to present an image of a unified nation: the *Hull Daily Mail* stated 'happily the religious upheaval which was of the time, so closely following the Reformation was not even introduced', whilst *Kinematograph Weekly* described James I's coronation in the film as symbolising 'the healing of the feud between the two countries' [England and Scotland].[61] A rampant jingoism was actively

---

[59] E. W. B., 'History on Screen. Fay Compton as Mary Stuart', *Kinematograph Weekly*, 6 November 1923, p. 7.
[60] 'Loves of Mary Queen of Scots', *Western Daily Press*, 17 Mary 1924, p. 11.
[61] 'Historical Drama Screened', *Hull Daily Mail*, 12 August 1924, p. 4; 'Long Shots and Close-Ups', *Kinematograph Weekly*, 31 August 1922, p. 32.

encouraged, with exhibitors being celebrated for 'flag-waving and the beating of the drums'.[62] *The Loves of Mary, Queen of Scots* was a distinctly national film.

The Loves of Mary, Queen of Scots built on the essentialist qualities of a 'British' film, propounded beforehand by West's *Mary, Queen of Scots* and *Romance of History*. There is a sustained focus on the perceived authenticity of the film and its educational value. The trade press praised Clift's 'careful and exhaustive research into all the historic facts connected with the story', which involved searching 'through all the official records at the British Museum', whereupon the script was scrutinised by 'two or three of the leading historical experts'.[63] Fay Compton was cast as Mary, being purportedly 'fortunate enough to possess a physiognomic resemblance to the tragic Queen . . . the actress's forehead and nose . . . phenomenally like the original'.[64] The *Hull Daily Mail* enthused of 'wild battle scenes, enacted almost on the same spots as these which really formed history are witnessed', and the *Nottingham Evening Post* rhapsodised about the use of 'actual relics', rather than 'mere studio imitations'.[65] All of this amounted to the film being described as a 'historical film which will appeal to all students of English history', with the aim 'not to teach history, but to make it' [before viewers' eyes].[66]

The film first depicts Mary in France, where she is mourning the passing of her betrothed boy-husband François II. This is portentously described as her 'first tragedy'. Mary is dressed in white, and stands against the dark interiors and black dress worn by Catherine de' Medici. Catherine questions Mary's fitness to be queen and warns her that she is 'only a passionate woman! To rule a Kingdom you must crush human desires, even love.' Catherine's stern bearing is set against that of the more expressive and emotional Mary. Encouraged by a cardinal to claim her heritage as queen of England as well as queen of Scotland, Mary responds, declaring that she will be 'Queen of England!! I shall seek my destiny!' The intertitles that are a staple of the silent film are important in *The Loves of Mary, Queen of Scots* because not only do they provide information relevant to forthcoming images, they also anticipate Mary's destiny and take a clear position on her character: 'With characteristic impulsiveness Mary at once despatched an ambassador to her cousin, Queen Elizabeth, to arrange a safe despatch to Scotland. And thus the political tragedy began.' The portrayal of Mary in this film conforms to the established gendered history that sets her in

---

[62] 'British Film Week', *The Bioscope*, 7 February 1924, p. 34.

[63] '*Mary Queen of Scots*. Denison Clift to Produce Historical Drama', *Kinematograph Weekly*, 24 November 1921, p. 67.

[64] Ibid.

[65] 'Historical Drama Screened', *Hull Daily Mail*, p. 4; 'Freeing Exhibitors from US "Bondage"', *Nottingham Evening Post*, 10 November 1921, p. 3.

[66] 'Public Amusements', *Torquay Times, and South Devon Advertiser*, 6 June 1924, p. 12; 'Pavilion', *Torquay Times, and South Devon Advertiser*, 30 May 1924, p. 12.

Figure 14.9 Production still from *The Loves of Mary, Queen of Scots* (1923), printed in the *Daily Mirror* (4 February 1924, p. 5) in support of the British Film Weeks
With thanks to The British Newspaper Archive (www.britishnewspaperarchive.co.uk)

poor relation to Elizabeth who is described as 'a born ruler, [who] had the heart of a man, not a woman'.

The film is based predominantly in Scotland and exploits the rich visual potential and symbolism of historical locations that featured in Mary's life such as Holyrood Palace, Borthwick Castle, Stirling Castle (see Figure 14.10) and Loch Leven. Despite this authentication the political claims of Mary and of Catholic Scotland are granted very little narrative space within the film. As Mary leaves France her destination is described as 'alien in its life and religion' from 'Edinburgh – stark sentinel of the land of political hatreds and religious fanaticism'. The political machinations of the earl of Moray and what the film refers to as 'the secret league' outmanoeuvre Mary throughout. Her marriage to Lord Darnley, while providing her with a son and heir, does little to strengthen her authority. Darnley is described as 'weak, vicious and dissolute', the antithesis of Bothwell. The lack of engagement with Mary's Catholic allies in Scotland means that she succumbs to her next 'love' via the romantic attentions and protection of Bothwell, as the intertitle unambiguously confirms: 'mistaking Bothwell's sensual passion for love and overcome by his brutal energy Mary impulsively surrendered herself'.

Fay Compton's performance as 'the lovely and 'ill-fated Queen' is complemented by relatively long takes and restrained cutting, but she remains an emotional and somewhat romanticised victim.[67] The liberal-leaning newspaper *The Daily News* pointedly expressed the wish that 'Denison Clift the producer and writer of the scenario had given us more the real Mary and not made her quite such a puppet. Film audiences ought to be told, for instance, why Mary proclaimed herself Queen of England, Ireland and Scotland.'[68] Mary's earlier marriage of convenience to Lord Darnley yields an heir to the throne that she desired. Elizabeth, played by Compton's sister Ellen, enjoys a much lesser, contained screen presence, and after approving her cousin Mary's execution, she concedes that 'she was a woman and I am but a Queen'.

The 'Britishness' of the film is intensified by frequent comparisons with its American counterparts. The trade press reported 'the picture has spaciousness of canvas, it moves with well-ordered sequences, and has none of that effect of bustle which mars most of the American historical films', whilst a local newspaper made a more implicit comparison: 'the story moves from incident to incident with scrupulous directness, dispensing with all the embroidery and "fanfaronade" that usually mar pictures of this kind'.[69] This dichotomy moves beyond formal characterising, to develop a moralistic and classist tone. E. A. Baugnan of the *Daily News (London)* disdainfully referred to America's 'half-educated flappers', and claimed they would fail to see the value of the film.[70] The *Dundee Courier* adopted a similar rhetoric, stating that there was a 'moral astigmatism about the American pictures', due to catering for 'incompletely educated classes in the States', before lamenting the effect of this 'moral poison' in Britain via film imports.[71] Here we see the dark underbelly of the utopian vision of unifying the nation through film, as it comes with an overtly didactic, moralistic, misogynistic and elitist precondition.

Despite the overwhelming jingoism that accompanied *The Loves of Mary, Queen of Scots*, criticisms sneaked through the cracks, and it ultimately failed in its ambition to reinvigorate the British industry. A reviewer for *Kinematograph Weekly* stated that the 'the story line is not strong . . . the action is jerky and gives little indication of the passage of time . . . [and] there has been little or no attempt to increase the story value beyond the facts'.[72] The *Oxford Chronicle and Reading Gazette* complained that the film was 'rather austere', whilst *The Bioscope* bemoaned 'characters whose identities one is scarcely able to grasp', and bordered on lampooning the film by pondering 'surely Elizabeth did not wear her

[67] 'British Films on their Mettle', *Dundee Courier*, p. 4.
[68] E. W. B., 'History on Screen', p. 7.
[69] Ibid.; 'Whiteladies Cinema', *Western Daily Press*, 20 May 1924, p. 3.
[70] E. A. Baugnan, 'Fine Acting in British Films', *Daily News (London)*, 12 November 1923, p. 9.
[71] 'British Films on their Mettle', *Dundee Courier*, p. 4.
[72] 'Reviews of the Week', *Kinematograph Weekly*, 8 November 1923, p. 54.

Figure 14.10 Denison Clift on set at Stirling Castle, filming *The Loves of Mary, Queen of Scots* (1923) (*Kinematograph Weekly*, 20 September 1923, p. 60) Reproduced by kind permission of the Syndics of Cambridge University Library (classmark NPR.B.415)

crown so persistently'.[73] Aside from these shortcomings in the film itself, Olly Gruner astutely argues that the British Film Weeks 'exemplified what was, and so often is, the negative effects of promoting a "national" culture: the interests of a select few were catered for, and the many ignored ... it was a "British" organisation in an extremely narrow sense of the word'.[74] The project was a failure in the colonies, too – by 1925, politicians were lamenting the dismal 1 per cent of British films shown on Empire screens.[75] In what almost seems like a definitive mark to punctuate BNFL's demise, and a conflicted acknowledgement

---

[73] 'Mary Queen of Scots', *Oxford Chronicle and Reading Gazette*, 2 May 1924, p. 23; 'The Loves of Mary Queen of Scots', *The Bioscope*, 8 November 1923, pp. 63–64.
[74] Gruner, '"Good Business, Good Policy, Good Patriotism"', p. 51.
[75] Ibid.

of America's dominance, the *Kinematograph Weekly* printed an article entitled 'Denison Clift to Produce for Fox', reporting:

> Having now put the final touches to the big Ideal production, *[The Loves of] Mary, Queen of Scots*, Denison Clift sails to-day (Thursday) for California, where he will produce for Fox, under contract recently signed by cable, a series of important pictures on a handsome scale.[76]

Conclusion

By the early 1920s, there was an emerging idea and critical mobilisation of what Britain's national cinema should be. In Andrew Higson's conceptualisation of national cinema, he argues that what is often at stake is a concern with what films' audiences are watching – how many foreign films, especially American films were in distribution within a particular nation-state.[77] In the decades following *The Loves of Mary, Queen of Scots* we see this 'Americanisation' growing in stature, epitomised by RKO's *Mary of Scotland* (1936), starring Katherine Hepburn and Fredric March. The film's flagrant appropriation and distortion of British history prompted a parliamentary debate, in which a motion to censor historical films was discussed. The motion was dismissed due to the impracticality of administering such a scheme, but it does point towards the very real anxieties the establishment felt about historical representation and national identity.[78] Repeatedly, since 1895, filmic versions of Mary Stuart have embodied this anxiety.

Over the course of this chapter, seven filmic productions of Mary Stuart have been discussed, spanning from 1895 to 1923. Each production reflects divergent national concerns, specific to time and place. We see an evolution of historicity and character portrayal, from the Punch-and-Judy-esque *The Execution of Mary, Queen of Scots*, to the sober and desperately 'British' *The Loves of Mary, Queen of Scots*. These productions embody the fascination Mary Stuart continued to hold, since still more could be discussed, albeit many remained unrealised.

In 1911, Gaumont produced the stencil-coloured *Marie Stuart et Rizzio*, whilst in 1912 Éclair released *The Favourite of Mary Queen of Scots* at 1,250ft, which was described as 'a sumptuous historical, grandly staged and acted. Éclair quality throughout.'[79] In 1915, the London-based distributor Artons Ltd was marketing a further Gaumont production entitled *Mary, Queen of Scots*, running at 910ft,

---

[76] 'Denison Clift to Produce for Fox', *Kinematograph Weekly*, 4 October 1923, p. 57.
[77] Andrew Higson, *Waving the Flag: Constructing a National Cinema in Britain* (Oxford, 1995), p. 5.
[78] 'Historical Films and Censorship', *Kinematograph Weekly*, 17 December 1936, p. 20.
[79] *Marie Stuart et Rizzio* has been newly acquired by the NLS for preservation, and is now viewable on site; 'Éclair', *Kinematograph Weekly*, 28 March 1912, p. 1224.

whilst The Pearl Film Service (also based in London) had a coloured version at 875ft.[80] In 1927, a German version entitled *Mary Stuart* was released, directed by Friedrich Feher and shot in Berlin. In 1933, Gaumont-British printed a full-page advertisement for their version of *Mary, Queen of Scots*, due to be filmed at Shepherd's Bush Studios. It was set to be directed by Victor Saville (who had reportedly read sixteen biographies in preparation), and to star Madeleine Carroll.[81] In 1934, British National Films scheduled *Mary, Queen of Scots*, for production at Ealing Studios.[82] In 1938, Warner released *This England*, a 963ft film that told 'the tragic story of Mary Queen of Scots, from the time of her last marriage until her abdication and flight from Scotland'.[83] *The Heart of the Queen* was directed by Walter Haag and shot in Berlin in 1940, acting as an anti-English propaganda film. In 1946, the British trade press reported that Carl Dreyer was to follow up *Day of Wrath* (1943) with *Mary Stuart* – he was actively working on a script at the time of the report.[84] In 1946, David Lean was set to direct *The Gay Galliard* – shooting was scheduled to begin immediately after *Great Expectations* (1946). It was billed as 'Margaret Irwin's love story of Mary, Queen of Scots and the Earl of Bothwell', and 'a record of the violent days in Scottish history'.[85] In 1957, ambitions for *The Gay Galliard* were revived by The Rank Organisation, which aimed to produce it at Pinewood Studios in Technicolor.[86] In 1956, Figaro, Inc. announced plans for an 'original screen story by Francis Winwar based on Elizabeth I of England and Mary, Queen of Scots', in conjunction with United Artists.[87] There were thus a plethora of further visions of Mary Stuart on film, whether realised or not, but we will stop here. With each new production, the relevance of Mary Stuart to contemporary society has been renewed and transformed, and the pliability and elusiveness of her legacy strengthened.

---

[80] 'Artons Ltd', *Kinematograph Weekly*, 17 June 1915, p. lxxxiv; 'The Pearl Film Service', *Kinematograph Weekly*, 3 February 1916, pp. xlii–xliii.

[81] Advertisement, *Kinematograph Weekly*, 23 November 1933, p. 50C; P. L. Mannock, 'Saville Up North', *Kinematograph Weekly*, 26 October 1933, p. 43.

[82] '*Cecil Rhodes* Not to be Made by British National', *Kinematograph Weekly*, 15 November 1934, p. 1; 'British National Films', *Kinematograph Weekly*, 11 October 1934, p. 5.

[83] 'Warner', *Kinematograph Weekly*, 31 March 1938, p. 49.

[84] 'About People', *Kinematograph Weekly*, 19 December 1946, p. 321.

[85] 'Scottish History on the Screen', *Kinematograph Weekly*, 28 June 1945, p. 31.

[86] Untitled, *Kinematograph Weekly*, 3 January 1957, p. 21; 'Pinewood', *Kinematograph Weekly*, 2 October 1947, p. v.

[87] 'Wagner joins Figaro to Produce for a UA Release', *Kinematograph Weekly*, 18 October 1956, p. 15.

FIFTEEN

Long Live the Queen: The Afterlife of Mary, Queen of Scots in Contemporary Visual Culture

Daniel Fountain and Alicia Hughes

Introduction

From subtle and nuanced to kitschy and outlandish, the cultural afterlife of Mary, Queen of Scots is varied and complex. The many dimensions of Mary and her story – Catholic martyr, tragic queen, Romantic heroine – invite creative experimentation and offer artists a vehicle through which to explore contemporary issues, particularly those relating to gender and identity. Helen Flockhart's series of seventeen paintings for the 2018 exhibition *Linger Awhile* (Arusha Gallery) depict key moments in Mary's life, reinterpreting her narrative and reimagining historical sources with rich symbolism to understand Mary as both queen and woman. In 2012, multi-media artist Rachel Maclean used Mary as inspiration for her acclaimed work *The Queen* (2013). This was part of a series entitled *I HEART SCOTLAND* that was created in response to the 2014 Scottish Referendum for Independence, in which Maclean explored Scottish national identity and the nation's romantic histories through a contemporary lens, drawing simultaneously on baroque motifs and twenty-first-century tourist kitsch. In 2021, the Scottish-born, New York City-based drag queen and performance artist Rosé referenced Mary explicitly in a series of performances that reinterpreted the historical figure in comedic, glamorous and dramatic fashion. For each of these artists, Mary acts as a historical touchstone through which to explore extremely different contemporary issues specific to each of their artistic practices and experiences.

This chapter takes the work of Flockhart, Maclean and Rosé as a prompt to consider how Mary's cultural afterlife manifests in work by artists in the image-driven twenty-first-century. It will think across a range of media including oil painting, digital media and performance art, and use the concept of 'refraction' to explore how contemporary artists draw on and re-imagine Mary's iconography to speak to contemporary issues of gender and identity. Evolving from the fields of memory studies, literary studies and literary history, in visual studies 'refraction' – a word taken from physics – critically engages with ways of seeing and knowing and the referential transmission of ideas and creation of art across time, geographical space and media.[1] Artistic interpretations of Mary mirror the preoccupations of societies in different historical periods, but these variations have themselves evolved and refracted over time, directly responding to and 'bouncing off' other 'Marys'. Just as light and energy waves change direction upon contact with the new media through which they are transmitted, so too has 'Mary' been altered and re-imagined against the backdrop of multiple other 'Marys' and other cultural sources and questions. The analysis in this chapter is informed by original artist interviews with Flockhart, Maclean and Rosé and will show how different types of layering, parody and the act of performing Mary offers a particularly twenty-first-century lens through which Mary is refracted, and which allows for creative re-imaginings of some of the most enduring aspects of the queen's story and legacy. This chapter thus considers how and why Mary not only endures but thrives in twenty-first-century visual culture.

Mary, Queen of Scots in visual culture

Before moving on to a focused analysis of works by Flockhart, Maclean and Rosé, we must first identify some key characteristics that artists have long found compelling in relation to Mary, and not just in the contemporary imagination. What is it about Mary's story that captivates and inspires artistic re-imagining?

In the eighteenth century, Mary was no longer a figure of recent history, but one rooted firmly in the past. She had been used in political propaganda, first by the Stuarts and their critics, and then by the Jacobite cause, which sought to restore a Catholic Stuart monarch to the throne.[2] In the late eighteenth century, the figure of Mary had transitioned in popular consciousness to a historical figure whose character and life were examined and defended in antiquarian histories of Scotland. These histories sought to discover the 'truth' about Mary

---

[1] For refraction in the field of memory studies, see Michael Rothberg, *Multidirectional Memory* (Stanford, CA, 2009); and Ann Rigney, 'Transforming Memory and the European Project', *New Literary History* 43 (2012): 607–28; and Rigney, 'Remaking Memory and the Agency of the Aesthetic', *Memory Studies* 14 (2021) no. 1: 10–23. For refraction in visual studies, see 'Introduction to "Refraction"', in *Refract: An Open Access Visual Studies Journal*, 1 (2018) no. 1: 7.

[2] See Murray Pittock, 'Treacherous Objects: Towards a Theory of Jacobite Material Culture', *Journal for Eighteenth-Century Studies* 34 (2011) no. 1: 39–63; Cailean Gallagher, 'Lies, Liberty, and the Fall of the Stuarts: James Steuart's Commentary on Hume's *History of England*', *History of European Ideas* 46 (2020) no. 4: 438–57; and Gallagher, 'Notes on Hume's *History* (James Steuart, 1760–1765)', *History of European Ideas* 46 (2020) no. 4: 458–537; Jayne Elizabeth Lewis, *Mary Queen of Scots: Romance and Nation* (London, 1998).

and rescue her from previous interpretations that cast her simply as either an innocent victim or an adulterous and treasonous villain.

It is within this context that the neo-classical artist Gavin Hamilton made the grand oil painting, *The Abdication of Mary, Queen of Scots* that was commissioned by James Boswell (an eighteenth-century author and biographer), painting it over the course of ten years between 1765 and 1775 (see Figure I.1). Mary is shown imprisoned in Lochleven Castle, being forced to sign her abdication in favour of her infant son James. Surviving correspondence between Hamilton and Boswell highlights their desire to identify the most accurate sources available to help create the depiction of Mary on canvas.[3] Hamilton researched Mary's true likeness, but the painting is a romantic composite representation of the queen, wherein Hamilton sought to present an idealised version of his subject as a 'beauty in distress'. There are many dramatic moments in Mary's life, but Hamilton and Boswell forgo depicting early successes such as the rebellions she put down, or personal misfortunes such as the murder of Lord Darnley and her abduction by the earl of Bothwell. In keeping with the conventions of eighteenth-century history painting, they choose instead to depict the moment of moral and political crisis at which, in 1567, Mary was forced to abdicate and sign away her claim to the crown, an act that she maintained she had not done willingly. Moments of moral crisis in a narrative are a key feature of grand history painting and speak to the historical moment of an artwork's creation.[4]

Similarly, popular twenty-first-century depictions of Mary reflect contemporary societal concerns. For example, as Elena Woodacre argues in her discussion of representations of queenship in popular film, 'each generation has overlaid its own interests and values on the lives of queens reinterpreting them to fit with the societal values and preconceptions of their era'.[5] Recent popular depictions include the CW television series *Reign* (2013–17), which follows the young queen during her early years at the French and later Scottish courts. Josie Rourke's film *Mary Queen of Scots* (2018) presents a strong-willed queen returning to her homeland determined to rule despite an entrenched patriarchy and includes queer romance and actors of colour. There has been a significant shift away from previous privileging of a 'love story' between Mary and Lord Bothwell and historical narratives of religious conflict towards more current

---

[3] See Lewis, *Mary Queen of Scots*, chapter 5, particularly the discussion of Hamilton's painting on pp. 113–19; and 'Hamilton's *Abdication*, Boswell's Jacobitism and the Myth of Mary Queen of Scots', ELH 64 (1997) no. 4: 1069–90; Helen Smailes and Duncan Thomson, *The Queen's Image* (Edinburgh, 1987). For the results of recent provenance research on Hamilton's painting by Anne Dulau-Beveridge, see the object file for the painting (GLAHA:43874) in The Hunterian archive. See also Chapters 1 and 2, this volume.

[4] The literature on 'history painting' in the history of art is vast.

[5] Elena Woodacre, 'Early Modern Queens of Screens: Victors, Victims, Villians, Virgins, and Viragoes', in *Premodern Rules and Postmodern Viewers: Gender, Sex and Power in Popular Culture*, ed. Janic North, Larl C. Alvestad and Elena Woodacre (Cham, 2018), p. 27.

questions about gender politics, sexual violence and racial representation.[6] Mary's Catholic martyrdom is no longer the narrative anchor or cipher for her reign's 'weakness' and religious division. Instead, it is Mary the woman who is brought to the foreground and narratives which might have historically been suppressed are now brought into focus.

These representations of Mary through contemporary film and TV have, quite literally, served to construct revised narratives around Mary's life with which contemporary audiences are now most familiar – queen, martyr, victim, but also woman, daughter, friend, wife and cousin. The stylised representations, through costume, makeup and *mise-en-scène*, have also built upon Mary's historical iconography – fiery red hair, pious dress, crucifix – to make visual and emotional connections with new audiences. These heavily stylised twin elements proved ripe for unpicking by the likes of Flockhart, Maclean and Rosé, to name but a few. It is to their work that we now turn.

Subtle yet seditious: Helen Flockhart's symbolism and layering

In 2018, the Glasgow School of Art-trained painter Helen Flockhart unveiled a series of seventeen paintings entitled *Linger Awhile* that were inspired by the events and personal tragedies that marked Mary's life. These include her marriage to François II of France; her escape from Lochleven Castle following her imprisonment, forced abdication and miscarriage of twins; her long imprisonment in England; and her execution. Unlike nineteenth-century artists whose depictions of Mary at key moments in her life take on a moralising tone that is characteristic of Victorian painting and wider ideas about ideal womanhood, Flockhart is interested in contemporary attitudes towards these moments in Mary's story. Historical understandings of Mary have often been binary with little room for complexity regarding Mary's identity and experience over time. As Flockhart observes, 'this polarisation of woman as either whore or virgin, victim or temptress[,] is still very much present and pertinent to the portrayal and perceptions of women today'.[7] The artist paints Mary in her own likeness (like Mary, Flockhart has red hair) but these are not self-portraits. She draws upon and subverts traditional iconography associated with Mary (such as the red hair, ruff and even the red bodice she wore to her execution). Archival sources and images (original, digital and reproductions in historiographies) are refracted in different directions through Flockhart's rich tapestry of symbolism and within

---

[6] See, for example, Jennifer M. DeSilva and Emily K. McGuire, 'Revising Mary Queen of Scots: from Protestant Persecution to Patriarchal Struggle', *Journal of Religion & Film* 25 (2021) no. 1, DOI: 10.32873/uno.dc.jrf.25.1.003; and Shelley Anne Galpin, 'Leaning in Or Opting Out? Women's Choices in *Little Women* and *Mary Queen of Scots*', *Feminist Media Studies* (2021): 1–14. DOI: 10.1080/14680777.2021.1979070.

[7] Helen Flockhart, artist notes.

Figure 15.1 Helen Flockhart, *Linger Awhile*, 2018, oil on linen, 102 × 152cm
Courtesy of Helen Flockhart and Arusha Gallery

the series of paintings itself. Altering our perception of the sources, Flockhart blurs and re-imagines the historical with the modern; her 'Marys' shift in and out of focus just as, despite the rich body of knowledge about the queen and the material culture associated with her, Mary the historical figure is never quite knowable.

Prior to beginning what evolved into a series of paintings, Flockhart's artistic process required in-depth research into the historiography of her subject. Responding to Jenny Wormald's narrative of failure in the life of the queen, Flockhart's approach to Mary is sympathetic and sensitive.[8] Her artistic process begins with extensive research into historical representations before harnessing an essential core of an idea in small, 'scratchy' sketches in small notepads. These ideas evolve via larger sketches in oil pastels or oil paintings on canvas.[9] Following this, her paintings are built up meticulously, layer by layer, technically and symbolically. For example, the painting *Linger Awhile* (2018) is the largest in the series and depicts Mary locked in an innocent embrace with her first husband, the *dauphin* of France, François II, whom she married when she was 15 and he was 14 in 1558 (see Figure 15.1). The pair, who were brought up together at the French court and enjoyed a close relationship before marriage, lie curled towards each other in the painting, engulfed in a cloud of textured lace from Mary's petticoat. The white fabric evokes Mary's gown on her

---

[8] Jenny Wormald, *Mary Queen of Scots: A Study in Failure* (London, 1988).
[9] Arusha Gallery, Helen Flockhart artist film, dir. by Ewan Marshall https://www.arushagallery.com/press/49-video-helen-flockhart, accessed 21 September 2023; see 0:36.

wedding; white was an unconventional choice for a bride in France in the sixteenth century, but Mary insisted, and contemporary accounts tell us that the joyous young queen made a striking vision to her new subjects.[10] The title of Flockhart's painting is taken from a section of *Faust*, the two-part play in which the eighteenth-century German dramatist Goethe tells the story of a man who sells his soul to the devil.[11] This transactional moment was a starting point for Flockhart, who wondered what Mary would have given to remain in this idyllic stage of life, given all the turbulent years that followed.

Along the top of *Linger Awhile* there is a small panel interlacing the initials of Mary and François, pointing to their shared future that disappeared in such a short space of time. The proportions of the painting give the sense that François could be Mary's child; in life, Mary's spirit outshone that of François, who had a reputation as a sickly child.[12] Despite this, there was genuine affection between the couple and Mary was devastated following his death (and with it the loss of her future as queen consort of France). As Jan Patience has described, the 'tender scene evokes a sense of peace and comfort, while bright tumbled wild flowers recall the abandonment and carelessness of youth'.[13] The historical episode provides a departure point, to offer an imagined contemplative and emotive space in which the 15-year-old girl grieves for her young friend and husband. It is a historical moment in a sense, but one that prioritises human emotion rather than moral choice.

Flockhart's paintings are layered with iconography and patterns that draw on archival material, transforming them into symbols. Repeated motifs such as monograms, initials and flowers are heavy with historical narratives and are woven into the fabrics of Mary's dresses, echoing Mary's own needlework practice, which Flockhart considers politically subversive. Mary embroidered during her imprisonment when she was manoeuvring to free herself and during political meetings where she gave, as Flockhart describes, 'the impression of a passive female presence, all the while being a shrewd and attentive witness'.[14] The cryptic symbols that Mary used to convey her own wry take on life resonate with Flockhart:

> As an artist I also like to smuggle in symbols and expression in the details of my paintings, in beadwork, pattern and texture, which render symbols about female sexuality and the human condition. I think this quiet expressionism is something which women have always done in craft in an under-the-radar way, quite different from the overt slash

---

[10] Fraser, *Mary Queen of Scots*.
[11] Johann Wolfgang von Goethe, *Faust* (Faust: a tragedy) trans. David Syme (Edinburgh and Leipzig, 1834).
[12] Fraser, *Mary Queen of Scots*; and Retha M. Warnicke, *Mary Queen of Scots* (Abingdon, 2006).
[13] Jan Patience, 'Artist Helen Flockhart's Compelling Works Tell Tragic Story of Mary, Queen of Scots', *The Herald*, 15 September 2018, accessed 10 January 2023.
[14] Helen Flockhart, artist notes. For Mary, Queen of Scots and her practice of embroidery, see Clare Hunter, *Embroidering Her Truth: Mary, Queen of Scots and the Language of Power* (London, 2022).

Figure 15.2 Helen Flockhart, *Lachrymose Window*, 2018, oil on board, 102 × 152cm
Courtesy of Helen Flockhart and Arusha Gallery

and gouge of male art, and I like the echo of what Mary was doing in her needlework being mirrored in my approach to my own work.[15]

In *Linger Awhile* we see intricate patterns of Scottish thistles, French *fleur de lys* and Tudor roses form in the lace of Mary's dress, symbolising the queen's familial and ancestral connections and providing a heavy portent for future events. In *Lachrymose Window* (2018) Mary's iconic white lace ruff is re-imagined at a reduced size that would be conservative and sedate if not for its screaming lemon colour, which shimmers transparently as light from a window to the left falls upon it (see Figure 15.2). Mary sits serenely and her blue-and-white

---

[15] Helen Flockhart, artist notes.

embroidered dress is packed with stories, including a crow to symbolise Reformation figurehead John Knox, and a dolphin for François. Also seen are images of a hare, which refers to Bothwell's coat of arms, symbolising lust, and a mermaid, symbolising a prostitute (as Debra Barrett-Graves notes).[16] These elements are taken from the inflammatory placard that emerged after Mary's wedding to Bothwell and are also repeated in Flockhart's *The Mermaid and The Hare* (2018). That union, which followed the assassination of Mary's second husband Lord Darnley, galvanised the queen's opponents and helped bring about her downfall. In *Lachrymose Window* Flockhart weaves into the fabric the voices of Mary (including several of her most famous mottos) and her critics: 'Wantons marry in the month of May'; 'an adulteress and a liar'; 'do not touch me or I will prick'; 'Sa Virtue M'atire'; the 'monstrous regiment of women'; 'a good neighbour, a dear sister'; and 'in my end is my beginning'. According to Arusha Gallery, '[w]earing her own legends, the images are so jumbled up it is impossible to tell facts from tales'.[17] Posed serenely in cavernous, castle-like interiors that speak simultaneously to Mary's historical imprisonment by her cousin and a psychological interiority, these competing narratives, voices and symbols swirl, embroidered onto the very fabric that confines Mary.

In contrast to the paintings that show the queen in interior spaces, Flockhart's nine portrait-style 'heads' within the series feature women connected to Mary, imagined in lush, natural enclosures that are rich in fruit and flowers. They include Mary of Guise (her mother), Elizabeth I (her cousin) and Philippa of Guelders (her great-grandmother). Again, historical documents (some of which date from Mary's time) provide motifs that are repeated on the subject's otherwise simple gowns: for example, in *I See and Keep Silent* (2018) (a saying associated with Elizabeth) Mary's green outfit bears multiple images taken from maps and locations in Scotland that have an association with the queen (see Figure 15.3). The images are overlaid with one another and woven into a rich tapestry in which spatial (and temporal) reference points jumble together, refracting in multiple directions.[18] In *Lover's Eye* (2018), inspired by Gerda Stevenson's poem

---

[16] See Debra Barrett-Graves's discussion of the portrayal of Mary in the Mermaid and Hare placard, in *The Emblematic Queen: Extra-Literary Representations of Early Modern Queenship* (New York, 2013), chapter 4, particularly pp. 69–70. The mermaid-siren was a symbol for prostitution in the early modern period. As Barrett-Graves notes, '[m]ermaids and sirens and their enervating effect on unsuspecting men who crossed their paths occur in many emblematic and literary works of the early modern period'.

[17] Arusha Gallery, Linger Awhile exhibition overview, https://www.arushagallery.com/exhibitions/30-linger-awhile-helen-flockhart/overview/, accessed 21 September 2023. See also Louise Elderton, 'By her Blood and Burnished Flame', in *Linger Awhile: Helen Flockhart* (Edinburgh, 2018).

[18] Thank you to Helen Flockhart for sharing the range of sources that were originally used in this painting. These include: https://maps.nls.uk/view/00001038; https://maps.nls.uk/view/74475427; https://maps.nls.uk/view/00001168, all accessed 21 September 2023 https://blog.nls.uk/map-of-the-month-edinburgh-in-1582/, accessed XX YYY ZZZZ.

Figure 15.3 Helen Flockhart, *I See and Keep Silent*, 2018, oil on board, 40 × 26cm
Courtesy of Helen Flockhart and Arusha Gallery

'The Abdication of Mary Queen of Scots' (2016), the repeated motif on the dress is the subject escaping Lochleven Castle, pushing a boat carrying two small figures – a reference to her miscarrying twins during her time at the castle (see Figure 15.4). Mary looks off to the side and holds up her hand from which dangles a lover's eye. Lover's eyes were a secret keepsake: people would have the eye of a loved one painted – a child, a lover, a husband – and wear it as a locket, ring or bracelet.[19] Flockhart paints the eye of Mary's son James, whom, after her imprisonment in Lochleven, Mary never saw again.

---

[19] See, for instance, Hanneke Grootenboer, 'Treasuring the Gaze: Eye Miniature Portraits and the Intimacy of Vision', *The Art Bulletin* 88 (2006) no. 3: 496–507.

Figure 15.4 Helen Flockhart, *Lover's Eye*, 2018, oil on board, 40 × 26cm
Courtesy of Helen Flockhart and Arusha Gallery

Most of the Marys in Flockhart's portraits are shown in profile, gazing steadfastly to the side, but the exception to this rule is found in a work called *Red Bodice* (2018), which depicts Mary at the very end of her life (see Figure 15.5). The painting takes its title from Mary's last moments in life, in which she wore a crimson undergown prior to being beheaded in front of an audience of noblemen at Fotheringhay Castle in England for her complicity in a plot to murder her cousin, Elizabeth I. Disrobed of her black gown, Mary revealed a crimson petticoat and bodice in her last moments before execution, an act of defiance and martyrdom. Flockhart's bodice is a deep red colour and the artist explains that

Figure 15.5 Helen Flockhart, *Red Bodice*, 2018, oil on board, 40 × 26cm
Courtesy of Helen Flockhart and Arusha Gallery

she 'added to her bodice a large, f**k-off corsage as a final gesture of defiance'.[20] Mary's life contained many betrayals, but this act of defiance is one that (as we will continue to see in the next sections of this chapter) inspires contemporary artists in different ways. These moments of assertion (whether openly or quietly defiant) resonate particularly with Flockhart because of the efforts that were made, as Flockhart says, to 'extinguish any trace of her', not only by imprisoning the queen but destroying her possessions after her death. While the original intention of these acts may have been to prevent Mary becoming queen of England and her possessions becoming relics imbued with religious and political power, these acts of erasure resonate in the twenty-first-century when women still endure a society

[20] Helen Flockhart, artist notes.

rife with misogyny and domestic abuse.[21] Flockhart's own features, including her red hair, provide a canvas on which Mary's narratives refract through the lens of rich symbolism, bouncing from the extensive historiography on Mary, to archival documents and to (and within) the paintings in the *Linger Awhile* series itself.

Ghostly glimmers and glitches: Rachel Maclean and 'Mary, Queen of Scots'

Just as female identity is a central concern for Flockhart, so too is it an important topic of investigation for Scottish multi-media artist Rachel Maclean. In her satirical film *The Lion and the Unicorn* (2012), from which the digital print *The Queen* (2013) spins off, the Scottish multi-media artist Rachel Maclean experiments with different dimensions of Mary to explore contemporary questions around female identity, Scottish heritage and national identity (see Figure 15.6). These works were part of a larger series commissioned and published by Edinburgh Printmakers in 2012 in response to the 2014 Scottish Referendum for Independence, and were displayed in an exhibition entitled 'I HEART

Figure 15.6 Rachel Maclean, *The Queen*, 2013, archival digital print, 50.5 × 40.5cm
Photo © Rachel Maclean

Figure 15.7 George Vertue, *Maria Scotorum Regina et Franciae Dotaria*, 1735, engraving, GLAHA:25597
Photo: The Hunterian, University of Glasgow

[21] There are countless other artistic representations of Mary in the contemporary imagination that respond to the queen's imprisonment and cultural erasure, and that also relate to notions of gender and identity, such as *Bower of Bliss* (2018), a short feminist retelling of Mary's imprisonment at Chatsworth House by contemporary artist Linder Sterling (known simply as Linder).

SCOTLAND'.[22] In her work, Maclean invokes a range of pop cultural references and creates an array of characters including contemporary and historical figures. She uses found audio and lip-syncs to it while wearing exaggerated costumes, leading to surreal scenes in which the historical and contemporary playfully come together. The 2012 film work includes Maclean's own performance as a queen who narrates the fantastical occasion on which a lion and a unicorn (symbolising Scotland and England and using audio from an interview between Jeremy Paxman and Alex Salmond) discuss the subject of oil and its role in financing Scottish independence.

In one sense the queen's bright auburn hair, her pale complexion, her lace cap and collar and prominently displayed crucifix make her instantly recognisable. However, Maclean's works are loaded with visual and gestural references (a practice that Maclean refers to as a maximalist approach) that make us question whether this queen is indeed Mary.[23] The visual iconography of the queen is present, but 'Mary's' dress is also draped in Union Jacks, a symbol of Great Britain, rather than the saltire of Scotland. In *The Lion and the Unicorn*, 'Mary' is ventriloquised, and speaks as Queen Elizabeth II, as if giving her annual televised Christmas message, from the library of Traquair House in the Scottish Borders (where Mary is rumoured to have spent a night at some point). 'Mary' later stands in front of the Bear Gates at Traquair House which, as the story goes, will not be opened until a Stuart monarch claims the crown. 'Mary' shifts in and out of focus as the film goes on, as audiences question whether the queen is indeed Mary, Queen of Scots. The representations of Mary appear ghostly and glitchy.

Mary's iconography and her fame as a historical female figure were part of what drew Maclean to the subject:

> There are few iconic Scottish figures who are historical or even contemporary who are women and who have this level of recognition . . . If you have grown up in Scotland, there is a good chance you will recognise an image of Mary, Queen of Scots, even if it is cartoonish or kitsch, so there is something there to play with because she is part of our cultural consciousness.[24]

---

[22] For the series and its 2013 exhibition, see Catriona McAra and David McCrone, *I HEART SCOTLAND: An Exhibition by Rachel Maclean* (Edinburgh, 2013).

[23] In a visual art context, maximalism describes labour-intensive practices that result in visually and referentially excessive works; a 'more is more' aesthetic. Maximalism is evident in a range of Maclean's art, which commonly appropriates compositions and formal properties of traditional renaissance or baroque paintings and tapestries, which are subverted and re-imagined through a contemporary lens, complete with a candy-coloured and saturated palette. For more on this in relation to Maclean's work see Sarah Neely and Sarah Smith, 'The Art of Maximal Ventriloquy: Femininity as Labour in the Films of Rachel Maclean', in *Women Artists, Feminism and the Moving Image*, ed. Lucy Reynolds (London, 2019), pp. 165–78, at p. 167.

[24] Artist interview with Alicia Hughes, 11 October 2022.

Maclean recalls learning about Mary, Queen of Scots in primary school, and one art class in which students crafted their own images of Mary, including cutting up white paper doilies to make lace caps for their pictures of the queen. The 'twenty-odd' Marys that covered the classroom wall at the end of the lesson gave Maclean a strong sense of the visual iconography of the Queen of Scots:

> Mary is visually iconic in a world where images take such a priority, so she has been able to endure. She is very easily reproducible in a way that, say, Robert the Bruce is not. She has a logo-like, brand-like image that is attached to her that can be easily simplified and transferred. Her endurance is about her as a visual symbol, which can take on different meaning and is part of why I was attracted to her; I could dress up as her and be recognised as her.[25]

Mary's visual iconography becomes blurry as Maclean plays not only with symbols of Scottishness and Britishness but also with baroque art-historical references and twenty-first-century tourist kitsch, realising Mary as 'logo' and 'brand'. In an accompanying digital print, titled *The Queen*, 'Mary' glances upward towards the heavens. Her expression and tears of ecstasy evoke previous historical paintings by seventeenth-century artists such as Guido Reni. The distinctive melodramatic emotion of baroque art speaks directly to Mary's evolution into both Catholic martyr and Romantic victim, even though it is re-imagined through digital art. Maclean describes how she is drawn to the extreme complexity of baroque art: 'It is overwrought to the point of being ridiculous. You feel unsettled by the complexity of it.'[26] However, rather than tears of religious devotion, Maclean's 'Mary' cries tears of North Sea oil in reference to the Scottish independence movement's devotion to the oil industry as a means of economic independence: religious martyrdom is transformed into political, nationalist martyrdom, which is also destabilised by its ridiculousness.

In addition to the allusions to baroque religious art, *The Queen* also has a compositional similarity with the eighteenth-century engraved portraits of Mary by George Vertue (see Figure 15.7).[27] Monochrome black and white is replaced with a highly saturated palette of purples, blues and reds. Mary is contained within the frame, but is now surrounded with the material trappings associated with twenty-first-century Scottish tourist culture. Tartan cloth is draped around the frame and a golf ball sits in the foreground. Instead of holding her crucifix (as in other representations of Mary as pious Catholic martyr), Mary

---

[25] Artist interview with Alicia Hughes, 11 October 2022.
[26] Artist interview with Alicia Hughes, 11 October 2022.
[27] See Steven Reid's discussion in the Introduction to this volume.

now clutches a golf club, perhaps humorously suggesting that the leisure sport of golf is the new religion of twenty-first-century Scotland. Here, Maclean not only points to the place of romanticised Scottish histories within twenty-first-century tourism (many of which have little or no basis in reality), but also plays with the power that we assign to the material belongings of historical figures. Precious objects in museums that have connections to Mary evoke wonder and awe and her connections to historic castles and houses in Scotland and England draw visitors from around the globe. As Maclean notes, 'people want that feeling of closeness to [Mary], to walk in her shoes, to see where she slept, to see her belongings, even when the links are dubious. She has a power that others don't have.'[28] The artist plays with this desire for relics and a search for the 'authentic' Mary in *The Queen*, but subverts it to emphasise that there is no sense of authenticity: the white dress 'Mary' dons is a second-hand wedding dress and the Union Jack tat that adorns her was chosen from the abundant selection in Poundland (thanks to the Jubilee of Queen Elizabeth II at the time of production). 'Mary' is blurred, unstable and, ultimately, unreachable.

Other examples of Scottish tourist kitsch abound in the image, including the tartan Tam O'Shanter cap which is worn by the grotesque, cadaverous/skeletal figure sporting a red beard and untamed eyebrows who intrudes into the frame and clutches at Mary's shoulder. In Vertue's engraving, the skeleton that similarly creeps into the frame is a *memento mori* who foresees Mary's death and reminds viewers of their moral obligations.[29] In Maclean's twenty-first-century print the skeleton takes on other possible interpretations. Is it John Knox, the misogynistic Protestant zealot who incited violence against the queen? Or is it intended to be another of the plethora of male characters in Mary's life who undermined her, plotted against her and betrayed her? This interpretation does not need to be limited to Mary's lifetime; what of the multitude of male authors who wrote of Mary's so-called crimes and failures in the centuries following her death? The possibilities are endless, intentionally confusing and darkly humorous. The colour palette may be playful and whimsical but the undertones are less so. Maclean's version can be heralded as a feminist (re-)interpretation, symbolically showing the men that tried to hold the queen back during her lifetime.

The visual iconography of Mary goes hand in hand with her story as a queen in a hostile, male-dominated society, and the many ways in which that story (and particularly its tragic elements) have been told and retold since her death

---

[28] Artist interview with Alicia Hughes, 11 October 2022.
[29] On the theme of *memento mori* and the *vanitas* still life see Kristine Koozin, *The Vanitas Still Lifes of Harmen Steenwyck: Metaphoric Realism* (Lampeter, 1990), pp. 7–83; Liana De Girolami Cheney, 'Dutch *Vanitas* Paintings: The Skull', in *The Symbolism of Vanitas in the Arts, Literature and Music. Comparative and Historical Studies*, ed. Liana De Girolami Cheney (Lampeter, 1992), pp. 113–76.

in 1587. The motivations behind the retellings and narrativisings of this historical female figure in a position of power are a subject of interest to Maclean:

> I am attracted to female figures in history who have been afforded power and the way that they are narrativised as failures or cautionary tales against female empowerment. Growing up in Scotland, Mary was the only [historical female] figure you were aware of, but you were aware most consciously of her failure, her demise and her tragedy. She is not, at least in popular consciousness, a heroic figure, so on some level I think I was attracted to that, and I wanted to do something that questioned it or subverted it.[30]

Mary's memorialisation is in a sense contradictory; she is a historical figure who has been canonised as a famous Scottish queen and yet the narratives of her personal and political 'failings' have become so sensationalised that the very process by which this has happened has become obscured. Artistic and literary interpretations of Mary and her story over the centuries since Mary's death are reflections of shifting political and societal attitudes and priorities at moments in history, but this process is not simply a mirroring (that would imply only a two-way, back-and-forth direction). Rather than that, Mary (the woman and the historical figure) is fractured and subsequently refracted in all directions.[31] The fracturing of female identity is particularly interesting to Maclean:

> Many of the characters in my work play with female identity in a way that is fractured. Characters are inconsistent and are being fractured through the lens of different perspectives or expectations of female identity. You don't even need to look too forensically at the historical reality but even in our collective consciousness there is a sense in which she represents victim or harlot or whore, which are all misogynistic perspectives on female identity, so it is interesting to dissect this. At some level, it is not about her, it is about what we project onto her.[32]

The instability of Maclean's Mary makes this refraction visible, with reference to multiple historical sources and contemporary questions.

Maclean's work explores Scottish national identity and the nation's romantic histories through a contemporary lens. In *Mary Queen of Scots: Romance and Nation*, Jayne Elizabeth Lewis considers Mary's name ('Mary, Queen of Scots') a 'tribal designation', one that identifies its referent not with a place but with a people.[33] For Lewis, this push and pull is fundamental to the relationship between Mary and the fiction of Britain, which merges a body of imaginative

---

[30] Artist interview with Alicia Hughes, 11 October 2022.
[31] 'Introduction to "Refraction"', p. 7.
[32] Artist interview with Alicia Hughes, 11 October 2022.
[33] Lewis, *Mary Queen of Scots*, p. 4.

expression and romance with the image and idea of the Queen of Scots.[34] With an over-the-top, baroque flair, Maclean explores the sense of power and absurdity in representations of Scottish national pride, asking 'What are the symbols that we attach to an idea of Scottishness? What do they mean? How malleable or ultimately empty are they?'[35] Ultimately, as she notes, '[i]t is not about her [Mary] but our sense of her'.[36] The role that history plays in forming our national identities and the blurriness and malleability of this process are of particular interest to Maclean:

> Realistically, national identity is something that is amalgamated through a large number of visual, iconographic references and many fuzzy versions of history. These come together to form a sense of self or a sense of nationhood. [In *The Lion and the Unicorn*] I wanted to play on this so that you are not taking something that is historically firm and accurate. You are playing with something that is intentionally confusing and blurry. Our identities are not fixed to objective facts or objective history.[37]

Blurring the boundaries of 'Mary' in *The Queen* and *The Lion and the Unicorn* and making the audience question what they are seeing and why they think they are seeing it is at the heart of Maclean's work: 'Artistically, there is something interesting about being ambiguous, in throwing something out and letting people come to their own understandings . . . confusion makes people question the baggage they are bringing to images or understandings'.[38]

Part of this confusion comes from Maclean's own performance techniques. She describes the act of 'performing Mary' as the creation of a character, rather than one of embodiment or self-portrait making: 'It is pretend. Imitating. It is the opposite of sincere acting style because there, intentionally, is not depth of emotion. It is the creation of a surface impression. It is not an embodiment but dressing up and pretending to be [Mary].'[39] The audience is kept on their toes, they are never allowed to lose themselves in the performance: 'There is always a shifting back and forth. It is unstable. "Me" always comes through. The audience is never allowed to be immersed.'[40] It is neither 'Mary' nor Maclean, but some sense of an enmeshed identity through which the artist's use of costume, props, makeup and green-screen technology produces a blurry, fuzzy and glitchy persona, and deliberately so.

---

[34] Lewis, *Mary Queen of Scots*, pp. 2–4.
[35] Artist interview with Alicia Hughes, 11 October 2022.
[36] Ibid.
[37] Ibid.
[38] Ibid.
[39] Ibid.
[40] Ibid.

Maclean's 'Mary' is a satirical representation in an age of digital art, that pokes fun at the romanticised myth of Mary within Scottish contemporary culture. Indeed, humour is a unique way in which Maclean plays with empowering her female characters. As the artist notes, '[t]here is something about humour that is traditionally in the realm of men, and particularly absurdist humour. There is something empowering about making a woman funny.' She adds:

> With humour you can really refract things in a way that it becomes much more on the viewer to make of it what they will. Humour affords you a much greater degree of complexity in the way that you treat something and it allows you to talk about Mary.[41]

As Maclean observes, humour is, in itself, a process of refraction that allows aspects of the subject's life to be exaggerated, performed, satirised, in ways that move beyond a one-dimensional representation.

Queens and queenship: Rosé performing Mary, Queen of Scots

Just as Maclean uses humour within her performance of Mary, so too have other artists. One form of performance art for which Mary has proved a popular (though perhaps unexpected) source of inspiration is drag. Drag is an art-form in which people dress up and perform (often in highly stylised ways) in order to exaggerate forms of gender expression. Drag is ultimately a form of creative and artistic expression, and as artists in other media have done throughout the ages, drag performers often look to contemporary and historical figures for sources of inspiration.

In early 2021, the Scottish-born, New York City-based drag queen Rosé took part in the American reality TV competition, *RuPaul's Drag Race*, and delighted audiences with her Mary, Queen of Scots persona. Rosé is the drag name of Ross McCorkell who was born in Greenock but moved to the USA when he was around 10 years old. He still maintains strong connections with Scotland and frequently visits, saying 'it still feels like home'.[42] Before considering Rosé's work in more depth, we should note that she is by no means the only drag queen to draw on Mary, Queen of Scots in their performances. The recent series of the BBC's *Drag Race UK* in 2021 saw not one, but two Scottish queens take to the stage – Dundee's Ellie Diamond and Glasgow's Lawrence Chaney. Chaney, who was crowned the winner of Season Two, even introduced themselves in the promotional video as 'kind of like Mary, Queen of Scots, only I hope one of these English drag queens doesn't chop off my head'.[43] Chaney humorously

---

[41] Ibid.
[42] Artist interview with Daniel Fountain and Alicia Hughes, 10 December 2022.
[43] BBC Three, 'Meet Lawrence Chaney', *YouTube*, https://www.youtube.com/watch?v=0LP9_FL-VVg, accessed 21 September 2023.

references the ill-fated rivalry between Mary and Elizabeth that has dominated much of the binary historical discourse around the two queens, and is reflected in the playful rivalries that are played out over the course of the drag competition. In doing so, they rhetorically position themselves as Scottish, without overt visual references to Mary within their dress, though they do wear a ruff reminiscent of the early modern period.

Mary is not the only historical queen to whom performers on *RuPaul's Drag Race* look for inspiration.[44] On Season Four of *Drag Race UK*, Manchester drag icon Cheddar Gorgeous performed as Queen Elizabeth I, and even corrected one of the show's celebrity guest judges (Mel B, a fellow Brit) as to the historical specificities of Elizabeth's story: no, she was not sister to Mary, nor did she shoot her dead; Mary was her cousin who she had executed by beheading. Host, judge and self-proclaimed 'supermodel of the world', RuPaul, portrayed Queen Elizabeth I and was photographed by Annie Leibovitz for the May 2019 issue of US *Vogue*.[45] RuPaul's signature use of highly stacked blonde wigs was replaced with auburn dreadlocks, fastened in an updo and decorated with pearls (which could reference representations of Elizabeth as the 'Virgin Queen'). Thai drag queen Pangina Heals – *RuPaul's Drag Race: UK vs the World* – took inspiration from historical representations of Elizabeth but fused this with influences from their own Thai culture and heritage. For example, the 'crown' that she wore on the main stage was a modernised version of a *chada* (also known as *Makuṭa*), a head-dress used in many south-east Asian monarchies as a form of royal regalia. Furthermore, although Pangina revealed that her makeup was inspired by Elizabeth's use of white lead for the purpose, it was equally inspired by the makeup worn by traditional Thai dancers (นางรำ) – usually a very stark white face with a heavy and bold use of black eye makeup.[46] Technically speaking, neither RuPaul nor Pangina establish historically accurate versions of Elizabeth in their portrayals. Rather, they each draw upon aspects of her iconography – the auburn hair and white makeup – and fuse these together with other influences from their own cultures that effectively assert various facets of their own identities, including their shared subversions of gender through drag, their social standing as internationally renowned queens, their race and ethnicity as drag queens of colour, and their pride in their own cultural heritage. As this

---

[44] For the longer history of people dressing as historical queens, and discussion of the numerous appearances of women dressed as Mary at masked balls in the nineteenth century, see Benjamin L. Wild, 'Romantic Recreations: Remembering Stuart Monarchy in Nineteenth-Century Fancy Dress Entertainments', in *Remembering Queens and Kings of Early Modern England and France: Reputation, Reinterpretation, and Reincarnation*, ed. Estelle Paranque (Cham, 2019), pp. 179–96.

[45] Abby Aguirre, 'How the World Fell Head Over Heels for RuPaul', *Vogue*, 15 April 2019, https://www.vogue.com/article/rupaul-interview-may-2019-issue, accessed 21 September 2023.

[46] @panginaheals, Instagram Post, 9 March 2022, https://www.instagram.com/p/Ca4xUgtLyrW/?hl=en, accessed 21 September 2023.

Figure 15.8 Rosé as Mary, Queen of Scots. Instagram, 6 March 2021. Photography by Robert Postotnik
Photo © Rosé

Figure 15.9 François Clouet, *Mary, Queen of Scots*, c. 1558, watercolour on vellum, 8.3 × 5.7cm, RCIN 401229
Photo: Royal Collection Trust/© His Majesty King Charles III, 2023

shows, drag as a form of cultural expression can bring history to new audiences, provoking fascinating new conversations about accuracy and authenticity, even if drag representations themselves are not necessarily accurate or authentic.

There is a wealth of examples of drag queens performing Elizabeth, and those of Mary are becoming more common. The most overt visual reference to Mary in drag can be seen in the work of Rosé, especially their performance in the 'Snatch Game' – perhaps the most popular challenge in the *RuPaul's Drag Race* franchise, which sees the drag queens embody various celebrities and icons of their choice and act as if they are competing on a gameshow together. Drawing on her Scottish roots, Rosé donned an auburn wig; a regal red gown; ruffled collar; and chalk-white foundation for her performance as Mary (see Figure 15.8). She spoke in an exaggerated Glaswegian accent and gave witty (and sometimes deliberately unintelligible) ripostes to questions from RuPaul in a way that, as she describes, reminded international audiences that 'what they are experiencing and enjoying is a Scottish artist'.[47] When asked about the significance of Mary to her, Rosé revealed that it is ultimately a sense of pride: 'Her pride in Scotland, her pride in herself. And using her image and storyline in my work

---

[47] Artist interview with Daniel Fountain and Alicia Hughes, 10 December 2022.

exemplifies my own pride in Scotland, and in myself.'[48] In Rosé's Snatch Game performance, she continued to draw attention to the queen-on-queen rivalries between Elizabeth and Mary. The performance was distinctly comical, certainly an embodiment of Mary, but an exaggeration that utilised artistic licence. Rosé acknowledges that the 'absence of information regarding historical figures' personalities past a certain date gives way for solid satirical interpretation'.[49] In regard to the Snatch Game performance, Rosé revealed that it was their first choice, a performance that had been imagined before she was selected to compete on *RuPaul's Drag Race*. 'I loved the idea of juxtaposing her classic, posh appearance with a rough, masculine and notably Glaswegian persona . . . I saw a gold mine of creative and comedic opportunity,' they said.[50]

Although the performance was both 'creative and comedic', Rosé's portrayal had a distinct visual resemblance to portraits painted of Mary in her life, such as the Sheffield portrait and the portrait by François Clouet (*c.* 1558) (see Figure 15.9).[51] The sumptuousness of sixteenth-century fabrics is evoked through the rich reds and oranges and the abundance of gold embroidery. As with Clouet's portraits, the composition of Rosé's photographs of her portrayal (later shared on the social media platform Instagram) showed mid-length portraits of the drag queen as Mary. While Clouet's portrait includes symbols of marriage and empowerment, such as the subtle touching of the ring on her fourth finger, Rosé compositions feature a of contemporary props including a leopard-print hip flask, a candelabra that was used to light a cigarette and a phone with which to take selfies: performance, pageantry, and pomp are evident in both portraits, despite the hundreds of years' time difference (see Figures 15.10 and 15.11).

Due to the overnight success of the performance (which went viral across social media), Rosé went on to create video portraits of Mary exploring New York City. Directed by Austin Nunes, they chronicle Mary's adventure through present-day New York. She is there with one mission in mind – to become a star. 'I think the biggest difference between now and before I was dead is that now I've got a head. When I died, my head was chopped off,' she explains dryly.[52] Following the video portrait's premiere, Rosé took to her Instagram stories to speak out against those who claimed that her interpretation was not historically

---

[48] Ibid.
[49] Ibid.
[50] Ibid.
[51] For the Sheffield portrait, see Jeremy L. Smith, 'Revisiting the Origins of the Sheffield Series of Portraits of Mary Queen of Scots,'', *Burlington Magazine* 152 (2010): 212–218; Marguerite A. Tassi, 'Martyrdom and Memory: Elizabeth Curle's Portrait of Mary, Queen of Scots,'', in *The Emblematic Queen: Extra-Literary Representations of Early Modern Queenship*, ed. Debra Barrett-Graves (New York, NY, 2013), pp. 101–132; Jeremy L. Smith, 'The Sheffield Portrait Types, Their Catholic Purposes, and Mary Queen of Scots's Tomb', *British Catholic History* 33: 1 (2016) no. 1: 71–90; and Chapter 2 in this volume.
[52] Artist interview with Daniel Fountain and Alicia Hughes, 10 December 2022.

Figure 15.10 Rosé as Mary, Queen of Scots with cigarette and candelabra. Instagram, 6 March 2021.
Photography by Robert Postotnik
Photo © Rosé

accurate, and especially those who questioned why Rosé had a Scottish accent and acted as if Mary was consistently fed up with life in contemporary New York City. In a comment, they responded: 'I did soo [sic] much research on MQoS! I am well aware she spoke with a French accent. I'm also aware that being miserable is a choice!'[53] Similar criticisms of historical inaccuracy were levelled against the 2018 film in which Mary and Elizabeth meet, forgetting that there is a long history of artists, playwrights and poets taking creative licence with Mary's story, and re-imagining it for their own narrative and creative purposes.[54] As early as the eighteenth century, there is evidence that women opted to embody Mary through their fashion choices on a range of occasions. For example, one of the most popular ladies' head-dresses in 1765 is said to have exactly resembled that of Mary, Queen of Scots as represented in her portraits.[55] Women

---

[53] Artist interview with Daniel Fountain and Alicia Hughes, 10 December 2022.
[54] See, for example, Friedrich Schiller's play *Mary Stuart* (1800), and Kate Mulvany's 2020 adaption of Schiller's play: Kate Mulvany and Friedrich Schiller, *Mary Stuart* (Strawberry Hills, New South Wales, 2020).
[55] Lewis, *Mary Queen of Scots*, p. 123

also sat for portraits in sixteenth-century costumes meant to identify them as the Stuart queen.[56] This practice rose further in popularity in the nineteenth century, particularly after Princess Alexandra dressed as Mary for a fancy dress ball.[57] Embodying or performing Mary as a form of artistic or self-expression has a longer history than one might think.

In addition to re-imagining Mary's general iconography of auburn hair, white ruff and crucifix, Rosé has also considered how fashion factored into key chapters in Mary's story, particularly the highly symbolic choice that Mary employed during her execution in 1587. Contemporary accounts of the execution tell us that, before being led to the executioner's block, Mary's ladies in waiting removed the queen's black dress, revealing a crimson velvet petticoat with red sleeves and crimson-brown satin bodice. On considering the symbolism of this fashion choice, Antonia Fraser has noted that the queen was 'thus wearing all red, the colour of blood, and the liturgical colour of martyrdom in the Catholic Church'.[58] Mary had a flair for the dramatic and Rosé spectacularly re-interpreted this act of defiance in glamorous and theatrical fashion with her own 'scarlet reveal stunt' within her performance piece 'Heads Will Roll' (see Figure 15.11). The piece begins with a male dancer brandishing a sword in a threatening manner, before 'Mary' (Rosé) is led onto the stage, her hands together and eyes downcast, as if being led to her execution. 'Mary' then frees herself, dancing and lip-syncing 'off with your head, heads will roll' (a song by American rock indie band Yeah Yeah Yeahs), before dancers dramatically pull apart Rosé's pseudo-historical black and blue gown (with black ruff collar and an oversize gold, jewelled crucifix hanging from the waist) to reveal a satin-esque scarlet dress with a plunging neckline. Daring, dramatic and diva-ish, Rosé's performances re-interpret Mary's last stance for contemporary audiences in a way that is entirely their own. The resulting performance is artistic and distinctively modern, but ultimately it is also based in historical fact and brings Mary's story to new audiences who may be unfamiliar with her tale and eventual plight.

Rosé's number evolved in her performance for the 'Night of the Living Dead' tour in 2021, which incorporated new visual graphic elements that further told Mary's story. Visual graphics on the stage's digital backscreens placed Rosé's performance in a dark, cavernous, castle-interior stage-setting, which changed throughout the production. In this performance, at the choreographed moment of the scarlet reveal stunt, as the supporting dancers pull apart Rosé's pseudo-historical dress visual graphics on the stage backscreen lit up with vigorous, moving splashes of bright red blood in reference to the executioner's axe falling. Rather than dying, Rosé smiles, dances and shimmies defiantly across the stage.

---

[56] Lewis, *Mary Queen of Scots*, p. 123.
[57] See Wild, 'Romantic Recreations', pp. 179–96.
[58] Fraser, *Mary Queen of Scots*, p. 538.

Figure 15.11 Stills from 'Night of the Living Drag' at MGM National Harbor, Maryland on 21 November 2021, with Rosé as Mary, Queen of Scots; YouTube Images reproduced with permission of Eric Brady

It is less of a scene of degradation and death, and more one of empowerment and empathy. This reflects Mary's own narrative, as Rosé notes: 'I was delighted to learn that Mary had a twisted flair for drama, as she famously performed a bold and shocking reveal moments before being executed. It was drag!'[59] Mary's crimson undergown certainly shocked onlookers at her execution and was a carefully constructed 'reveal' in the moments before her execution. As Rosé acknowledges,

> Mary is probably so renowned amidst many prominent Scottish historical figures because she was a defiant woman. And her story is remembered as cinematic (and very dramatic) highs and lows. Her legend is a vessel for me because I can take what we all know and agree upon as historical, and paint vividly within those lines.[60]

The etymology of terms such as 'drag' and 'drag queen' are also interesting to reflect upon here in regard to Rosé's embodiment of Mary and portrayals

---

[59] Artist interview with Daniel Fountain and Alicia Hughes, 10 December 2022.
[60] Ibid.

of royalty, or queenship. Although its origins are uncertain, the term 'drag' is thought to have been derived from stage directions used in Elizabethan England where it has been rumoured that 'DRAG' was written into the stage directions and stood for 'dressed resembling a girl'. While this has long been debated and disputed by scholars, many of whom claim it is a form of folk etymology, Shakespearean theatre is still widely considered to be one of the earliest examples of drag.[61] During an age in which women were not allowed to perform on stage, men (and usually young boys) would play all the female roles, and would wear women's clothing and makeup. Although drag is now considered a much more inclusive and diverse phenomenon (anyone, regardless of their gender identity or sexuality, may perform or exaggerate gender signifiers) the original referent of the term 'drag queen' referred to a 'male' who would typically exaggerate 'female' gender signifiers and roles for entertainment purposes, hence the gendered referent 'queen'.[62] The idea of drag queens as members of royalty was particularly common as part of the ballroom culture in the United States of America, which emerged in New York City. The ballroom scene was an LGBTQ+ sub-culture primarily for African American and Latinx communities who found themselves ostracised in society and many of whom experienced overt forms of racism, transphobia and violence among the drag queen pageant circuit. The ballroom originated in the late twentieth century, and the culture was especially common in the 1980s. These balls saw participants compete in various categories with events usually including 'walking' (as in walking a fashion runway) or 'voguing' (a highly stylised form of dance). Members often competed in their 'houses', which functioned as alternative familial systems in which people often lived together or supported one another, usually presided over by an elder member of the community who would be referred to as the 'house mother' or 'house father'. Many of these 'houses' directly referred to themselves as royalty, such as the Royal House of LaBeija. Particularly successful houses who would continuously score highly in balls were often referred to explicitly as 'drag royalty', a phrase that is often still used today for popular or internationally acclaimed drag performers, including Rosé.

Mary, Queen of Scots was no stranger to the pageantry or defiance of gender conventions that now characterises drag as a performance art-form. Her court

---

[61] Roger Baker, *Drag: A History of Female Impersonation in the Performing Arts* (New York, 1995).
[62] For example, many historic texts discuss drag as an artform purely carried out by cisgender gay men, as a form of female impersonation. This implies that drag was the exclusive domain of gay men, which of course is not true; lesbian women, trans women, trans men, straight men, straight women, non-binary people, genderfluid people and many others have long engaged in drag. For more contemporary scholarship on drag, see Mark Edward and Stephen Farrier (eds), *Contemporary Drag Practices and Performers: Drag in a Changing Scene*, Vol. 1 (London, 2020) and Mark Edward and Stephen Farrier (eds), *Drag Histories, Herstories and Hairstories: Drag in a Changing Scene*, Vol. 2 (London, 2022).

was 'exceptionally devoted to performance and display' – excessive costuming, performance and cross-dressing or 'masking' would often be used to show gratitude or to obtain courtly allegiances.[63] It is claimed that Mary herself enjoyed wearing men's clothing on occasion. She adopted the daring habit of wearing men's breeches under her skirts when riding and hunting (a fashion introduced by Catherine de' Medici) and her father-in-law (the earl of Lennox) claimed that she loved to wear 'man's apparel . . . secretly with the King her husband' and would often wear 'masks by night through the streets'.[64] On 11 February 1565, Mary and her lady's maids were recorded to be wearing 'men's apperell [sic]' during a visit to court by the French ambassador.[65] The queen even reportedly wished she *were* a man: 'to know what life it was to lie all night in the fields, or to walk upon the causeway with a jack [an armoured outer garment] and knapscall [helmet]'.[66] Although we can only speculate about Mary's defiance of expected gender norms, her competitive spirit, rebelliousness and love of pageantry certainly lives on today, as emphasised and personified through Rosé's performances. As Rosé's characterisation exemplifies, we can see similarities between drag queens and royalty, from the performative nature of fashion and costume to embody a persona, to the use of makeup, props and so on. Through Rosé's performance, Mary also becomes refracted once more, but still with glimmers of historical accuracy.

Conclusion

Just as cheap, black-and-white-printed engravings reproduced Mary's image for people in Europe in the sixteenth and seventeenth centuries, twenty-first-century digital and social media have enabled representations of Mary by contemporary artists and creative practitioners to spread around the globe with Mary becoming a site for re-invention and re-imagining. This chapter has provided an important examination of Mary's afterlife in contemporary visual culture, using works by three different artists working in three different mediums as a site for analysis. As we have shown, Flockhart's use of symbolism in her oil paintings, Maclean's use of baroque and tourist kitsch in her video and digital art, and Rosé's humour and style in her performances, enable new and exciting representations of Mary to emerge. Mary continues to speak to contemporary audiences today and artists continue to take inspiration from the Queen of Scots, just as they have for almost 450 years.

---

[63] Sarah Carpenter, John J. McGavin and Greg Walker, *Early Performance: Courts and Audiences: Shifting Paradigms in Early English Drama Studies* (Abingdon, 2021).
[64] Fraser, *Mary Queen of Scots*, p. 240.
[65] Fraser, *Mary Queen of Scots*, p. 240.
[66] Quoted in Sarah Carpenter, 'Performing Diplomacies: The 1560s Court Entertainments of Mary Queen of Scots', *SHR* 82 (2003): 194–225, at p. 218.

Mary's cultural afterlife is itself subject to creative and artistic investigation and re-imagining. The individual historical figure has been refracted and fragmented into multiple 'Marys' that themselves become the site for creative and artistic experimentation. Although many scholars have previously analysed re-imaginations of Mary through TV and film, other art-forms have not received significant attention. We have therefore highlighted the ways in which a greater range of contemporary artists working in a range of media, such as oil painting, digital media and performance, have also used artistic licence to re-imagine various facets of Mary's life and eventual death, particularly to explore present-day debates on gender and identity. In doing so, we have also raised questions about the role of authenticity and historical accuracy in the cultural afterlife of Mary, Queen of Scots, arguing that in addition to the recognisable iconography of Mary, it is also her fragmentation and instability that inspires the vast range of representations within contemporary visual culture. In our analysis, we have utilised oral history, retaining the original voices of the artists, and preserving quotations from each artist to enable and encourage future scholarship in this area. Our analysis has also been foregrounded by the concept of refraction to highlight how representations of Mary are always multi-layered, glitchy and ghostly, and indeed performative. Clearly, this is the beginning of a much longer conversation that will play out over the course of many more years but we hope that the apparatus we have set out here will enable future scholarship on the cultural afterlife of Mary in contemporary visual culture to emerge. Long live the Queen!

INDEX

Act of Settlement, 127
Anderson, James
  life, 127
  reception, 134
  work, 126–33
Annan, Robert, 227–8
antiquarianism, 125–9, 135, 228, 253, 262, 266, 273, 344
audience response (online), 24, 114, 122
Austen, Jane, 171
authenticity
  artefacts/objects, 5–6, 107, 116, 223–8, 232, 240, 262, 268–9, 273, 278–80, 289–90, 337, 357
  costume, 65–8, 80, 362
  letters, 115, 125; *see also* Casket Letters
  likeness (portraits), 58–9, 63–8, 78, 187
  replicas, 24, 107, 114, 116
  setting (heritage site), 241, 257, 259
  textual, 5
  visual (film), 329–30, 332, 334, 357

Bardari, Giuseppe, 300–1
'The Battle of Corrichie', 295, 315
Beale, Robert, 85, 109
Blackwood, Adam, 16–17, 45, 85
Blairs Memorial Portrait, 45, 58–61, 68, 78–80, 84
books of hours, 86–105
Boswell, James, 11, 138, 163–4, 248
British Magazine, 147–9
The Briton, 144–5
Bruce, Robert, 237–8, 356

Buchanan, George, 7, 128, 132–3, 152, 161
Burns, Robert, 10, 158, 165–8, 222, 225
  Burns Club, 28

Camden, William, 17, 128, 130–2
Carissimi, Giacomo, 296–7, 315
Caroline Matilda of Great Britain, 155–6
Cartland, Barbara, 192
Casella, Pietro, 299
Casket Letters, 8, 108–9, 138, 144–5, 147, 165, 185–6, 190
'Casket Sonnets', 143, 153, 159
Cecil, Robert, first Earl of Salisbury, 148
Cecil, William, Lord Burghley, 132, 148
Chalmers, George, 127, 134, 137
Charles I, 50, 247
Clouet, François, 12, 37
  comparison of his works, 67, 70, 362–3
Coccia, Carlo, 300
community souvenirs, 231, 240
Cotton, Sir Robert, first Baronet of Connington
  library, 131
Covenanters, 127, 237
Craig, Cairns, 318
crucifixes, 5, 43, 68, 85, 150
  Craigmillar, 271–5, 279

Darnley, Lord (Henry Stuart)
  coinage, 38–9
  depictions, 295, 303, 308, 338
  Mary and his murder, 140, 142, 144, 182, 245
  relationship with Mary, 6–7, 156

Day, John, 133
de Bourbon, Antoinette, 76–7
de Bourbon, Louise, 87
de Lorraine, Anne, 89
de Lorraine, Renée, 87
Defoe, Daniel, 149
DiDonato, Joyce, 311–12
Donaldson, Gordon, 2, 189–94
Donizetti, Gaetano, 293–4, 299–305, 313, 314
drag, 25, 360; *see also* Rosé
dress *see* Mary, Queen of Scots
Dudley, Robert, earl of Leicester, 204
  portrayal in Donizetti's *Maria Stuarda*, 300, 306, 309

Edinburgh, 9, 26, 85, 106, 140, 166, 197, 200, 254, 257, 283, 311, 338
Edward Burne-Jones window, 116
Elizabeth I, 51, 108–9
  depictions and comparisons to Mary, Queen of Scots, 19, 20–1, 120, 149–50, 158–9, 161–2, 165, 170, 202–5, 217, 301–2, 304, 307–9, 311, 314–15, 323–4, 327–8, 338, 350, 361, 363
  drag, 25, 361, 362, 363
Elstrack, Renold (Reginold), 47
embroidery, 4, 251, 262, 348
emotion
  affect, 5, 7, 9, 151, 285, 286, 290
  empathy, 6, 8, 142, 222, 275–80, 368
  personal connection, 276–7
  Sensibility, 9, 142, 146, 151, 159, 160, 167
  sentimentality, 154, 285, 299
  sympathy, 9, 10, 24, 142, 144, 145, 146, 152, 158, 159, 162, 193, 236, 240, 276, 347
engravings, 7, 15, 18, 38, 44–8, 69, 71–2, 356–7, 368
Erskine, David, earl of Buchan, 154–5
Evelyn, John, 109
  grandson of (John Evelyn of Wotton), 248
execution (of Mary), 3, 68, 77, 85–6, 112, 183, 365
  literary depictions of, 8, 11, 150–1, 211–12, 216, 296, 301
  visual depictions of, 13, 15, 16, 19, 21, 45, 84–5, 281, 285, 308, 315, 319–23, 325, 352, 365–6

exhibitions, 5, 12, 22–4, 112, 180, 187, 222–3, 229–40, 258, 259, 267–8, 273, 277–9, 286, 323, 343, 354–5

face tracings, 14, 58–9, 63, 78
Ferguson, Adam, 144
Fergusson, James, of Kilkerran, 190
film, 9, 18–23, 28, 121–1, 189, 305–11, 31–4, 317–41, 345–6, 354–5, 364–5
Flockhart, Helen, 24, 343–69
Franklin, Benjamin, 139
Fraser, Antonia, 1, 10, 28, 179–80, 189–95, 365

Gardyn, Beatrix, of Banchory, 5, 225
gender, 2, 7–9, 11, 118, 120–1, 150, 192–3, 196, 198–200, 202–5, 208–9, 212, 217, 328, 337–8, 360–1, 367–8
Gentleman's Magazine, 152, 156, 157
gift-giving, 4, 5, 79, 87, 113, 267, 271
Glasgow, 180, 213, 229, 231, 237, 238
Goodall, Walter, 9, 143–6, 153
Goodall, William, 138–9
Grave Digger, 294
Gregory, Phillippa, 120
Guy, John, 108, 290, 305

Hamilton, Gavin, 4, 11–12, 138, 163, 210
Hatton, Sir Christopher, 148–9
Hay Fleming, David, 10, 180–9, 191
heirlooms *see* authenticity
Henderson, T. F., 188, 192
Hepburn, James, fourth earl of Bothwell, 2, 39, 206, 214–16, 245
Hilliard, Nicholas, 40, 54, 57, 61–2, 65–6
Hogg, James, 225
Hume, David, 125, 138, 147, 150, 152
humour (satire), 26, 360
Hunter, William, 126, 135–40
Hutcheson, Francis, 142

iconoclasm, 50–1, 82
iconography, 13–15, 18, 36–9, 52, 176, 346, 348, 355–6, 361
identity
  'British', 24, 318, 323, 333
  changing, 86, 100, 346
  cultivating, 101, 105, 111
  gender, 21, 215, 343, 358, 367
  Scottish national, 21, 28, 180, 212–13, 315, 343, 358–9

imperialism, 19, 21, 27–8, 318–19, 322–3, 325, 332–5
  jingoism, 324, 331, 333, 336–7, 339

Jacobitism, 9, 164–5, 239, 286
James VI and I, 15, 35, 44, 49–50, 62, 211, 242, 245, 336, 351
  rehabilitation of Mary's reputation, 48, 54, 128
Jebb, Samuel, 127, 143
jewels, 6, 286
  cameos, 280–6
  Craigmillar Crucifix *see* crucifix
  Penicuik Jewels, 269–71, 279–80, 286
Johnson, Samuel, 152–3, 164–5, 248

Killigrew, Sir William, 149
Knox, John, 82, 152, 182, 187, 244, 284, 312, 350
  depictions of, 200–1, 206–9, 215, 306–7

Labanoff, Prince Alexander, 99, 109, 118–19
Lang, Andrew, 179, 182–9, 191–2
lantern slides, 320–5
Law, Thomas Graves, 181
Leslie, John, Bishop of Ross, 7, 15, 69, 88, 128, 132
letterlocking, 114
Loch Leven
  Castle (captivity), 11, 39, 210, 226, 351
  keys from, 225–8
Lochhead, Liz, 11, 120, 194, 197–217
Lockey, Rowland, 42, 44
London, 11, 24, 35, 44, 48, 107, 126, 138, 140, 156, 161, 171, 180, 205, 231, 242, 246, 293, 296, 300, 320

McCready, Marion, 198, 200, 210, 211–12, 217
Mackenzie, Henry, 142, 146
Mackie, J. D., 188
McLean, Linda, 198, 200, 202, 204, 206–8, 217, 276, 290
Maclean, Rachel, 23–4, 27, 343–6, 354–60, 368
McVicar, Sir David, 311–12
Maitland, John, of Thirlestane, 14–15, 33–5
  'Maitland Mary' portrait, 33, 43, 50, 53, 72–83

Maitland, William, 109, 144–5
Maitland, William of Lethington, 33, 109, 190
'Marian Controversy', 147, 153
Marot, Clément, 95, 100
Marshall, H. E.,190
Mary of Guise, 41, 226, 242–3, 350
Mary, Queen of Scots
  biographies of, 1–2, 47–8, 53, 175, 179–96, 259, 305
  book ownership, 8, 85–6, 105, 137
  coinage, 4, 36–9, 174
  comparison with Elizabeth *see* Elizabeth I
  contemporary description, 76–7, 365
  depictions in film and television, 19–22, 23, 28, 120–1, 189, 305–11, 313, 314, 317–42, 342, 345–6, 354–5
  depictions in literature, 6–9, 111–12, 117, 120, 156–9, 160–79, 197–217, 225, 226, 253, 259, 296, 351
  dress, 3, 14, 36, 52, 65–8, 84, 186, 232, 315, 350, 352, 365
  embroidery, 4, 232, 251, 262, 348, 262, 348, 350
  hair (appearance and significance), 17, 38, 150, 234, 283, 309, 346
  martyrdom, 8, 13, 15–16, 26, 40, 45, 85, 105, 143, 169, 172, 194, 197, 202, 211, 212, 231, 236–7, 267, 275, 277, 305, 311, 313–14, 323–4, 329, 352, 356
  miscarriage, 11, 346
  portraits of, 11–18, 33–52, 53–83, 84–5, 186–7, 201, 223, 236, 265, 269–70, 280, 352, 363
Master of François de Rohan, 87
material culture, 3–6
  Andrew Lang, 183, 185–7
  commemorative items/memorabilia, 5, 24–5, 221, 259, 261
  kitsch, 27, 343, 355–7
  relics, 5, 84, 108, 221, 223–6, 231–2, 234, 239–40, 267, 273, 284, 289, 353
  theory, 222, 268, 274
  see also authenticity
memorial inscriptions, 87–8, 92
memorialisation, 6, 14, 53, 75, 83, 84, 89, 105, 107, 119, 152, 222, 236, 241, 246, 253, 266, 280, 283, 285–6, 289, 358

Mickle, William Julius, 161–3
Mulgrew, Gerry, 202
museums, 267–90
  curators, 6, 268, 271, 273, 287, 288
  visitors, 5, 180, 235, 236, 238, 240, 246, 247–8, 251–2, 252–9, 266, 268–9, 271, 275, 277, 278–9, 290
music, 226, 293–316

opera, 293–5, 299–305, 311–15
Order of the White Rose, 231, 239

Pakenham, Elizabeth, Countess of Longford, 192
Phellipes, Thomas, 109
Philippa of Guelders, 350
Pinkerton, John, 115
Pinter, Harold, 193
plays, 9, 156, 161, 168–71, 194, 197–217, 276, 300, 348
portraits, 40–1
  cameos, 280–1, 284–6
  circulation, 15, 69–71, 75, 83
  French portraiture, 63–6, 81
  miniatures, 40
  Sheffield portrait, 13–15, 39, 41–52, 53–83, 363
Presbyterian, 128, 155, 161, 167, 180, 206, 234, 272, 275
provenance *see* authenticity
public history, 268, 287

Queen Elizabeth II, 355, 357
Queen Mary Harp, 5, 224–5, 228, 273
Queen Victoria, 230, 233–4, 241, 252, 254–6, 257, 262, 266

race, 27–8, 361
Reformation, 2, 10, 51, 83, 88, 95, 143, 151, 175, 181–3, 195, 202, 207, 275, 287, 336
refraction, 343–4, 358, 360, 369
Reni, Guido, 356
Richter, Max, 305–9, 311, 313, 315
Rizzio, David, 5, 177, 182, 241, 245, 247–8, 250–5, 257, 260, 266, 303, 306, 341
Robertson, William, 7, 9–10, 125, 137–8, 140, 146–7, 153–5, 165–6
romantic period, 10, 160, 165
Rosé, 25, 343, 360, 360–8
  reactions to, 25–7

Rourke, Josie, 28, 120, 305–11, 314, 345

Said, Edward, 319–20, 332
St John, John, 156, 159
Schiller, Friedrich, 9, 120, 168–75
Schumann, Robert, 297–9
Scott, Walter, 7, 117, 173–7, 253
Scottish Enlightenment, 10, 142, 144, 159–60, 163, 165–6
Scudamore, John, 149
sexuality, 10, 348, 367
Shrewsbury, Elizabeth Hardwick, countess of, 4, 41, 56, 147, 262
Shrewsbury, George Talbot, earl of, 41, 43, 111, 148
Siddons, Sarah, 156
Smith, Adam, 142
Smith, Alexander Howland ('Antique Smith'), 115
Smollett, Tobias, 144–6, 153
social media, 363, 368
Society of Antiquaries of Scotland, 180, 223, 225, 228, 259–60
'spiral lock' *see* letterlocking
Steuart, Sir James, third Baronet of Goodtrees, 152–3, 225
Stevenson, Gerda, 198, 210–11, 217, 350
Stevenson, Joseph, 184–5
Stewart, James, Earl of Moray, 39, 65, 184, 295–6, 308, 338
Strickland, Agnes, 116–19, 192, 225, 259
Strong, Roy, 54–5, 63, 195
Struensee, Johan Friedrich, 155
Stuart, Gilbert, 9, 153
Stuart, Charles Edward, 152, 239, 247, 258
Stuart, James Francis Edward, 152
Stuart, John, third Earl of Bute, 144–5
symbolism, 211–12, 338, 343, 346–54, 365

technical studies (evidence from and interpretation of), 56–7
television, 19, 345–6, 360–3
Thatcher, Margaret, 11, 197, 205
Thomson, George Malcolm, 165, 191
tourism, 241, 246–52, 357
Traquair House, 355
Tytler, William, 10, 138–40, 147, 151–3, 165–8

Udall, William, 17–18, 47–8, 128, 139

Vanson, Adrian, 14, 35–6, 40, 53, 72–5
Vertue, George, 27, 354, 356–7

Walsingham, Francis, 62, 108
Whig, 127–8, 134, 160, 164, 166, 173, 179

Whitaker, John, 147
Wilkes, John, 144–5
Wordsworth, William, 10, 171–3
Wormald, Jenny, 128, 194–5, 347
Wortley Montagu, Mary, 160–2

EU representative:
Easy Access System Europe
Mustamäe tee 50, 10621 Tallinn, Estonia
Gpsr.requests@easproject.com